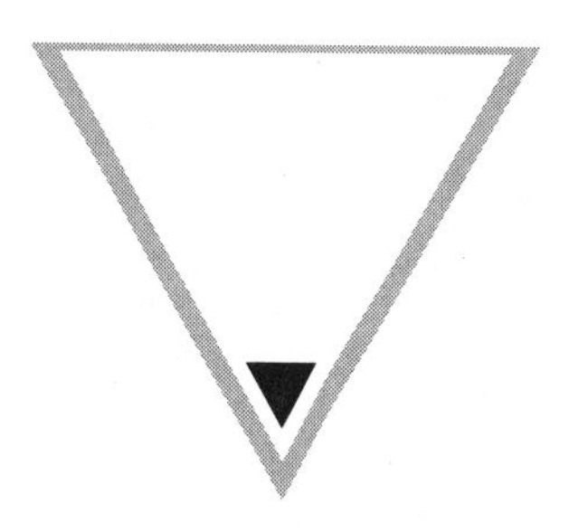

Do-It-Yourself Web Publishing with HoTMetaL

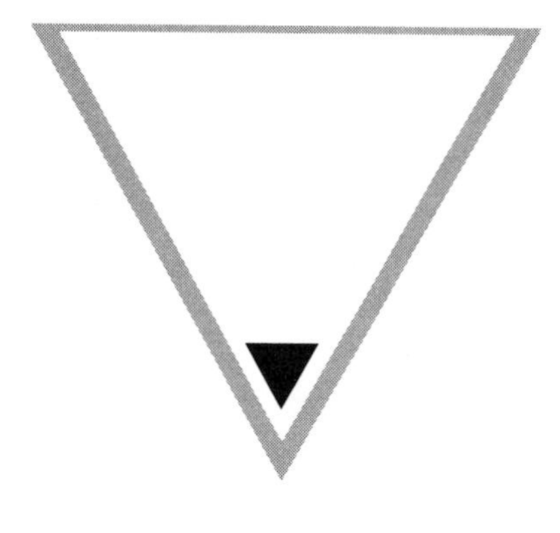

Do-It-Yourself Web Publishing with HoTMetaL™

James Jaworski

San Francisco • Paris • Düsseldorf • Soest

Associate Publisher: Carrie Lavine
Acquisitions Manager: Kristine Plachy
Developmental Editors: Dan Brodnitz and Brenda Kienan
Editor: Valerie Potter
Technical Editor: Miles Pratt
Production Coordinator: Kim Wimpsett
Desktop Publisher: Bob Bihlmayer of London Road Design
Proofreader: Vicki Wilhite of London Road Design
Book Designer: Jan Haseman of London Road Design
Technical Artists: Kelly and Tony Jonick
Indexer: Nancy Guenther
Cover Designer: Design Site
Cover Illustrator: Jack D. Myers

Library of Congress Card Number: 95-73268
ISBN: 0-7821-1691-4

Manufactured in the United States of America
10 9 8 7 6 5 4 3 2

Warranty

SYBEX warrants the enclosed CD-ROM to be free of physical defects for a period of ninety (90) days after purchase. If you discover a defect in the CD during this warranty period, you can obtain a replacement CD at no charge by sending the defective CD, postage prepaid, with proof of purchase to:

SYBEX Inc.
Customer Service Department
2021 Challenger Drive
Alameda, CA 94501
(800) 227-2346
Fax: (510) 523-2373

After the 90-day period, you can obtain a replacement CD by sending us the defective CD, proof of purchase, and a check or money order for $10, payable to SYBEX.

Disclaimer

SYBEX makes no warranty or representation, either express or implied, with respect to this medium or its contents, its quality, performance, merchantability, or fitness for a particular purpose. In no event will SYBEX, its distributors, or dealers be liable for direct, indirect, special, incidental, or consequential damages arising out of the use of or inability to use the software even if advised of the possibility of such damage.

The exclusion of implied warranties is not permitted by some states. Therefore, the above exclusion may not apply to you. This warranty provides you with specific legal rights; there may be other rights that you may have that vary from state to state.

Shareware Distribution

This CD contains various programs that are distributed as shareware. Shareware is a distribution method, not a type of software. The chief advantage is that it gives you, the user, a chance to try a program before you buy it.

Copyright laws apply to both shareware and commercial software, and the copyright holder retains all rights. If you try a shareware program and continue using it, you are expected to register it. Individual programs differ on details—some request registration while others require it. Some request a payment, while others don't, and some specify a maximum trial period. With registration, you get anything from the simple right to continue using the software to program updates.

Copy Protection

None of the files on the CD is copy-protected. However, in all cases, reselling or redistributing these files, except as specifically provided for by the copyright owners, is prohibited.

To Lisa, Emily, and Jason

ACKNOWLEDGMENTS

I'd like to thank everyone who helped to see this book to completion. In particular, I'd like to thank George Stones for the initial motivation, Margo Maley for making it possible, and everyone at Sybex for their great support—especially Valerie Potter and Dan Brodnitz. I'd also like to thank my daughter, Emily, for her help in developing the sample graphics and my wife, Lisa, for her patience, love, and understanding.

A number of people have contributed software to this book's CD. I'd like to thank Bernd Richter for giving me permission to include the UdiWWW browser and Andrew Bulhak for WHAM. I'd also like to thank Duplexx Software, Inc. for permission to include NET TOOB, Q&D Software Development for WebForms, and last, but definitely not least, Microsoft Corporation for use of its fine viewers.

TABLE OF CONTENTS

Introduction

If you'd like someone to teach you how to develop and publish documents on the World Wide Web, this book is for you. You might expect that creating Web documents is a time-consuming, complicated task. In fact, part of the secret to the Web's popularity is its ease of use. Once you learn the basics, preparing a Web document is about as easy as applying styles in Word or WordPerfect. The lessons in this book use illustrated, step-by-step instructions to teach you these basics and then take you several steps beyond. By the time you're finished, you'll be a master at creating exciting, attractive, and informative Web documents.

To make the process as accessible as possible, we've included HoTMetaL Light 2.0, an award-winning Web authoring program, on the CD in the back of this book. HoTMetaL helps make Web publishing easier by turning it into a series of straightforward points and clicks. This book teaches you how to use HoTMetaL to quickly develop high quality Web pages. By Lesson 2, you'll create your own home page. In subsequent lessons, you'll learn how to format text, how to insert graphics in your Web documents, and how to create links to other Web pages. You'll also learn how to use advanced HoTMetaL features such as forms and tables. Perhaps most importantly, you'll learn to create your Web pages with a style that ensures they are eye-catching, easy to use, and equipped with the capabilities that Web users expect.

Why Publish on the Web?

The benefits of publishing on the Web are enormous. Websites are registered in every major country on every continent. These websites are maintained by a wide variety of private individuals, educational institutions, governments, businesses, and other organizations. A large part of the Web's power is that it lets these people and organizations distribute information globally at minimal expense.

People use personal Web pages in many different ways. Some pages describe or advance their authors' hobbies and interests and cover topics ranging from hamsters to *Hamlet.* Others offer online magazines and galleries that feature original stories, articles, and art. Some people use the Web to distribute their résumés online. They write about their work, accomplishments, and professional interests and then publish this information for prospective employers. Many people design their Web pages as a collection of links to interesting websites. The Yahoo website (an extensive catalog of websites) began in this way. Others, such as the famous Cool Site of the Day, maintain Web pages that review or highlight other websites. A few personal Web pages have already become so popular that their publishers can sell advertising space!

Web publishing is especially attractive to businesses. A number of budding entrepreneurs use their sites to affordably promote their startups. A Web home page costs much less than most full-page magazine ads and can be seen by millions of people around the world. Web documents are also interactive and easily updated. They can be used to provide customers with the information they need, when they need it. Many businesses use their Web pages to provide 24-hour-a-day customer information. Other businesses use their Web pages to provide online catalogs or electronic storefronts. The capacity to perform secure business transactions on the Internet is paving the way for completely online shopping and financial services, allowing worldwide sales to be conducted through the Web.

The Web: Past, Present, and Future

Before you begin contributing to the Web's future, it will help to learn a bit about its past. The Internet has witnessed explosive growth in the last few years. An estimated 30 million people have Internet access, and the number of users is rapidly increasing. The *World Wide Web,* or *WWW,* or simply *the Web,* is the most exciting development in Internet services. With its attractive graphical interface, worldwide links, and multimedia features, it has become the Internet service of choice.

The Web was created in 1989 by Tim Berners-Lee, a computer scientist at CERN, the European Laboratory for Particle Physics, located in Geneva, Switzerland. (The acronym CERN comes from the French title of the lab: *Conseil Européen pour la Recherche Nucléaire.*) Berners-Lee developed the Web to allow increased collaboration between particle physicists, but it quickly spread to millions of users around the globe. Part of the reason for the Web's growth was that its underlying structure made it easy for anyone to join and it allowed its users to publish information on any subject.

Another reason for the Web's popularity was the development of Mosaic at the National Center for Supercomputing Applications at the University of Illinois, Urbana-Champaign. Mosaic was developed by Marc Andreessen, an undergraduate student at NCSA, in 1992. The initial version was released in February of 1993. By September 1993, NCSA had released versions for Microsoft Windows and Macintosh. Mosaic's success resulted from its ease of use, its remarkable melding of a graphical user interface to the Web framework, and the hard work and dedication of Marc Andreessen in advancing its cause.

NCSA freely distributed Mosaic, and the Web explosion began. Universities, government agencies, businesses, and private individuals began to link to the Web at a phenomenal rate. Software companies realized the importance of the Web and began to release commercial versions of Web client and server software. A number of outstanding freeware programs were also made available over the Web.

Almost all who came in contact with the Web realized its power and commercial potential. Thousands of businesses developed home pages and joined the Web in 1994. The World Wide Web Organization was announced in July 1994 as a collaboration between CERN and the Laboratory for Computer Science at the Massachusetts Institute of Technology (MIT). It later became the World Wide Web Consortium (W3C). The consortium is open to industry and other institutions and has the mission of coordinating the development of the Web and promoting its use in business, education, research, and government.

The current focus of Web development is in the areas of security, electronic commerce, and online entertainment. Web security enhancements are oriented toward the development of capabilities to support online sales and financial services. If you are interested in using the Web to sell a product or service, these capabilities will allow you to sell globally with minimal overhead expense.

Online entertainment is in its infancy. Short audio files and primitive videos are freely available on the Web. This book will show you how to incorporate multimedia features into your Web pages. Significant increases in the data rates of client connections will provide the basis for advanced online entertainment in the near future.

Required Experience

This book is aimed at the Web neophyte. It assumes that you have heard about the Web and have minimal experience using a Web browser, such as Netscape Navigator or Microsoft Internet Explorer. It also assumes that you know how to use Windows to perform basic tasks such as creating a directory, copying files, starting a program, and connecting to the Internet.

No matter how little experience you have using the Internet or the World Wide Web, you can develop expert-level skills in writing Web pages by working through the lessons in this book. Learning to use HoTMetaL is not difficult. All you need to do is start with Lesson 1 and learn one feature at a time, letting this book be your guide.

Hardware and Software Requirements

To use this book with the HoTMetaL program, you'll need the following:

- A 100% PC-compatible computer with a 386 or better CPU
- At least 8MB of RAM
- At least 10MB of available hard disk space
- A VGA color monitor
- A mouse
- A CD drive
- Windows 95, Windows 3.1, Windows for Workgroups, or Windows NT
- An HTML 2.0-compatible browser

What Browser Should I Use?

The examples in this book are displayed using Netscape Navigator 2.0. Any browser that is compatible with version 2.0 of the Hypertext Markup Language (HTML) may be used. NCSA Mosaic 2.0 and Microsoft Internet Explorer 2.0 are popular alternatives to the Netscape browser. If you don't already have a browser, I recommend that you look into getting the Netscape browser. It is the world's most popular browser and is widely available. You can purchase it at most software stores for about forty dollars. If you currently have a different browser, and you are interested in obtaining the Netscape browser, you may be able to download an evaluation copy from the Netscape website by pointing your browser at **http://home.netscape.com**.

► ► ► If you are planning on purchasing a new browser, first check with your service provider to make sure that it is supported by your Internet connection.

Using Other Versions of Windows

The lessons in this book use HoTMetaL with Windows 95. You can also run HoTMetaL with Windows 3.1, Windows for Workgroups, or Windows NT. If you are using a version of Windows other than Windows 95, simply substitute its commands for the Windows 95 commands you encounter. This will not be difficult because most Windows 95 commands used in this book are limited to creating directories, copying files, and starting programs.

How This Book Is Organized

The lessons in this book have three basic elements: background information, procedural steps, and visual references. The background information is provided to help you understand what you're learning and why you're learning it. The procedural steps show you how to do things such as using HoTMetaL to develop Web documents. They consist of numbered steps that you'll carry out using your keyboard and mouse. The accompanying illustrations show you what your screen should look like when you perform each step so you will know if you are doing things correctly.

If you're using a browser other than Netscape 2.0 or a version of Windows other than Windows 95, your display will not look exactly like the screens in this book.

Before you get into Lesson 1, here's a quick look at the terrain that lies ahead:

- Lesson 1 explains the process of Web publishing and introduces the HoTMetaL program provided on the companion CD. You'll learn how to install HoTMetaL, then you'll take a tour of its features.
- Lesson 2 gets you started using HoTMetaL. You'll learn the syntax and structure of Web documents and you'll create your first Web home page.
- In Lesson 3, you'll learn to use HoTMetaL's basic text formatting features.
- Lesson 4 introduces you to more complex text formatting features that are extensions to basic HTML.
- Lesson 5 shows you how to insert inline graphics in your Web pages.

- In Lesson 6, you'll learn to organize your documents using lists and horizontal rules.
- Lesson 7 shows you how to link your Web pages to other Web documents and Internet services.
- Lesson 8 covers interactive forms. You'll learn how to create a basic form, then add such features as menus, buttons, and text input fields. Finally, you'll learn how to use these features to gather information from Web users.
- Lesson 9 introduces the Common Gateway Interface. You'll learn how to create Web documents that interface with external programs, called scripts. You'll also learn how to use image maps to create advanced graphical applications.
- Lesson 10 shows you how to use HoTMetaL to quickly and easily create complex tables.
- In Lesson 11, you'll learn how to incorporate multimedia files into your Web pages. You'll also learn all about external viewers.
- Lesson 12 covers additional HoTMetaL features, such as templates, styles, and macros, that will make the development of Web documents easier than ever before.
- Lesson 13 provides a Web publishing guide. You'll learn the minimum features that every Web application should provide and how to satisfy the high expectations of Web users. You'll also learn how to check your documents for correct spelling and validate them with respect to the latest Web document formats. Finally, you'll learn how to put your pages on the Web.
- Lesson 14 ties everything together with an extended example of developing a Web application. You'll use what you've learned in Lessons 1 through 13 to create and publish the example application.
- The Appendix identifies the shareware programs that are provided on the CD and explains how to install and begin using them. It also provides pointers to additional HTML reference information on the CD.

You should proceed through all these lessons in order. Subsequent lessons build on the concepts and skills taught in preceding lessons. Work through the book, page by page, and when you have completed it you will be an expert in using HoTMetaL to publish Web pages. You can then use this book as a HoTMetaL reference manual.

Conventions Used in This Book

Certain conventions are used in this book to make it easier for you to work with.

For instance, opposite each lesson's opening page is a large stopwatch that tells you the estimated number of minutes it will take you to read and work through the examples in that lesson. You can look at the stopwatch and set aside enough time to get through the whole lesson in one sitting.

▶ ▶ ▶ Throughout the book, notes call out important details. Some notes also cross-reference related topics elsewhere in the book.

▶ ▶ ▶ Tips provide information on ways to make Web publishing with HoTMetaL even easier.

▶ ▶ ▶ Warnings alert you to potential trouble spots.

Sidebars

Sidebars discuss interesting Web publishing and Internet-related topics in more detail.

Whenever you see the ↵ symbol, it signifies the Enter or Return key on your keyboard. We use this symbol because some keyboards label this key *Enter* and some label it *Return,* but almost all include the ↵ symbol.

The Companion CD

Inside the back cover of this book is the companion CD. The CD contains HoTMetaL Light 2.0, some HTML files that contain extra information about certain topics in the book, and additional shareware that you may find useful. See the inside back cover for a complete listing of the CD's contents.

1

GETTING STARTED

In this lesson, you'll get an overview of the Web's architecture and its key elements. You'll also learn the steps involved in Web publishing and how HoTMetaL helps simplify this process. You'll then install HoTMetaL and take an initial tour of its features.

How the Web Works

This section contains valuable background information on the structure and operation of the Web. Learning this information is necessary to understand the process of Web publishing. In the following paragraphs you'll study the key elements of the Web—pages, links, servers, browsers, and HTML. You'll learn what each element is and how it interacts with other elements to produce the dynamic entity known as the Web.

You should approach this material in a relaxed and casual manner. It may be new to you, but it is very easy to understand, and it helps set the stage for the following section on Web publishing. Just try to get an overall feel for what the Web is and how it works by becoming acquainted with its basic elements. Understanding these elements will be very useful, not only while you read this book, but as you continue to explore the Web itself.

► ► ► If you are already familiar with the Web's operation, you may want to skim this section and move on to the section entitled "How Web Pages Are Published."

Pages and Links

The goal of the Web, in the words of its creator Tim Berners-Lee, is to create "a seamless world in which all information, from any source, can be accessed in a consistent and simple way." Berners-Lee helped to achieve this goal by designing the Web as a simple collection of connected documents called *Web pages*. Web pages are used to store information and are connected via *links*. Links also connect Web pages to other files and Internet services. This basic structure is illustrated below.

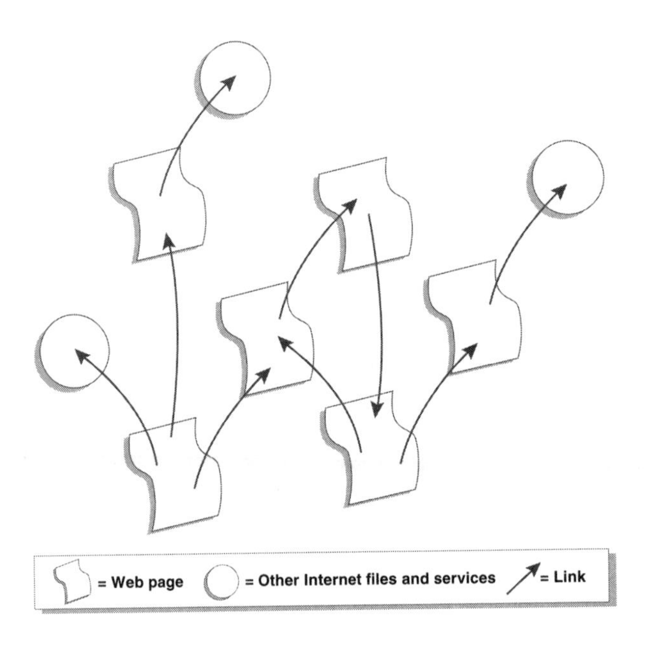

The linked pages of the Web are an example of an organizational system called *hypertext*. Hypertext is a way of connecting and presenting information that enables the user to explore a variety of paths through the information. The term was coined by Ted Nelson in the mid-1960s to refer to "nonsequential writing." Windows Help files are good examples of hypertext. These files contain key words (usually identified by color) that link related pages. By clicking on a key word, you immediately switch to the page to which that word is linked. The following illustration shows how a typical hypertext document works. Hypertext links on the Web connect text, graphics, multimedia, and Internet services in a flexible, easy to use manner.

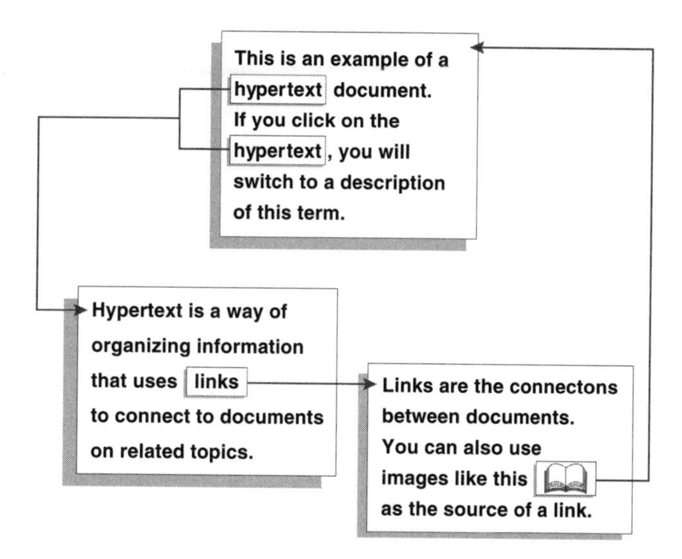

Servers and Browsers

Web pages are stored at various locations on the Web called *websites*. A website consists of a collection of Web pages that are accessed through a Web *server*. A Web server is a special program that makes the Web pages available for viewing by Web *browsers*, such as Netscape and Internet Explorer. Browsers are programs that retrieve pages from Web servers and display them to Web users. The Web pages are said to be *published* via the Web server.

Communication between Browsers and Servers

Now that you're familiar with the basic elements of the Web, let's take a look at how they interact.

If you're accessing the Web at home, you probably connect your computer to the Internet via an Internet service provider, a company that sells Internet access. This connection is usually made using a modem and a telephone line. Once your connection is established, you can use your computer to run your browser. This program fetches Web pages and displays them in a window on your computer. It fetches them from the World Wide Web, the collection of all websites on the Internet.

Your browser locates a Web page using the *universal resource locator*, or *URL*, for that page. The URL identifies the Internet location of the website containing the Web page, as well as the location of the page within the Web server. A URL is similar in function to a street address or phone number. For example, to find out about Internet books published by Sybex, you would tell your browser to fetch the Web page addressed by the URL **http://www.sybex.com/internet.html**. This URL identifies the location of the Sybex website as **www.sybex.com** and the file to be retrieved as *internet.html*.

Your browser talks to Web servers using a language called the *Hypertext Transfer Protocol*, or *HTTP*. This language is used to exchange information between browsers and servers. Your browser uses HTTP to request a Web page from a Web server, and the server then sends that page to your browser for display on your computer, as illustrated below. HTTP can also be used to send information to a Web server.

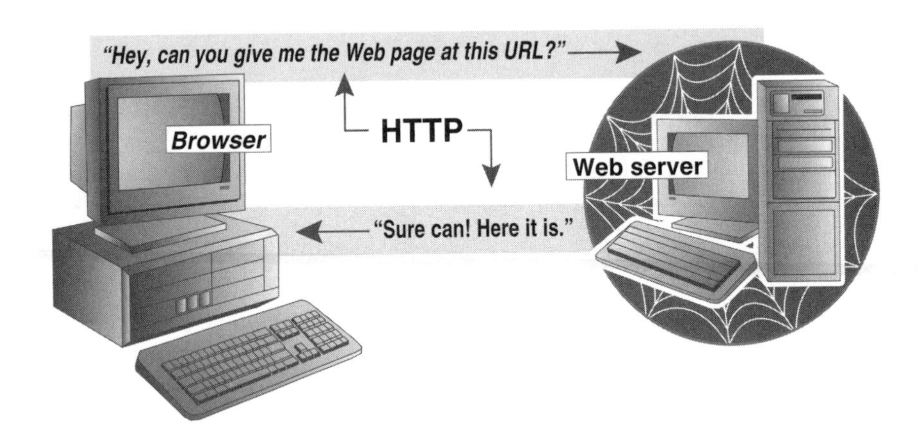

When your browser displays a Web page on your computer, there are usually links from that page to other Web pages. Most of today's browsers identify these links by using colored, highlighted, or underlined text, or images with colored borders. When you select a link by clicking on it with a mouse, or using special keyboard commands, your browser fetches the Web page associated with that link.

Web browsers and servers work together to implement the conceptual architecture of the Web shown earlier in the lesson. When you use your browser to access several Web pages in sequence, they appear to be seamlessly connected via the hypertext links. Your browser works with the Web servers that publish these pages to create this impression.

HTML

Now that you have a good understanding of how the Web works, there are only two more background topics that need to be covered—How are Web pages written? and How are they displayed by Web browsers? These questions are obviously very important to Web publishing. Their answers both involve HTML.

Web pages are written in the *Hypertext Markup Language*, or *HTML*. It is a very simple language that uses ordinary text files to identify what information is contained in a Web page and how that information is structured. HTML is very similar to word processor styles. You use it to identify the different parts of a Web page, such as its title, headings, lists, tables, and paragraphs. HTML also lets you specify links to other documents and include graphics and multimedia in your Web pages.

HTML is not a difficult language to learn. It's far simpler than any programming language, such as C or Pascal. HTML's major drawback is that it is cumbersome. If you want your Web page to be organized in a particular manner, you have to specify that organization in HTML, and that involves inserting the proper HTML formatting codes, called *tags*. Fortunately, HoTMetaL greatly simplifies the process of working with tags. In the next lesson, you'll learn all about tags and how to work with them using HoTMetaL.

The major benefit of HTML is that it focuses more on how a Web page is structured than on how it is displayed. This feature allows browsers to make the decision as to how a page may be best displayed using a particular computer system. It is an important feature of HTML because it allows Web pages to be operating system- and machine-independent.

The earliest browsers did not support graphical displays. They could only display Web pages in text mode. Lynx is an example of a text mode browser and is still popular with some DOS and Unix users. The Netscape Navigator is the most popular browser today. It supports many graphics formats and has many features that aren't supported by text mode browsers. The following illustration shows how Lynx and Netscape display the same Web page.

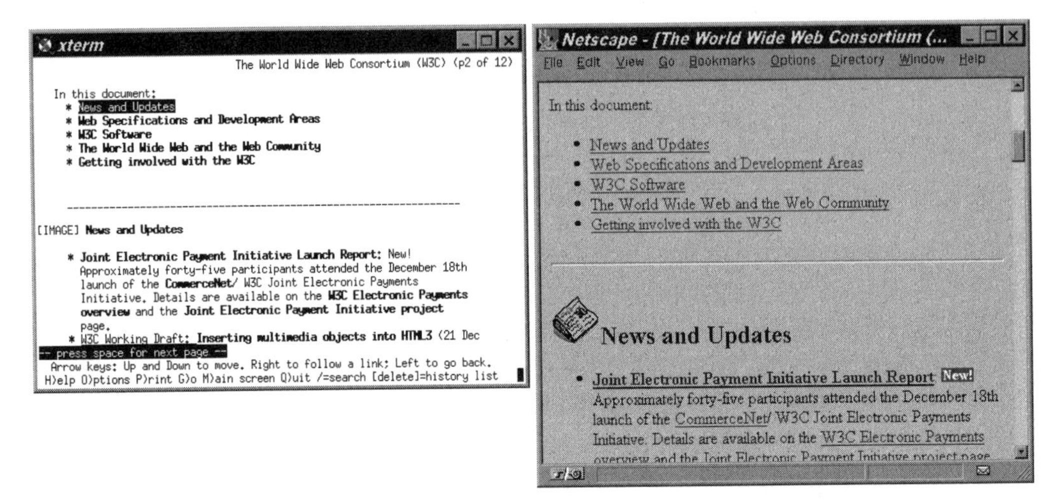

Lynx browser ***Netscape browser***

As you can see, the same Web page can look very different when viewed by different browsers. The fact that both browsers can read this page at all is the result of HTML's flexible design. If a Web page is carefully written, all browsers will display the page to the best of their abilities. For example, the Netscape browser is able to display all the features of the sample Web page above. The Lynx browser, although much less powerful, still adequately displays the sample page and identifies the fact that the page contains an image, even though it can't display the image.

▶ ▶ ▶ As you prepare your own Web pages, keep in mind that Web pages are not displayed in the same way by all browsers. Whenever possible, try to design your Web pages so that they will work well with both text- and graphics-oriented browsers.

How Web Pages Are Published

Now that you know how the Web works, it is easy to understand the process of Web publishing. First you create your Web pages, then you put them under the control of a Web server, and finally you let the world know they exist, as illustrated below. Of these three steps, the first is by far the most involved, and it is the primary subject of this book. The second step, described in Lesson 13, involves moving the pages that you have created from your computer to a Web server. Lesson 13 also covers step 3, registering and publicizing your Web pages.

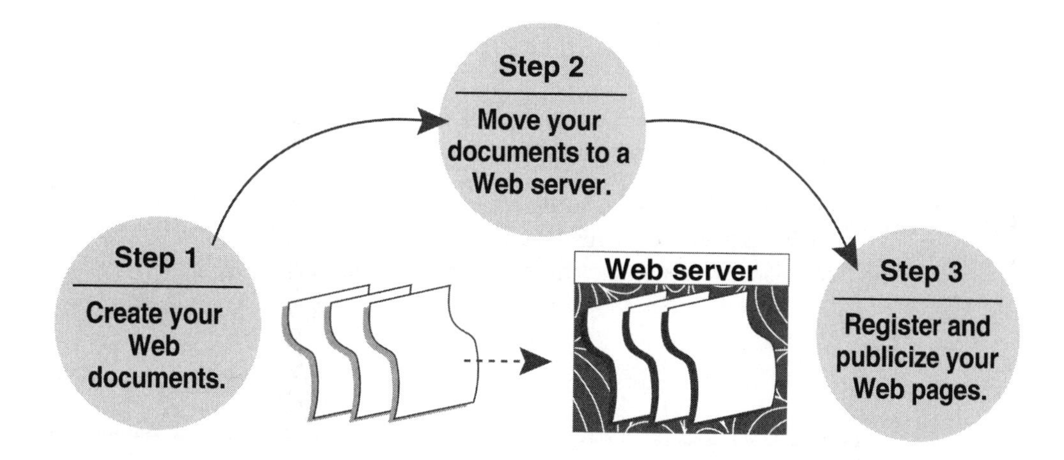

From here on, you'll learn how to create documents for publication on the Web using HoTMetaL. As you can probably guess from the way HoTMetaL is spelled, it has something to do with HTML.

Why Should I Use HoTMetaL?

There are two main reasons for using HoTMetaL: simplicity and correctness. HoTMetaL simplifies the process of creating Web pages by providing buttons and menus from which HTML elements may be selected and edited. These menus free you from having to memorize the details of the language syntax. They also allow you to create Web pages with a lot less typing.

HoTMetaL checks Web pages for correctness with respect to established standards. It ensures that your pages are correctly written and compatible with current and future Web browsers.

Installing HoTMetaL

Installing HoTMetaL is easy. It comes with an installation program that uncompresses the software, installs it in the correct directories, and sets up the SoftQuad HoTMetaL Light 2.0 program group. The CD contains both Windows 95 and Windows 3.1 versions of HoTMetaL. The Windows 95 version is installed by running the setup program located in the \hotmetal\win95 directory of the CD. The Windows 3.1 version is installed by running the setup program in the \hotmetal\windows3.1 directory.

►►► HoTMetaL Light is the same program as the award-winning HoTMetaL Pro 2.0 with the exception that the Pro version contains additional commands to import files from word processors such as Word and WordPerfect.

►►► These installation instructions assume that you are installing the Windows 95 version of HoTMetaL. If you are installing the Windows 3.1 version, the dialog boxes you encounter will differ slightly from the ones shown here.

1 Click on the **Start** button and select **Run** from the Start menu.

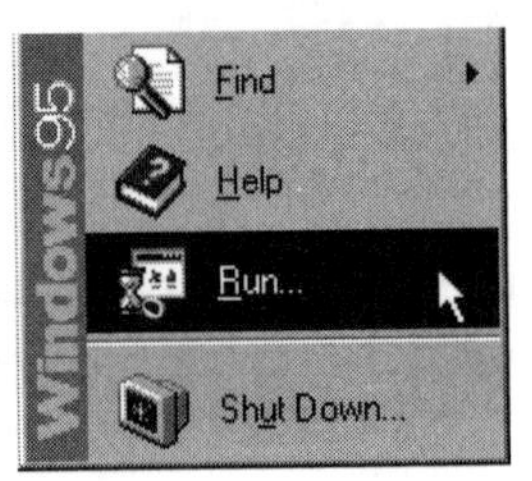

▶ The Run dialog box is displayed.

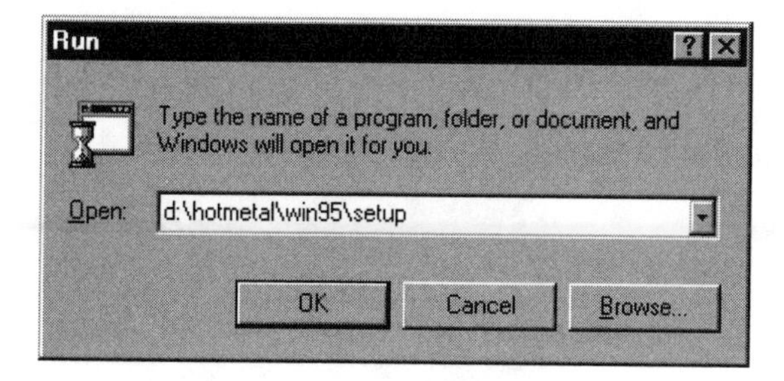

2 Type **d:\hotmetal\win95\setup** in the Run dialog box. If your CD-ROM uses a different drive letter, substitute that drive letter for *d*.

3 Click on **OK**.

▶ The Setup program notifies you that it is initializing, and then the Welcome Message dialog box appears.

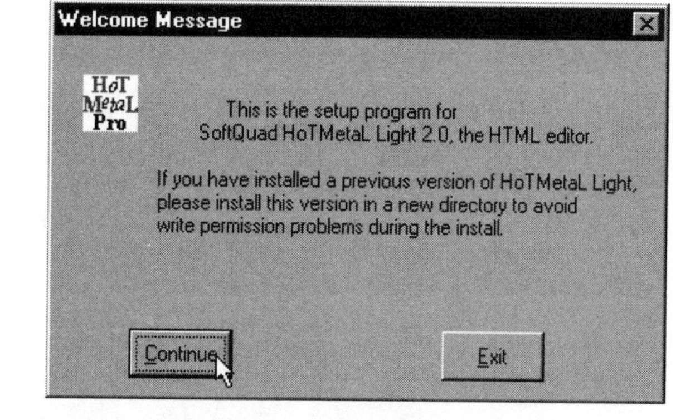

4 Click on **Continue**.

▶ The Installation Location dialog box appears.

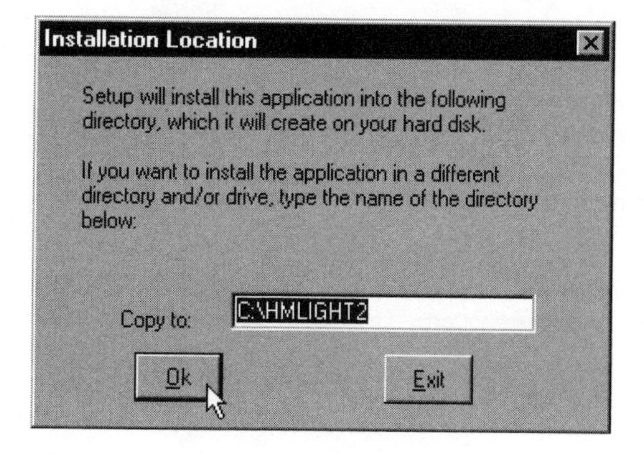

5 Click on **Ok** to install HoTMetaL in the c:\hmlight2 directory.

▶ The Setup program installs HoTMetaL files in the specified directory. Vertical and horizontal gauges indicate the progress of the installation.

▶ When all of the files have been installed, the Setup program prompts you to approve the creation of the SoftQuad HoTMetaL Light 2.0 program group.

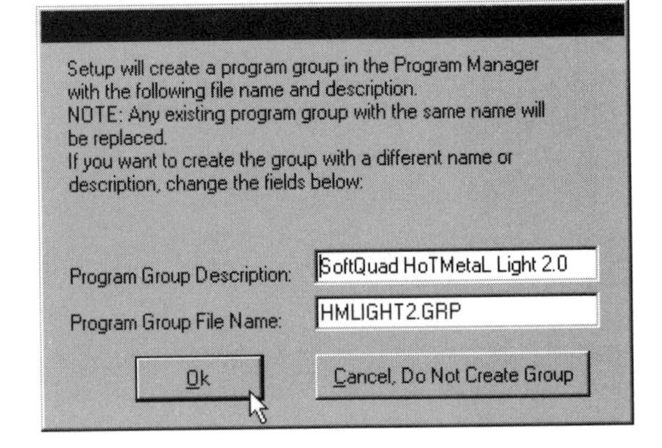

6 Click on **Ok** to create the program group.

▶ The program group is created. The Setup program then informs you that installation is complete and prompts you to view the readme file.

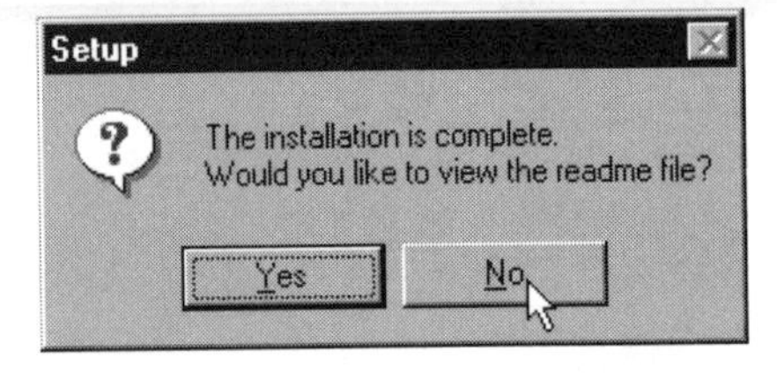

7 Click on **No**.

▶ The Setup program terminates, leaving the HoTMetaL program group window open. Icons for the HoTMetaL Light program and the readme file are shown.

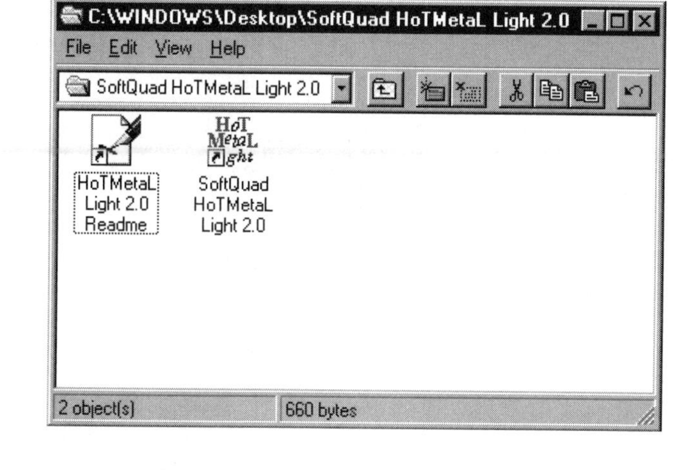

8 Close the program group window by clicking on the **Close** icon (the X in the upper-right corner of the window).

▶ If you look at the icons on your Windows 95 Desktop, you will notice the SoftQuad HoTMetaL Light 2.0 folder. This folder contains the icons for the HoTMetaL program and readme file.

Congratulations! You've installed HoTMetaL Light 2.0.

▶ ▶ ▶ You can view the HoTMetaL readme file at any time by selecting it from the SoftQuad HoTMetaL Light 2.0 program group. It contains information on registration and product support, new features, and known problems.

Starting HoTMetaL

Now that you've installed HoTMetaL, I'm sure that you're anxious to start it up and see how it runs. You could have double-clicked on the SoftQuad HoTMetaL Light 2.0 program icon when the HoTMetaL program group window was open, but I'll show you how you can always start HoTMetaL, even when the program group window is not visible.

1 From the Windows 95 Desktop, open the SoftQuad HoTMetaL Light 2.0 folder, then double-click on the **SoftQuad HoTMetaL Light 2.0** program icon to launch the HoTMetaL program.

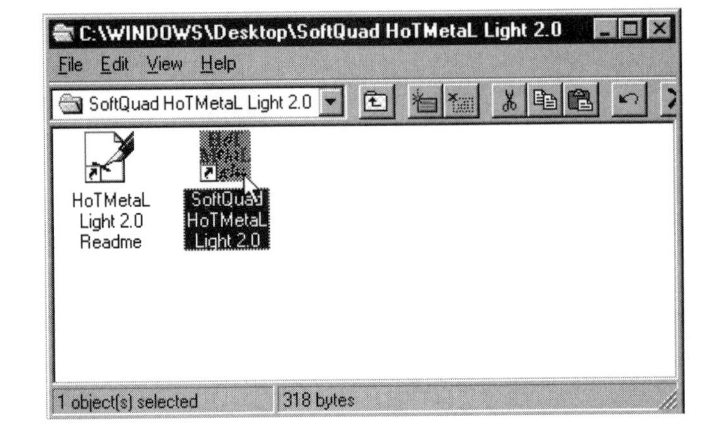

▶ The HoTMetaL Light opening window is displayed, followed by the Register Now dialog box.

2 Click on **OK** to dismiss the dialog box. (You can register later by selecting Registration from the Help menu.)

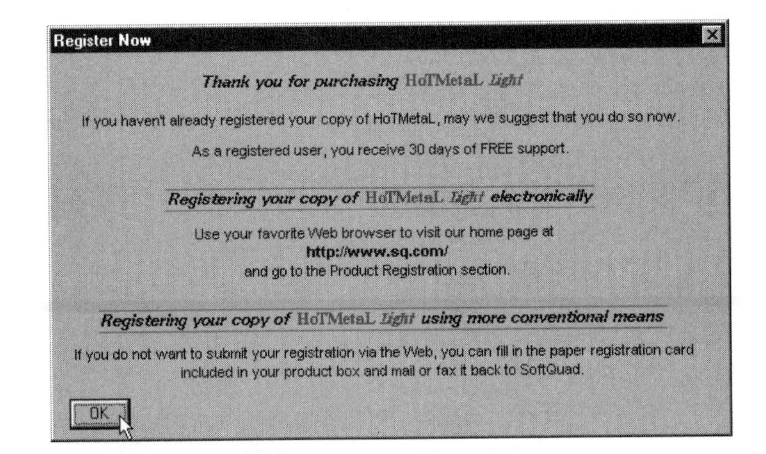

▶ The HoTMetaL Light program window appears. Notice that most of the program's toolbar buttons are dimmed.

3 Click on the **Maximize** button.

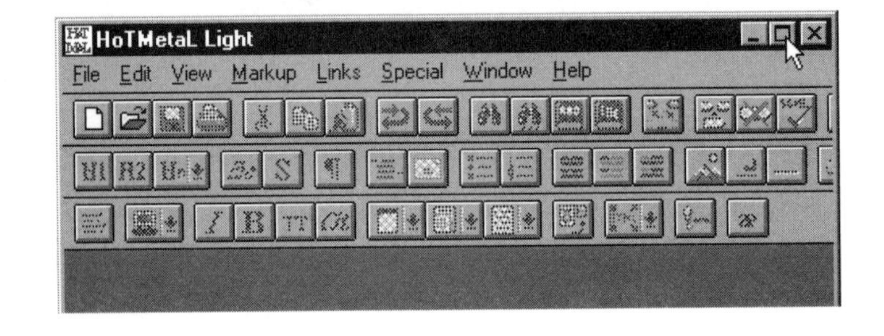

The window is maximized and all toolbar buttons are visible. Next we'll go on a tour of HoTMetaL's features.

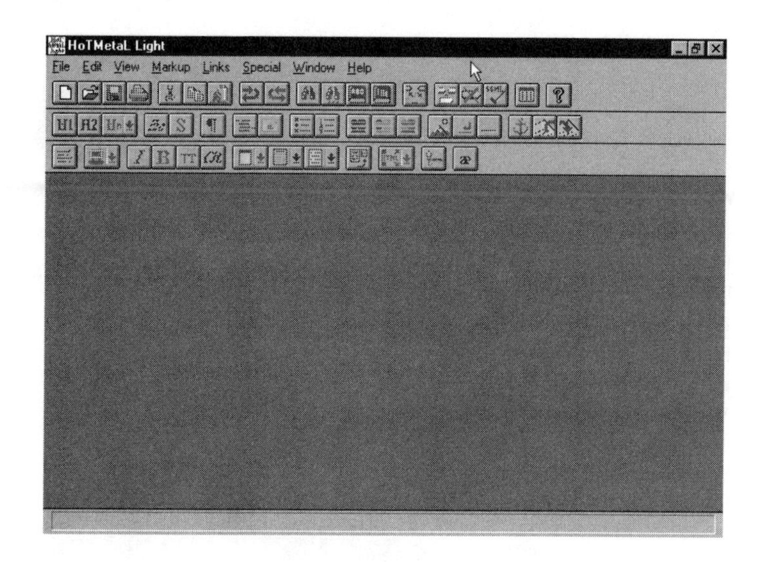

A Tour of HoTMetaL's Features

Having installed and launched HoTMetaL, you're ready to explore some of its features. This section will provide you with an overview of the HoTMetaL graphical user interface. Don't worry about learning the specific details of each feature. Just try to become familiar with the basic layout of the program. You will learn how each feature works over the course of the lessons in this book.

1 Click on the **New** icon to open a new HoTMetaL document.

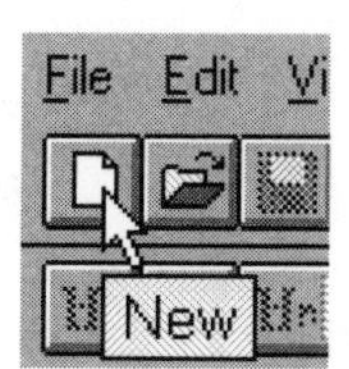

▶ A new HoTMetaL document is created. All the toolbar buttons light up and the document contains some pointy-looking objects. These pointy objects are how HoTMetaL displays the HTML tags that you learned about earlier in this lesson. Tags represent HTML syntax elements. You'll learn much more about tags in Lesson 2. For now, just be aware of how they are displayed.

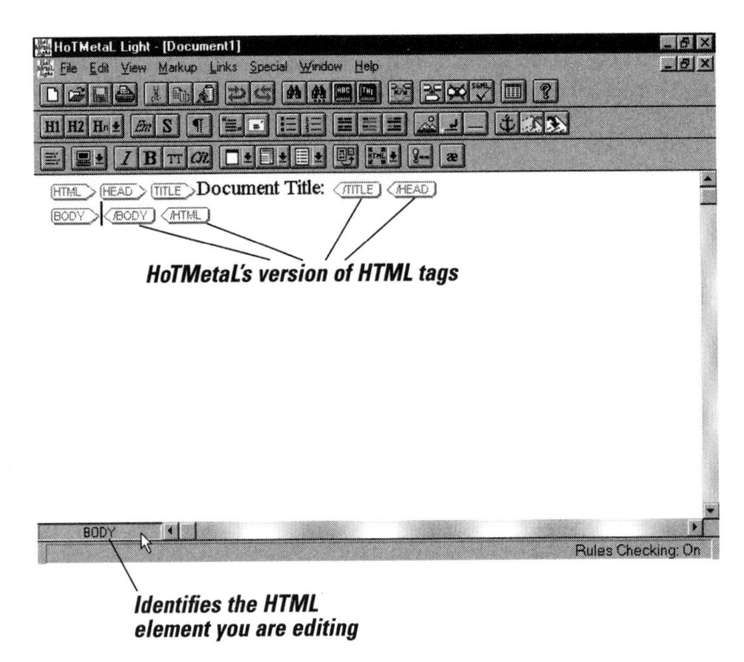

▶ The little bar in the lower-left corner of the HoTMetaL window containing the text *BODY* is used to identify the HTML element that you are currently editing. If you click your mouse in other parts of the document, it will change to tell you that you are editing another HTML element.

▶ The lower-right corner of the HoTMetaL window indicates that rules checking is on. This means that HoTMetaL is checking your document to make sure that it contains valid HTML.

Now let's get back to the toolbars and the menu bar.

The HoTMetaL Toolbars

HoTMetaL has three toolbars. The HoTMetaL Pro documentation refers to these toolbars as the *standard, common HTML,* and *other HTML* toolbars. I find it clearer and easier to refer to them as the *top, middle,* and *bottom* toolbars.

The buttons in the top toolbar support file operations, editing tools, document tools, and help.

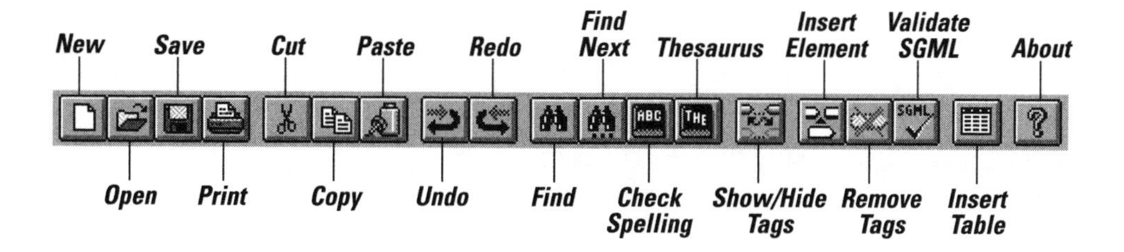

The buttons in the middle toolbar support the insertion of common HTML elements: text formatting tags, lists, images, and hypertext links.

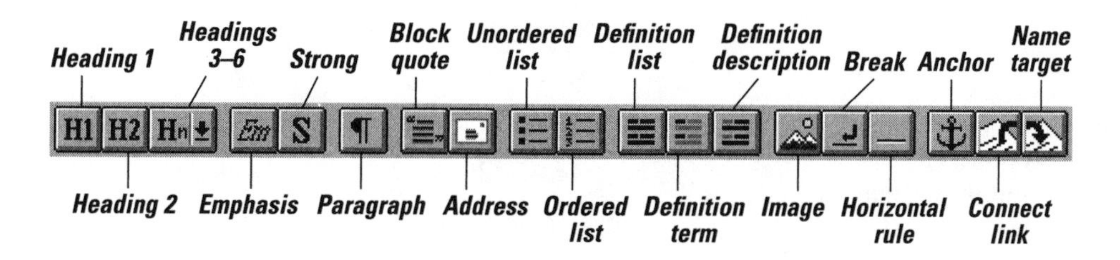

The buttons in the bottom toolbar support the insertion of text formatting tags, forms, lists, HTML extensions, comments, and special characters.

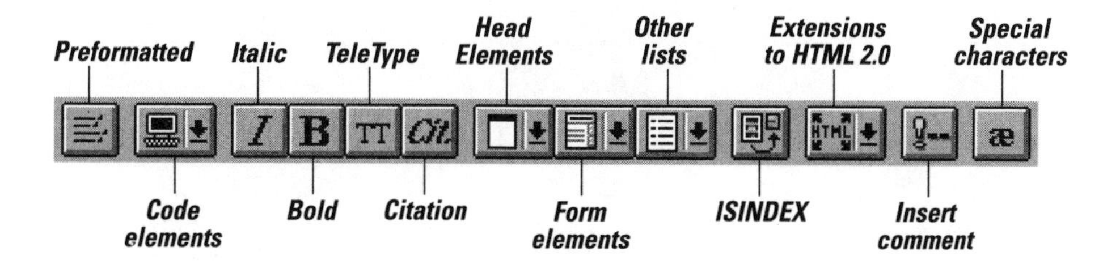

The HoTMetaL toolbars provide the ultimate convenience for developing Web pages. You'll learn how to use all of the toolbar buttons in the next few lessons. By learning to use these buttons, you will greatly simplify the process of developing your Web pages.

The HoTMetaL Menu Bar

The HoTMetaL menu bar consists of eight pull-down menus: File, Edit, View, Markup, Links, Special, Window, and Help.

1. Click on **File** to see the File menu. This menu lets you perform common file operations such as opening, closing, saving, and printing. The Preview feature allows you to preview a HoTMetaL document using your Web browser.

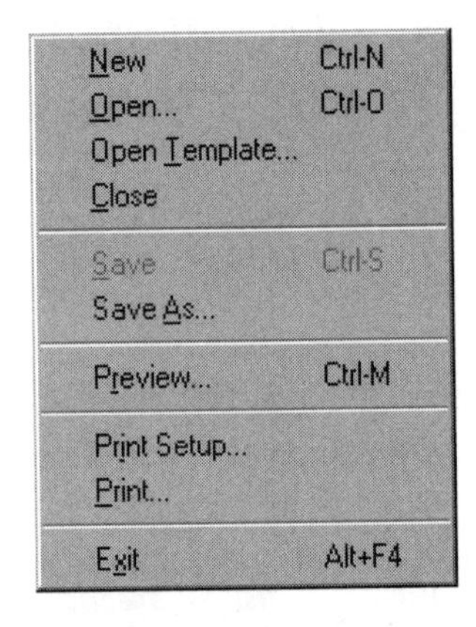

2. Click on **Edit** to see the Edit menu. This menu lets you perform common edit operations such as cutting and pasting. It also provides access to the spell checker and thesaurus.

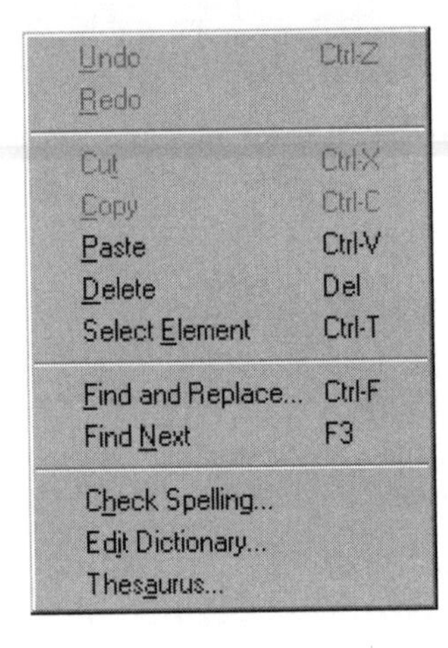

3 Click on **View** to see the View menu, which allows you to look at your HoTMetaL documents from a variety of perspectives. It also allows you to change the appearance of the HoTMetaL window.

Hide Tags Ctrl-W
Show Invisibles
Show Outline View F11
View Image...
Hide Inline Images
Hide URLs
Styles... Ctrl-B
Load Styles...
Save Styles...
Toolbars...

4 Click on **Markup**. The Markup menu lets you edit the HTML tags in the HoTMetaL document window as well as insert tables and special characters.

Insert Element... Ctrl-I
Change... Ctrl-L
Split Element Ctrl-P
Join to Preceding Ctrl-J
Remove Tags Ctrl-D
Edit SGML Attributes... F6
Insert Table...
Cell Properties...
Row Properties...
Edit Table...
Special Characters... Ctrl-E
Insert Comment F8

5 Click on **Links** to access the Links menu, which lets you develop and maintain hypertext links.

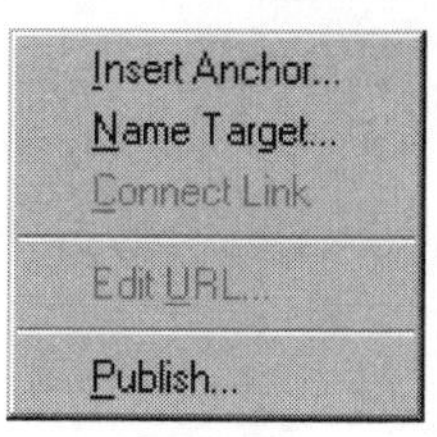

6 Click on **Special**. This menu allows you to validate documents; record, edit, and run macros; and select user preferences.

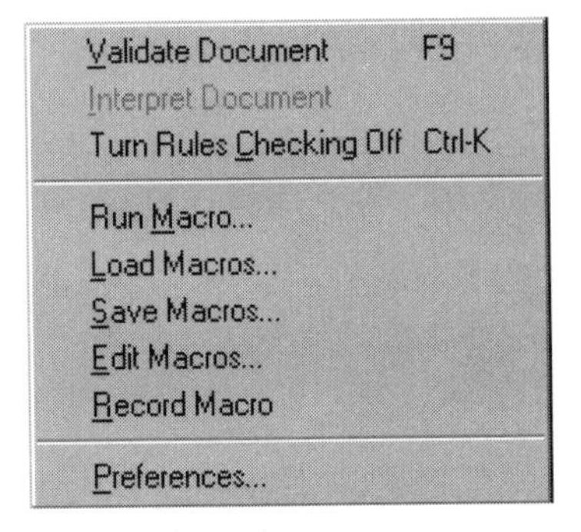

7 Click on **Window**. The Window menu allows you to switch between documents and change the manner in which windows are displayed.

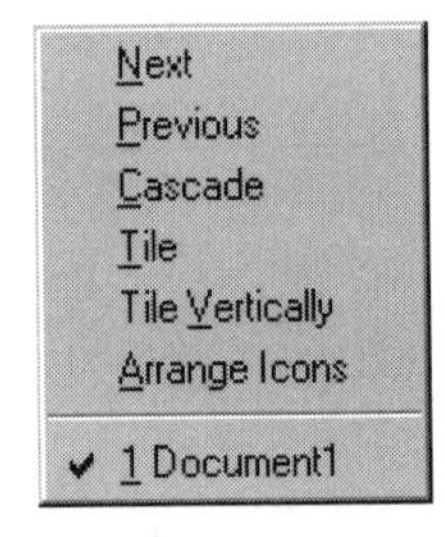

8 Finally, click on **Help**. The Help menu provides extensive help features, including an HTML tutorial and quick reference manual. The Help menu also supports online registration and communication with SoftQuad.

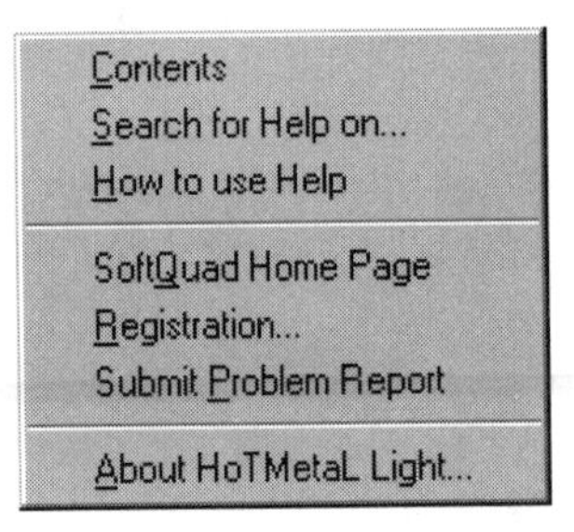

Our tour of HoTMetaL's features is at an end.

9 To exit HoTMetaL, click on the **Close** button.

► The HoTMetaL program closes and you return to your desktop.

Creating a Working Directory

In subsequent lessons, you will be using HoTMetaL to develop Web pages that explore the features of HTML. You should now create a working directory where you can save the pages that you develop while carrying out the lessons in this book. To create the new directory c:\html:

1 In the Start menu, click on **Programs**.

2 In the Programs menu, click on **Windows Explorer**.

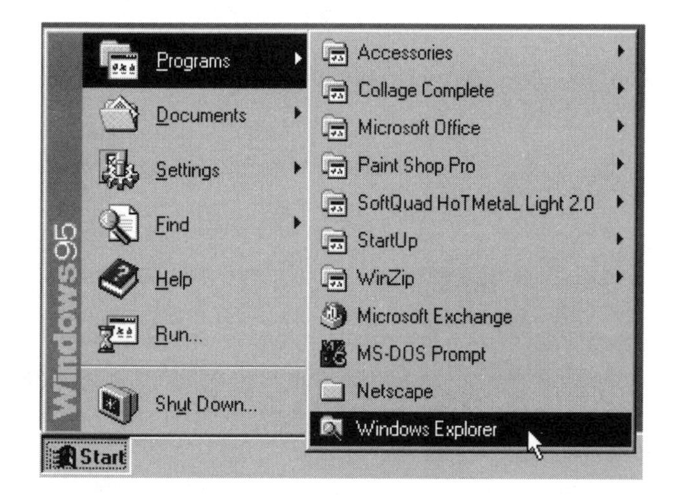

▶ The Windows Explorer window pops up.

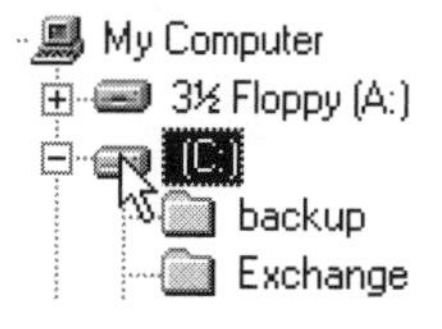

3 Click on your **C:** hard drive icon to change to the c: directory.

4 Select **File ➢ New ➢ Folder**.

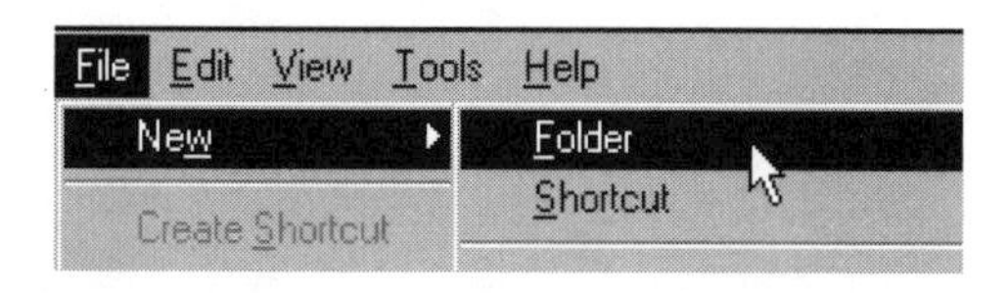

▶ The New Folder icon appears.

5 Type **html** and press ↵. (The ↵ symbol stands for the Enter or Return key on your keyboard.)

► You have created the c:\html directory as your working directory.

► ► ► If you want to use a different directory, you may do so. However, subsequent lessons will assume that you are using c:\html as your working directory.

In this lesson, you learned how the Web works and how to use HoTMetaL to publish documents on the Web. You installed HoTMetaL, took a tour of its features, and set up a working directory for saving your Web pages. Now you're all set to go on to Lesson 2 and develop your first Web page.

2

USING HOTMETAL

In this lesson, you'll learn how to use HoTMetaL and your Web browser to create and view your first Web page. You'll be introduced to the syntax of HTML, and you'll learn how to use tags to specify the structure of Web pages. You'll use HoTMetaL to work with tags that support text formatting. When you finish this lesson, you'll be able to create basic Web pages.

▶ ▶ ▶ This lesson introduces the syntax of HTML and the structure of Web pages. Understanding the information contained in this lesson is required before going on to subsequent lessons.

Creating Your First Web Page

You're going to create your first Web home page using HoTMetaL and then view it using your Web browser. Your home page is the first Web page that people see when they link to your website. It may provide links to other Web pages that you've created or to pages and services at locations around the Web. The home page that you create during this lesson will not be accessible from the Web.

Before you begin, you need to run HoTMetaL. If you have not already installed HoTMetaL, or you want a refresher on how to start the program, go back to Lesson 1 and follow the instructions under the heading "Starting HoTMetaL." Once the program is running, the following steps will walk you through creating a new document, giving it a name, entering two lines of text, and saving your first Web page.

1 Select **File > New.**

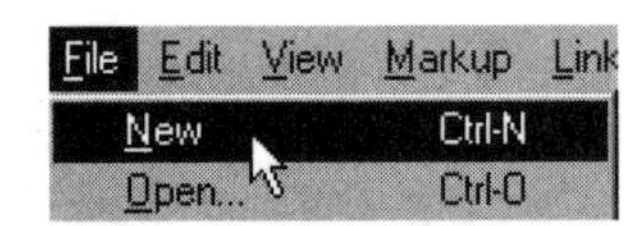

▶ A new HoTMetaL document is created. Note that the new document opens with the cursor between the **BODY** and **/BODY** tags.

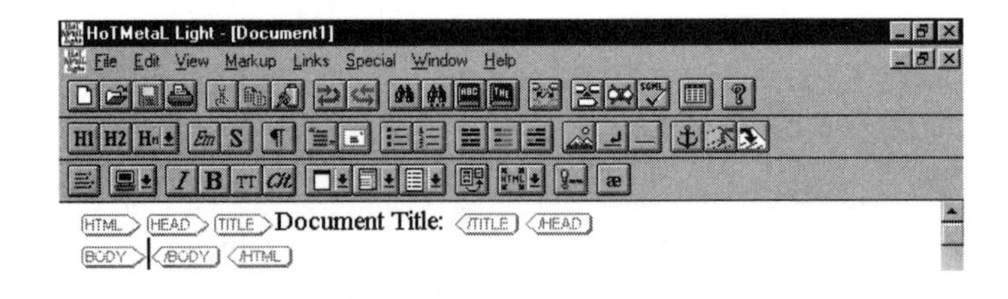

2 Move the cursor immediately to the left of the **/TITLE** tag and type **My First Home Page**.

HTML HEAD TITLE Document Title: My First Home Page /TITLE /HEAD
BODY /BODY /HTML

3 Move the cursor back between the **BODY** and **/BODY** tags.

4 Type **Hello World!**

BODY P Hello World! /P /BODY /HTML

▶ HoTMetaL inserts **P** and **/P** tags around the text.

5 Click on the **Break** toolbar button.

▶ **BR** and **/BR** tags appear in your document.

BODY P Hello World!
BR /BR /P /BODY /HTML

6 Type **Welcome to my home page.**

BODY P Hello World!
BR /BR
Welcome to my home page. /P /BODY /HTML

► HoTMetaL inserts your text after the **/BR** tag.

7 Select **File ➢ Save** and save your Web page in the c:\html directory, using the name ch02-01.htm.

Using Your Browser to View Your Home Page

Having created and saved your home page, you'll now view it with your Web browser. Your browser must be installed and working properly to complete this lesson. Consult your browser's documentation for installation and operation instructions. The examples in this book use Netscape Navigator 2.0. You may use any browser that fully supports HTML 2.0, the Netscape extensions, and HTML 3.0 tables. To avoid any confusion, I recommend getting Netscape 2.0.

1 Select **File ➢ Preview.**

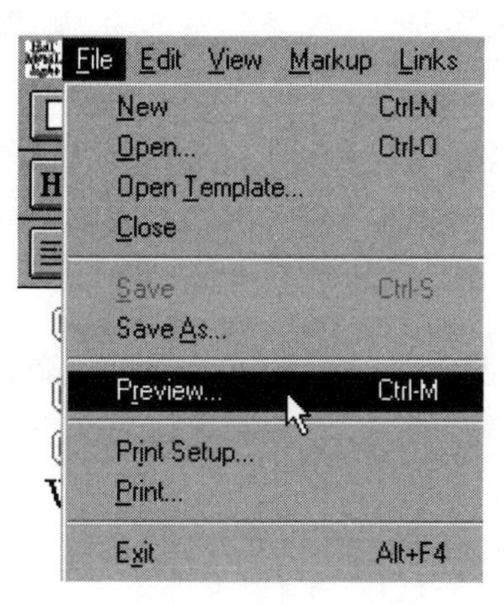

▶ The Choose Browser dialog box appears.

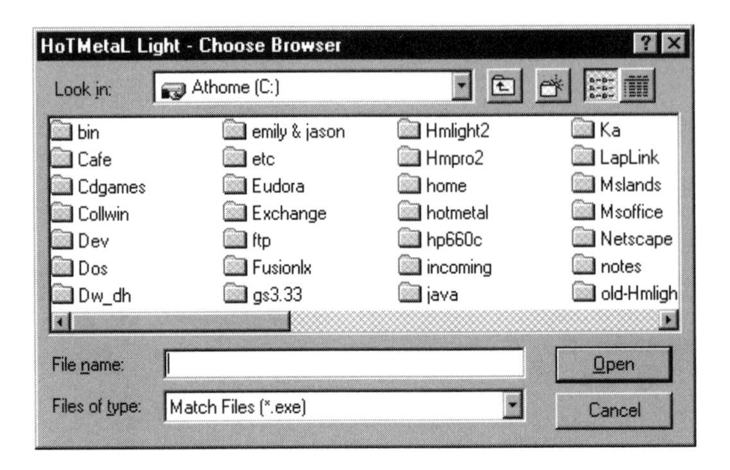

2 Use the dialog box to navigate to the directory where your browser's program file is located.

3 Double-click on the executable file name of your browser.

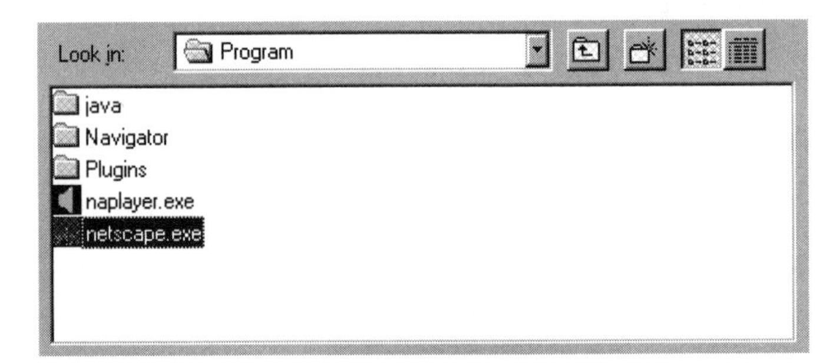

▶ Another Choose Browser dialog box appears.

4 Click on the **Preview** button.

▶ HoTMetaL launches the browser that you selected and points the browser at your Web page.

▶ The selected browser displays your Web page.

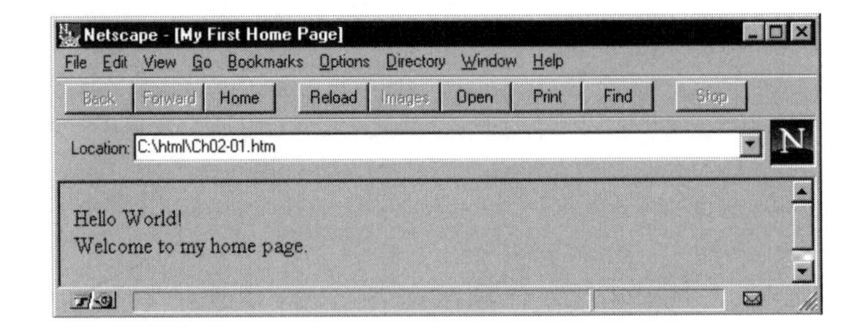

Congratulations! You have just built and displayed your first home page. Leave your browser running and move on to the next section.

Tagging and HTML Syntax

As you learned in Lesson 1, HTML uses *tags* to specify the structure of Web pages. There are two basic types of HTML tags: *surrounding* tags and *separating* tags. If you look at the ch02-01.htm file we created earlier in the lesson, you will see examples of both types of tags.

The actual text files generated by HoTMetaL are referred to as HTML *source files* or *source documents*. You can view these files using a word processing program or text editor. In addition, most Web browsers provide commands that allow you to view source files. The illustration below shows the relationship between HoTMetaL, source files, and your Web browser.

You use HoTMetaL to generate a source HTML file containing your Web page.

You use your browser to display the source HTML file in local mode (i.e., without having to request it from a Web server).

You can also use your browser to view the contents of the source file.

1 Use your browser's View Document Source command to look at the source HTML file that HoTMetaL created.

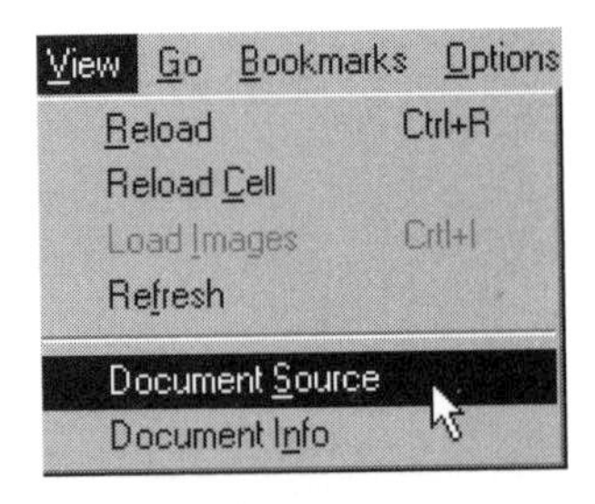

▶ The source document appears in a separate window.

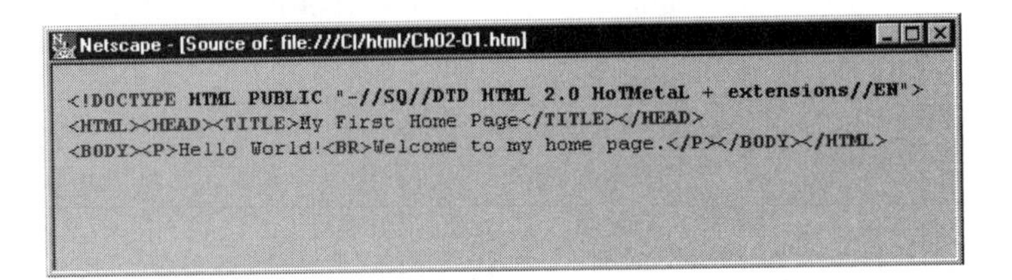

The first line of the source document displays the document type declaration for your Web page. This line was automatically inserted by HoTMetaL. It tells browsers that your Web page contains HTML version 2.0 tags and, possibly, some extensions to HTML 2.0. HoTMetaL will always insert this line at the beginning of your Web pages.

The actual HTML in your Web page begins with the **<HTML>** tag and ends with the **</HTML>** tag. These tags are examples of surrounding tags. Your document contains other surrounding tags: **<HEAD>** and **</HEAD>**, **<TITLE>** and **</TITLE>**, **<BODY>** and **</BODY>**, and **<P>** and **</P>**.

Surrounding tags are written in the form

<TAG_NAME>text that is surrounded</TAG_NAME>

The first tag is referred to as the *opening* tag and the second tag is referred to as the *closing* tag. Closing tags always begin with a slash (/) and opening tags do not.

Separating tags are placed between the items that are to be separated. For example, in your home page, the tag **
** is used to separate the first line, "Hello World!," from the second line, "Welcome to my home page."

The use of tags to identify the structure of a document is known as *markup*. HTML is referred to as a *markup language*.

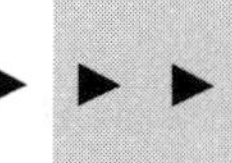

Tags may be written in any combination of upper- and lowercase. The examples in this book use uppercase to distinguish tags from other text.

As you learned in Lesson 1, HoTMetaL displays surrounding tags using arrow-like shapes. The right-pointing arrows indicate opening tags. The left-pointing arrows identify closing tags. HoTMetaL displays separating tags as if they were surrounding tags, with an opening tag followed by a closing tag. However, this is for display purposes only. It still inserts the correct separating HTML tag in your Web pages, as illustrated below.

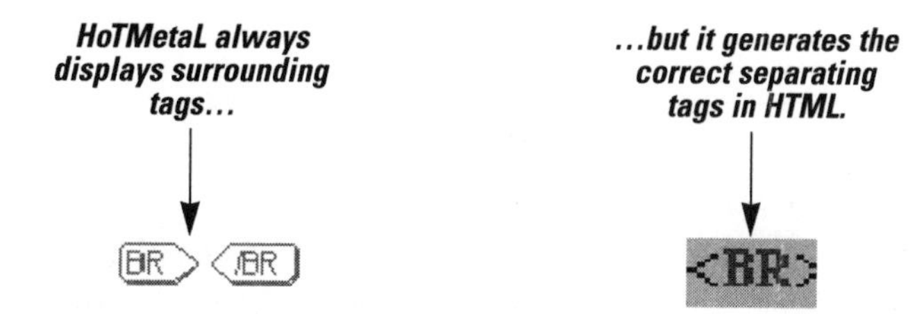
HoTMetaL always displays surrounding tags...
BR
/BR
...but it generates the correct separating tags in HTML.

Why does HoTMetaL do this? Some surrounding and separating tags contain additional information, known as *attributes.* To access a tag's attributes, you click immediately after the opening tag, then select Markup ➢ Edit SGML Attributes. By displaying all tags as surrounding tags, HoTMetaL provides a consistent, easy to use graphical interface for accessing tags and their attributes.

Creating Basic Web Pages

Now that you've created and displayed your first home page and learned about HTML tags, let's look at some of the tags used to create basic Web pages. Although the goal of this book is to show you how to write Web pages using HoTMetaL, it is useful to learn about the HTML tags generated by HoTMetaL. By learning the purpose of these tags, you will have a better understanding of how HoTMetaL operates, and you'll feel more confident and comfortable using it to develop your Web pages.

Basic Structure Tags

The top-level structure of a Web page is defined by three surrounding tags: the *HTML* tag, the *head* tag, and the *body* tag. You used these tags in your first home page. Almost all browsers would correctly display your page even if you left these tags out, but to be on the safe side, HoTMetaL automatically inserts them in new documents. These basic tags are shown below.

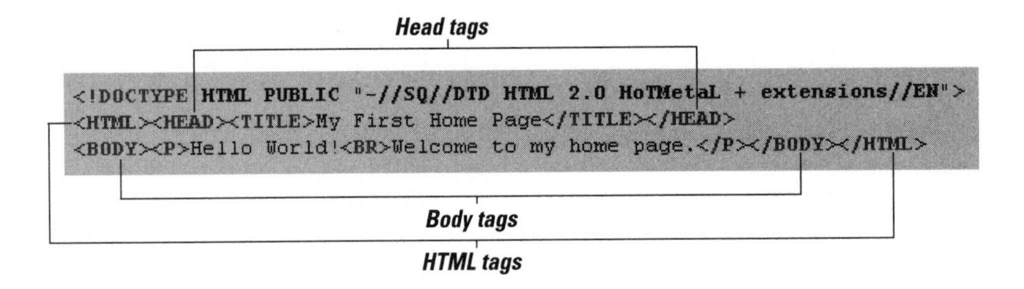
Head tags
<!DOCTYPE HTML PUBLIC "-//SQ//DTD HTML 2.0 HoTMetaL + extensions//EN">
<HTML><HEAD><TITLE>My First Home Page</TITLE></HEAD>
<BODY><P>Hello World!
Welcome to my home page.</P></BODY></HTML>
Body tags
HTML tags

- The *HTML* tag is used to indicate the beginning and end of a Web page. Each page should begin with **<HTML>** and end with **</HTML>**. The HTML tags surround the entire document.
- The *head* tag is used to identify the head of a Web page. The primary element of the head is the title. The head begins with **<HEAD>** and ends with **</HEAD>**. Notice that the head surrounds the title but not the main body of the document.
- The *body* tag is used to identify the main body of a Web page. The body of the document begins with **<BODY>** and ends with **</BODY>**. It contains everything except for the head and the HTML tags.

Giving Your Web Page a Title

The title of a Web page is analogous to the title of a book, article, or report. It is the human-readable name associated with the page. Just as every book should have a title, so should every Web page. The title is usually displayed at the top of the browser Window.

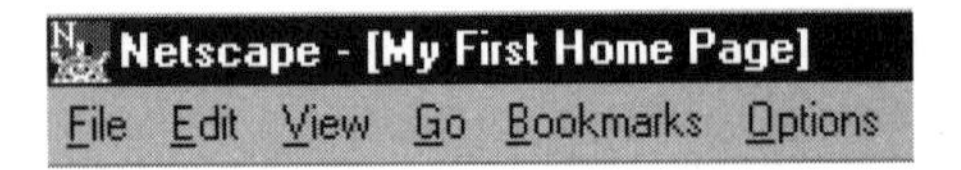
Netscape - [My First Home Page]
File Edit View Go Bookmarks Options

The title is identified using the **<TITLE>** and **</TITLE>** tags and is placed in the head. A page can have only one title. No other tags may be embedded in the title.

```
<!DOCTYPE HTML PUBLIC "-//SQ//DTD HTML 2.0 HoTMetaL + extensions//EN">
<HTML><HEAD><TITLE>My First Home Page</TITLE></HEAD>
<BODY><P>Hello World!<BR>Welcome to my home page.</P></BODY></HTML>
```

Title tags

It is important to select good titles for your pages. You may not be able to judge a book by its cover, but you should be able to judge a Web page by its title. The title should summarize what your page is all about. If someone decides to save a reference to a particular page on their browser hotlist, the title of the page will be saved on the list. Choosing a good title will help them remember what was contained on your page.

Specifying Heading Levels

HTML headings are analogous to the headings that may be found in books, articles, or reports. In these documents, various levels of section and subsection headings are used to organize the presentation of written material. HTML headings serve the same purpose. They are used to organize Web pages into sections and subsections.

HTML provides up to six heading levels with the first level being the most prominent and the sixth level being the least prominent. HTML uses the nested tags **<H1>**, **<H2>**, **<H3>**, **<H4>**, **<H5>**, and **<H6>** to denote the six heading levels. For example,

```
<H3>this is a third level heading</H3>
```

It is not necessary to use a lower numbered heading before a higher numbered heading, but it is recommended for clarity and consistency.

The following example shows how all six heading levels are displayed by your browser.

► ► ► This example and all subsequent examples assume that you know how to open HoTMetaL and use it with your browser. If you do not, go back and review Lesson 1 and the beginning of this lesson.

1 Close all browser windows and exit your browser.

2 Close the HoTMetaL document we were working on before by selecting **File ➢ Close**, but leave HoTMetaL running.

3 Click on the **New** toolbar button.

► A new document window opens.

HTML HEAD TITLE Document Title: Using Heading Levels /TITLE /HEAD
BODY /BODY /HTML

4 Move the cursor immediately before the **/TITLE** tag and type **Using Heading Levels**.

5 Move the cursor between the **BODY** and **/BODY** tags.

6 Click on the **Heading 1** (H1) toolbar button.

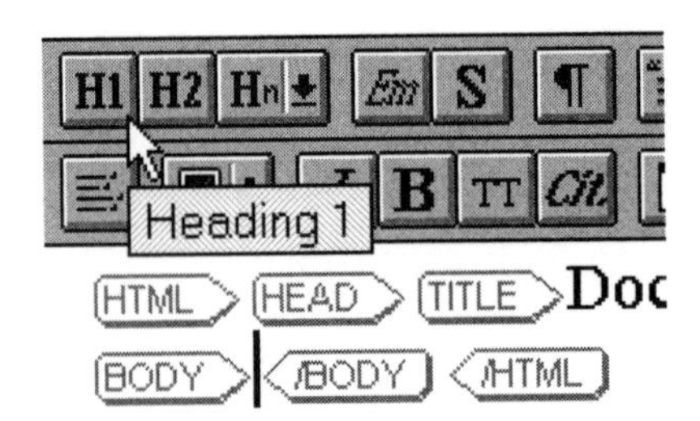

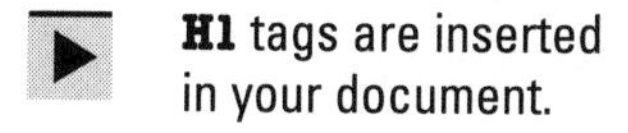

H1 tags are inserted in your document.

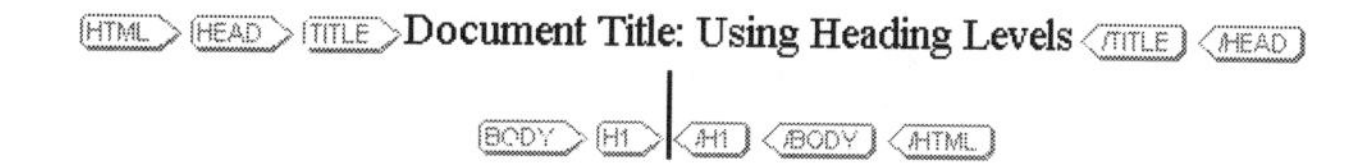

7 Type **This is a level 1 heading.**

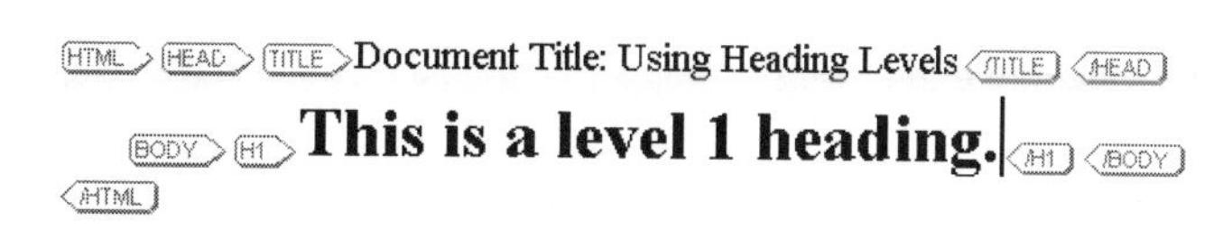

8 Move the cursor between the **/H1** and **/BODY** tags and click on the **Heading 2** (H2) toolbar button.

H2 tags are inserted.

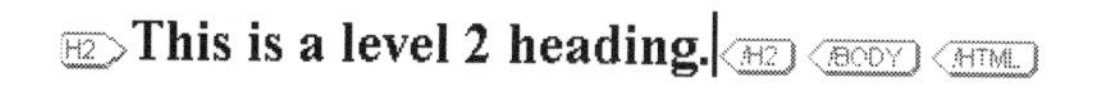

9 Type **This is a level 2 heading.**

H2 This is a level 2 heading. /H2 /BODY /HTML

10 Move the cursor between the **/H2** and **/BODY** tags and click on the down-arrow on the right side of the **Headings 3–6** (Hn) toolbar button.

A menu pops up.

11 Select **H3**.

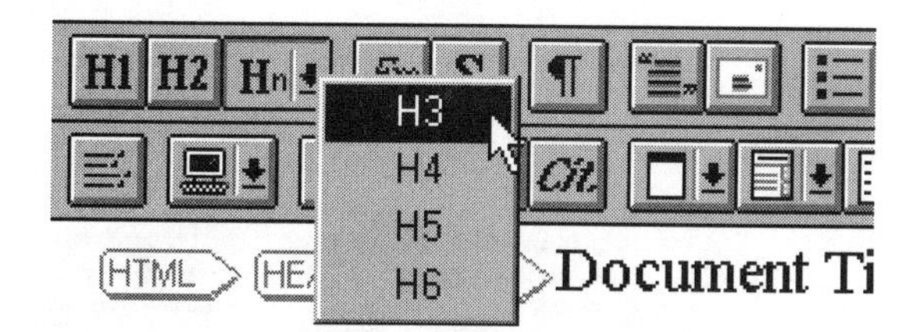

▶ **H3** tags are inserted in your document.

BODY H1 **This is a level 1 heading.** /H1

H2 **This is a level 2 heading.** /H2

H3 ***This is a level 3 heading.*** /H3 /BODY /HTML

12 Type **This is a level 3 heading.** and move the cursor between the **/H3** and **/BODY** tags.

13 Repeat steps 10–12 for level 4, 5, and 6 headings.

▶ The finished product has all six headings, from large to small.

HTML HEAD TITLE Document Title: Using Heading Levels /TITLE /HEAD

BODY H1 **This is a level 1 heading.** /H1

H2 **This is a level 2 heading.** /H2

H3 ***This is a level 3 heading.*** /H3

H4 **This is a level 4 heading.** /H4

H5 *This is a level 5 heading.* /H5

H6 **This is a level 6 heading.** /H6 /BODY /HTML

Now we'll save the file and view it with a browser.

14 Select **File ➢ Save As** and save your file as c:\html\ch02-02.htm.

15 Press **Ctrl+M**.

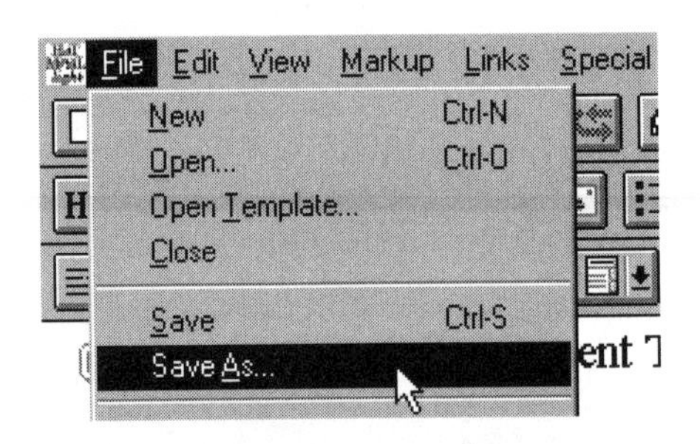

▶ The **Choose Browser** dialog box appears.

16 Click on the **Preview** button to launch your browser.

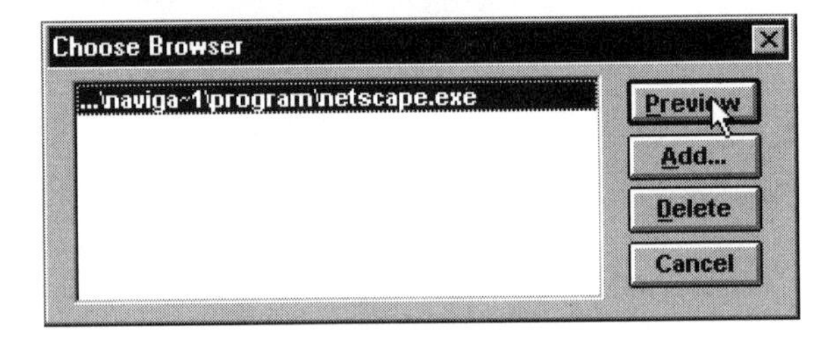

▶ Your browser displays the headings page. Notice how the fonts gradually get smaller for higher numbered headings.

This is a level 1 heading.
This is a level 2 heading.
This is a level 3 heading.
This is a level 4 heading.
This is a level 5 heading.
This is a level 6 heading.

17 Use your browser's View Document Source feature to look at the HTML file that HoTMetaL generated.

```
<!DOCTYPE HTML PUBLIC "-//SQ//DTD HTML 2.0 HoTMetaL + extensions//EN">
<HTML><HEAD><TITLE>Using Heading Levels</TITLE></HEAD>
<BODY><H1>This is a level 1 heading.</H1>
<H2>This is a level 2 heading.</H2>
<H3>This is a level 3 heading.</H3>
<H4>This is a level 4 heading.</H4>
<H5>This is a level 5 heading.</H5>
<H6>This is a level 6 heading.</H6></BODY></HTML>
```

18 Close all browser windows and exit your browser.

19 Close the ch02-02.htm HoTMetaL document, but do not exit HoTMetaL.

▶ ▶ ▶ If your browser displays the heading levels differently, don't worry. Every browser is allowed to determine the best way to display heading levels on the system it is running. Some browsers even allow you to select the fonts used to display heading levels.

Identifying Paragraphs

When you write a letter, memo, or report using your word processor, you usually organize it as one or more paragraphs. You probably do this automatically for most documents that you write.

When you use HTML, you must explicitly mark your paragraphs. This is necessary to differentiate paragraphs from other types of tagged text. Paragraphs are indicated by placing the **<P>** tag at the beginning of a new paragraph and the **</P>** tag at the end of the paragraph. For example,

```
<P>this is a paragraph</P>
```

The trailing **</P>** tag is optional, but is useful for clearly defining the end of a paragraph. HoTMetaL will insert it automatically.

Why all the big fuss over a simple paragraph? The answer lies in the way Web browsers treat traditional line and paragraph markers: spaces, carriage returns, and tabs. These characters are referred to as *white space characters*. When a browser encounters one or more white space characters, it usually treats them as a single space character. This eliminates the traditional way you position a line or format a paragraph.

As with all other HTML elements, the actual formatted display of paragraphs is browser-dependent. Most browsers do not indent paragraphs but instead place a half to a whole line of blank space between paragraphs.

The following example illustrates the use of paragraph tags.

1. Click on the **New** button to open a new document.

2. Move the cursor immediately before the **/TITLE** tag and type **Using Paragraphs**.

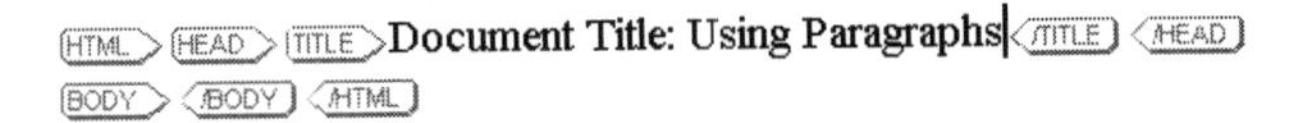
HTML HEAD TITLE Document Title: Using Paragraphs /TITLE /HEAD
BODY /BODY /HTML

3 Move the cursor between the **BODY** and **/BODY** tags and click on the **Heading 1** toolbar button.

▶ **H1** and **/H1** tags appear between the body tags.

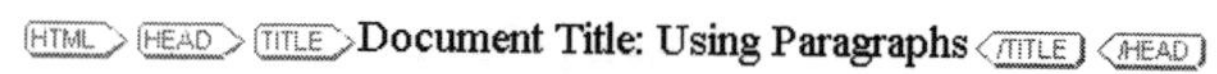
HTML HEAD TITLE Document Title: Using Paragraphs /TITLE /HEAD

BODY H1 **Examples of Paragraph Formatting** /H1 /BODY /HTML

4 Type **Examples of Paragraph Formatting**.

5 Move the cursor between the **/H1** and **/BODY** tags and click on the **Paragraph** (¶) toolbar button.

¶
Paragraph

▶ Paragraph tags are inserted into your document.

HTML HEAD TITLE Document Title: Using Paragraphs /TITLE /HEAD

BODY H1 **Examples of Paragraph Formatting** /H1

P This is paragraph 1. /P /BODY /HTML

6 Type **This is paragraph 1.**

7 Press ↵.

▶ A new set of paragraph tags is automatically inserted into your document.

HTML HEAD TITLE Document Title: Using Paragraphs /TITLE /HEAD

BODY H1 **Examples of Paragraph Formatting** /H1

P This is paragraph 1. /P

P This is paragraph 2. /P /BODY /HTML

8 Type **This is paragraph 2.**

9 Type 10 to 20 spaces followed by **Oops! This was tacked on the end of paragraph 2.**

<P>This is paragraph 2.   Oops! This was tacked on the end of paragraph 2.</P> </BODY> </HTML>

10 Press ↵ three times.

▶ HoTMetaL inserts additional sets of paragraph tags.

<P>This is paragraph 1. </P>

<P>This is paragraph 2.   Oops! This was tacked on the end of paragraph 2. </P>

<P> </P>

<P> </P>

<P>This is paragraph 3.</P> </BODY> </HTML>

11 Type **This is paragraph 3.**

12 Click on the **Save** toolbar button and save your file as c:\html\ch02-03.htm.

13 Press **Ctrl+M** and follow the steps outlined earlier in the chapter to view ch02-03.htm using your browser.

Examples of Paragraph Formatting

This is paragraph 1.

This is paragraph 2. Oops! This was tacked on the end of paragraph 2.

This is paragraph 3.

▶ Notice that the extra line we typed appears as part of paragraph 2 instead of on a separate line. Also, notice that the multiple spaces and carriage returns that we entered have no effect on the way the browser displays the Web page.

14 Use your browser's View Document Source capability to take a look at the HTML file generated by HoTMetaL.

```
<!DOCTYPE HTML PUBLIC "-//SQ//DTD HTML 2.0 HoTMetaL + extensions//EN">
<HTML><HEAD><TITLE>Using Paragraphs</TITLE></HEAD>
<BODY><H1>Examples of Paragraph Formatting</H1>
<P>This is paragraph 1.</P>
<P>This is paragraph 2.                    Oops! This was tacked on to the
of paragraph 2.</P>
<P></P>
<P></P>
<P>This is paragraph 3.</P></BODY></HTML>
```

15 Close your browser.

Using Line Breaks

Now that you can use HoTMetaL to work with paragraphs, you can move your new novel over to the Web. However, if you are a poet, you are probably wondering how you would tell a browser to end a line of text without starting a new paragraph. *Line breaks* are your answer. They force a browser into ending a line of text without beginning a new paragraph.

Line breaks are specified by putting the **
** tag where the break is desired. The text following the line break begins on a new line.

The following example illustrates the use of line breaks.

1 In the HoTMetaL document title, double-click on **Paragraphs** and type **Line Breaks.**

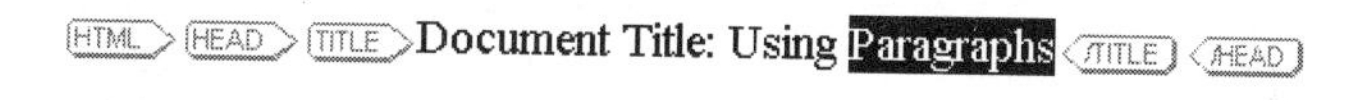
HTML HEAD TITLE
Document Title: Using Paragraphs
/TITLE /HEAD

2 In the headline, select **Paragraph Formatting** and type **Line Breaks.**

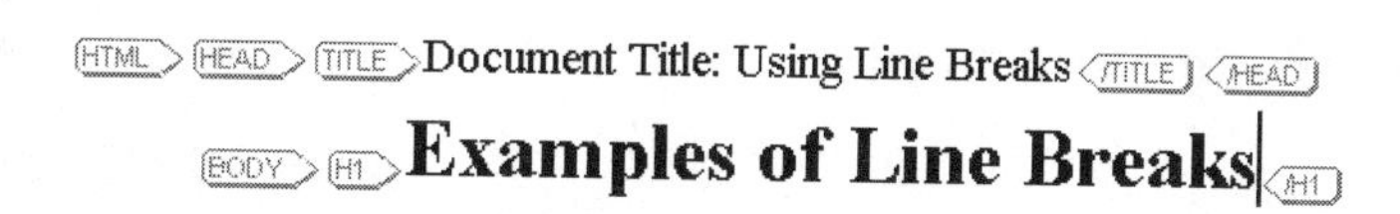
HTML HEAD TITLE
Document Title: Using Line Breaks
/TITLE /HEAD
BODY H1
Examples of Line Breaks
/H1

3 Move the cursor immediately before **Oops!** and click on the **Break** toolbar button.

Break

▶ Break tags are inserted.

This is paragraph 2.
Oops! This was tacked on the end of paragraph 2.

4 Move the cursor immediately before **end** and click on the **Break** toolbar button.

This is paragraph 2.
Oops! This was tacked on the
end of paragraph 2.

▶ Break tags are inserted.

5 Save your Web page as c:\html\ch02-04.htm.

6 View your Web page with your browser.

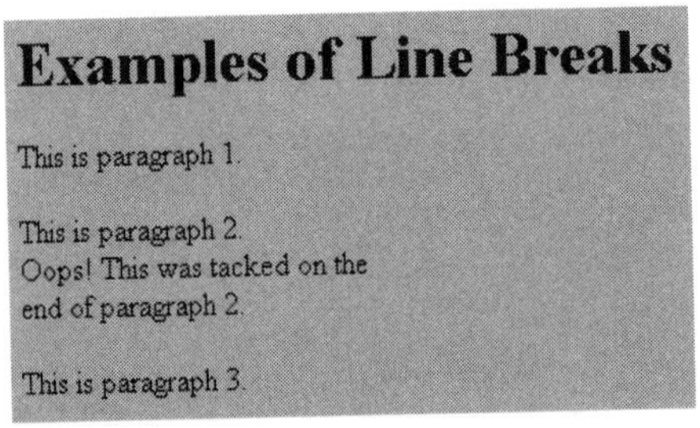

Examples of Line Breaks

This is paragraph 1.

This is paragraph 2.
Oops! This was tacked on the
end of paragraph 2.

This is paragraph 3.

▶ Notice how the line break differs from the paragraph tag. Paragraph tags generally cause a blank line to appear at the beginning of a paragraph. Line breaks do not.

Inserting Comments

When you are developing a Web page, it is sometimes convenient to write a little note to yourself. In HTML, these little notes are referred to as *comments*. They are similar to WordPerfect comments, Microsoft Word annotations, and the comments used in programming languages. You might use comments to remind yourself why you put something in a Web page or when it should be updated. I usually use them to include a to do list in pages that are in progress. HTML comments are not displayed by Web browsers; they are just there to record your notes.

Comments are inserted into Web pages using the following syntax:

<!—this is a comment—>

All text between **<!—** and **—>** is treated as a comment.

►►► **H**oTMetaL displays comment tags using **.COMMENT** and **/.COMMENT** but inserts the **<!—** and **—>** tags into the Web pages that it generates.

Comments may be placed within other HTML tags, such as headings and paragraphs, although this is generally not a good idea, since it makes it harder to distinguish your comments from the contents of your Web page. The following example shows what happens when a comment is haphazardly inserted into a Web page.

1. Close your browser, but do not close the HoTMetaL document.

2. Move the cursor to the middle of the word *paragraph*.

3. Click on the **Insert comment** toolbar button.

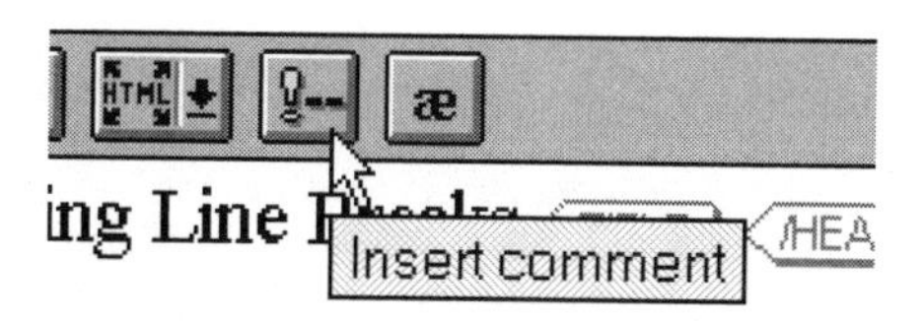

► Comment tags are inserted in your document.

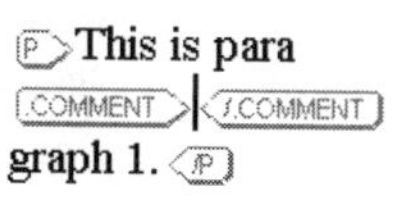

4 Type **This comment is in the middle of a paragraph.**

```
<P>This is para
<COMMENT>This comment is in the middle of a paragraph.|</COMMENT>
graph 1.</P>
```

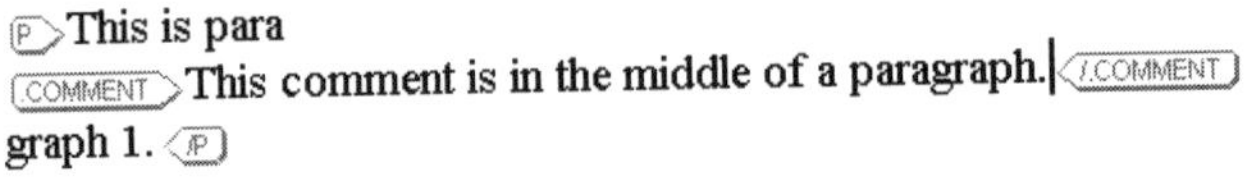

5 Save your Web page as c:\html\ch02-05.htm.

6 View it with your browser.

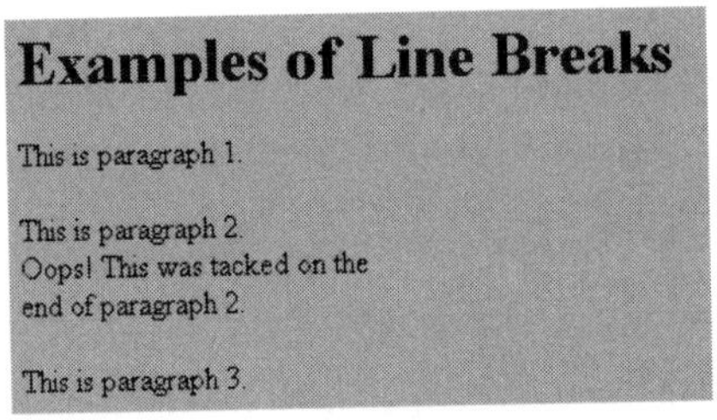

Examples of Line Breaks

This is paragraph 1.

This is paragraph 2.
Oops! This was tacked on the
end of paragraph 2.

This is paragraph 3.

▶ The page appears the same as before you added the comment.

7 View the source HTML document generated by your browser.

```
<!DOCTYPE HTML PUBLIC "-//SQ//DTD HTML 2.0 HoTMetaL + extensions//EN">
<HTML><HEAD><TITLE>Using Line Breaks</TITLE></HEAD>
<BODY><H1>Examples of Line Breaks</H1>
<P>This is para<!--This comment is in the middle of a paragraph.-->graph 1.
<P>This is paragraph 2.                    <BR>Oops! This was tacked on th
<BR>end of paragraph 2.</P>
<P></P>
<P></P>
<P>This is paragraph 3.</P></BODY></HTML>
```

▶ Notice that HoTMetaL inserted the correct comment tags and that the tags were inserted exactly in the middle of the word *paragraph*. Luckily our browsers weren't confused.

8 Exit your browser and HoTMetaL.

You have covered a lot of ground in this lesson. You learned how HoTMetaL uses tags to specify the structure of Web pages. You then learned how to use HoTMetaL to work with these tags. Most importantly, you got some hands-on experience using HoTMetaL to create several small Web pages. Lesson 3 will build upon the material that you've covered so far. You'll learn how to use HoTMetaL to work with additional text formatting tags.

3

Enhancing Text

In this lesson, you'll learn how to format text and insert special characters in your Web pages. You'll learn the difference between logical and physical formatting tags. You'll learn how to use preformatted text to place multiple spaces, tabs, and hard returns in your Web pages. You'll also learn to use special tags for inserting quotations and addresses. When you finish this lesson, you will know how to use HoTMetaL to work with most text formatting tags.

Working with Different Character Formats

Almost any attractive document, be it a magazine article, book, or Web page, uses a variety of text formats to add emphasis and structure to the text it contains. HTML provides the Web publisher with many formatting tags to specify the meaning and appearance of tagged text. Character formatting tags are used to specify the format of small units of text. They are typically used within a single paragraph or heading.

There are two major types of character formatting tags: logical and physical. *Logical* formatting tags are used to format text based upon its meaning or use. For example, you can specify that certain text is to be emphasized. Browsers will then emphasize the text using the local formatting capabilities that are available to them—boldface, italics, underline, and so on. *Physical* formatting tags differ from logical formatting tags in that they specify the exact manner in which text is to appear. For example, instead of using a logical formatting tag to identify emphasized text, you can use a physical formatting tag to tell browsers that they should always use italics.

Logical formatting tags are preferred to physical formatting tags because logical tags specify how text is to be used rather than how it is to be displayed, which allows different browsers to display tagged text according to the capabilities of their local operating environments.

Logical Character Formatting

Logical character formatting tags specify the meaning of tagged text and let browsers determine how it should be displayed. Some browsers may use a different font to display a particular logical style, others may use italics, boldface, or underline, and others still may display the text in the same way as normal text. Logical formatting tags are analogous to the formatting styles found in popular word processors such as Word and WordPerfect.

There are seven logical character formatting styles that are officially part of the HTML 2.0 standard. Additional styles have been proposed, but they are not widely supported. Some of the logical formatting styles that are currently part of HTML may seem a little odd. For example, there are styles that help you include snippets of program code, display program variables, and identify text that is to be typed by a user at a keyboard. This is because some of these styles were originally intended for use by computer scientists and physicists at CERN, where HTML was developed (see this book's introduction for details). Other styles, such as citation, emphasis, strong emphasis, and sample text, are more general and are intended for the now larger base of Web publishers.

We will now cover the seven logical character formatting styles. While reading through the descriptions of these tags, you'll use HoTMetaL to insert them in a Web page. After you have covered all seven tags, you'll be able to see them in action by viewing them with your Web browser.

Citation

The citation tag is used to cite a particular document as a reference. The citation tag is written like so:

```
<CITE>the citation</CITE>
```

For example, suppose you are writing a Web page and you want to reference your favorite newspaper. You could write it as follows:

I read about it in <CITE>Weekly World News</CITE>.

Most Web browsers display cited text using italics.

Let's use HoTMetaL to insert the above HTML.

1. Launch HoTMetaL as described in Lesson 2.

2. Open a new document and place the cursor immediately before the **/TITLE** tag.

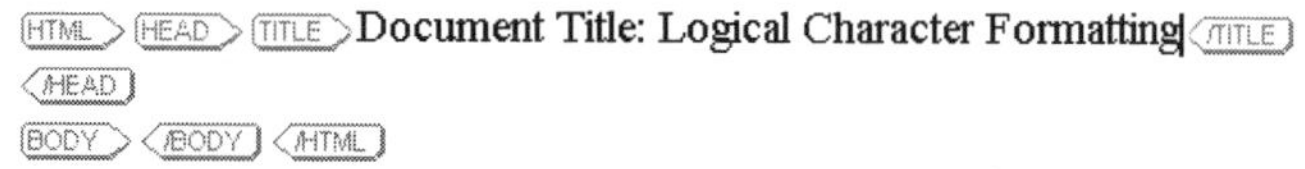

   HTML HEAD TITLE Document Title: Logical Character Formatting /TITLE /HEAD
   BODY /BODY /HTML

3. Type **Logical Character Formatting** for the document title.

4. Move the cursor between the **BODY** and **/BODY** tags.

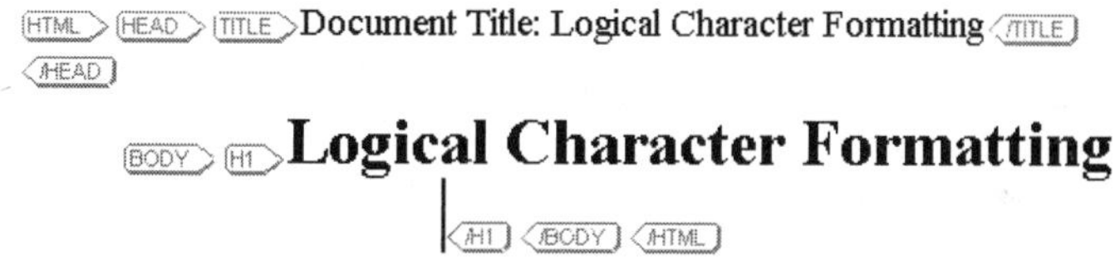

   HTML HEAD TITLE Document Title: Logical Character Formatting /TITLE /HEAD
   BODY H1 **Logical Character Formatting** /H1 /BODY /HTML

5. Click on the **H1** toolbar button to insert **H1** tags.

6. Type **Logical Character Formatting** for the heading.

7. Move the cursor between the **/H1** and **/BODY** tags.

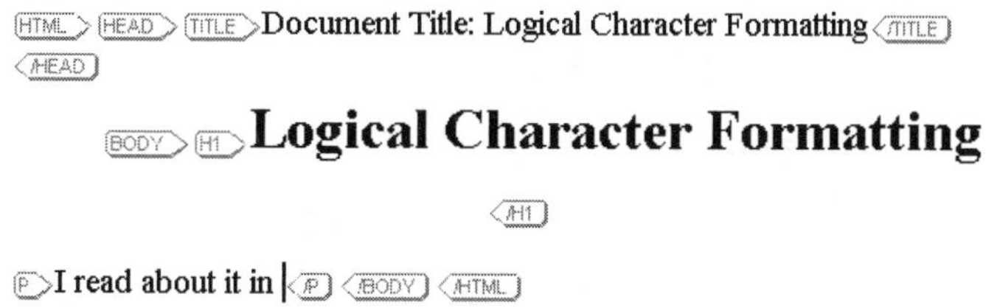

   HTML HEAD TITLE Document Title: Logical Character Formatting /TITLE /HEAD
   BODY H1 **Logical Character Formatting** /H1
   P I read about it in /P /BODY /HTML

8. Type **I read about it in** followed by a space.

▶ **P** and **/P** tags are automatically inserted by HoTMetaL.

9 Click on the **Citation** (*Cit.*) toolbar button.

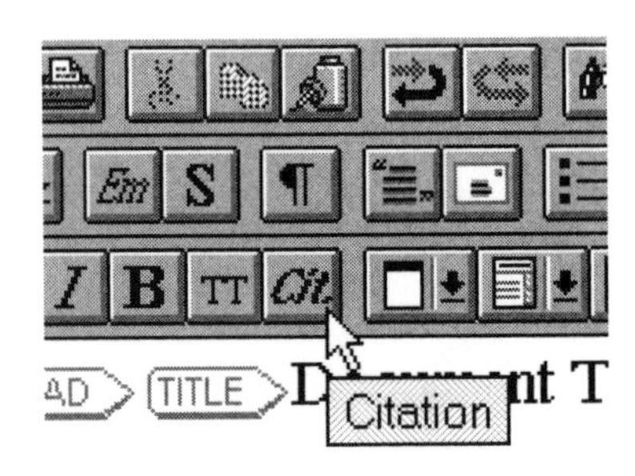

▶ **CITE** and **/CITE** tags appear in the document.

P I read about it in CITE /CITE /P /BODY /HTML

10 Type **Weekly World News**.

HTML HEAD TITLE Document Title: Logical Character Formatting /TITLE /HEAD

BODY H1 **Logical Character Formatting** /H1

11 Move the cursor between the **/CITE** and **/P** tags and type a period.

P I read about it in CITE *Weekly World News* /CITE . /P /BODY /HTML

▶ Keep this HoTMetaL document open. You'll add additional logical formatting tags to this example.

Emphasis

The emphasis tag is used to identify text that is to be set apart and emphasized. Emphasized text is written like so:

<EM>this is emphasized text</EM>

For example, if you wanted to emphasize the word *not* in the following text, you would write it as shown:

Do <EM>not</EM> call before 9 a.m.

Emphasized text is usually displayed in italics.

1. Press ↵ and type **Do not call before 9 a.m. and never on weekends.**

▶ HoTMetaL automatically inserts new paragraph tags.

2. Select the word **not** by double-clicking on it.

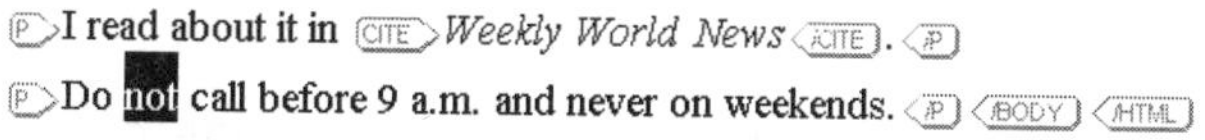

3. Click on the **Emphasis** (*Em*) toolbar button.

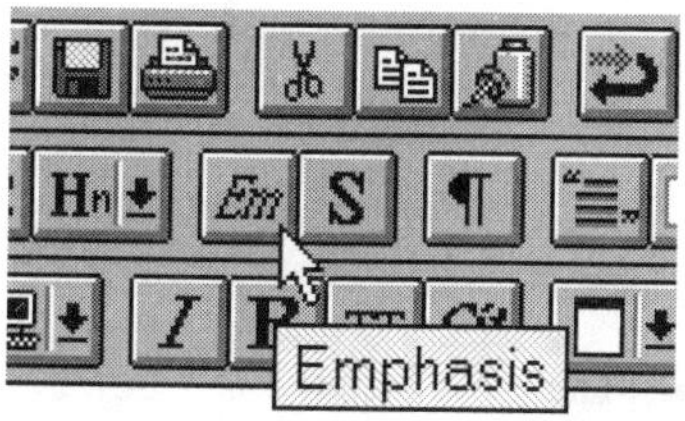

▶ **EM** tags are placed around the word *not*.

Strong

The strong tag is used to identify text that is to be strongly emphasized. Strongly emphasized text is written like this:

<STRONG>this is strongly emphasized text</STRONG>

For example, if you wanted to emphasize the word *never* more than the word *not* in the following text, you could write it as follows:

Do <EM>not</EM> call before 9 a.m. and <STRONG>never</STRONG> on weekends.

Strongly emphasized text is usually displayed using a bold font.

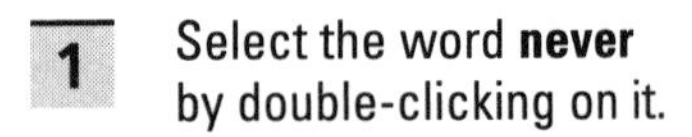

1 Select the word **never** by double-clicking on it.

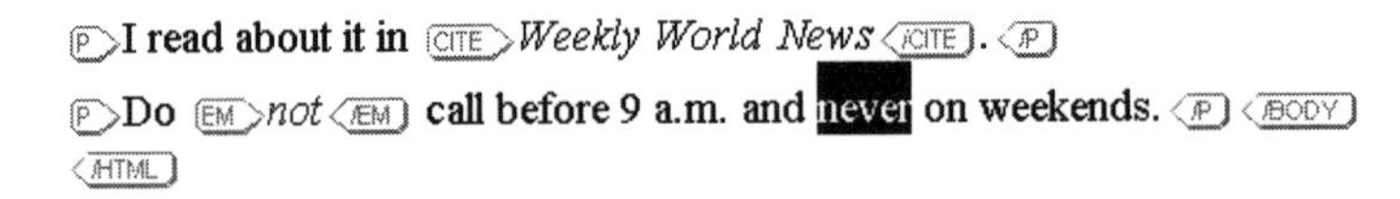
P I read about it in CITE *Weekly World News* /CITE . /P
P Do EM *not* /EM call before 9 a.m. and never on weekends. /P /BODY
/HTML

2 Click on the **Strong** (S) toolbar button.

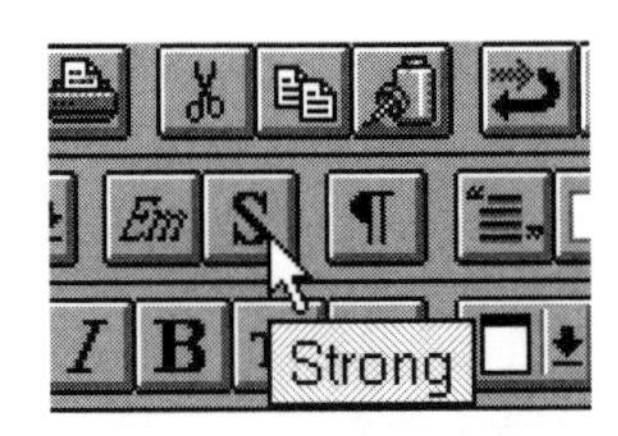
Em
S
B
Strong

▶ **STRONG** tags are placed around *never*.

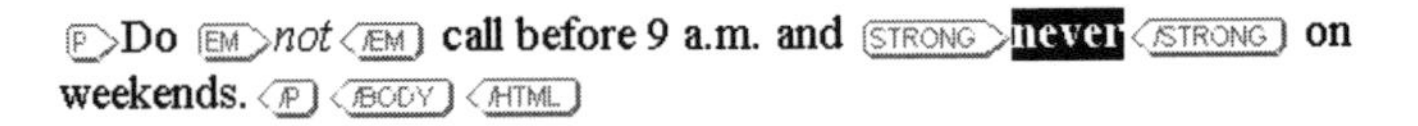
P Do EM *not* /EM call before 9 a.m. and STRONG never /STRONG on
weekends. /P /BODY /HTML

Code

The code tag is used to identify an example of program code. The code tag is written like this:

```
<CODE>this is program code</CODE>
```

For example, suppose that you want to include a C programming language statement in a Web page. You could write it as follows:

```
The statement that defines the pi constant is: <CODE>#define
PI 3.14159</CODE>
```

Code examples are usually displayed using a *monospaced* font, i.e., a font in which all characters have the same width.

1 Place the cursor immediately before the **/BODY** tag and type **The statement that defines the PI constant is:** followed by a space.

P The statement that defines the PI constant is: | /P /BODY /HTML

2 Click on the **Code elements** toolbar button and select **CODE** from the menu that pops up.

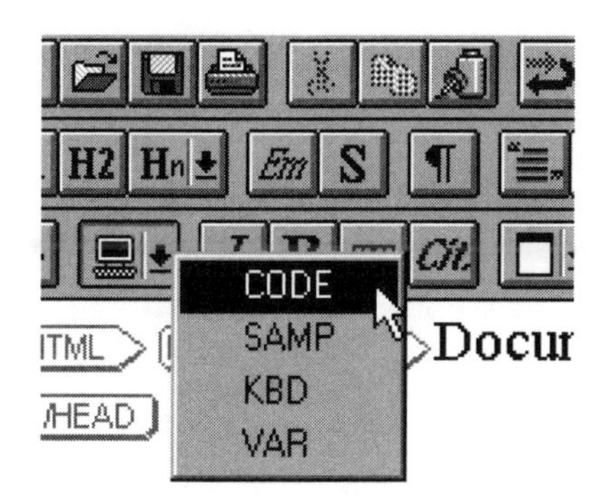

▶ **CODE** tags appear in your document.

<P>The statement that defines the PI constant is: <CODE>|</CODE> </P> </BODY> </HTML>

3 Type **#DEFINE PI 3.14159**.

<P>The statement that defines the PI constant is: <CODE>#DEFINE PI 3.14159|</CODE> </P> </BODY> </HTML>

Sample

The sample tag is used to identify a sequence of literal characters. The sample tag is written like so:

<SAMP>this is sample text</SAMP>

For example, suppose that you are writing a training manual as a Web page and that you want the reader to search for the string *xsum* using a text editor. You would write it as follows:

Search for <SAMP>xsum</SAMP> with your text editor.

Sample text is usually displayed using a monospaced font.

1 Place the cursor immediately before the **/BODY** tag and type **Search for xsum with your text editor.**

<P>The statement that defines the PI constant is: <CODE>#DEFINE PI 3.14159</CODE> </P>
<P>Search for xsum with your text editor.|</P> </BODY> </HTML>

2 Double-click on **xsum**.

<P>Search for xsum with your text editor. </P> </BODY> </HTML>

3 Click on the **Code elements** toolbar button and select **SAMP** from the pop-up menu.

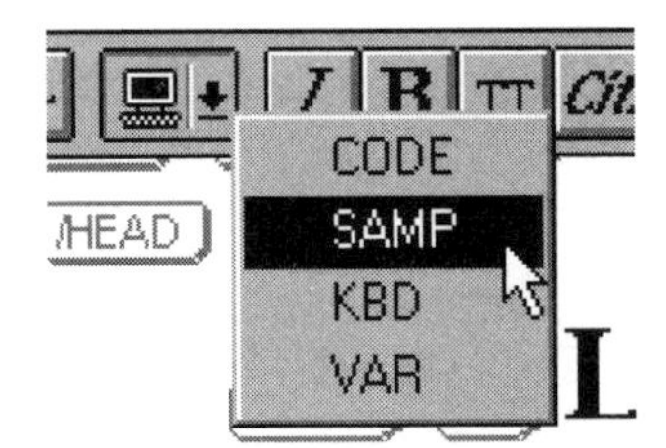

▶ **SAMP** tags are inserted.

Keyboard

The keyboard tag is used to identify text typed by a user. The keyboard tag is written like so:

<KBD>this is text that is typed at a keyboard</KBD>

For example, suppose you want to show the reader how to type in a command to obtain a directory listing. You could write it as follows:

To get a complete directory listing, type <KBD>ls -al | more</KBD>.

Keyboard input is usually displayed using a monospaced font.

1 Place the cursor immediately before the **/BODY** tag and type **To get a complete directory listing, type ls -al | more.**

Search for xsum with your text editor.
To get a complete directory listing, type ls -al | more.

2 Select **ls -al | more** with your mouse.

ls -al | more.

3 Click on the **Code elements** toolbar button and select **KBD**.

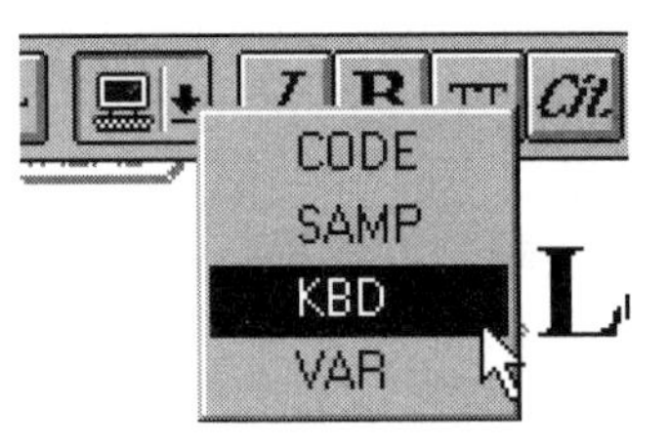

▶ **KBD** tags are inserted.

To get a complete directory listing, type ls -al | more.

Variable

The variable tag is used to identify a variable name. It is written like this:

<VAR>this is a variable</VAR>

For example, suppose you want to identify the variable used to hold the value of total sales in a description of an accounting program. You could write it as follows:

The value of total sales is stored in <VAR>$sales-total</VAR>.

Variables are usually displayed using italics.

1 With the cursor between the **/P** and **/BODY** tags, type **The value of total sales is stored in $sales-total.**

P The value of total sales is stored in $sales-total. /P /BODY /HTML

2 Select **$sales-total** with your mouse.

stored in $sales-total. /P /BODY /HTML

3 Click on the **Code elements** toolbar button and select **VAR**.

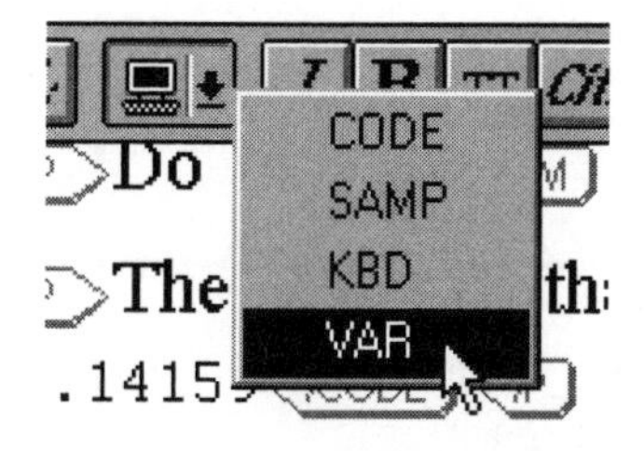

▶ **VAR** tags are inserted.

P The value of total sales is stored in VAR *$sales-total* /VAR . /P /BODY /HTML

4 Click anywhere in your document to deselect the text.

5 Save your document as c:\html\ch03-01.htm.

6 Press **Ctrl+M** to view your document using your browser.

Logical Character Formatting

I read about it in *Weekly World News*.

Do *not* call before 9 a.m. and **never** on weekends.

The statement that defines the PI constant is: `#DEFINE PI 3.14159`

Search for `xsum` with your text editor.

To get a complete directory listing, type `ls -al | more`.

The value of total sales is stored in *$sales-total*.

▶ Notice how your browser displays the various types of tagged text.

7 Use your browser to view the source HTML document generated by HoTMetaL.

```
<!DOCTYPE HTML PUBLIC "-//SQ//DTD HTML 2.0 HoTMetaL + extensions//EN">
<HTML><HEAD><TITLE>Logical Character Formatting</TITLE></HEAD>
<BODY><H1>Logical Character Formatting</H1>
<P>I read about it in <CITE>Weekly World News</CITE>.</P>
<P>Do <EM>not</EM> call before 9 a.m. and <STRONG>never</STRONG> on weekends
<P>The statement that defines the PI constant is: <CODE>#DEFINE PI 3.14159</
<P>Search for <SAMP>xsum</SAMP> with your text editor.</P>
<P>To get a complete directory listing, type <KBD>ls -al | more</KBD>.</P>
<P>The value of total sales is stored in <VAR>$sales-total</VAR>.</P></BODY>
```

8 When you're finished, close your browser and your HoTMetaL document (but not the HoTMetaL program).

Your browser may render logical formatting tags using a scheme that is different from Netscape.

Physical Character Formatting

Physical character formatting tags are used to tell browsers the exact manner in which text is to be displayed. Physical formatting tags are especially useful when no appropriate logical formatting tags are available. There are three physical character formatting styles that are defined in the HTML 2.0 standard: bold, italic, and teletype. In the next lesson, you will learn additional physical character formatting tags that have been introduced by Netscape and the HTML 3.0 standard.

▶ ▶ ▶ **A**lthough you may specify that text be displayed using a physical format such as italics, if the style cannot be displayed by a browser, it may be displayed using an alternative style such as underline.

Bold

The bold tag is used to identify text that is to be displayed in boldface. It is used as follows:

<B>this is bold text</B>

Italic

The italic tag is used to identify text that is to be displayed in italic font. It is used as follows:

<I>this is italic text</I>

Teletype

The teletype tag is used to identify text that is to be displayed in a fixed-width typewriter font. It is used as follows:

<TT>this is teletype text</TT>

Let's create a Web page using these physical formatting tags and then see how they are displayed.

1. Open a new document.

2. Type **Physical Character Formatting** as the title.

HTML HEAD TITLE Document Title: Physical Character Formatting /TITLE /HEAD

BODY H1 **Physical Character Formatting**

3. Click on the **H1** button to create a level 1 heading and type **Physical Character Formatting**.

4 Place the cursor after the **/H1** tag and type **This is normal text.**

HTML HEAD TITLE Document Title: Physical Character Formatting /TITLE
/HEAD

BODY H1 **Physical Character Formatting**

/H1

5 Press ↵.

P This is normal text. /P
P /P /BODY /HTML

▶ Another set of paragraph tags is automatically inserted.

6 Click on the **Bold** (**B**) toolbar button.

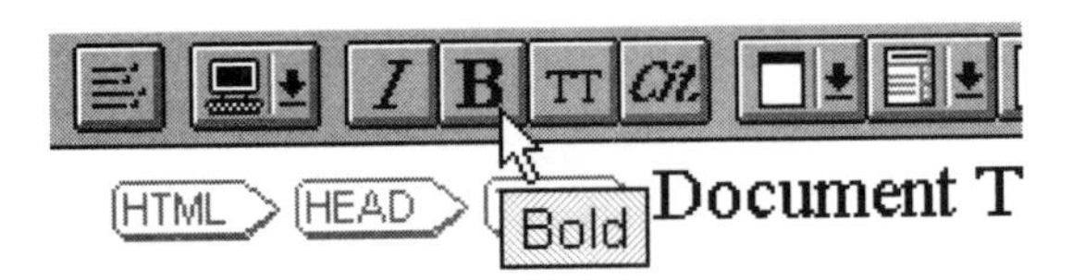

▶ **B** tags are inserted.

7 Type **This is bold text.** and press ↵.

P This is normal text. /P
P B **This is bold text.** /B /P
P /P /BODY /HTML

8 Click on the **Italic** (*I*) toolbar button.

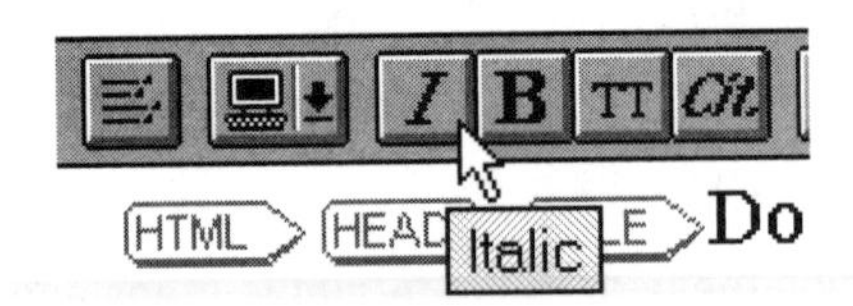

▶ **I** tags are inserted.

9 Type **This is italic text.** and press ↵.

P This is normal text. /P
P B **This is bold text.** /B /P
P I *This is italic text.* /I /P
P /P /BODY /HTML

10 Click on the **TeleType** (TT) toolbar button.

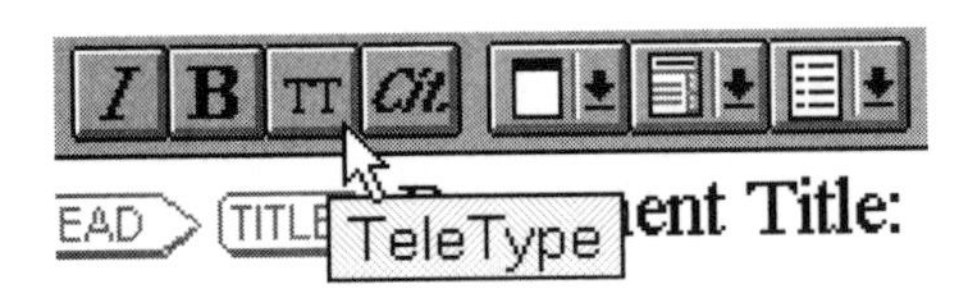

▶ **TT** tags are inserted.

```
<P><I>This is italic text.</I></P>
<P><TT>This is teletype text.</TT></P>
<P>|</P></BODY></HTML>
```

11 Type **This is teletype text.** and press ↵.

12 Press the **Bold** button, then the **Italic** button, then the **TeleType** button.

▶ Bold, italic, and teletype tags are inserted in nested fashion.

```
<P><B><I><TT>|</TT></I></B></P></BODY></HTML>
```

13 Type **This is bold italic teletype text.**

```
<P><B><I><TT>This is bold italic teletype text.|</TT></I></B>
</P></BODY></HTML>
```

14 Save your document as c:\html\ch03-02.htm.

15 View the document using your browser.

16 When you're finished, close your browser and the HoTMetaL document (but stay in HoTMetaL).

Physical Character Formatting

This is normal text.

This is bold text.

This is italic text.

`This is teletype text.`

`This is bold italic teletype text.`

▶ ▶ ▶ **B**oth logical and physical formatting tags may be nested. However, not all browsers display nested styles as a combination of styles; some just display the outermost style in the nesting.

Using Escape Sequences

The Web, by design, is international in nature and its users speak a multitude of languages. Along with this international flavor comes the need to develop pages using characters from other languages, such as ñ, ü, £, ¥, and ¿, and other symbols, such as © and ®, that just aren't available from most keyboards. *Escape sequences* are the mechanism used by HTML to insert international and special characters into Web pages.

Web pages are written using a subset of the 7-bit U.S. ASCII character set. The allowed characters are the printable ASCII characters from 33 (!) through 126 (~) and space, tab, carriage return, and line feed. You can type all of these characters on your keyboard. Four of these characters (&, ", <, and >) are reserved by HTML and must be coded using escape sequences in order to be used as text (as opposed to being used as part of a tag). Other characters, such as international characters and special symbols, may be inserted in Web pages by using either *named character references* or *numbered character references*, both of which are coded using escape sequences. You'll learn more about these terms later in this section.

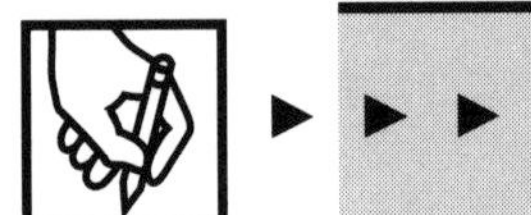

Escape sequences are used to insert international characters and special symbols in Web pages.

Inserting Reserved Characters

As previously mentioned, four ASCII characters are reserved by HTML: the left angle bracket (<), the right angle bracket (>), the ampersand (&), and the double quote ("). These characters may not be directly used in tagged text because they are used as part of HTML tags. In order to use these characters in text, they must be identified using an escape sequence. The following escape sequences are required to use the four reserved characters:

left bracket	<
right bracket	>
ampersand	&
double quote	"

Identifying Characters by Name

In addition to specifying the four reserved characters, escape sequences are used to insert characters by name or by numeric value. *Named character references* identify characters by name and are used primarily to insert international characters into Web pages.

For example, to insert the word *inglés* into a Web page, you would write it as *inglés*, where *é* is the named character entity for the Spanish character *é*.

For a complete list of HTML 2.0 named character references, see the \support\chars.htm file on this book's CD.

Identifying Characters by Numeric Value

Escape sequences may also be used to insert characters by numeric value. HTML supports an international character set known as Latin-1. Latin-1 includes characters from most Western European languages, as well as a number of other special symbols. *Numbered character references* identify characters by numeric value and can be used to insert any Latin-1 character into a Web page. The file named \support\chars.htm on the CD identifies the Latin-1 characters and the numeric escape sequences used to code these characters.

For example, you could also write the word *inglés* as *inglés* using the numeric character reference: *é* is used to encode the character *é*.

HoTMetaL's Support of Escape Sequences

HoTMetaL simplifies the process of inserting escape sequences. The reserved characters ("&<>) are automatically converted into escape sequences when you type them into an HTML document. HoTMetaL lets you insert Latin-1 characters and special symbols by selecting them from the special characters palette. In fact, you don't have to worry about escape sequences at all when you use HoTMetaL.

1 Open a new document in HoTMetaL.

2 Type **Escape Sequences** as the document title.

HTML HEAD TITLE Document Title: Escape Sequences /TITLE /HEAD

BODY H1 **Escape Sequences** /H1

3 Create a level 1 heading and type **Escape Sequences**.

P These are the reserved characters: /P /BODY /HTML

4 Place the cursor between the **/H1** and **/BODY** tags and type **These are the reserved characters:** followed by a space.

5 Click on the **Code elements** button and select **SAMP**.

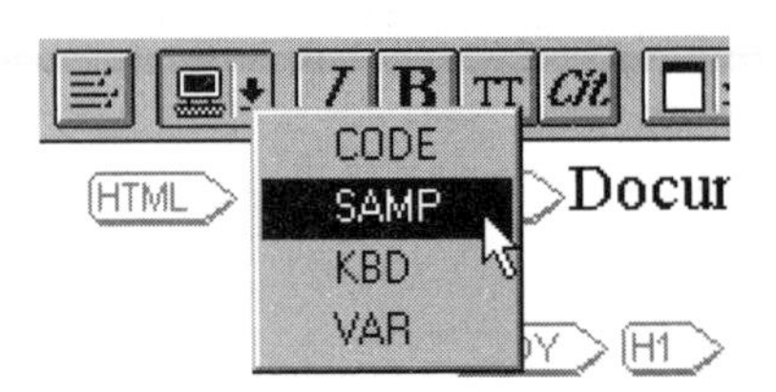

6 Type **"&<>** and press ↵.

P These are the reserved characters: SAMP "&<> /SAMP /P /BODY

▶ HoTMetaL inserts a new set of paragraph tags.

HTML HEAD TITLE Document Title: Escape Sequences /TITLE /HEAD

BODY H1 **Escape Sequences** /H1

7 Type **These are Latin-1 characters:** followed by a space.

P These are the reserved characters: SAMP "&<> /SAMP /P

P These are Latin-1 characters: SAMP /SAMP /P /BODY /HTML

8 Click on the **Code elements** button and select **SAMP**.

9 Click on the **Special characters** toolbar button.

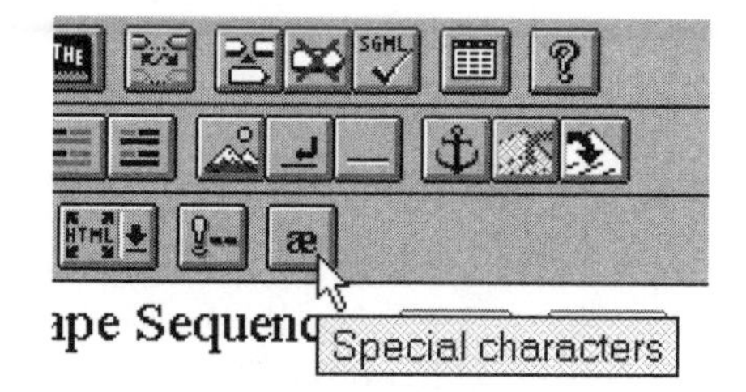

▶ The Special Characters palette appears, offering you a wide variety of symbols and international characters, including common fractions, letters with accents, and superscript numbers.

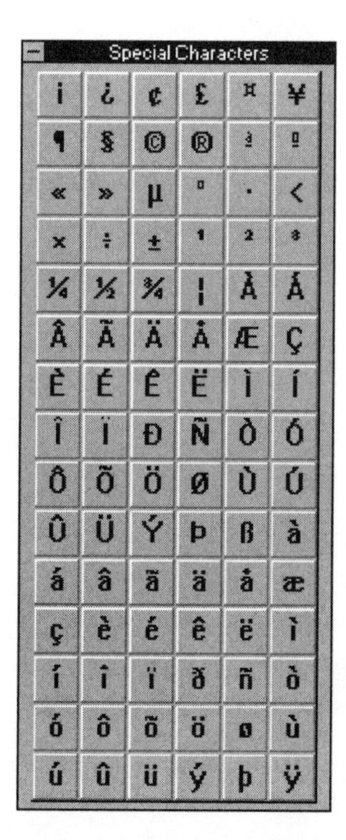

10 Click on the **ccedil** button (the *ç* character).

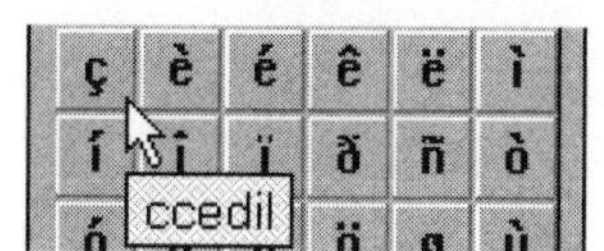

11 Click on the **ntilde** button (the *ñ* character).

12 Click on the **eacute** button (the *é* character).

▶ The *ç*, *ñ*, and *é* characters appear in your document.

characters: <SAMP>çñè</SAMP>

13 Press ↵ and type **Here are some other symbols:** followed by a space.

<P>These are Latin-1 characters: <SAMP>çñè</SAMP> </P>

<P>Here are some other symbols:

14 Click on the **Code elements** button and select **SAMP**.

15 On the **Special Characters** palette, click on the © (copyright) symbol.

16 Click on the ® (registered trademark) symbol.

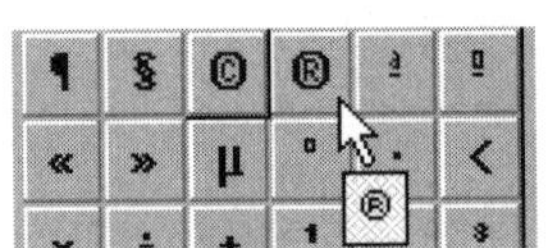

17 Click on the ÷ (division) symbol.

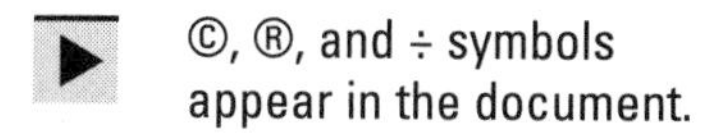

▶ ©, ®, and ÷ symbols appear in the document.

```
HTML HEAD TITLE Document Title: Escape Sequences /TITLE /HEAD
BODY H1 Escape Sequences /H1
P These are the reserved characters: SAMP "&<> /SAMP /P
P These are Latin-1 characters: SAMP çñè /SAMP /P
P Here are some other symbols: SAMP ©®÷ /SAMP /P /BODY /HTML
```

18 Close the **Special Characters** palette.

19 Save your document as c:\html\ch03-03.htm.

20 View the document using your browser.

Escape Sequences

These are the reserved characters: "&<>

These are Latin-1 characters: çñè

Here are some other symbols: ©®÷

21 Use your browser's View Document Source command to look at the HTML file that was generated by HoTMetaL.

```
<!DOCTYPE HTML PUBLIC "-//SQ//DTD HTML 2.0 HoTMetaL + extensions//EN">
<HTML><HEAD><TITLE>Escape Sequences</TITLE></HEAD>
<BODY><H1>Escape Sequences</H1>
<P>These are the reserved characters: <SAMP>&quot;&amp;&lt;&gt;</SAMP></P>
<P>These are Latin-1 characters: <SAMP>&ccedil;&ntilde;&egrave;</SAMP></P>
<P>Here are some other symbols: <SAMP>&#169;&#174;&#247;</SAMP></P></BODY>
```

▶ Notice that HoTMetaL inserted a combination of escape sequences for the reserved characters, Latin-1 characters, and special symbols.

22 When you have finished, exit your browser and close the HoTMetaL document (but do not exit HoTMetaL).

HoTMetaL's support of special characters allows you to quickly and easily insert any valid HTML character into your Web pages.

Block Formatting Tags

The tags we've covered so far in this lesson are used to mark up short phrases and insert special characters. Block formatting tags are used to format larger units of text. You already know one block formatting tag—the paragraph tag—from Lesson 2. Other block formatting tags are used to identify preformatted text, quotations, addresses, and lists. Lists are covered in Lesson 6.

Working with Preformatted Text

Sometimes you'll want to use carriage returns, spaces, and tabs to break up, line up, and position your content. In a traditional word processed document you can just type these characters. In HTML, however, all three of these elements are normally treated as if they were spaces. You can get around these limitations by identifying these sections as preformatted text using the **<PRE>** and **</PRE>** tags.

Preformatted text is displayed in a fixed-width font. This makes it possible to precisely align characters relative to each other on the browser's display. In addition, HTML provides the width attribute to set the maximum number of characters to be displayed on a line.

Suppose you wanted to limit the width of a preformatted text display to 50 characters. You would mark up your text as follows:

```
<PRE WIDTH="50">this is the text to be displayed</PRE>
```

The default width is 80 characters per line. Line widths between 40 and 132 characters are generally supported by most browsers.

When preformatted text is used, tab stops are set at every column that is a multiple of 8.

1 Open a new HoTMetaL document.

2 Type **Preformatted Text** as the document title.

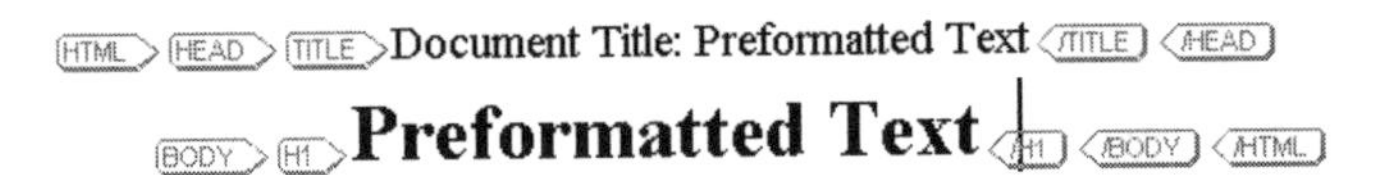

3 Create a level 1 heading and type **Preformatted Text**.

4 Click on the **Preformatted** toolbar button.

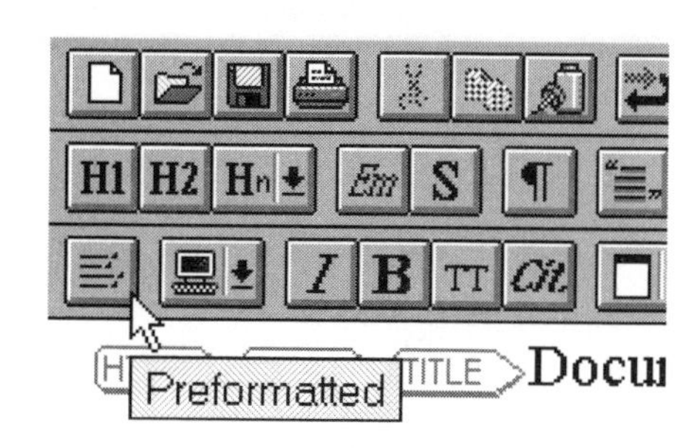

▶ **PRE** tags are inserted into your document.

PRE /PRE /BODY /HTML

5 Select **Markup ➢ Edit SGML Attributes** (or press the **F6** key).

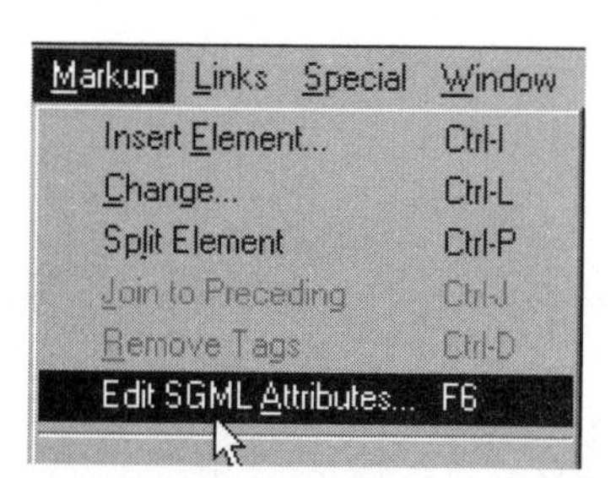

▶ The Edit Attributes dialog box appears.

6 In the WIDTH field, type **50**.

7 Click on the **Apply** button.

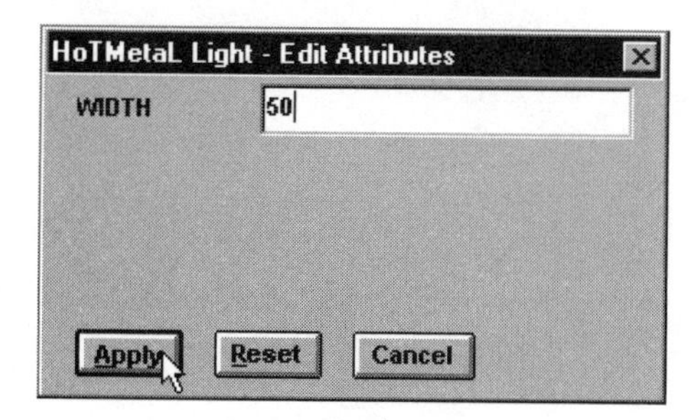

8 Type **This is preformatted text.**, then type five spaces, then type **Notice that I skipped several spaces.**

9 Press ↵ three times.

10 Type **Pressing Enter results in a new line.** and press ↵ twice.

11 Type **See how**, press **Tab** three times, type **tabs**, press **Tab** three times, and type **work.**

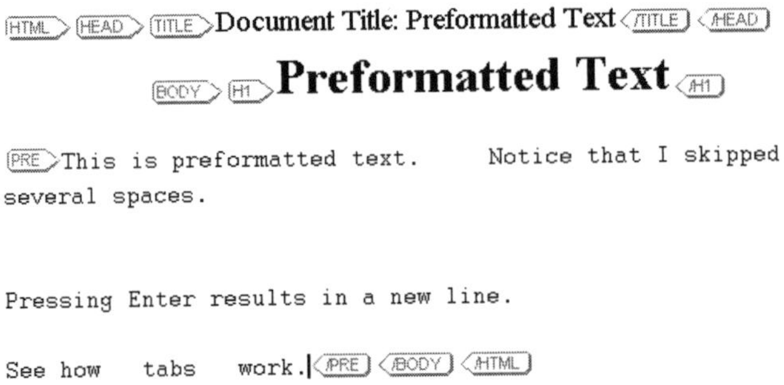

<HTML> <HEAD> <TITLE>Document Title: Preformatted Text</TITLE> </HEAD>

<BODY> <H1>**Preformatted Text**</H1>

```
<PRE>This is preformatted text.     Notice that I skipped
several spaces.


Pressing Enter results in a new line.

See how    tabs    work.</PRE> </BODY> </HTML>
```

12 Save your document as c:\html\ch03-04.htm.

13 View the HTML document using your browser.

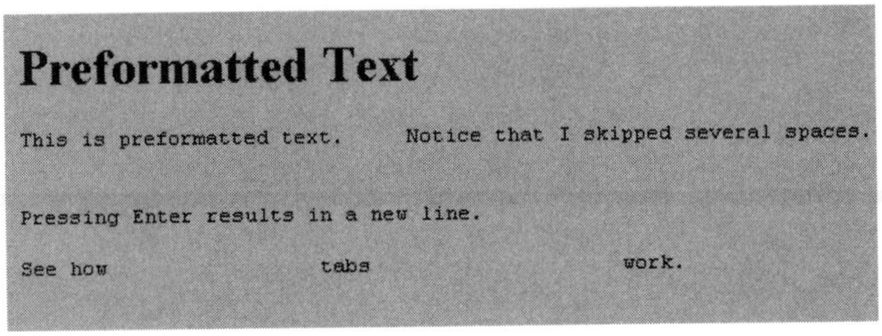

Preformatted Text

```
This is preformatted text.     Notice that I skipped several spaces.


Pressing Enter results in a new line.

See how                        tabs                        work.
```

▶ Unlike with text that is not preformatted, now your browser displays the embedded spaces, carriage returns, and tabs. Also, note that a monospaced font is used to display the preformatted text.

14 When you're finished, close your browser and the HoTMetaL document (but don't exit HoTMetaL).

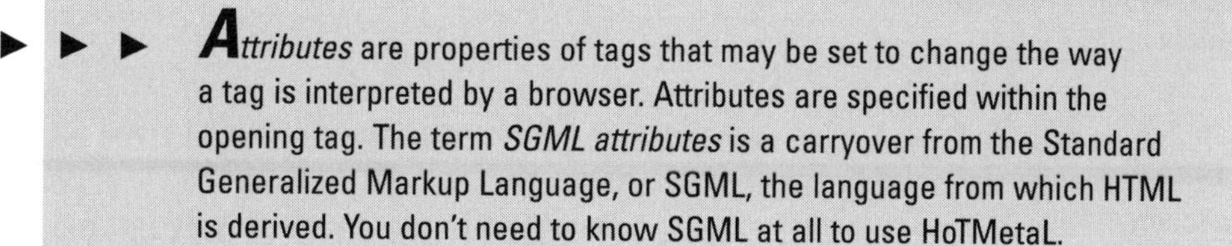

► ► ► *Attributes* are properties of tags that may be set to change the way a tag is interpreted by a browser. Attributes are specified within the opening tag. The term *SGML attributes* is a carryover from the Standard Generalized Markup Language, or SGML, the language from which HTML is derived. You don't need to know SGML at all to use HoTMetaL.

Using Quotations

HTML provides the block quotation tag to identify text that should be displayed in the form of a quotation. The block quotation tag is written like so:

<BLOCKQUOTE>this is a quotation</BLOCKQUOTE>

Text that appears between these tags is usually indented, italicized, and set apart from surrounding text.

Specifying Addresses

HTML provides a feature for specifying the name and address of the author of a Web page. The address tag is written as follows:

<ADDRESS>this is my name and address signature</ADDRESS>

The address tag is usually placed at the bottom of a Web page, along with the date of the page's creation and a copyright notice, if appropriate. Browsers usually display an address in italics.

It is usually a good idea to sign all of your Web pages with your e-mail address. This will help interested Web users contact you with their comments or requests for more information.

Let's create a document using the quotation and address block tags.

1. Open a new HoTMetaL document.

2. Type **Quotations and Addresses** as the document title.

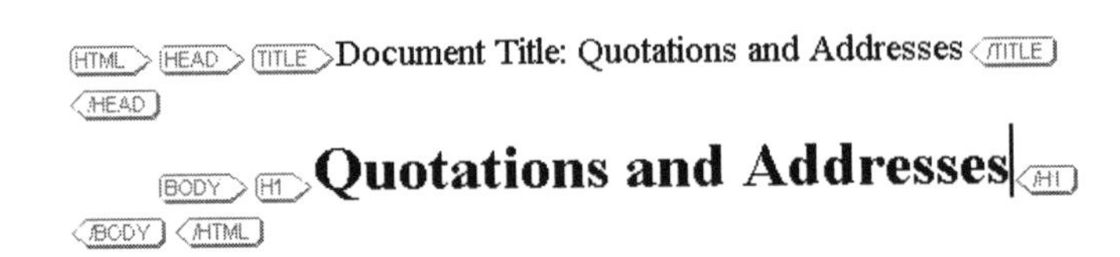
HTML HEAD TITLE Document Title: Quotations and Addresses /TITLE
/HEAD
BODY H1 Quotations and Addresses /H1
/BODY /HTML

3. Create a level 1 heading and type **Quotations and Addresses**.

4. Move the cursor between the **/H1** and **/BODY** tags and type **This is the paragraph before the quotation.**

BODY H1 **Quotations and Addresses** /H1

P This is the paragraph before the quotation. /P /BODY /HTML

5. Move the cursor between the **/P** and **/BODY** tags and click on the **Block quote** toolbar button.

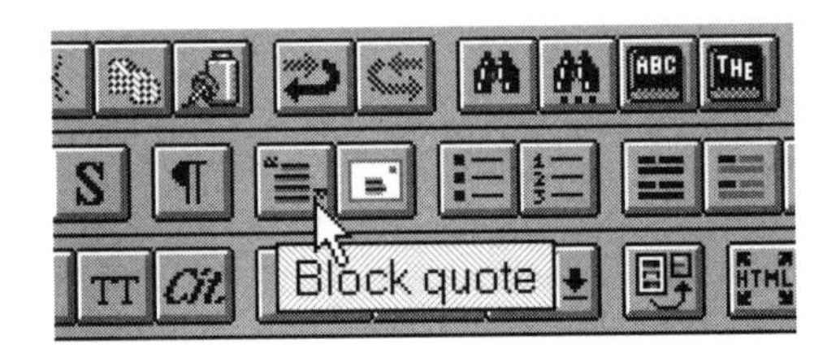
Block quote

▶ **BLOCKQUOTE** tags are inserted into your document.

BODY H1 **Quotations and Addresses** /H1

P This is the paragraph before the quotation. /P

BLOCKQUOTE P To be, or not to be, /P /BLOCKQUOTE /BODY /HTML

6. Type **To be, or not to be,**.

▶ Paragraph tags are automatically inserted within the block quote tags.

7 Click on the **Break** toolbar button.

SGML
Break

▶ **BR** tags are inserted into your document.

P This is the paragraph before the quotation. /P
BLOCKQUOTE P To be, or not to be,
BR /BR
That is the quotation! /P /BLOCKQUOTE /BODY /HTML

8 Type **That is the quotation!**

▶ The text you typed is inserted after the line break tags.

9 Select the entire first paragraph (including the paragraph tags).

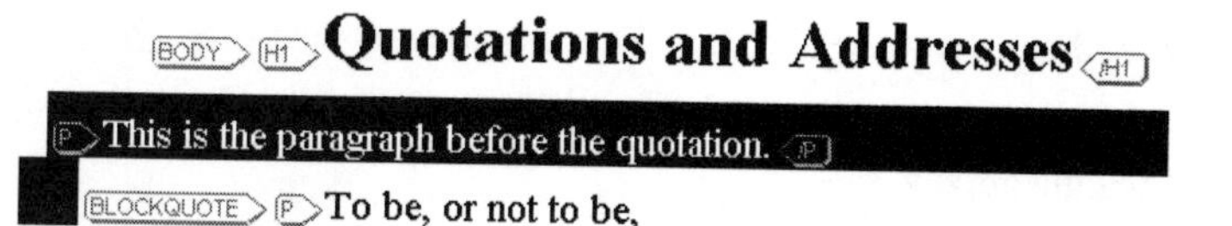
BODY H1 Quotations and Addresses /H1
P This is the paragraph before the quotation. /P
BLOCKQUOTE P To be, or not to be,

10 Click on the **Copy** button.

Copy

11 Place the cursor between the **/BLOCKQUOTE** and **/BODY** tags.

BR /BR
That is the quotation! /P /BLOCKQUOTE /BODY /HTML

12 Click on the **Paste** button.

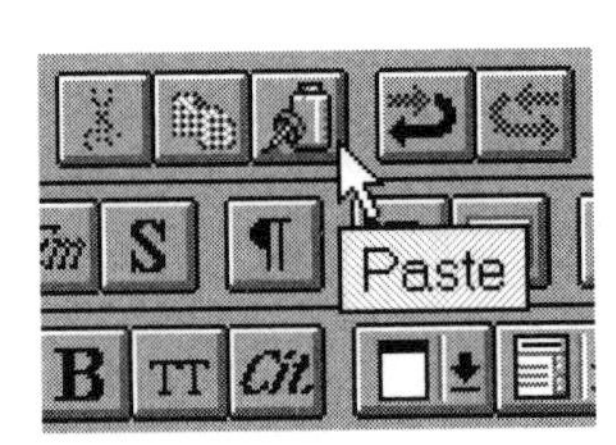

▶ HoTMetaL inserts the copied text inside paragraph tags below the block quote.

<P>This is the paragraph before the quotation. </P>

<BLOCKQUOTE> <P>To be, or not to be,

 </BR>
That is the quotation! </P> </BLOCKQUOTE>

<P>This is the paragraph before the quotation. </P> </BODY> </HTML>

13 Select the word **before** in the last paragraph.

That is the quotation! </P> </BLOCKQUOTE>

<P>This is the paragraph before the quotation. </P> </BODY> </HTML>

14 Type **after**.

That is the quotation! </P> </BLOCKQUOTE>

<P>This is the paragraph after the quotation. </P> </BODY> </HTML>

15 Move the cursor immediately before the **/BODY** tag.

16 Click on the **Address** button.

▶ **ADDRESS** tags are inserted into your document.

<P>This is the paragraph after the quotation. </P>
<ADDRESS>*shakespeare@globe.theater.com* </ADDRESS> </BODY> </HTML>

17 Type **shakespeare@globe.theater.com**.

18 Save your document as c:\html\ch03-05.htm and view it with your browser.

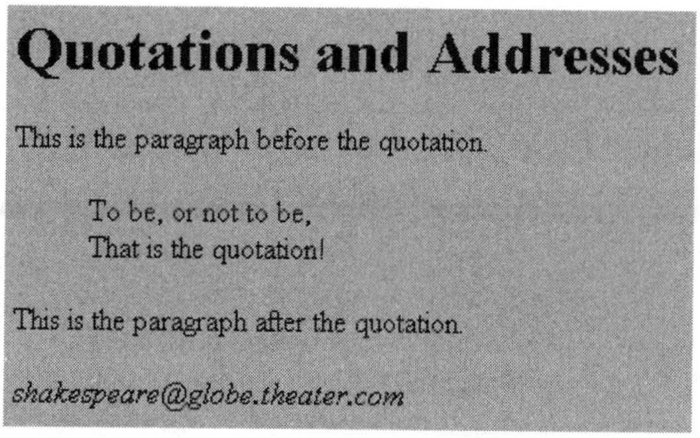

Quotations and Addresses

This is the paragraph before the quotation.

> To be, or not to be,
> That is the quotation!

This is the paragraph after the quotation.

shakespeare@globe.theater.com

▶ Notice how your browser rendered the quotation and Shakespeare's e-mail address.

19 Close your browser and the HoTMetaL program.

Congratulations! You now know how to use most of the text formatting features of HTML 2.0, and you are well on your way to mastering HoTMetaL. You've covered logical and physical character formatting, escape sequences, and block formatting tags.

In the following lesson, you will learn extensions to HTML 2.0, introduced by Netscape, and some HTML 3.0 tags that are supported by current browsers. These tags complement the tags that you have just studied.

4

Using HTML 2.0 Extensions

In this lesson, you'll learn to use new text formatting elements that extend the capabilities provided by HTML 2.0. These elements consist of tags and attributes that have recently been added to the language and are supported by popular browsers. When you finish this lesson, you will know how to work with HoTMetaL to include these new elements in your Web pages.

Where Do New Elements Come From?

HTML is a dynamic language. Although version 2.0 has been standardized, new tags are continually being developed. These extensions are incorporated into popular browsers and become part of HTML as it is "spoken" on the Web. One major source of new language features is the Netscape Communications Corporation, the maker of Netscape Navigator, the most popular browser on the Web. When the folks at Netscape define a new tag and implement it with Netscape Navigator, the tag quickly becomes part of the current standard. Another major source of new language features is the World Wide Web Consortium, or W3C. The W3C is supporting the development of HTML 3.0. Many 3.0 features have already been adopted by popular browsers and have become part of HTML as it is currently practiced.

In addition to providing complete support of HTML 2.0, HoTMetaL also supports new tags from Netscape and HTML 3.0. In this lesson, you'll learn how to use HoTMetaL to work with these new tags.

Netscape Extensions

The Netscape Navigator supports a number of new formatting features that enhance text display. These features can be either new tags or new attributes for existing tags. HoTMetaL provides access to the new Netscape tags through the Extensions to HTML 2.0 toolbar button and to the new attributes via the Edit SGML Attributes option in the Markup pull-down menu.

A description of the Netscape extensions can be found at **http://www.netscape.com/assist/net_sites/html_extensions.html**.

The new Netscape tags are introduced in the following paragraphs.

Blink

The *blink* tag causes text to be repeatedly flashed on and off in the browser window. It is used as follows:

<BLINK>blinking text</BLINK>

The blink tag is considered by some to be superficial and is not widely used.

Center

The *center* tag causes all text between the opening and closing tags to be centered. It may enclose multiple paragraphs and text elements. It is used as follows:

<CENTER>text to be centered</CENTER>

HTML 3.0 also provides the alignment attribute to support the formatting of headings, paragraphs, and other elements. You'll learn how to use the alignment attribute later in this lesson.

Font

The *font* tag allows the user to specify a range of seven font sizes to be used with tagged text. The font size is specified via the **SIZE** attribute. The font tag is used as follows:

```
<FONT SIZE=3>affected text</FONT>
```

A size 1 font is rendered in a very small point size. A size 7 font is rendered in a large point size. The specific font sizes to be used are individually determined by each browser.

Let's create a document that displays the blink, center, and font tags.

1. Launch HoTMetaL.

2. Type **New Netscape Elements** as the document title.

3. Create a level 1 heading and type **New Netscape Elements**.

HTML HEAD TITLE Document Title: New Netscape Elements /TITLE /HEAD
BODY H1 New Netscape Elements /H1 /BODY
/HTML

4. Move the cursor between the **/H1** and **/BODY** tags.

5. Type **This text blinks.**

HTML HEAD TITLE Document Title: New Netscape Elements /TITLE /HEAD
BODY H1 New Netscape Elements /H1
P This text blinks. /P /BODY /HTML

6. Select the word **blinks**.

P This text blinks. /P /BODY /HTML

7 Click on the **Extensions to HTML 2.0** toolbar button and select **BLINK**.

▶ **BLINK** tags are inserted in your document.

8 Press ↵ to start a new paragraph.

<P>This text <BLINK>blinks</BLINK>. </P>
<P>This text is centered.</P> </BODY> </HTML>

9 Type **This text is centered.**

10 Click on the **Extensions to HTML 2.0** toolbar button and select **CENTER**.

BIG
BLINK
CENTER
DFN

▶ The paragraph tags are replaced with center tags.

11 Move the cursor to the right of the **/CENTER** tag.

<P>This text <BLINK>blinks</BLINK>. </P>
<CENTER>This text is centered. </CENTER>
<P>This text is displayed using a size 1 font.</P> </BODY> </HTML>

12 Type **This text is displayed using a size 1 font.**

13 Select the text you just typed.

<P>This text is displayed using a size 1 font.</P> </BODY> </HTML>

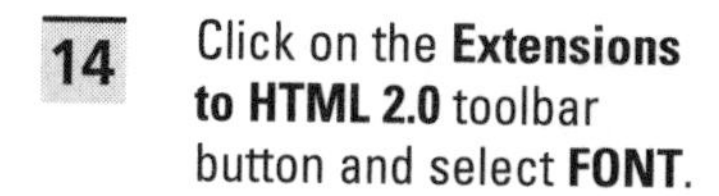

14 Click on the **Extensions to HTML 2.0** toolbar button and select **FONT**.

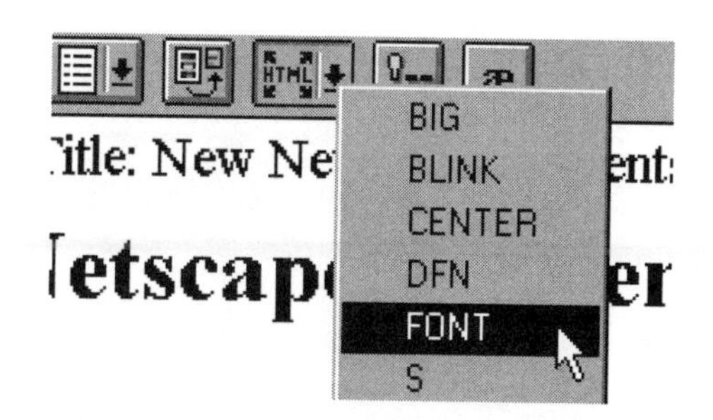

▶ The Edit Attributes dialog box appears.

15 Type **1** in the SIZE field and click on **Apply**.

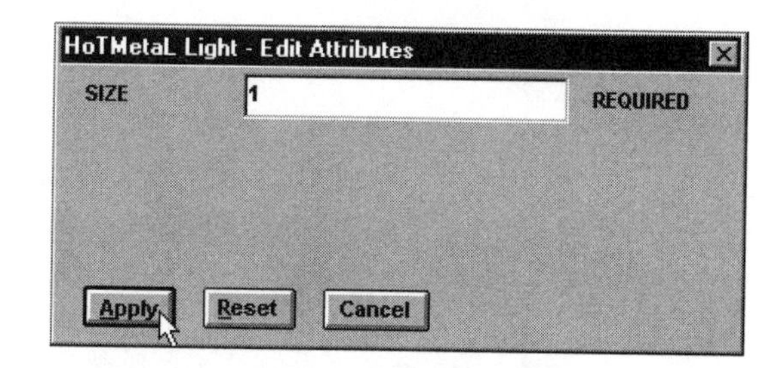

16 Select the entire last paragraph (including the paragraph tags).

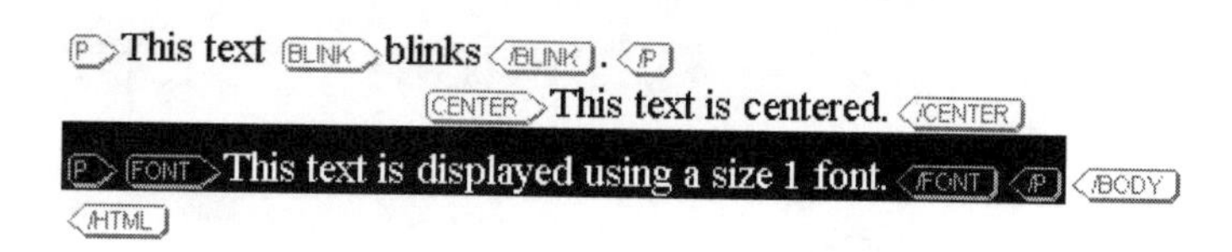

17 Press **Ctrl+C** to copy the paragraph to the clipboard.

18 Move the cursor immediately before the **/BODY** tag.

19 Press **Ctrl+V** to paste the paragraph that you just copied.

P This text BLINK blinks /BLINK . /P
CENTER This text is centered. /CENTER
P FONT This text is displayed using a size 1 font. /FONT /P
P FONT This text is displayed using a size 1 font. /FONT /P /BODY
/HTML

20 In the paragraph that you just pasted, select **1** and type **7** over it.

P FONT This text is displayed using a size 1 font. /FONT /P
P FONT This text is displayed using a size 7 font. /FONT /P /BODY
/HTML

21 Press the **F6** function key to bring up the Edit Attributes dialog box.

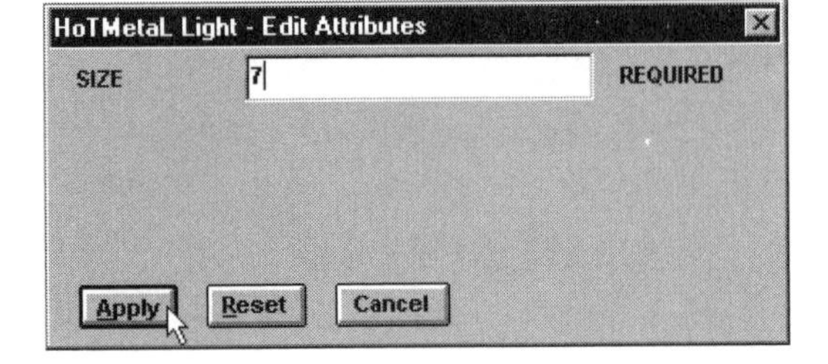

22 Type **7** in the SIZE field and click on **Apply**.

23 Save your document as c:\html\ch04-01.htm.

24 View the document using your browser.

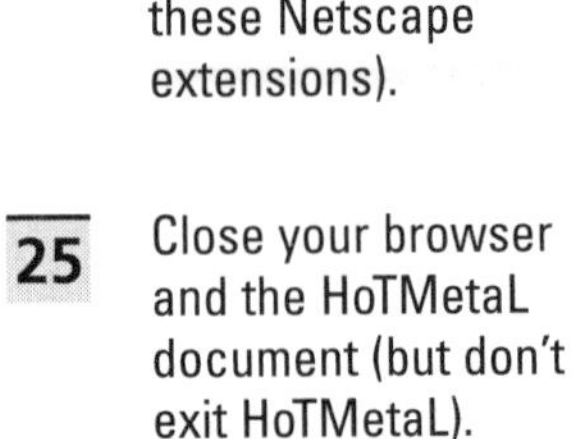

▶ The word *blinks* in the first paragraph is blinking on and off, the second paragraph is centered, the third paragraph is displayed in a very small font, and the fourth is displayed in a very large font (provided your browser supports these Netscape extensions).

25 Close your browser and the HoTMetaL document (but don't exit HoTMetaL).

No Break and Word Break

In Lesson 2, you learned how the line break attribute is used to force browsers to move to a new line when displaying formatted text. In some cases, you may want to do the opposite—inhibit a browser from wrapping text to the next line.

The *no break* and *word break* tags control how browsers wrap lines of text. Text enclosed by no break tags should not be wrapped by a browser and should be displayed on a single line up to the edge of the browser window. If the text extends beyond the visible window, the horizontal scroll bar can be used to view the extended text. The no break tag is used as follows:

<NOBR>This text should be displayed on a single line in the browser window even if it extends beyond the visible window boundary.</NOBR>

The word break tag is used within the no break tags. The word break tag allows you to identify exactly where a line of text may be wrapped. It does not force a line break, but informs the browser where a line break is permitted.

<NOBR>This text should be displayed on a single line in the browser window <WBR>even if it extends beyond the visible window boundary. However, it may be wrapped right before the word "even."</NOBR>

► ► ► The following example assumes that you are using a standard 640 by 480 screen resolution. If you are using a higher screen resolution, such as 800 by 600, your browser's display will not match the one that is shown.

Let's practice using no break and word break tags.

1. Open a new HoTMetaL document.

2. Type **No Break and Word Break** as the document title.

3. Create a level 1 heading and type **No Break and Word Break**.

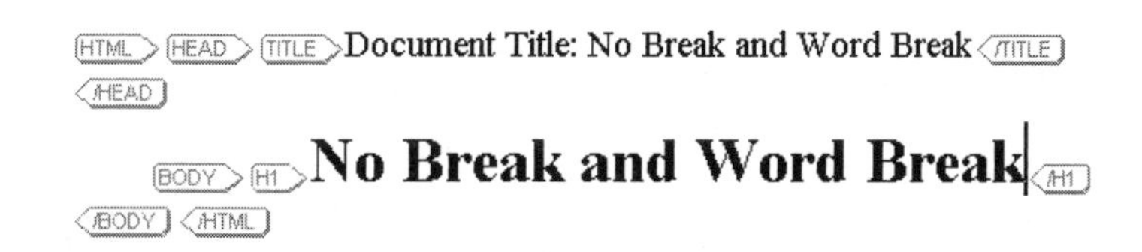

4 Move the cursor to the right of the **/H1** tag and type **This is an example of a paragraph that does not use the No Break tags to keep text from breaking to the next line.**

<HTML> <HEAD> <TITLE>Document Title: No Break and Word Break</TITLE> </HEAD>

<BODY> <H1>**No Break and Word Break**</H1>

<P>This is an example of a paragraph that does not use the No Break tags to keep text from breaking to the next line.</P> </BODY> </HTML>

5 Select the words **does not** and click on the **Emphasis** toolbar button.

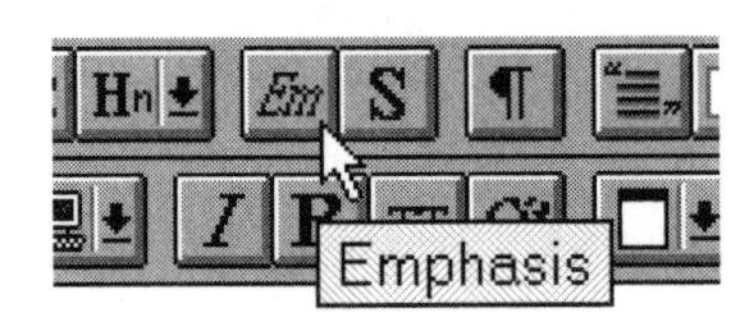

▶ **EM** tags appear around *does not.*

<P>This is an example of a paragraph that <EM>*does not*</EM> use the No Break tags to keep text from breaking to the next line. </P> </BODY> </HTML>

6 Copy the whole paragraph (including its paragraph tags) and paste it between the **/P** and **/BODY** tags.

<P>This is an example of a paragraph that <EM>*does not*</EM> use the No Break tags to keep text from breaking to the next line. </P>

<P>This is an example of a paragraph that <EM>*does*</EM> use the No Break tags to keep text from breaking to the next line. </P> </BODY> </HTML>

7 In the paragraph that you just pasted, delete the word *not.*

8 Select the entire last paragraph, but not its enclosing paragraph tags.

<P>This is an example of a paragraph that <EM>*does not*</EM> use the No Break tags to keep text from breaking to the next line. </P>

<P>This is an example of a paragraph that <EM>*does*</EM> use the No Break tags to keep text from breaking to the next line. </P> </BODY> </HTML>

9 Click on the **Extensions to HTML 2.0** toolbar button and select **NOBR**.

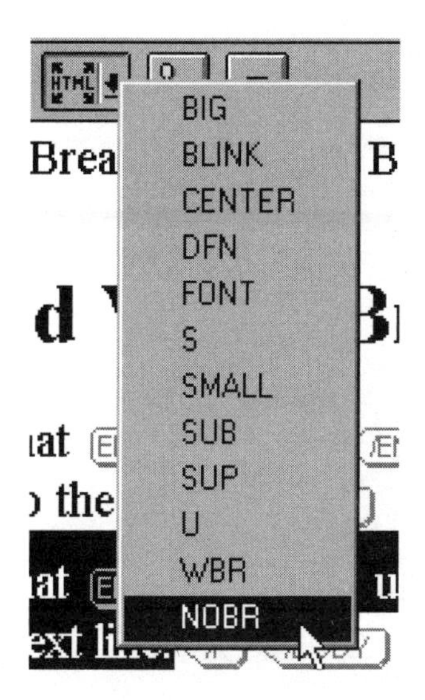

► **NOBR** tags are nested inside the paragraph tags.

10 Select the entire last paragraph (including the paragraph tags).

<P>This is an example of a paragraph that <EM>*does not*</EM> use the No Break tags to keep text from breaking to the next line.</P>

<P><NOBR>This is an example of a paragraph that <EM>*does*</EM> use the No Break tags to keep text from breaking to the next line.</NOBR></P></BODY>
</HTML>

11 Copy the paragraph and paste it between the **/P** and **/BODY** tags.

<P>This is an example of a paragraph that <EM>*does not*</EM> use the No Break tags to keep text from breaking to the next line.</P>

<P><NOBR>This is an example of a paragraph that <EM>*does*</EM> use the No Break tags to keep text from breaking to the next line.</NOBR></P>

<P><NOBR>This is an example of a paragraph that <EM>*does*</EM> use the No Break tags to keep text from breaking to the next line.</NOBR></P></BODY>
</HTML>

12 Move the cursor before the word *next* in the last paragraph.

<P><NOBR>This is an example of a paragraph that <EM>*does*</EM> use the No Break tags to keep text from breaking to the next line.</NOBR></P></BODY>
</HTML>

13 Click on the **Extensions to HTML 2.0** toolbar button and select **WBR**.

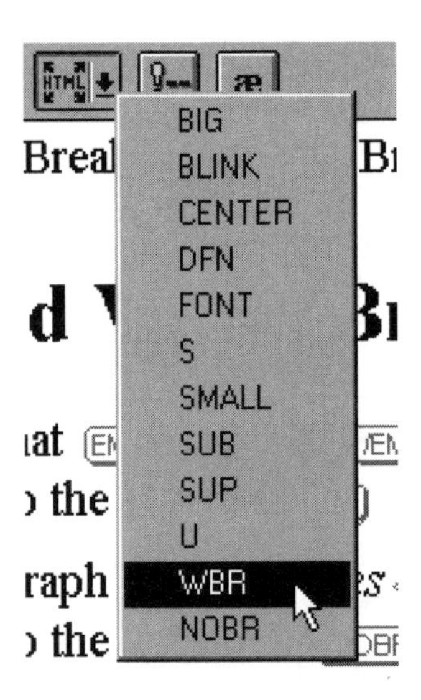

▶ **WBR** tags are inserted in your document.

<P> <NOBR>This is an example of a paragraph that <EM>*does*</EM> use the No Break tags to keep text from breaking to the
<WBR> </WBR>
next line. </NOBR> </P> </BODY> </HTML>

14 Move the cursor immediately before the final **/NOBR** tag and type **It also uses the Word Break tag to enable breaking at the word "next" in the first sentence.**

<P> <NOBR>This is an example of a paragraph that <EM>*does*</EM> use the No Break tags to keep text from breaking to the
<WBR> </WBR>
next line. It also uses the Word Break tag to enable breaking at the word "next" in the first sentence.</NOBR> </P> </BODY> </HTML>

15 Save your document as c:\html\ch04-02.htm.

16 View it with your browser.

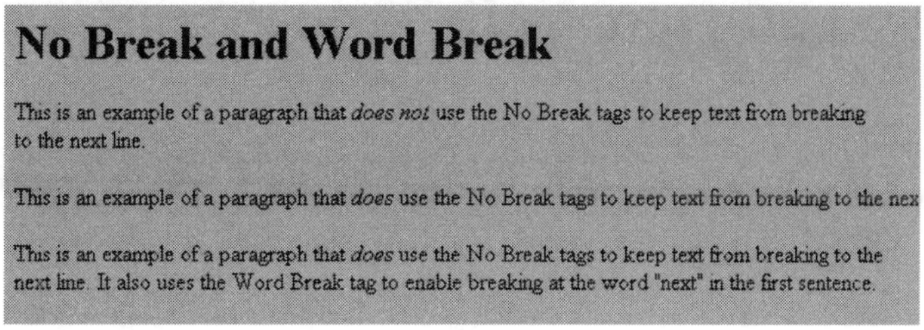

No Break and Word Break

This is an example of a paragraph that *does not* use the No Break tags to keep text from breaking to the next line.

This is an example of a paragraph that *does* use the No Break tags to keep text from breaking to the nex

This is an example of a paragraph that *does* use the No Break tags to keep text from breaking to the next line. It also uses the Word Break tag to enable breaking at the word "next" in the first sentence.

▶ Notice how the no break and word break tags affect the display of the second and third paragraphs.

17 Close your browser and the document, but keep HoTMetaL open.

Document Color Attributes

Some of the most popular Netscape extensions are the new attributes for the document body tag. These attributes allow you to change the color of the document background and text. You will learn how to use HoTMetaL to work with these attributes in this section. Netscape extensions also include attributes that allow you to use an image as background wallpaper and to change the color of links. These other attributes are covered in Lessons 5 and 7.

The BGCOLOR Attribute

The **BGCOLOR** attribute allows you to change the color of the document background. Instead of using a dull gray or white background, you can now change the background color of your Web pages to any color that fits your needs. The **BGCOLOR** attribute is used with the body tag, like so:

<BODY BGCOLOR="*#rrggbb*"> ... </BODY>

The red, green, and blue color intensities of your color are substituted for *rr*, *gg*, and *bb* above. These color intensities range from 0 to 255. The higher the color intensity, the more that color influences the composite color that is produced.

The color intensities are written as two-digit hexadecimal numbers. To convert the numbers 0 through 255 to their two-digit hexadecimal equivalents, use the table provided on the Web at **http://www.jaworski.com/htmlbook/rgb.htm**.

The hexadecimal numbering system is based on a scale of 16 instead of our standard decimal system's scale of 10. From lowest to highest, the scale consists of the digits 0, 1, 2, 3, 4, 5, 6, 7, 8, 9, a, b, c, d, e, and f.

Using these hexadecimal numbers, you can experiment with the red, green, and blue color intensities to select a very large range of custom colors. Here are some example color values:

Color	rr	gg	bb
White	ff	ff	ff
Red	ff	00	00
Yellow	ff	ff	00
Green	00	ff	00
Cyan	00	ff	ff
Blue	00	00	ff
Magenta	ff	00	ff
Brown	a5	2a	2a
Black	00	00	00

The TEXT Attribute

The **TEXT** attribute allows you to change the color of all text in your Web page except text that is used as part of a link. (You'll learn how to change the color of links in Lesson 7.) The **TEXT** attribute is similar to the **BGCOLOR** attribute.

<BODY TEXT="*#rrggbb*"> ... </BODY>

The red, green, and blue color intensities of your color are substituted for *rr*, *gg*, and *bb* in the same manner as with the **BGCOLOR** attribute.

Let's experiment with colors.

1 Open a new HoTMetaL document.

2 Type **Background and Text Colors** as the document title.

3 Create a level 1 heading and type **Background and Text Colors**.

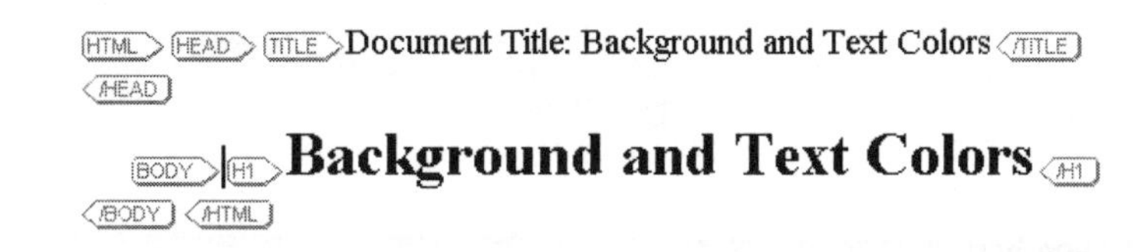
HTML HEAD TITLE Document Title: Background and Text Colors /TITLE
/HEAD
BODY H1 Background and Text Colors /H1
/BODY /HTML

4 Move the cursor between the **BODY** and **H1** tags and press the **F6** function key.

► The Edit Attributes dialog box appears.

HoTMetaL Light - Edit Attributes

BACKGROUNI	
BGCOLOR	#0000ff
TEXT	#ffff00
LINK	
VLINK	
ALINK	

Apply Reset Cancel

5 In the BGCOLOR field, type **#0000ff**.

6 In the TEXT field, type **#ffff00**.

7 Click on the **Apply** button.

8 Save your document as c:\html\ch04-03.htm.

9 View the document using your browser.

Background and Text Colors

► Your document background is blue and the text is yellow (provided your browser supports the HTML 2.0 extensions).

10 View the source HTML document generated by HoTMetaL.

```
<!DOCTYPE HTML PUBLIC "-//SQ//DTD HTML 2.0 HoTMetaL + extensions//EN">
<HTML><HEAD><TITLE>Background and Text Colors</TITLE></HEAD>
<BODY BGCOLOR="#0000ff" TEXT="#ffff00"><H1>Background and Text Colors</H1>
```

▶ Notice how HoTMetaL inserted the **BGCOLOR** and **TEXT** attributes into the **BODY** tag.

11 Close your browser and the document, but don't exit HoTMetaL.

HTML 3.0 Elements

HTML 3.0 introduces several text formatting features. Six new physical formatting tags and one new logical formatting tag are currently supported by HoTMetaL. In addition, HoTMetaL supports additional attributes for existing tags. HoTMetaL provides access to the HTML 3.0 text formatting tags through the Extensions to HTML 2.0 toolbar button and to the new attributes through the Edit SGML Attributes option in the Markup pull-down menu.

▶ ▶ ▶ The HTML 3.0 specification can be found on the Web at **http://www.w3.org/pub/WWW/MarkUp/MarkUp.html**.

The HTML 3.0 text formatting tags supported by HoTMetaL are introduced in the following paragraphs.

Big and Small

The *big* and *small* tags are used to increase and decrease the size of displayed text. They are used as follows:

```
<BIG>this text is displayed using a larger point size</BIG>
<SMALL>this text is displayed using a smaller point size</SMALL>
```

Subscript and Superscript

The *subscript* and *superscript* tags are used to specify subscripts and superscripts. They are used as follows:

```
<P>x sub 1 is written as x<SUB>1</SUB></P>
<P>x squared is written as x<SUP>2</SUP></P>
```

Underline

The *underline* tag causes tagged text to be underlined. It is used as follows:

```
<U>this text is underlined</U>
```

Strikeout

The *strikeout* tag causes tagged text to be displayed using strikeout. It is used as follows:

```
<S>this text is displayed using strikeout</S>
```

Definition

The *definition* or *defining instance* tag is a logical formatting tag that is used to indicate a term that is being defined. It is used as follows:

```
A <DFN>geodesic</DFN> is the shortest line between two points over a given
surface.
```

Let's try out some HTML 3.0 features.

1. Open a new HoTMetaL document.

2. Type **HTML 3.0 Elements** as the title.

3. Create a level 1 heading and type **New Physical Formatting Tags**.

<HTML> <HEAD> <TITLE>Document Title: HTML 3.0 Elements </TITLE> </HEAD>
<BODY> <H1>**New Physical Formatting Tags**
</H1> </BODY> </HTML>

4. Press ↵ to start a new heading and type **A New Logical Formatting Tag**.

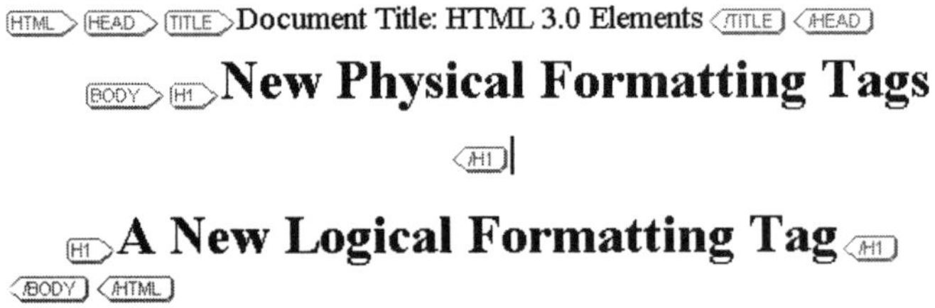

5. Place the cursor between the two headings.

<HTML> <HEAD> <TITLE>Document Title: HTML 3.0 Elements </TITLE> </HEAD>
<BODY> <H1>**New Physical Formatting Tags**
</H1>
<H1>**A New Logical Formatting Tag** </H1>
</BODY> </HTML>

6. Type **This is big., This is small., This is underlined., This is strikeout., This is an example of subscripting: x1**, and **This is an example of superscripting: x3**, pressing ↵ at the end of each sentence except the last.

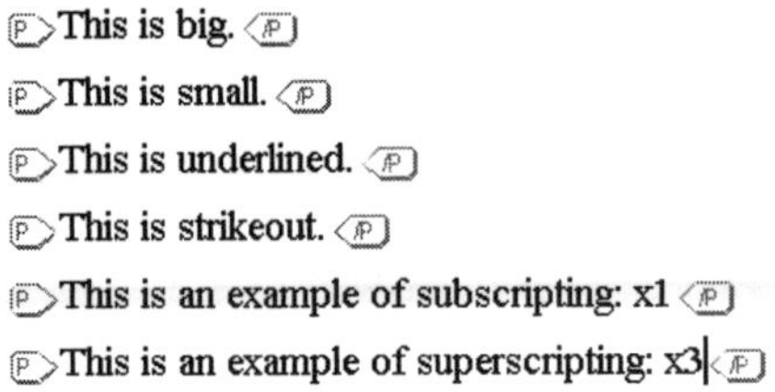

<P>This is big. </P>
<P>This is small. </P>
<P>This is underlined. </P>
<P>This is strikeout. </P>
<P>This is an example of subscripting: x1 </P>
<P>This is an example of superscripting: x3 </P>

7. Move the cursor before the **/BODY** tag and type **This is a definition.**

<P>This is an example of superscripting: x3 </P>
<H1>**A New Logical Formatting Tag** </H1>
<P>This is a definition. </P> </BODY> </HTML>

8. Select the word **big** in the first paragraph.

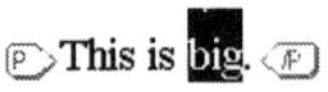

<P>This is big. </P>

9 Click on the **Extensions to HTML 2.0** button and select **BIG**.

▶ **BIG** tags are inserted.

10 Select the word **small** in the second paragraph, click on the **Extensions to HTML 2.0** button, and select **SMALL**.

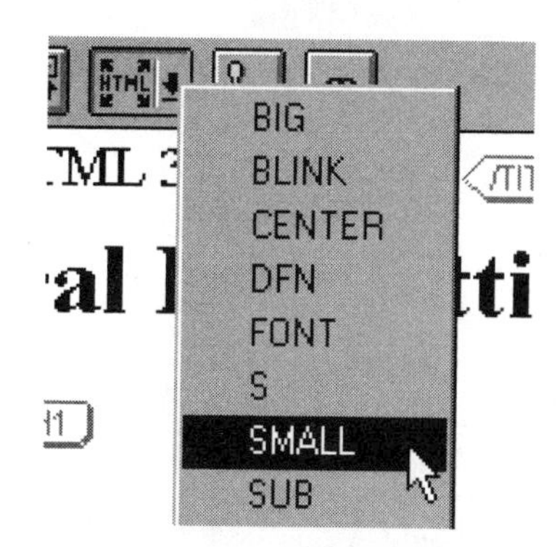

▶ **SMALL** tags are inserted.

11 Select the word **underlined** in the third paragraph, click on the **Extensions to HTML 2.0** button, and select **U**.

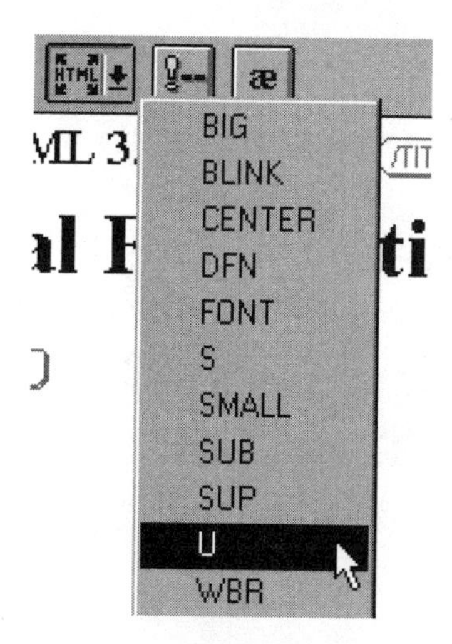

▶ **U** tags are inserted.

12 Select the word **strikeout** in the fourth paragraph, click on the **Extensions to HTML 2.0** button, and select **S**.

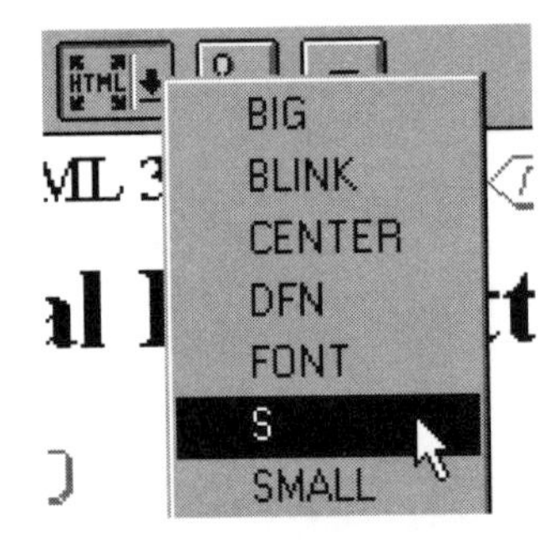

▶ **S** tags are inserted.

<P>This is <S>strikeout</S>. </P>

13 Select the number **1** in the fifth paragraph, click on the **Extensions to HTML 2.0** button, and select **SUB**.

▶ **SUB** tags are inserted.

<P>This is an example of subscripting: x₁ </P>

14 Select the number **3** in the sixth paragraph, click on the **Extensions to HTML 2.0** button, and select **SUP**.

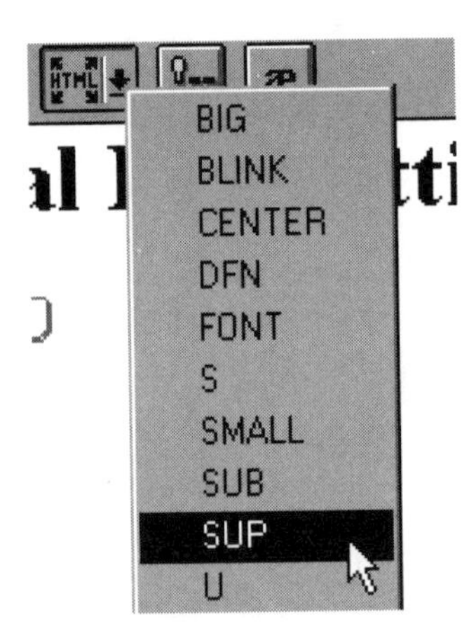

SUP tags are inserted.

This is an example of superscripting: x³</P>

15 Select the word **definition** in the last paragraph, click on the **Extensions to HTML 2.0** button, and select **DFN**.

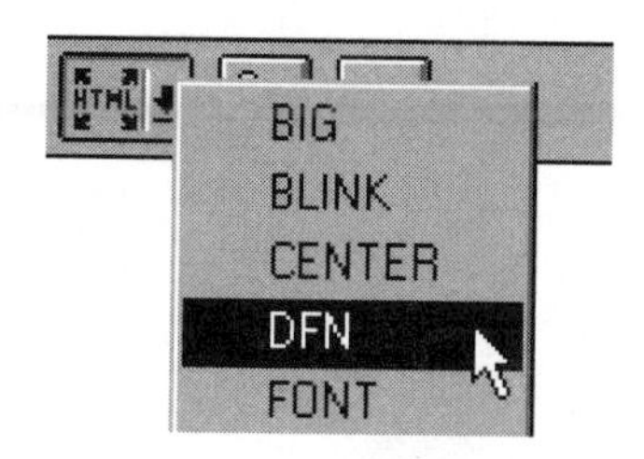

DFN tags are inserted.

This is a DFN definition /DFN . /P /BODY /HTML

16 Save your document as c:\html\ch04-04.htm and view it using your browser.

Netscape Navigator supports the big, small, subscripting, and superscripting tags, but not the underlined, strikeout, and definition tags.

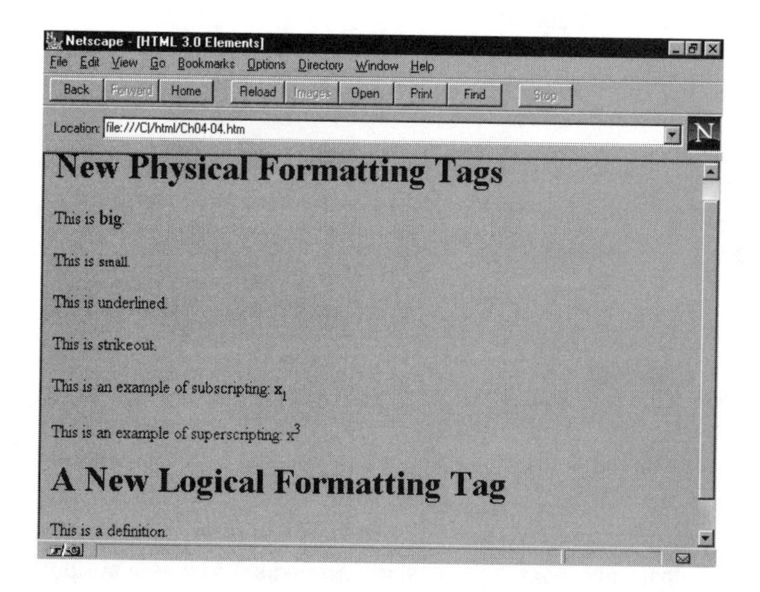

Microsoft's Internet Explorer supports exactly those tags that the Netscape Navigator doesn't support.

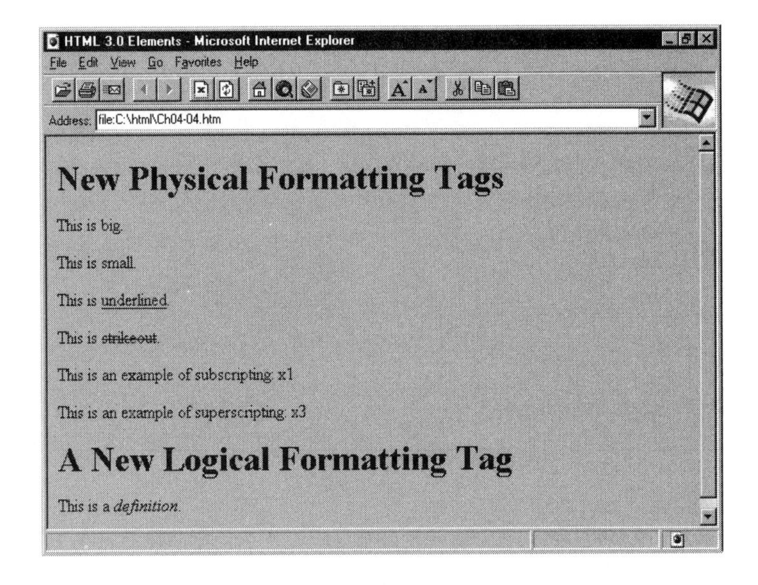

17 Exit your browser and close the HoTMetaL document, but stay in HoTMetaL.

Since current browsers provide limited HTML 3.0 support, you may wish to delay use of the new HTML 3.0 tags.

HTML 3.0 Attributes

HoTMetaL supports many new Netscape and HTML 3.0 attributes. You can access these attributes by choosing the Edit SGML Attributes option from the Markup pull-down menu or by pressing the F6 function key. New text formatting attributes apply to headings, paragraphs, line breaks, horizontal rules, and lists. The new attributes for line breaks, horizontal rules, and lists include support of graphics and are deferred to Lesson 7. We'll cover heading and paragraph attributes now.

HoTMetaL supports the HTML 3.0 **ALIGN** attribute for both headings and paragraphs. The **ALIGN** attribute may take on the values **LEFT**, **CENTER**, **RIGHT**, or **JUSTIFY**. The default value is **LEFT**. The **JUSTIFY** attribute value specifies full justification, where possible, but defaults to left justification in most cases.

1. Open a new HoTMetaL document.

2. Type **New SGML Attributes** as the document title.

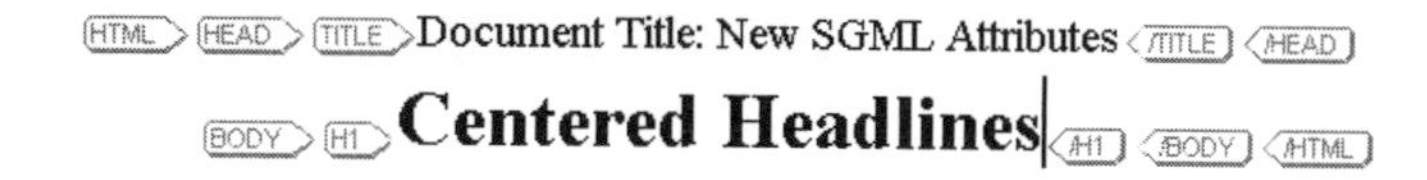

3. Create a level 1 heading and type **Centered Headlines**.

4. With the cursor anywhere between the **H1** tags, select **Markup ➢ Edit SGML Attributes**.

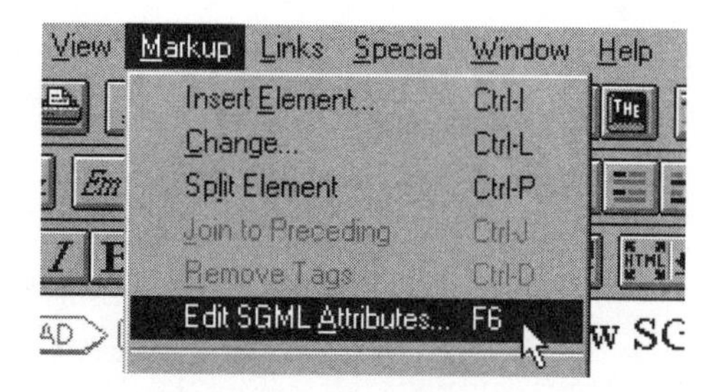

▶ The Edit Attributes dialog box appears.

5. Click on the down-arrow to the right of the ALIGN field and select **CENTER**.

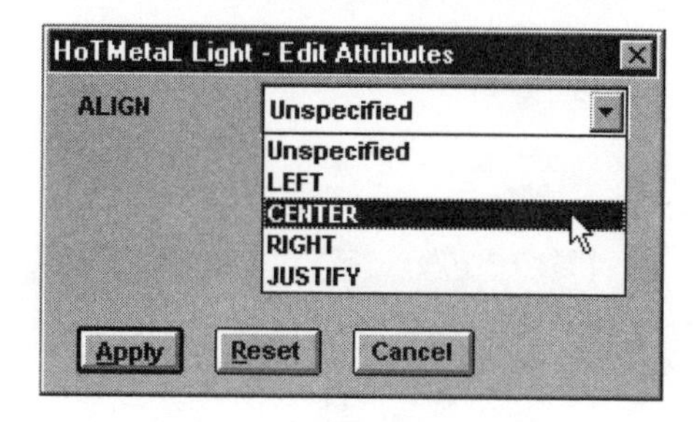

6. Click on **Apply**.

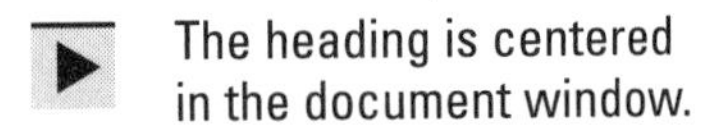
The heading is centered in the document window.

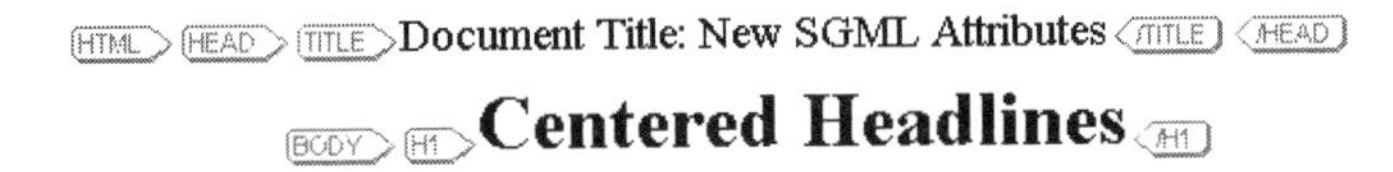

7 Move the cursor immediately before the **/BODY** tag and type **Centered paragraphs.**

BODY H1 **Centered Headlines** /H1

P Centered paragraphs. /P /BODY /HTML

8 Press the **F6** key to bring up the Edit Attributes dialog box.

9 Select **CENTER** in the ALIGN field and click on **Apply**.

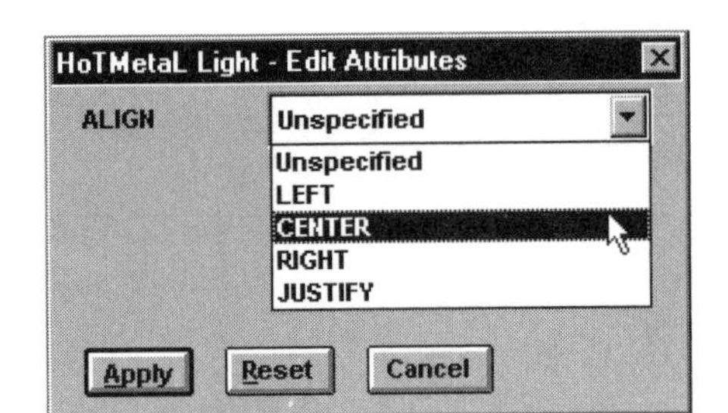

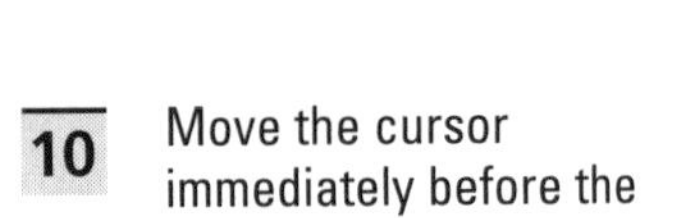
The paragraph moves to the center of the document window.

10 Move the cursor immediately before the **/BODY** tag and press the **H1** toolbar button.

P Centered paragraphs. /P

H1 **Right Justified Headlines** /H1 /BODY /HTML

11 Type **Right Justified Headlines**.

12 Press the **F6** key to bring up the Edit Attributes dialog box.

13 Select **RIGHT** in the ALIGN field and click on **Apply**.

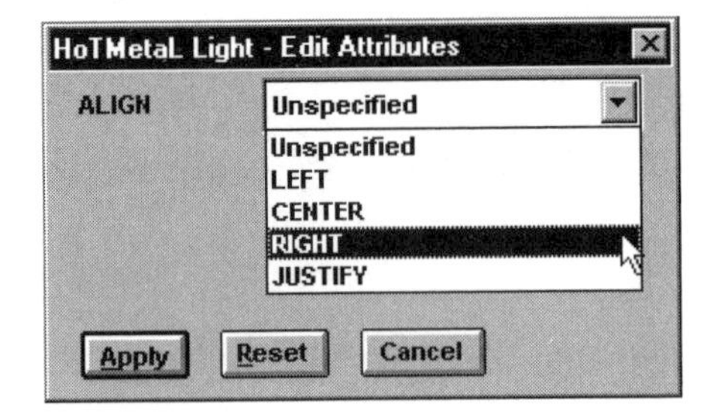

14 Move the cursor immediately before the **/BODY** tag and type **Right justified paragraphs.**

H1 **Right Justified Headlines** /H1

P Right justified paragraphs. /P /BODY /HTML

15 Press the **F6** key to bring up the Edit Attributes dialog box.

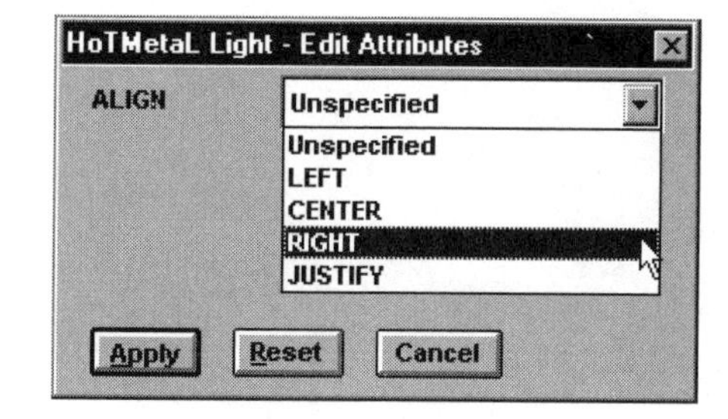

16 Select **RIGHT** in the ALIGN field and click on **Apply**.

▶ The paragraph moves to the right.

H1 **Right Justified Headlines** /H1

P Right justified paragraphs. /P /BODY /HTML

17 Save the file as c:\html\ch04-05.htm and view it with your browser.

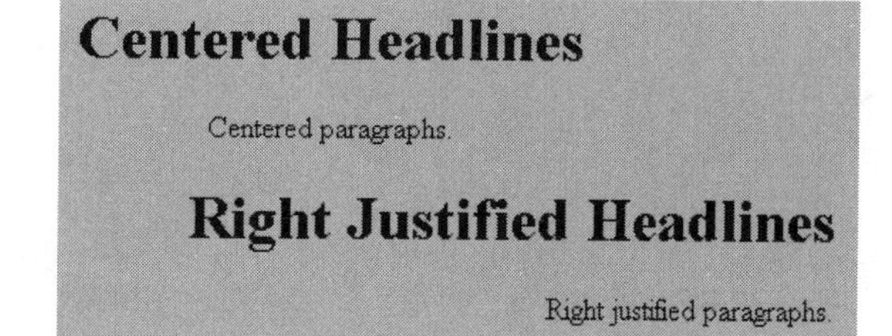

18 When you're done, close your browser and HoTMetaL.

You are well on your way to learning HoTMetaL. You can now use it to work with many HTML 2.0 tags, the Netscape extensions, and some HTML 3.0. In the next lesson, you will learn how to use HoTMetaL to insert inline graphics into your Web pages.

Adding Graphics

Part of the appeal of the World Wide Web is its integrated, operating system-independent support of inline images. Images make Web pages more interesting and informative. By integrating images within text, Web pages become more diverse and visually appealing and can be used to communicate more effectively. The old adage "a picture is worth a thousand words" has never been more appropriate.

In this lesson, you'll learn how to insert images into your Web pages. You'll learn what graphics formats are supported by Web browsers and what formats are best for different types of images. You'll learn how to align your images with surrounding text and create special effects using transparent and interlaced graphics. You'll also learn how to use images for your page background. When you finish this lesson, you'll be able to effectively use inline images in your Web pages.

► ► ► Full support of inline images is one of the primary reasons for the Web's popularity. Learning to use these graphics capabilities is essential to developing attractive Web pages.

Two types of graphic images are supported by Web browsers: inline graphic images and external graphic images. Inline images are loaded and displayed as part of a Web page. External images are downloaded and displayed outside a Web page. External images are not displayed by your Web browser, but by a separate program, referred to as an external viewer. This lesson covers inline images. External images will be discussed in Lesson 11.

Not all browsers support images. Some viewers, such as Lynx, can only display Web pages as formatted text. It is important to design Web pages so they will still make sense when viewed by nongraphical browsers.

Inline Graphics Formats

Early Web browsers supported two graphics formats for inline images: GIF and XBM. Second generation browsers, such as Netscape 2.0, Mosaic 2.0, and Internet Explorer 2.0, also support inline JPEG images.

The Graphics Interchange Format, or GIF, developed by CompuServe, is by far the most popular graphics format. GIF supports compressed storage of 8-bit color images. There are two upwardly compatible standards, GIF87 and GIF89, named after the years they were released. Web browsers are capable of displaying images in either format.

The X Bitmap, or XBM, format is a graphics format developed for displaying images on Unix workstations running the X Window System graphical user interface. Since the first Web browsers were developed to run on Unix systems, the XBM format was supported early on. XBM graphics files can also be displayed on Microsoft Windows and Macintosh-based browsers.

JPEG is another popular image format. JPEG stands for Joint Photographic Experts Group, the name of the group that created the standard. It uses a *lossy* compression algorithm to compress stored images. Lossy algorithms discard information from the original graphic in order to reduce the size of the compressed image. The JPEG algorithm exploits known limitations of the human eye in order to decide which information can be discarded. The advantages of JPEG over GIF are 24-bit color and reduced file size. JPEG has replaced GIF as the standard for storing photographic images.

Which Format Should I Use?

The GIF format is the most popular graphics format for inline graphics. Since GIF does not use lossy compression, all images may be represented using the GIF format. To ensure that your graphics can be viewed by the widest possible audience, you should use the GIF format. However, if your graphics consist of photographic images, using the JPEG format will result in a significant reduction in graphic file size.

There is one potential difficulty in using the GIF format. The format is copyrighted by CompuServe, and CompuServe has indicated that it may charge fees for programs that use GIF images. If this does come to pass, the Web community will surely adopt a public domain replacement format.

Installing Sample Graphics

Several graphics images are used in the examples of this lesson. The files containing these images may be copied from the CD included with this book. You'll install the graphics in the c:\html\images directory by copying the images directory from your CD to your hard disk. The following steps describe how this is done.

1. In the Windows 95 Start menu, click on **Programs ➢ Windows Explorer**.

2. Click on the drive icon for your CD-ROM.

3. Click on the **html** directory of your CD-ROM and then on the **images** subdirectory.

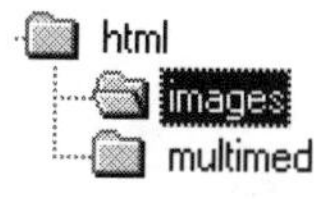

4 Select **Edit ➢ Copy**.

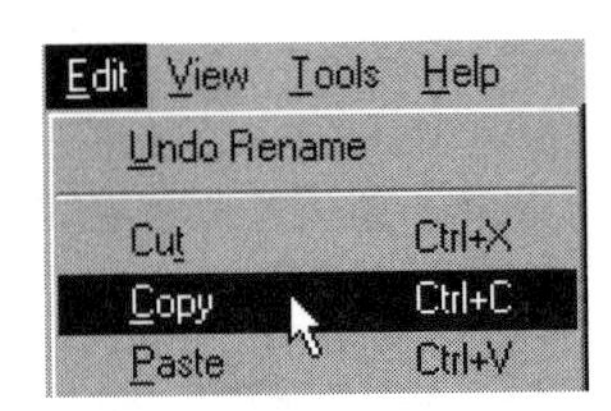

5 Click on your **C:** hard drive icon.

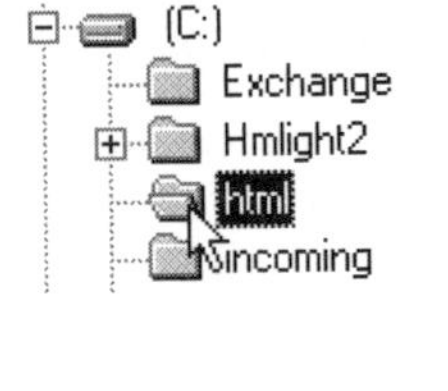

6 Double-click on the **c:\html** directory.

7 Select **Edit ➢ Paste**.

► The images directory is copied from the CD to your c:\html directory.

8 Close Windows Explorer.

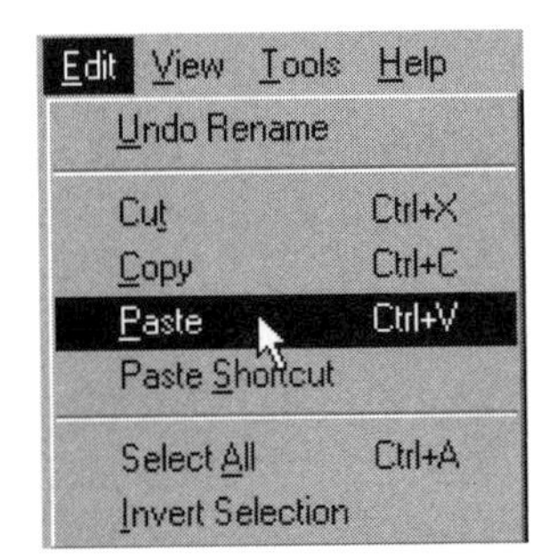

Using Images in Your Web Pages

Inline images are inserted in Web pages using the **<IMG>** tag. The image tag is a separating tag and has several attributes used to specify properties of the image.

Every image tag must identify the location of the graphic image to be displayed. This is accomplished using the image source attribute. The simplest way to insert an inline image is to use an image tag like this:

```
<IMG SRC="myimage.gif">
```

In the above example, *myimage.gif* is the name of the image file.

The file name extension of your image file must identify the format of the image it contains. Valid extensions include .gif for GIF files, .xbm for XBM files, and .jpg for JPEG files.

HoTMetaL does not insert just one image tag in the document window. Instead, it inserts a pair of tags: **IMG** and **/IMG**. However, it inserts the correct **<IMG>** tag in the HTML files that it generates.

Adding a Simple Image

Let's put a simple image in a Web page. One of the graphics files included on the CD, web.gif, is an image of a web. If you have copied the image files to your hard disk, it will be in the c:\html\images directory.

1. Launch HoTMetaL and open a new document window.

2. Type **A Simple Image Tag** as the document title.

3. Create a level 1 heading and type **A Simple Image Tag**.

HTML HEAD TITLE Document Title: A Simple Image Tag /TITLE /HEAD

BODY H1 **A Simple Image Tag** /H1 /BODY /HTML

4. Save your file as c:\html\ch05-01.htm.

5. Move the cursor between the **/H1** tag and the **/BODY** tag and type **A Spider Web**.

HTML HEAD TITLE Document Title: A Simple Image Tag /TITLE /HEAD

BODY H1 **A Simple Image Tag** /H1

P A Spider Web /P /BODY /HTML

6 Move the cursor between the **P** tag and the letter *A* and click on the **Image** toolbar button.

▶ The Edit Image dialog box appears.

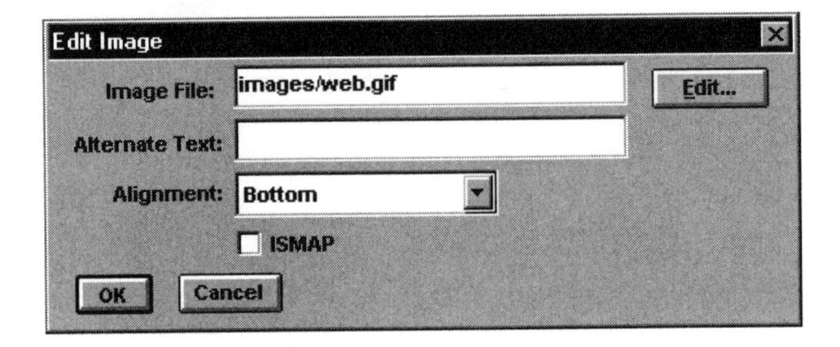

7 Type **images/web.gif** in the Image File field.

8 Click on the **OK** button.

▶ An image appears in your document.

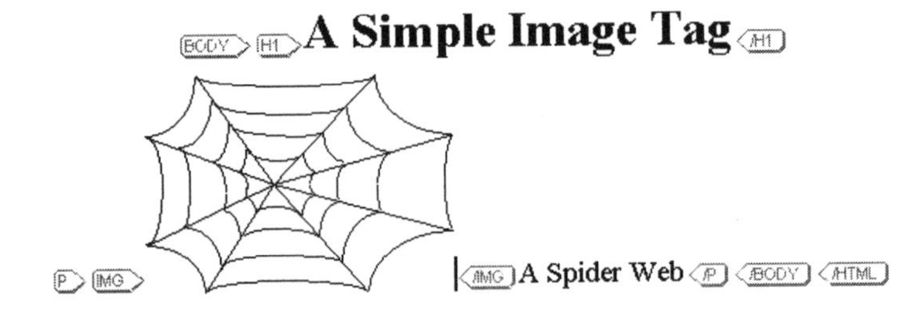

9 Select **View ➢ Hide Inline Images**.

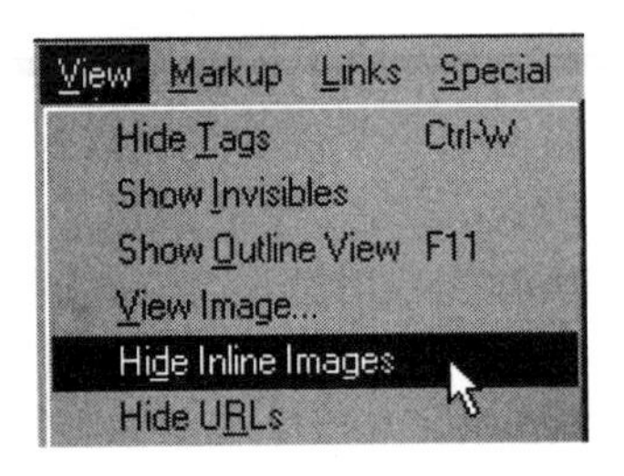

▶ The image is replaced with *[images/web.gif]*, its file name.

P IMG [images/web.gif] /IMG A Spider Web /P /BODY /HTML

10 Select **View ➢ Show Inline Images** to redisplay the image.

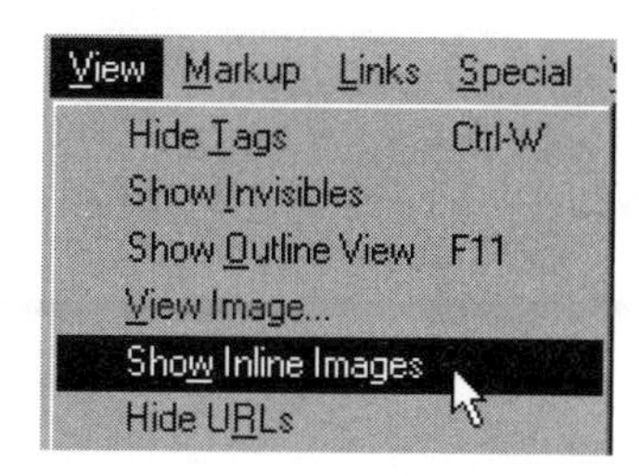

11 Save your document and view it with your browser.

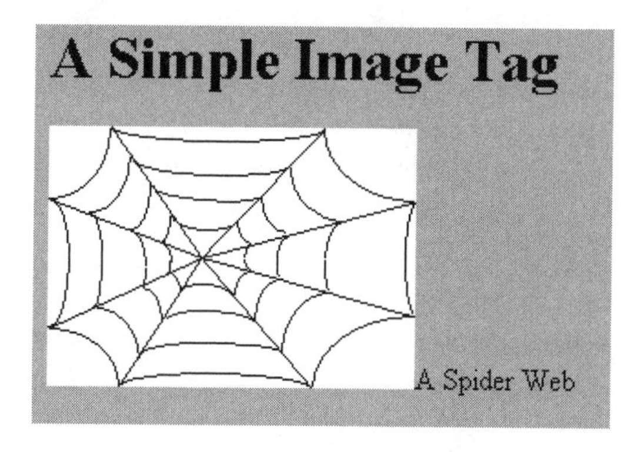

12 View the source document generated by HoTMetaL.

```
<!DOCTYPE HTML PUBLIC "-//SQ//DTD HTML 2.0 HoTMetaL + extensions//EN">
<HTML><HEAD><TITLE>A Simple Image Tag</TITLE></HEAD>
<BODY><H1>A Simple Image Tag</H1>
<P><IMG SRC="images/web.gif" ALIGN="BOTTOM">A Spider Web</P></BODY></HTML>
```

► Note that HoTMetaL inserted the correct image tag.

13 Close your browser, but leave the HoTMetaL document open.

► ► ► If your browser does not display the image, make sure the browser is configured to automatically display inline images.

If your browser does not use a white background, the background of the image and your browser display will differ. Later in this lesson, I will show you how to use a transparent background with GIF images.

Using Relative Path Names

The previous example illustrates the use of *relative path names.* The source attribute **"images/web.gif"** identifies the image file, web.gif, as being located in the image subdirectory of the directory of the Web page (c:\html\ch05-01.htm) from which it is referenced.

Path names in HTML are written using the Unix slash (/) rather than the DOS backslash (\).

Relative path names provide a convenient way to identify files in other directories. They are called *relative* because the location of a file is specified relative to the directory containing the Web page in which it is referenced.

In Windows, DOS, Unix, and most operating systems, files are organized using a hierarchical, tree-like file system. Relative path names can be used to identify files in any branch of these file systems. The special directory name (**..**) refers to the directory containing the current directory. By using **..**, you can climb up and down the file system directory tree until you reach the file you want. For example, suppose you want to reference the file c:\html\images\spider.gif from the Web page c:\html\newpage\test\web.htm. The relative path name would be **"../../images/spider.gif"**. Starting in the c:\html\newpage\test directory, the first **..** says to start looking in the c:\html\newpage directory. The second **..** says to look in the c:\html directory. From here, we go to the c:\html\images subdirectory where the file spider.gif is located.

Using Absolute Path Names

When referencing a graphic image, you can also specify the full path name of the file containing the graphic image. The full or *absolute path name* identifies the drive and complete path to the file. For example, suppose you want to identify the file d:\graphics\spider.gif to be used as the source for a graphic image. You could use the following image tag:

<IMG SRC="/d|/graphics/spider.gif">

In the above example, **"/d|/graphics/spider.gif"** is an absolute path to the graphics file.

Full path names always begin with /, followed by the drive specifier (with | substituted for :).

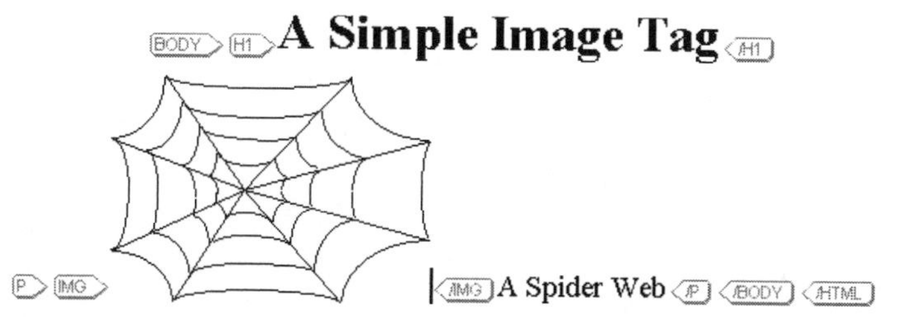

1. Using the document ch05-01.htm from earlier in this lesson, click the cursor between the **IMG** and **/IMG** tags.

2. Press the **F6** key.

▶ The Edit Attributes dialog box opens.

3. Place the cursor at the beginning of the SRC field and type **/c|/html/** (so the field reads */c|html/images/web.gif*).

4. Click on the **Apply** button.

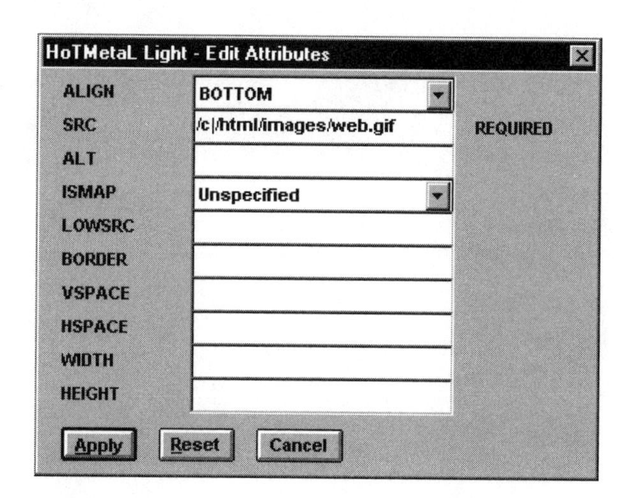

▶ HoTMetaL changes the image to a graphic saying *Image not available*. (This is a shortcoming of HoTMetaL. Sometimes it can't find the images that are specified in the SRC field. Browsers are smarter, as we'll soon see.)

HTML HEAD TITLE Document Title: A Simple Image Tag /TITLE /HEAD

BODY H1 **A Simple Image Tag** /H1

P IMG Image not available /IMG A Spider Web /P /BODY /HTML

5 Type **Absolute Path Names** over the old document title and level 1 heading.

HTML HEAD TITLE Document Title: Absolute Path Names /TITLE /HEAD
BODY H1 Absolute Path Names /H1
P IMG Image not available /IMG A Spider Web /P /BODY /HTML

6 Save your document as ch05-02.htm and view it with your browser.

▶ The browser is able to trace the absolute path name and display the image.

Absolute Path Names
A Spider Web

7 View the source document generated by HoTMetaL.

```
<!DOCTYPE HTML PUBLIC "-//SQ//DTD HTML 2.0 HoTMetaL + extensions//EN">
<HTML><HEAD><TITLE>Absolute Path Names</TITLE></HEAD>
<BODY><H1>Absolute Path Names</H1>
<P><IMG ALIGN="BOTTOM" SRC="/c|/html/images/web.gif">A Spider Web</P></BODY>
```

▶ Notice how HoTMetaL stores the absolute path name for your document.

8 Close your browser and the current HoTMetaL document, but leave HoTMetaL running.

If you can't get HoTMetaL to display an inline image with an absolute reference, try typing the full URL in the SRC field.

Relative Path Names vs. Absolute Path Names

Relative path names are preferred to absolute names for two reasons:

- Relative path names are more portable. If you want to move the location of your Web pages and graphics files to a different drive or subdirectory, relative path names generally require less modification.
- Relative path names result in more efficient browser operation. If an image is referenced several times on a Web page, it may be downloaded each time an absolute path name is encountered. If relative path names are used to reference the image, more intelligent browsers will download the image file only once.

The source of an image may also refer to graphics files stored on computers at other locations on the Internet. In this case, a URL is used to identify the image location.

Aligning Images

In the previous two examples, you may have noticed that HoTMetaL stored the attribute **ALIGN="BOTTOM"** in the **IMG** tag of the HTML files it generated. This tells the browser how to align the image with respect to the current line. The alignment attribute, **ALIGN**, may be specified in the image tag as any of the values in the following table.

VALUE	RESULT
LEFT	The image is placed on the left side of the browser window. Subsequent text and images are allowed to fill any available space along the right side of the image.
RIGHT	The image is placed on the right side of the browser window. Subsequent images and text are allowed to fill any available space along the left side of the image.
TOP	The image is placed as it occurs in a given line and aligned with the top of the tallest element occurring in the line.
TEXTTOP	The image is placed as it occurs in a given line and aligned with the tallest text occurring in the line.
MIDDLE	The baseline of the current line is aligned with the middle of the image.
ABSMIDDLE	The middle of the current line is aligned with the middle of the image.
BASELINE or **BOTTOM**	The bottom of the image is aligned with the baseline of the current line.
ABSBOTTOM	The bottom of the image is aligned with the bottom of the current line.

If the alignment attribute is omitted, most browsers will default to bottom alignment.

► ► ► Many browsers support only the **TOP**, **MIDDLE**, and **BOTTOM** alignment attribute values. The other attribute values are Netscape extensions.

The following example illustrates the use of alignment attributes.

1 Open a new HoTMetaL document, create a level 1 heading, and type **Image Alignment** for the title and heading.

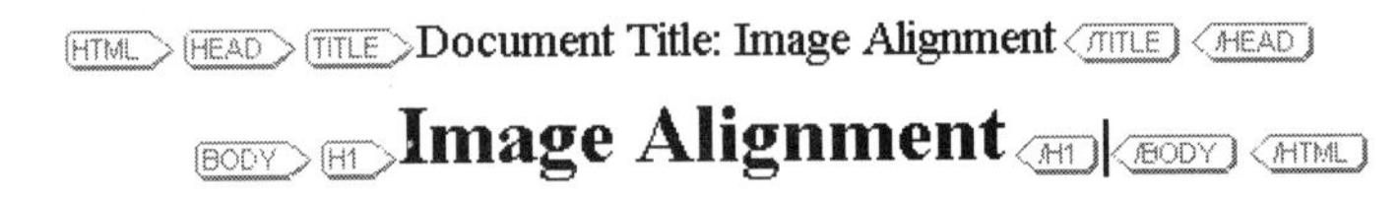

2 Save the file as c:\html\ch05-03.htm.

3 Move the cursor between the **/H1** and **/BODY** tags.

4 Click on the **Paragraph** button.

5 Click on the **Image** button.

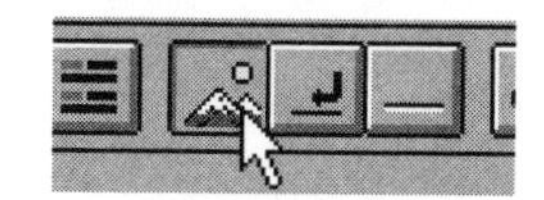

▶ The Edit Image dialog box appears.

6 Type **images/spider.gif** in the Image File field and click on **OK**.

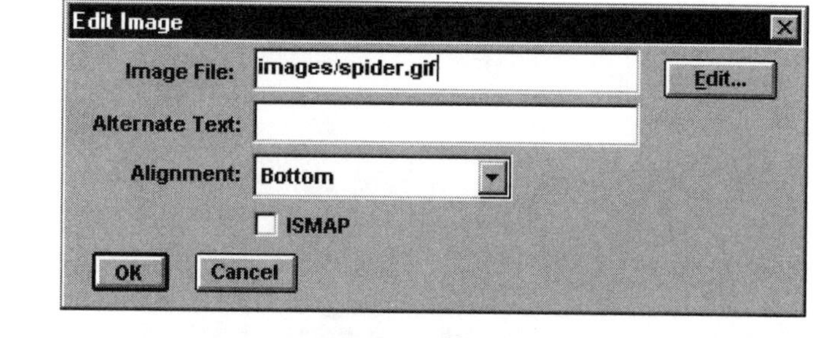

▶ The spider image is inserted in the document.

7 Press the **F6** key.

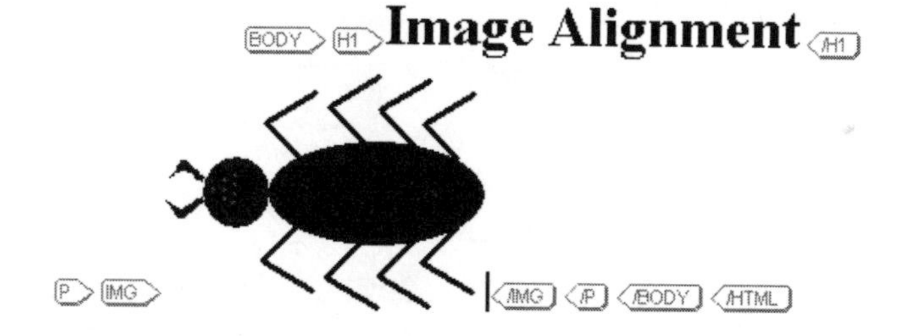

▶ The Edit Attributes dialog box appears.

8 Select **LEFT** in the ALIGN field and click on the **Apply** button.

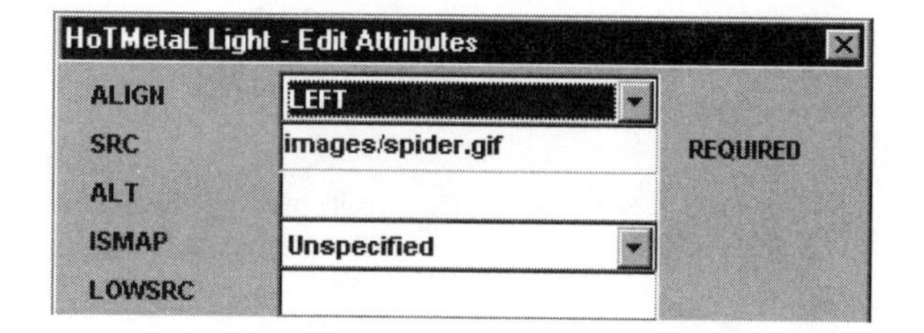

9 Move the cursor between the **/IMG** and **/P** tags.

10 Type **This spider is aligned using left alignment. This results in text being filled in to the right of the spider.**

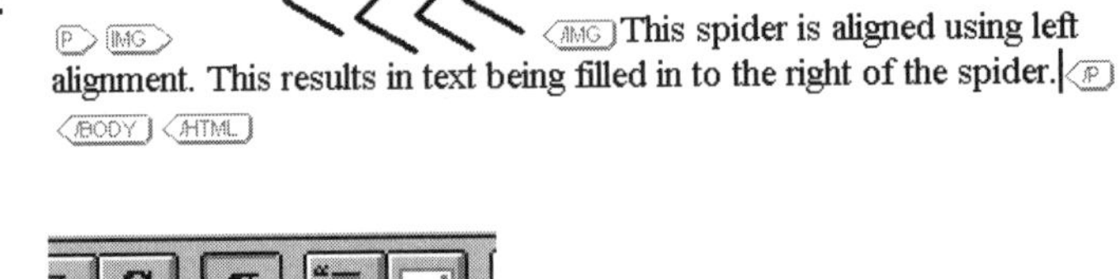

11 Move the cursor between the **/P** and **/BODY** tags and click on the **Paragraph** button.

12 Click on the **Image** button.

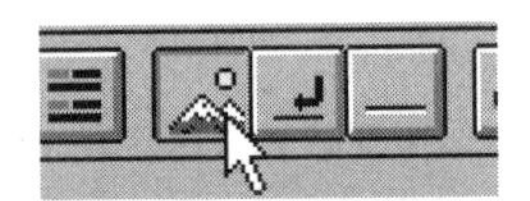

▶ The Edit Image dialog box appears.

13 Type **images/web.gif** in the Image File field and click on **OK**.

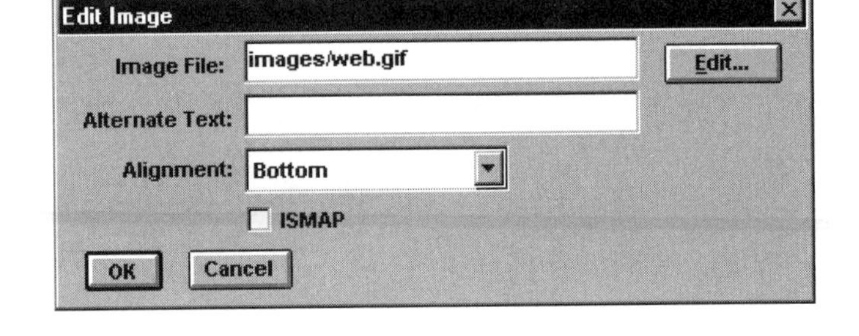

▶ The web image is inserted in the document.

14 Press the **F6** key.

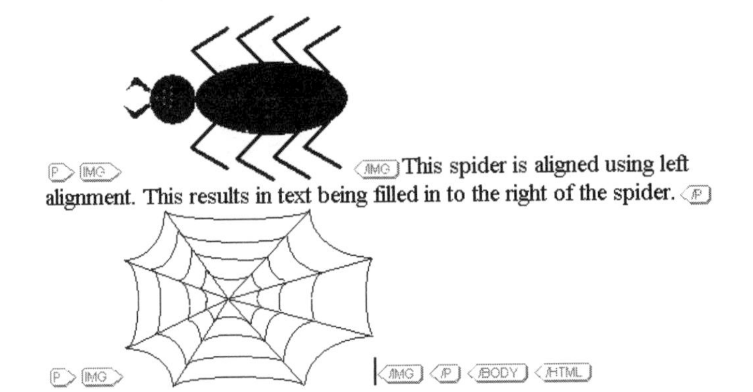

▶ The Edit Attributes dialog box appears.

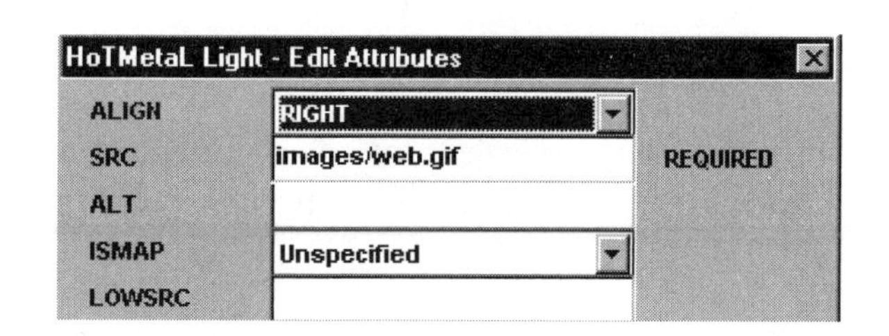

15 Select **RIGHT** in the ALIGN field and click on the **Apply** button.

16 Move the cursor between the **/IMG** and **/P** tags.

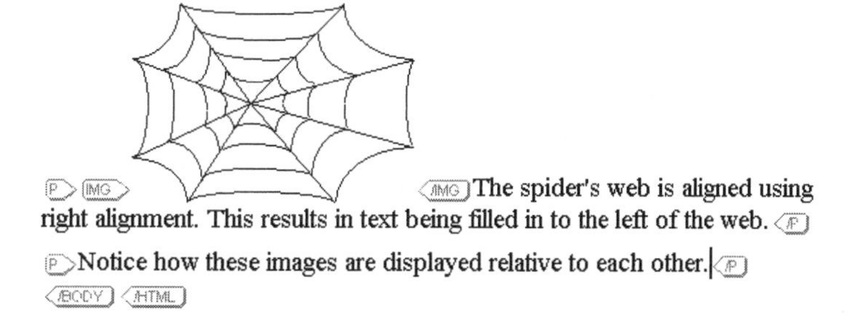

17 Type **The spider's web is aligned using right alignment. This results in text being filled in to the left of the web.** and press ↵.

18 Type **Notice how these images are displayed relative to each other.**

19 Save your document and view it with your browser.

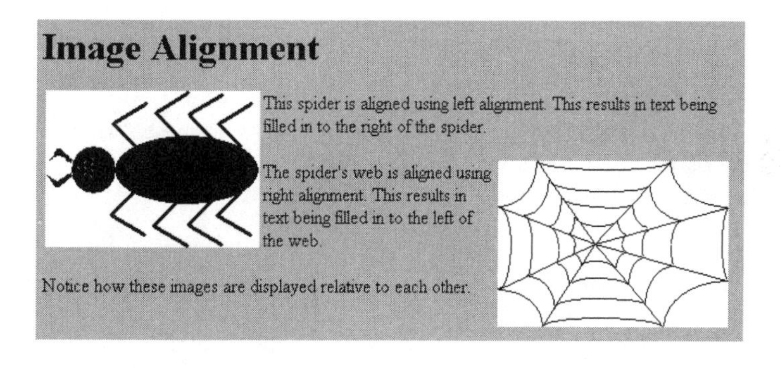

▶ Notice how the images are aligned relative to the paragraphs. Also, notice how the text is filled and wrapped relative to the images.

20 Close your browser, but keep the HoTMetaL document open.

Adding Alternative Text

The alternative text attribute provides a method by which text may be substituted for inline images. This attribute is used by browsers such as Lynx that do not support inline graphics and by browsers in which image display is disabled by the user. For example, suppose you want to display an inline image of a spider on your home page. The following image tag will substitute the text *[Picture of a Spider]* for the image contained in spider.gif:

```
<IMG SRC="images/spider.gif" ALT="[Picture of a Spider]">
```

If alternative text is not specified, most nongraphical browsers will display a default graphic placeholder such as *[IMAGE]* where the inline image is to appear.

▶ ▶ ▶ The alternative text tag should always be used instead of the default placeholder unless surrounding text clearly identifies the contents of the image.

The following example illustrates the use of alternative text.

1. Save the current HoTMetaL document as c:\html\ch05-04.htm.

2. Type **Alternative Text** over the old document title and heading.

3. Move the cursor between the first pair of image tags and press the **F6** key.

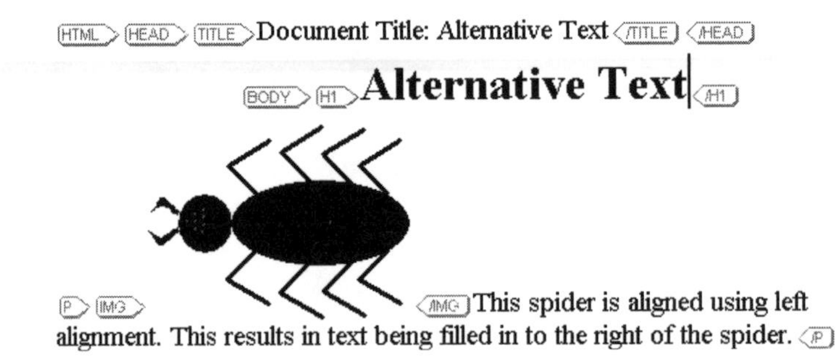

▶ The Edit Attributes dialog box appears.

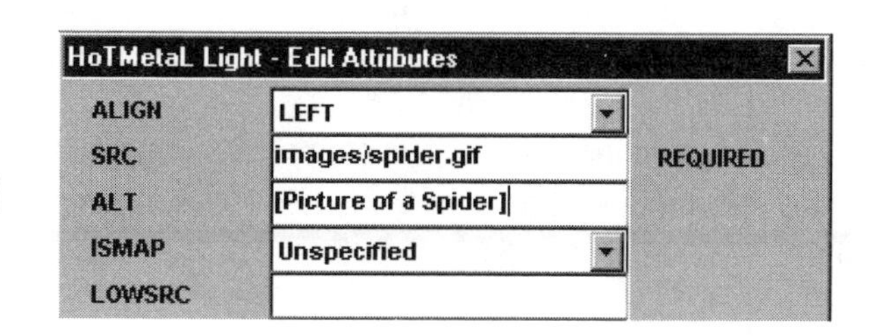

4 Type **[Picture of a Spider]** in the ALT field and click on the **Apply** button.

5 Move the cursor between the second pair of image tags and press the **F6** key.

▶ The Edit Attributes dialog box appears.

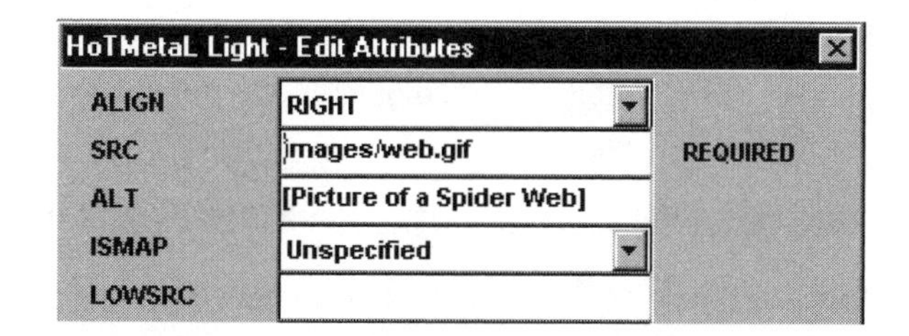

6 Type **[Picture of a Spider Web]** in the ALT field and click on the **Apply** button.

7 Save your document and view it with your browser.

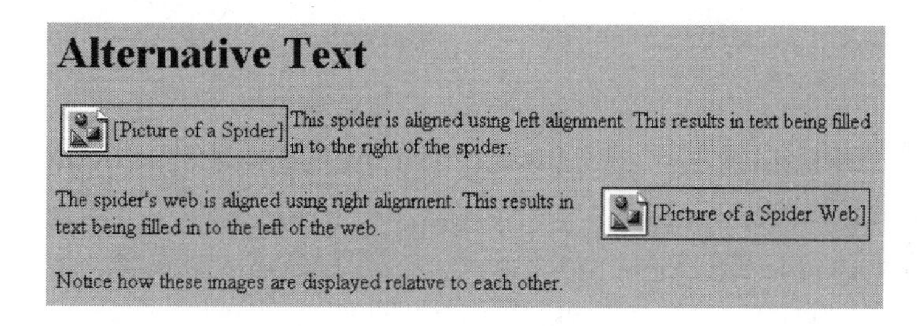

8 Disable your browser's inline image display.

▶ The pictures disappear and the alternative text appears in their place.

9 Turn your browser's image display back on.

10 Close your browser and your HoTMetaL document, but leave HoTMetaL running.

Using Netscape Image Attributes

Earlier in this lesson, you learned the new Netscape attribute values for text alignment. Now you'll learn other Netscape image attributes supported by HoTMetaL. These attributes are becoming part of the common HTML base supported by most graphical browsers.

Scaling the Image Size

The image **WIDTH** and **HEIGHT** attributes speed up page layout and display. When a browser tries to lay out a Web page for display, it must download all images and calculate their size. If the image width and height attributes are specified, the browser can lay out the Web page faster and quickly proceed with its display. The size of an image is specified in pixels. For example, the following image tag causes the Web image to be displayed in a 200 by 200 pixel box:

```
<IMG SRC="images/web.gif" WIDTH=200 HEIGHT=200>
```

If the specified width and height attributes are different from the actual image size, the image is scaled to fit. This may cause distortion in the image display.

Browsers that do not support image scaling ignore the width and height attributes.

Combining Low- and High-Resolution Images

The **LOWSRC** attribute enables browsers to implement a two-pass page display. In the first pass, the browser loads the image specified by the **LOWSRC** attribute. After all images have been loaded, the browser begins a second page display, loading the images specified by the SRC attribute. For example, the following tag causes the browser to load the lowres.gif image on its first pass and the highres.gif image on its second pass:

```
<IMG SRC="highres.gif" LOWSRC="lowres.gif">
```

The two-pass image display scheme provides users with a quick picture of the contents of the Web page. If users are interested after viewing the **LOWSRC** images, they can wait for the full page display. If users are not interested, they can move on to another Web page.

► ► ► If the **WIDTH** and **HEIGHT** attributes are not specified in the **IMG** tag, then the second (**SRC**) image is scaled to fit in the dimensions of the first (**LOWSRC**) image.

The following example shows how to use the **LOWSRC** attribute to implement a two-pass image display.

1 Open a new HoTMetaL document, create a level 1 heading, and type **Low and High Resolution Images** as the document title and heading.

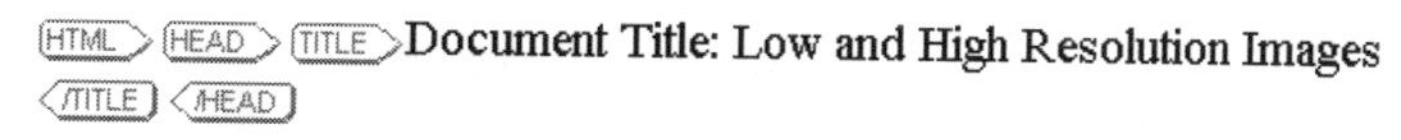
HTML
HEAD
TITLE
Document Title: Low and High Resolution Images
/TITLE
/HEAD

BODY H1 **Low and High Resolution Images** /H1 /BODY /HTML

2 Save the document as c:\html\ch05-05.htm.

3 Move the cursor between the **/H1** and **/BODY** tags and click on the **Image** button.

► The Edit Image dialog box appears.

4 Type **images/hiweb.gif** in the Image File field and click on **OK**.

Edit Image
Image File: images/hiweb.gif [Edit...]
Alternate Text:
Alignment: Bottom
ISMAP
[OK] [Cancel]

▶ The image is displayed in the document.

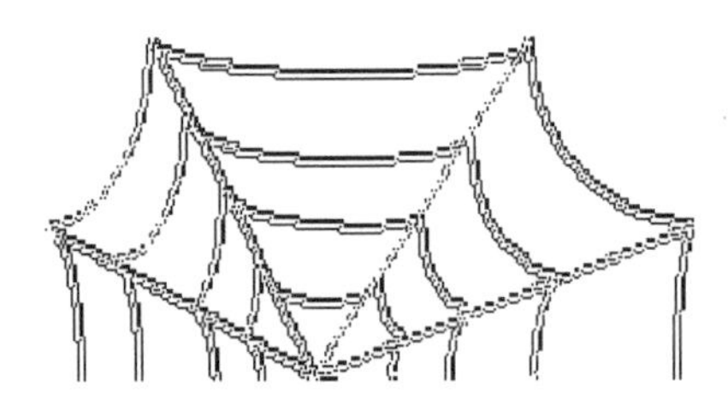

5 Press the **F6** key.

▶ The Edit Attributes dialog box appears.

6 Type **images/loweb.gif** in the LOWSRC field and click on the **Apply** button.

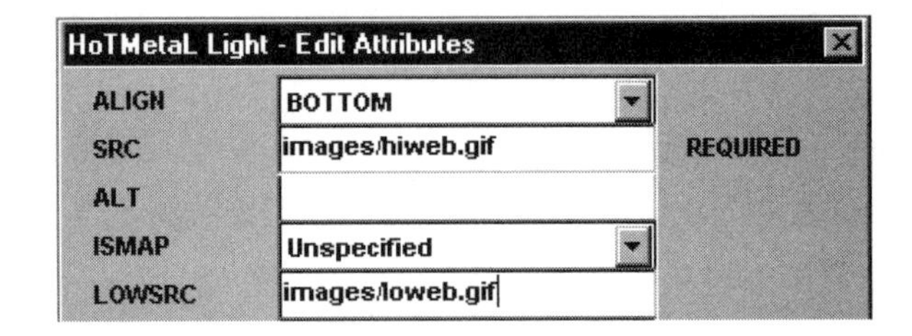

7 Save your document and view it with your browser.

▶ A blurred image appears…

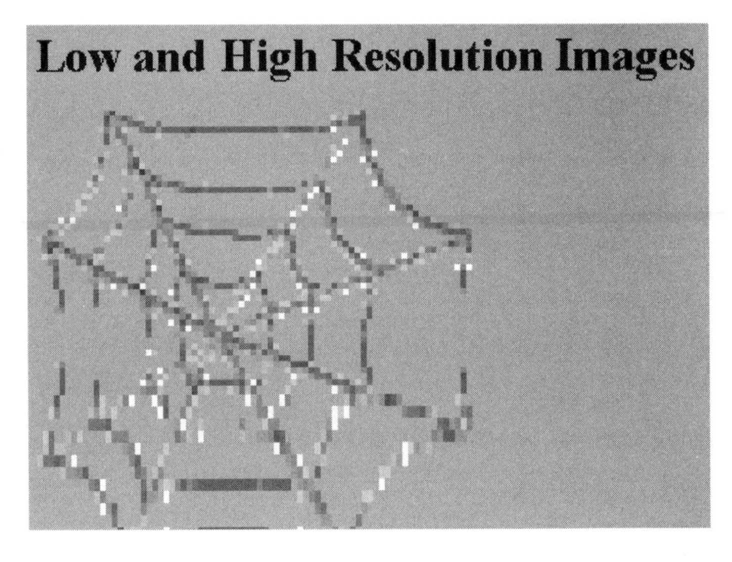

▶ ...followed by a more detailed image.

8 Close your browser and the HoTMetaL document, but leave HoTMetaL running.

▶ ▶ ▶ The **LOWSRC** and **SRC** images may be of different image types. For example, the **LOWSRC** image may be a **JPEG** image, and the **SRC** image may be a **GIF** image.

Controlling Border Thickness

The **BORDER** attribute is used to specify the thickness of the border (measured in pixels) around an inline image. For example, the following image is displayed with a border thickness of five pixels:

```
<IMG SRC="images/web.gif" BORDER=5>
```

Browsers that do not support the **BORDER** attribute simply ignore it and use a default border thickness.

Setting the Spacing around Images

When text wraps around an image, you may wish to control the spacing between the image and text. This is where the **VSPACE** and **HSPACE** attributes come in. The **VSPACE** attribute controls spacing above and below an image. The **HSPACE** attribute controls spacing to the left and right of an image. Both attributes are measured in pixels. The following image tag sets a vertical spacing of 10 pixels and a horizontal spacing of 15 pixels around the web.gif image:

```
<IMG SRC="images/web.gif" VSPACE=10 HSPACE=15>
```

Browsers that do not support the **VSPACE** and **HSPACE** attributes ignore them and use a default spacing.

Controlling Text Placement around Images

Another way to control how text and images appear together is the **CLEAR** attribute of the line break tag. This attribute's possible values are **LEFT**, **RIGHT**, and **ALL**. If the clear attribute is set to **LEFT**, a line break causes the following text to move to the left margin; if there is an image to the left of the text, the text will move down below that image so that it can reach the left margin. Likewise, if the clear attribute is set to **RIGHT**, a line break causes the text to move below the image so that it is able to reach the right margin. Setting **CLEAR=ALL** means that a line break moves the text below images on both the left and right side. For example, the following line break will move the text to the left margin, below any left-aligned images:

```
<BR CLEAR=LEFT>
```

The following example illustrates border thickness, image spacing, and the line break **CLEAR** attribute.

1. Open the HoTMetaL document c:\html\ch05-03.htm.

2. Type **Border Thickness and Spacing** over the old title and heading.

3. Save the document as c:\html\ch05-06.htm.

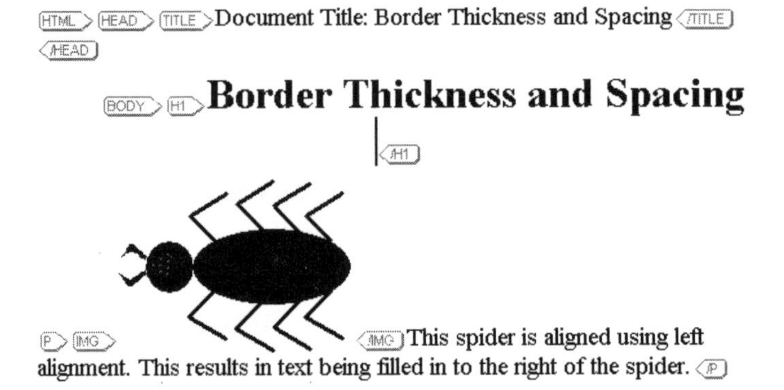

4 Click on the spider graphic and press the **F6** key.

▶ The Edit Attributes dialog box appears.

5 Type **10** in the HSPACE field and click on **Apply**.

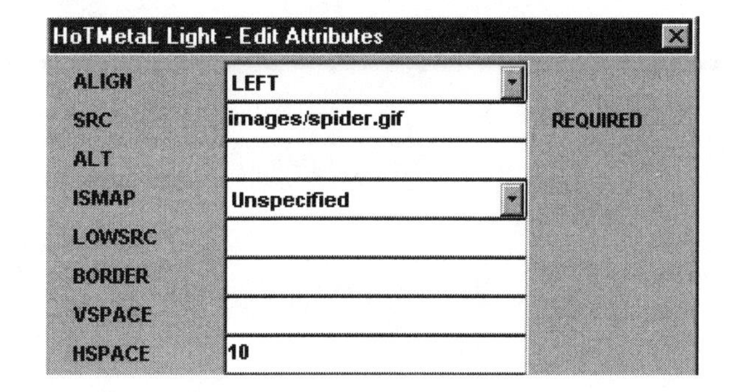

6 Click on the web graphic and press the **F6** key.

▶ The Edit Attributes dialog box appears.

7 Type **5** in the BORDER field and click on **Apply**.

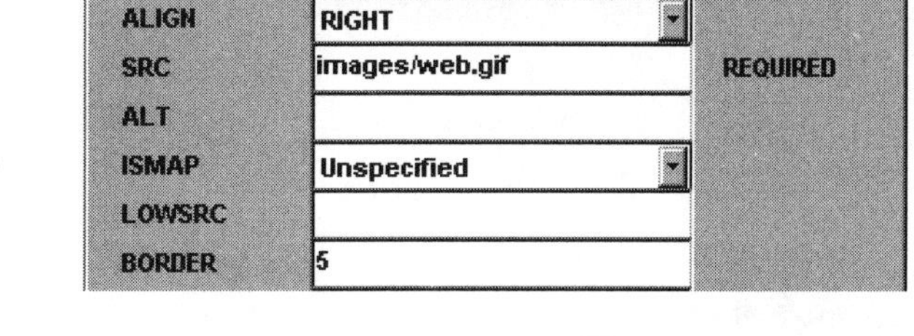

8 Move the cursor immediately before the second sentence of the second paragraph and click on the **Break** button to insert **BR** tags.

The spider's web is aligned using right alignment.

This results in text being filled in to the left of the web.

9 Press the **F6** key.

▶ The Edit Attributes dialog box appears.

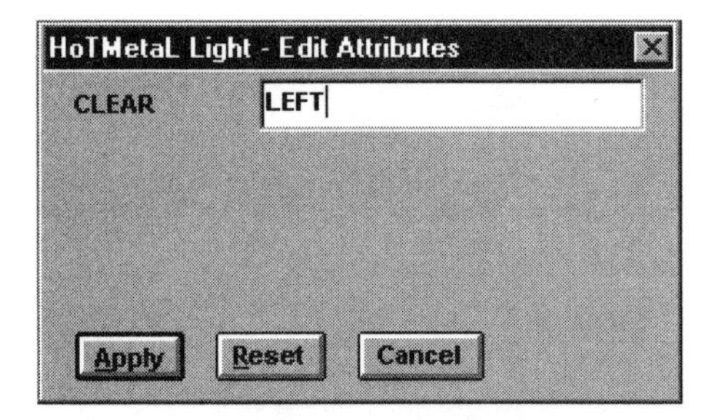

10 Type **LEFT** in the CLEAR field and click on **Apply**.

11 Save the document, then view it with your browser.

▶ Three things have changed. First, the spacing around the spider image has changed; because we set the **HSPACE** attribute to 5, the text no longer comes as close as it did before. Second, because we inserted a line break with a **CLEAR=LEFT** attribute just before the second sentence of the web text, that sentence now appears at the left margin of the display area, just below the spider. Finally, the web image has a border that is 5 pixels wide.

12 When you're done looking, close your browser and the HoTMetaL document, but keep HoTMetaL running.

Using Background Images

In Lesson 4, you learned how to change the background color of your Web pages using the **BGCOLOR** attribute. A new body attribute, **BACKGROUND**, allows you to go beyond a simple color change and use an image for your page background. Browsers that support background images use them to create tiled wallpaper for the page background. The **BACKGROUND** attribute is used as follows:

<BODY BACKGROUND="images/spray.gif">...</BODY>

The background attribute may use a relative path name, absolute path name, or URL to identify the location of the background image.

Let's give it a try.

1 Open a new HoTMetaL document, create a level 1 heading, and type **Background Images** as the title and heading.

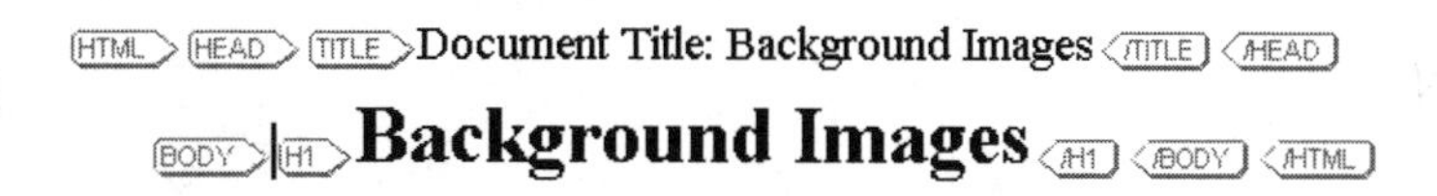

2 Move the cursor between the **BODY** and **H1** tags and press **F6** to edit the attributes of the **BODY** tag.

▶ The Edit Attributes dialog box appears.

3 Type **images/spray.gif** in the BACKGROUND field and click on **Apply**.

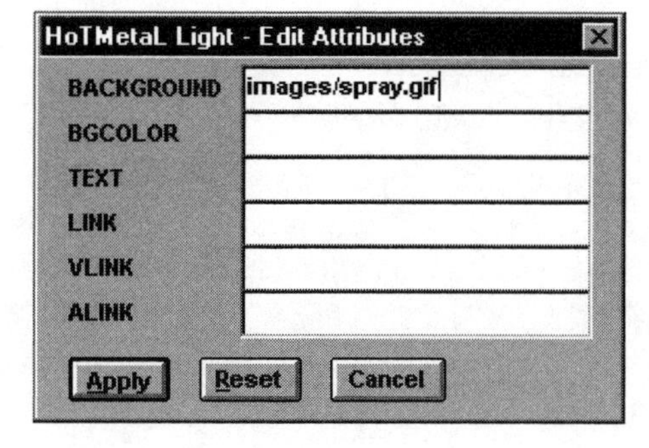

4. Save your document as c:\html\ch05-07.htm and view it with your browser.

5. When you're done, close your browser and HoTMetaL.

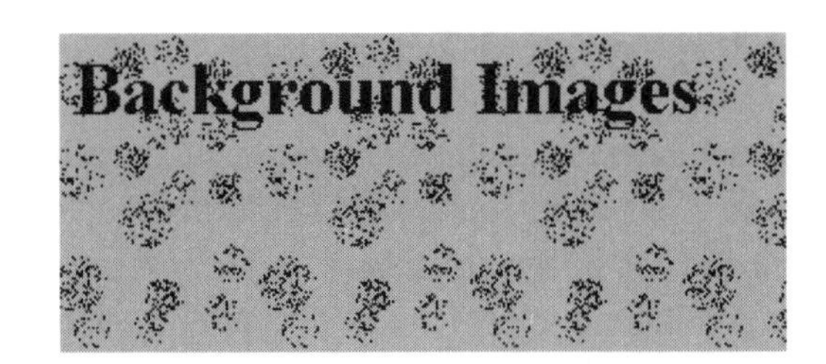

Making Graphics Transparent

Many graphical Web browsers have followed NCSA Mosaic's lead in using a light gray background color as a default. However, not all browsers do so. Some browsers, such as some of the commercial versions of Mosaic, use a default white background. And not all browsers support the Netscape extensions for changing the color and image associated with the page background. Because different browsers may display graphics using different background colors, it is difficult to create graphics that are displayed consistently by all browsers.

Images produced in the GIF89 format may make use of a transparent background option that enables the image to blend in with whatever background is being used. In order to use this feature, you must first create your image and then select a color to be your background color. A conversion program is used to convert the selected background color to a transparent background. All pixels with this color are converted to transparent and are displayed with the background color of the browser.

There are a number of freeware and shareware programs that support the conversion of GIF images to a transparent background color. Among these are giftrans, Paint Shop Pro, and LView Pro. The Transparent/Interlaced GIF Resource Page, located at **http://dragon.jpl.nasa.gov/~adam/transparent.html**, provides links to these programs as well as instructions on how to use them to create transparent GIF backgrounds.

(continued)

I used the Paint Shop Pro program to convert the spider and web images used in the previous examples to images with a transparent background. The converted files are stored in your c:\html\images directory in the files spidert.gif and webt.gif. As you can see below, transparent GIF images are displayed without a background square or border around them.

Using Interlaced GIF Images

GIF images may be stored in either *interlaced* or *noninterlaced* form.

The scan lines of noninterlaced images are stored sequentially beginning at the top of the image and ending at the bottom of the image. As a result, Web browsers load noninterlaced GIF images from the top down.

The scan lines of interlaced images are stored as a set of samples of the original image. When interlaced GIF images are loaded by Web browsers, they appear to fade in. The image is displayed as a sequence of successively more detailed images.

(continued)

The illustration below compares noninterlaced to interlaced GIFs.

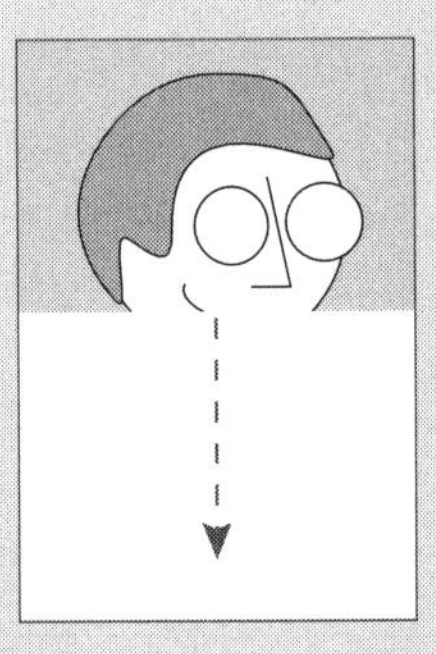

Noninterlaced GIFs are displayed in a top-down fashion.

Interlaced GIFs appear to fade in when they are displayed.

There are a number of freeware and shareware programs, available via the Internet, that convert between noninterlaced and interlaced GIF formats. Among these are Paint Shop Pro and LView Pro. The Transparent/Interlaced GIF Resource Page, located at **http://dragon.jpl.nasa.gov/~adam/transparent.html**, provides links to these programs and instructions on how to use them.

SoftQuad, the maker of HoTMetaL, has come out with a new image processing program called MetalWorks. It provides all the features you need to produce high-quality Web images. For more information, check out SoftQuad's home page at **http://www.sq.com**.

Obtaining Graphics

Now that you know how to display inline images using HTML, you are probably wondering how you go about obtaining graphics for your Web pages. There are several options.

- You can create a graphic using a paint or draw program and convert it to the GIF format.

- You can scan a graphic into your computer and convert it to JPEG or GIF.
- You can download images from Internet FTP sites or local bulletin board systems.
- You can buy a commercial clip-art package.

Each of these options has its advantages and disadvantages. By developing your own graphics, you can design them exactly as you like and display them as you wish without having to consider copyrights or royalties. The Windows Paint accessory allows you to create bitmapped graphics that can easily be converted to GIF format, and most popular Windows word processing programs include vector-based drawing programs. The downside of creating your own graphics, of course, is that it requires a lot of work.

► ► ► If you are going to develop your own graphics, I highly recommend using the Paint Shop Pro shareware program, available at **http://www.jasc.com**, to do your graphics conversion. If you decide to use this program, register it; it is far less expensive and more capable than many commercial graphics packages.

If you have access to a scanner, you may scan graphics and convert them to GIF or JPEG format for use as inline images. Make sure the images you scan are not copyrighted. A major advantage of using a scanner is that it allows you to use photographs in your Web pages. The disadvantage of using a scanner is the cost of purchasing one, although the cost of high-quality scanners has dropped quite a bit in recent years.

Downloading graphics is a very easy way to start an image collection, but you must take extra care to make sure that the graphics you download are not illegal copies of copyrighted images. (This may not be an easy task if you cannot contact the creator of the image.) To be on the safe side, you can use the Web Developer's Virtual Library located at **http://www.stars.com**, which provides links to publicly available images for use in Web pages.

Purchasing a clip-art package gives you access to thousands of royalty-free graphic images for a small price and saves you the time and trouble of developing your own inline images. The downside to clip-art packages is that you may not get the exact image you want. However, some clip-art is in a format that may be easily modified by drawing tools and thus tailored to your exact needs. Be sure to check the license agreement included with your package to make sure that you can distribute your images in electronic form. Some packages only allow you to use their graphics in printed form.

▶ ▶ ▶ Most drawing packages, such as CorelDRAW, include extensive clip-art collections. The clip-art provided by these packages can be easily modified using the drawing software. These packages usually provide a complete solution to developing Web images.

In this lesson, you learned how to use HoTMetaL to insert inline images in your Web pages. You learned how to use the image tag and several attributes that control image display. You can now use this information to develop appealing Web pages.

In the next lesson, you will learn how to organize your Web pages using lists and horizontal rules. You will also learn how to use images with these new features.

6

WORKING WITH LISTS AND RULES

In this lesson, you'll learn to use lists and horizontal rules. Lists provide a convenient way to organize Web pages. They display sequences of related items and are often used to structure larger documents. Horizontal rules divide Web pages into logical sections. They are used to visually organize browser displays. You will learn how to use list and rule attributes to control the way these elements are displayed. You will also learn to develop custom lists and rules in order to add icons, bullets, and graphical dividers to your Web pages. When you finish this lesson, you will be able to create Web pages that are well-organized and visually attractive.

Formatting Lists

Lists are a common way to organize information. We use them so much that we often fail to recognize them. For example, a telephone book is a list of names and phone numbers. A bank statement is a list of financial transactions. A table of contents is a list of chapters and page numbers. There are lists that keep track of the best sports teams, the best- and worst-dressed people, and the most wanted criminals. Many Web pages contain lists of related websites.

HTML supports three basic types of lists: ordered, unordered, and definition lists, which are covered in the following sections. HTML currently supports two additional types of lists: menu and directory lists. But because they are very similar to unordered lists, they are likely to be phased out soon; I recommend that you avoid using them.

You may use the **COMPACT** attribute with all types of lists to tell browsers to display the list in a more compact manner. See "Definition Lists" below for how to apply the **COMPACT** attribute in HoTMetaL. When using this attribute, keep in mind that some browsers ignore it.

Ordered Lists

Ordered lists, also called *numbered* lists, number the items in the list sequentially, beginning with 1. You might want to use an ordered list in your Web page to show the top ten music videos, the ranking of heavyweight boxers, or the lessons in this book. The following is the syntax for ordered lists:

```
<OL>
<LI>first item
<LI>second item
   .
   .
   .
<LI>last item
</OL>
```

The list is enclosed between the **<OL>** and **</OL>** tags. Each list item is identified by the **<LI>** tag. An optional **</LI>** tag may be used at the end of each list item. HoTMetaL automatically inserts this tag.

The following example shows how to use HoTMetaL to construct an ordered list.

1 Launch HoTMetaL, open a new document, create a level 1 heading, and type **Ordered Lists** for the title and heading.

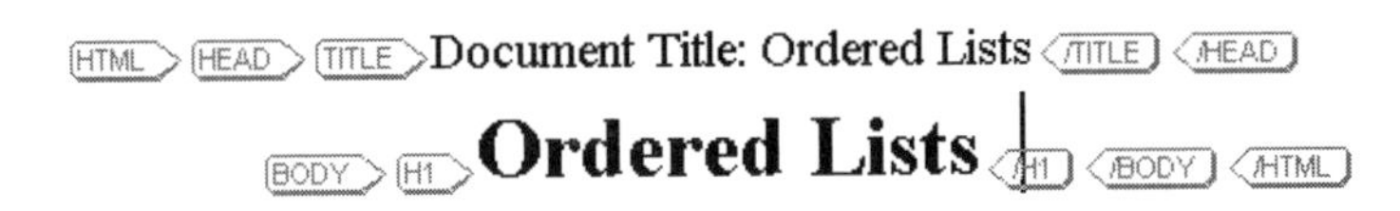
HTML HEAD TITLE Document Title: Ordered Lists /TITLE /HEAD
BODY H1 Ordered Lists /H1 /BODY /HTML

2 Place the cursor between the **/H1** and **/BODY** tags and click on the **Ordered list** button.

▶ HoTMetaL inserts **OL** tags and a set of **LI** tags nested within the **OL** tags.

BODY H1 **Ordered Lists** /H1

OL LI /LI /OL /BODY /HTML

3 Type **Wake up** and press ↵.

HTML HEAD TITLE Document Title: Ordered Lists /TITLE /HEAD

BODY H1 **Ordered Lists** /H1

OL LI Wake up /LI
LI Fall out of bed /LI
LI Drag a comb across my head /LI /OL /BODY /HTML

▶ A new set of **LI** tags is automatically inserted. This will happen every time you press ↵ with your cursor inside **LI** tags.

4 Type **Fall out of bed** and press ↵.

5 Type **Drag a comb across my head**.

6 Save your document as c:\html\ch06-01.htm and view it with your browser.

Ordered Lists

1. Wake up
2. Fall out of bed
3. Drag a comb across my head

▶ Your browser automatically numbers the list items.

7 Close your browser and the current HoTMetaL document.

Unordered Lists

Unordered lists, also called *bulleted* lists, display bullets rather than numbers next to the items in the list. You would use an unordered list instead of an ordered list when the items need not appear in a strict order, for example, in a "to do" list or grocery list. Unordered lists are syntactically similar to ordered lists. They differ only in their beginning and ending tags, as shown here:

```
<UL>
<LI>item
<LI>item
<LI>item
</UL>
```

The unordered list is enclosed between the **<UL>** and **</UL>** tags. Each list item is identified by the **<LI>** tag.

The following example shows how to create an unordered list using HoTMetaL.

1. Open a new document, create a level 1 heading, and type **Unordered Lists** as the title and heading.

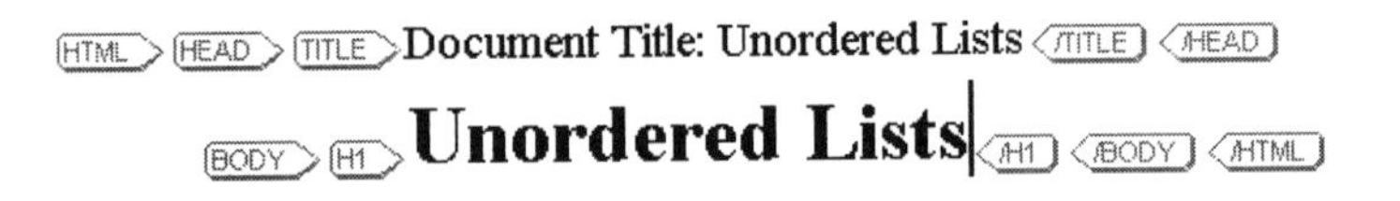

2. Move the cursor between the **/H1** and **/BODY** tags and click on the **Unordered list** button.

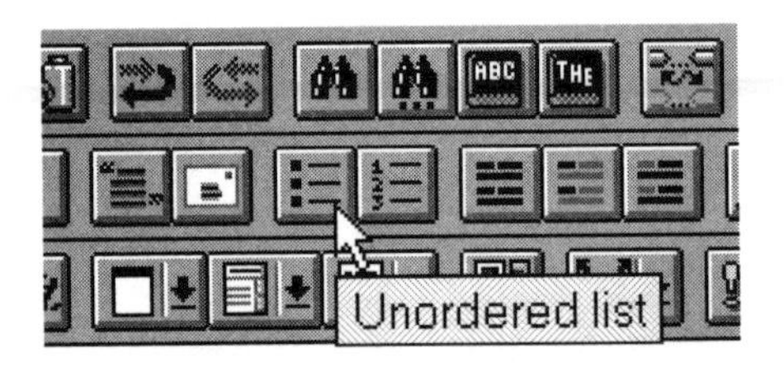

▶ HoTMetaL inserts **UL** tags with a set of **LI** tags nested within.

3 Type **Do laundry** and press ↵.

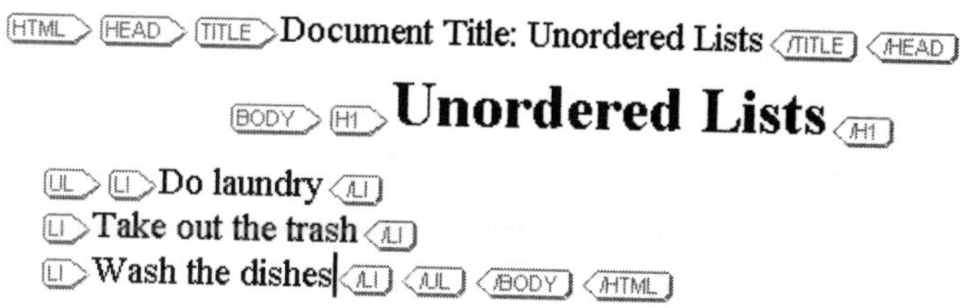

4 Type **Take out the trash** and press ↵.

5 Type **Wash the dishes**.

<HTML> <HEAD> <TITLE>Document Title: Unordered Lists </TITLE> </HEAD>

<BODY> <H1>**Unordered Lists**</H1>

<UL> <LI>Do laundry </LI>
<LI>Take out the trash </LI>
<LI>Wash the dishes </LI> </UL> </BODY> </HTML>

6 Save your document as c:\html\ch06-02.htm and view it with your browser.

Unordered Lists

- Do laundry
- Take out the trash
- Wash the dishes

▶ Your browser displays bullets next to the list items.

7 Close your browser and the current HoTMetaL document.

Definition Lists

Definition lists display text in two columns: items to be defined in the first column and their definitions in the second column. An example of a definition list is a glossary.

Definition lists are enclosed between **<DL>** and **</DL>** tags. The items to be defined are identified by a **<DT>** tag, and the definitions are identified by a **<DD>** tag. The following is the syntax of definition lists:

```
<DL>
<DT>item to be defined
<DD>definition
<DT>item to be defined
<DD>definition
</DL>
```

Optional closing **</DT>** and **</DD>** tags may be added to the end of the list items. HoTMetaL inserts these tags automatically.

In the following example we'll develop a definition list and use the **COMPACT** attribute to make the list more compact.

1 Open a new HoTMetaL document, create a level 1 heading, and type **Definition Lists** for the title and heading.

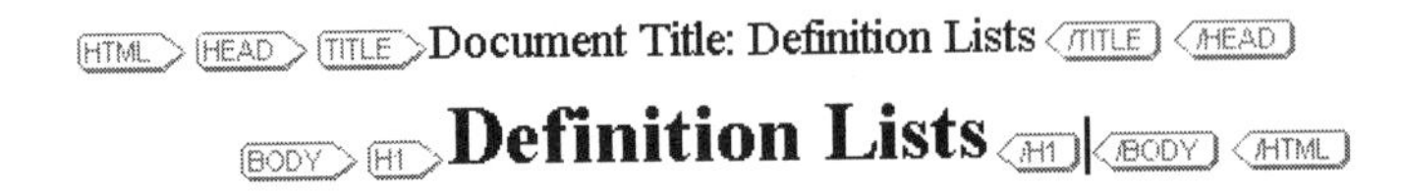

2 Move the cursor between the **/H1** and **/BODY** tags and click on the **Definition list** button.

▶ **DL** tags are inserted into your document.

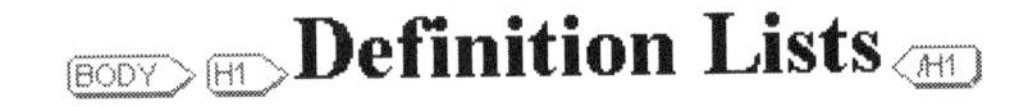

3 Select **Markup ➢ Edit SGML Attributes**.

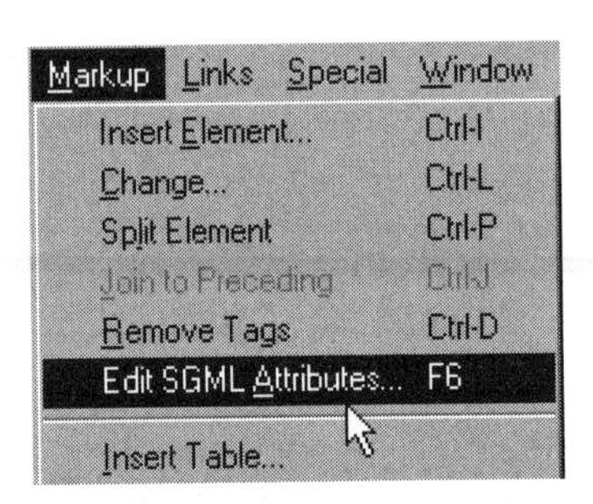

▶ The Edit Attributes dialog box appears.

4 Click on the down-arrow to the right of the COMPACT field and select **COMPACT**.

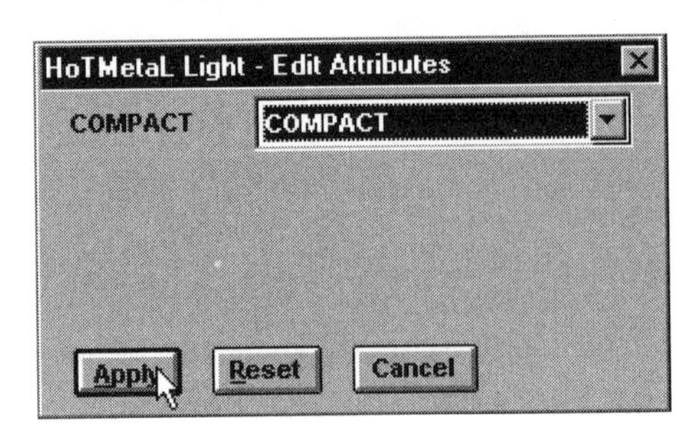

5 Click on the **Apply** button.

6 Click on the **Definition term** button.

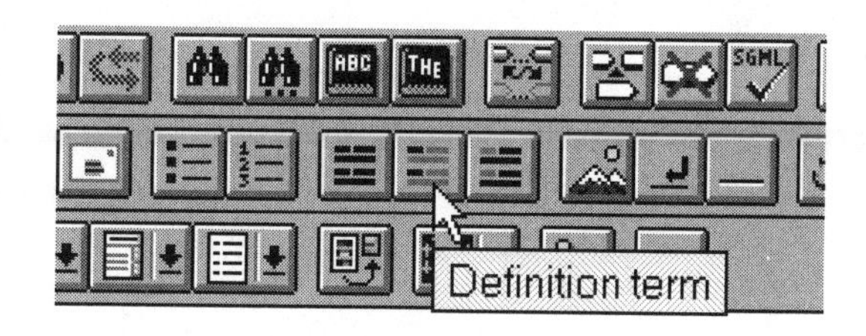

▶ **DT** tags are inserted into your document.

<DL> <DT> </DT> </DL> </BODY> </HTML>

7 Type **man**.

<DL> <DT>**man**</DT> </DL> </BODY> </HTML>

8 Place the cursor between the **/DT** and **/DL** tags and click on the **Definition description** button.

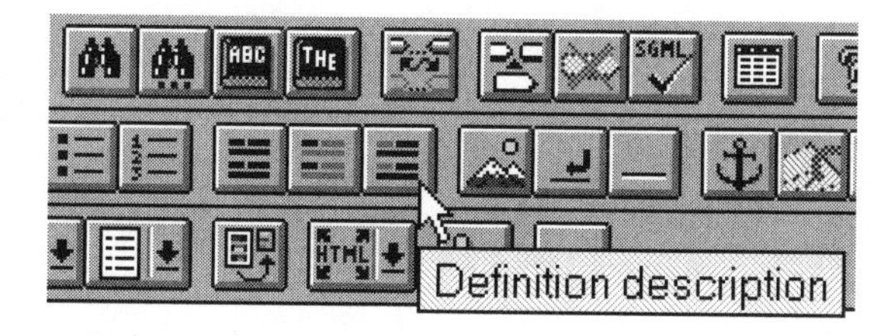

▶ **DD** tags appear in the document.

<DL> <DT>**man**</DT>
<DD> </DD> </DL> </BODY> </HTML>

9 Type **an adult male human** and move the cursor between the **/DD** and **/DL** tags.

<DL> <DT>**man**</DT>
<DD>an adult male human</DD> </DL> </BODY> </HTML>

10 Fill out the rest of the list as shown here, remembering to move the cursor just before the **/DL** tag and click on the appropriate button before typing each item.

<DL> <DT>**man**</DT>
<DD>an adult male human</DD>
<DT>**mortal**</DT>
<DD>subject to death</DD>
<DT>**Socrates**</DT>
<DD>a Greek philosopher</DD> </DL> </BODY> </HTML>

11 Save your document as c:\html\ch06-03.htm and view it with your browser.

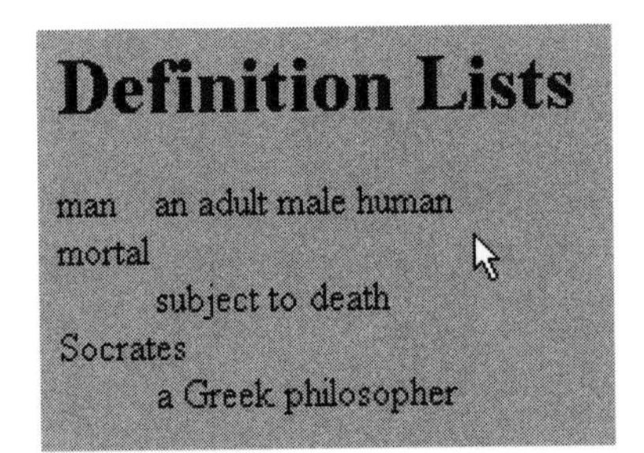

▶ Notice that the first term and definition are compacted.

12 Close your browser and the current HoTMetaL document.

▶ ▶ ▶ Definition lists aren't strictly limited to definitions. You can use them to present any logically related sequence of items and descriptions.

Using New List Attributes

HoTMetaL provides access to a number of Netscape and HTML 3.0 attributes that control how lists are displayed. The Netscape attributes are supported by most browsers. The HTML 3.0 list attributes are not yet supported by current browsers—not even by the prototype Arena browser, developed by the World Wide Web Consortium, the lead sponsor of HTML 3.0.

The new list attributes apply to ordered and unordered lists and are summarized in the following table. The following sections show how to work with HoTMetaL to develop Web pages that use the Netscape attributes.

ATTRIBUTE	TYPE	USED WITH TAG	EFFECT
TYPE	Netscape	**OL**	Sets the list numbering scheme
		UL	Sets the bullet type
		LI (ordered and unordered lists)	Changes the list numbering scheme or bullet type
START	Netscape	**OL**	Sets the sequence number of the first list item
VALUE	Netscape	**LI** (ordered lists only)	Changes the sequence number of the list item
CONTINUE	HTML 3.0	**OL**	Continues numbering from the previous list
SEQNUM	HTML 3.0	**OL**	Sets the sequence number for the first list item
WRAP	HTML 3.0	**UL**	Used to create multicolumn lists
PLAIN	HTML 3.0	**UL**	Suppresses the display of bullets
DINGBAT	HTML 3.0	**UL**	Identifies an icon to be used as a bullet
		LI (unordered lists only)	Identifies an icon to be used as a bullet
SRC	HTML 3.0	**UL**	Identifies an image to be used as a bullet
	HTML 3.0	**LI** (unordered lists only)	Identifies an image to be used as a bullet
SKIP	HTML 3.0	**LI** (ordered lists only)	Increases the sequence number by the skip value

Attributes for Ordered Lists

There are three new Netscape attributes that control the display of ordered lists: the **TYPE** attribute, the **START** attribute, and the **VALUE** attribute. These attributes are very easy to work with and provide great flexibility in the way ordered lists are displayed.

The **TYPE** attribute selects or changes the list numbering scheme. Typically a list is numbered using the integers 1, 2, 3, etc. The **TYPE** attribute lets you use letters or Roman numerals to number your lists. The following table identifies the available **TYPE** values.

VALUE	NUMBERING SCHEME	EXAMPLE
TYPE = 1 (default)	Integers	1, 2, 3, ...
TYPE = a	Lowercase letters	a, b, c, ...
TYPE = A	Uppercase letters	A, B, C, ...
TYPE = i	Lowercase Roman numerals	i, ii, iii, ...
TYPE = I	Uppercase Roman numerals	I, II, III, ...

The **TYPE** attribute may be used with either the **OL** or the **LI** tag. When it is used with the **OL** tag, it sets the numbering scheme for the entire list. When it is used with the **LI** tag, it changes the numbering scheme for the list item and all subsequent list items.

The **START** attribute is used to set the starting sequence number for a list. It is used with the **OL** tag, and it always takes a positive integer as its value. For example, **<OL START=100> ... </OL>** would display an ordered list numbered 100, 101, 102, etc. The list **<OL TYPE=a START=9> ... </OL>** would be numbered i, j, k, etc. The **START** tag works with all **TYPE** attribute values.

The **VALUE** attribute is used to change the sequence number of a list item. It is similar to the **START** attribute, but it is only used with the **LI** tag. The **VALUE** attribute changes the sequence number for the list item, as well as all subsequent list items.

The following example shows how to use these attributes to change the way ordered lists are displayed.

1. Open a new HoTMetaL document, create a level 1 heading, and type **Ordered List Attributes** for the title and the heading.

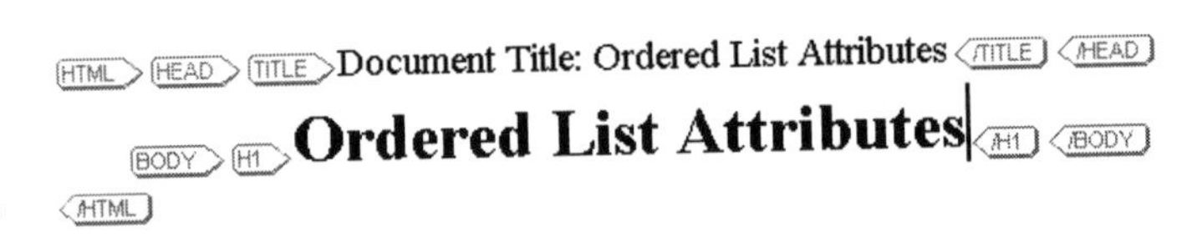

2. Move the cursor between the **/H1** and **/BODY** tags and click on the **Ordered list** toolbar button.

3 Type list items **one**, **two**, **three**, **four**, **five**, and **six**, pressing ↵ after all but the last.

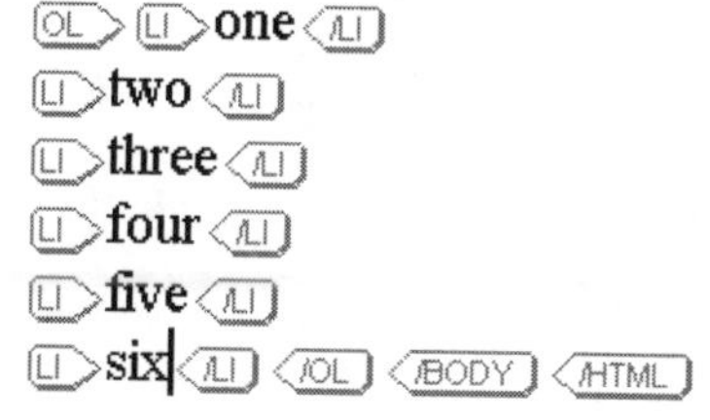

4 Place the cursor immediately after the **OL** tag and press **F6**.

OL LI one /LI
LI two /LI

► The Edit Attributes dialog box appears.

5 Type **a** in the TYPE field and **9** in the START field.

6 Click on **Apply**.

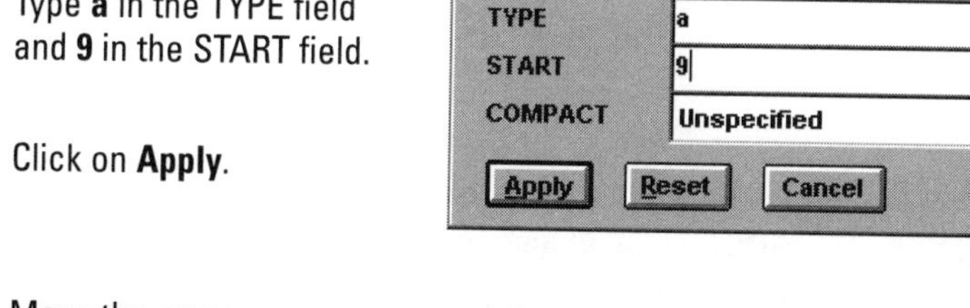

7 Move the cursor immediately before the word **four** and press **F6**.

LI three /LI
LI four /LI
LI five /LI

► The Edit Attributes dialog box appears.

8 Type **A** in the TYPE field and **24** in the VALUE field.

9 Click on **Apply**.

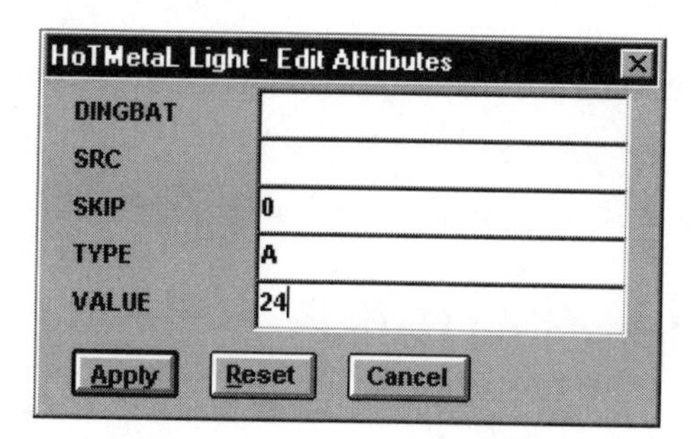

10 Save your document as c:\html\ch06-04.htm and view it using your Web browser.

Ordered List Attributes

i. one
j. two
k. three
X. four
Y. five
Z. six

▶ The first three items in the list are "numbered" with lowercase letters, starting with *i* (the 9th letter of the alphabet), and the last three are "numbered" with uppercase letters, starting with *X* (the 24th letter of the alphabet).

11 Close your browser and the current HoTMetaL document.

The HTML 3.0 attributes **CONTINUE**, **SEQNUM**, and **SKIP** also apply to ordered lists, although they are not supported by current browsers:

- The **CONTINUE** attribute is used with the **OL** tag. It enables number sequencing to continue from list to list.
- The **SEQNUM** attribute is identical to the Netscape **START** attribute. It sets the initial sequence number for a list.
- The **SKIP** attribute is used with list items. It causes the sequence number of a list item to be increased by the skip value before it is displayed.

You can access these attributes in the same manner you did the Netscape attributes.

Attributes for Unordered Lists

The Netscape **TYPE** attribute also controls the display of unordered lists. When used with unordered lists, it selects the type of bullet to be displayed. Valid bullet types are disc, circle, or square.

The **TYPE** attribute is used with either the **UL** tag or the **LI** tag. When it is used with the **UL** tag, it selects the bullet type for the entire list. When it is used with an **LI** tag, it selects the bullet type for the list item and all subsequent list items.

The following example shows how to use the **TYPE** attribute to modify the way unordered lists are displayed.

1. Open a new HoTMetaL document, create a level 1 heading, and type **Unordered List Attributes** for the title and heading.

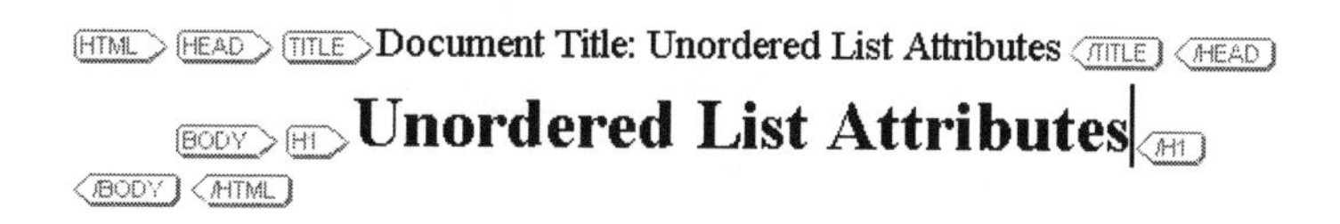

2. Move the cursor between the **/H1** and **/BODY** tags and click on the **Unordered list** toolbar button.

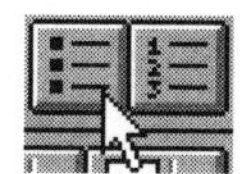

3. Enter the list items **box #1**, **box #2**, **ball #1**, and **ball #2**, as shown.

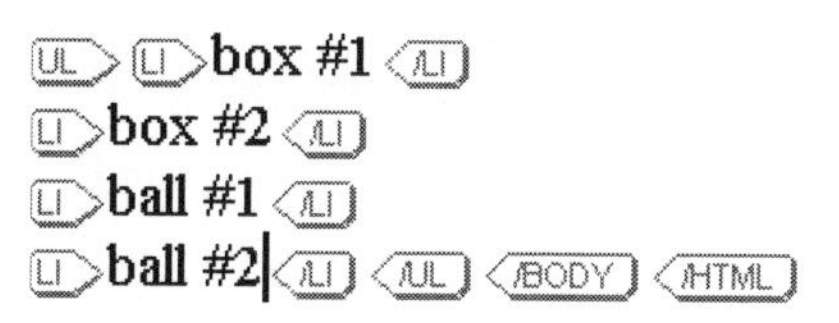

4. Place the cursor immediately after the **UL** tag and press **F6**.

▶ The Edit Attributes dialog box appears.

5. Select **SQUARE** in the TYPE field and click on **Apply**.

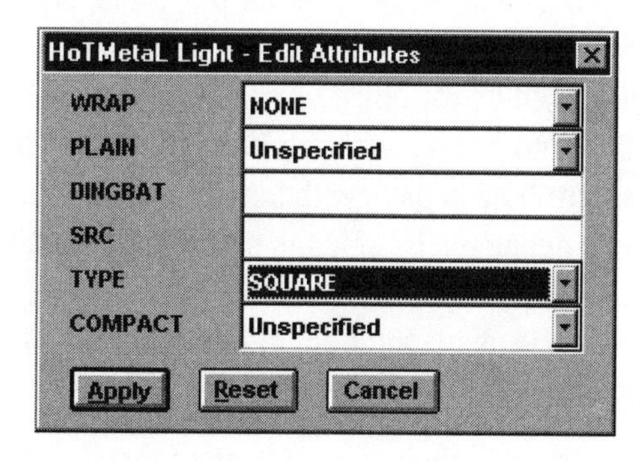

6 Move the cursor immediately before **ball #1** and press **F6**.

▶ The Edit Attributes dialog box appears.

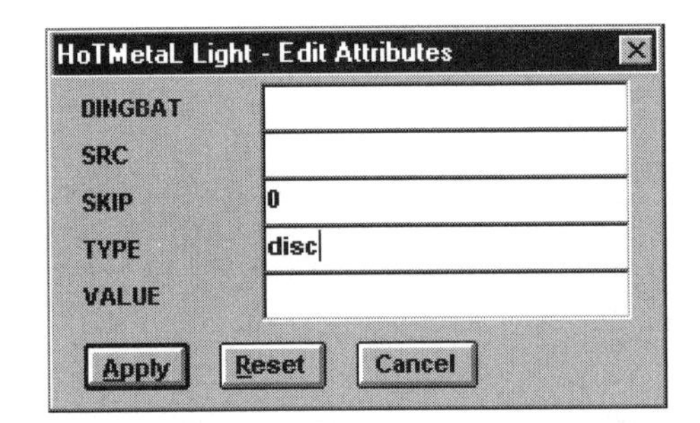

7 Type **disc** in the TYPE field and click on **Apply**.

8 Save your document as c:\html\ch06-05.htm and view it with your browser.

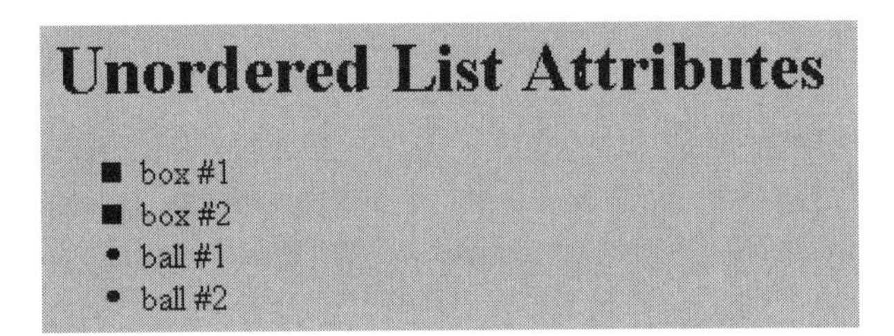

▶ The first two bullets are square and the second two are round.

9 Close your browser and the HoTMetaL document.

The HTML 3.0 attributes **WRAP**, **PLAIN**, **DINGBAT**, and **SRC** are also used with unordered lists, although they are not supported by current browsers:

- The **WRAP** attribute is used with the **UL** tag to display multicolumn lists. Setting **WRAP=vert** causes lists to be displayed by column. Setting **WRAP=horiz** causes lists to be displayed by row.
- The **PLAIN** attribute is used with the **UL** tag to suppress the display of bullets.
- The **DINGBAT** attribute is used with both the **UL** and **LI** tags to select a named icon. HTML 3.0 defines a list of icons from the dingbat font that can be used as bullets.
- The **SRC** attribute is used with both the **UL** and **LI** tags. It allows an image to be used as a bullet.

These attributes are accessed in the same manner as the Netscape attributes.

Custom-Building Lists

At this point, you may think that you've seen more types of lists and list attributes than you'll ever care to use. Think again. For some reason, the variety of lists presented so far doesn't seem to be enough to satisfy some Web users, so many of them have gone off and developed custom-built lists. You probably have seen instances of them on several Web pages: they are the ones with colorful icons and bullets.

Most of these customized lists aren't lists at all—not in the HTML sense. They are usually sequences of headings or paragraphs that begin with bullet-like images. This causes them to look like lists, only more eye-catching. Even though a list by any other name is not the same, it's hard, even for an HTML purist, to resist using such colorful Web page designs.

The following example shows how to construct a customized list using paragraphs and blue bullet images.

1. Open a new HoTMetaL document, create a level 1 heading, and type **Custom-Built Lists** for the title and heading.

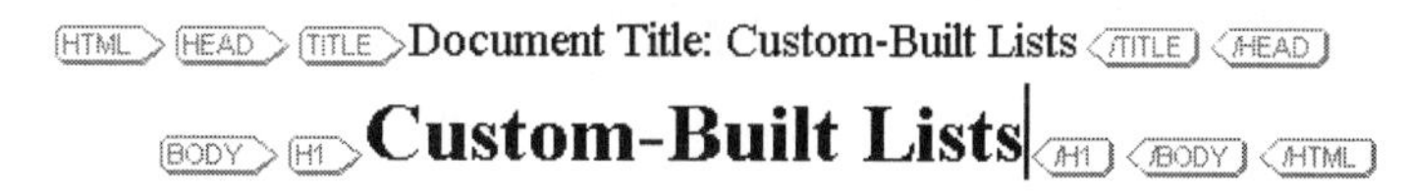
HTML HEAD TITLE Document Title: Custom-Built Lists /TITLE /HEAD
BODY H1 Custom-Built Lists /H1 /BODY /HTML

2. Move the cursor between the **/H1** and **/BODY** tags.

3. Type **list item #1**, press ↵, type **list item #2**, press ↵, and type **list item #3**.

P list item #1 /P
P list item #2 /P
P list item #3 /P /BODY /HTML

▶ As always, HoTMetaL inserts **P** tags when you begin typing and when you press ↵ at the end of each line.

4 Move the cursor immediately before the first list item and click on the **Image** toolbar button.

list item #1

list item #2

▶ The Edit Image dialog box appears.

5 Click on the **Edit** button.

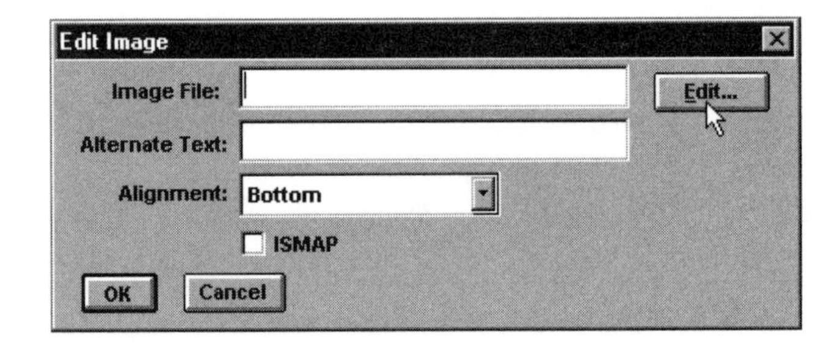

▶ The Edit IMG Source dialog box appears.

6 Click on the **Choose File** button.

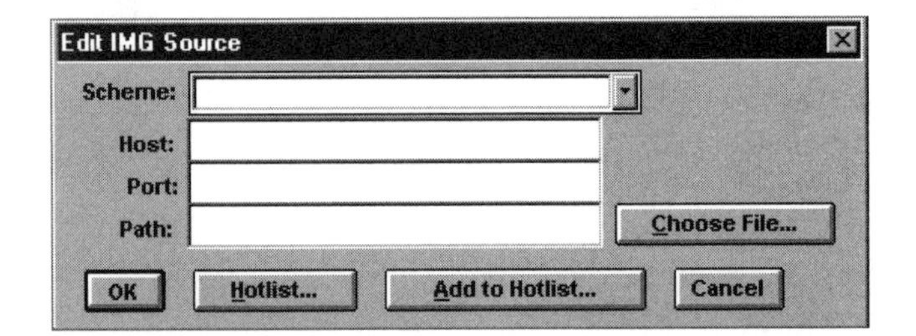

▶ The Choose Image File Image dialog box appears.

7 Type **c:\html\images\blueball.gif** in the File name field.

8 Click on **Open** to close the Choose Image File Image dialog box.

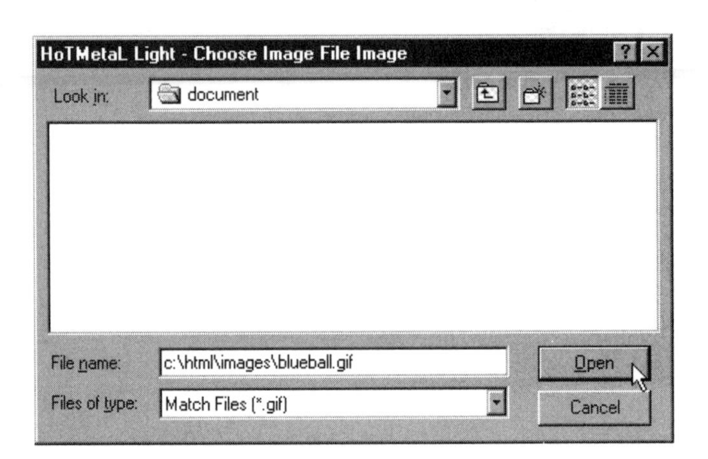

9 Click on **OK** to close the Edit IMG Source dialog box.

10 Click on **OK** to close the Edit Image dialog box.

► An image of a blue ball is placed before list item #1.

11 Repeat steps 4 through 10 to insert a blue ball before the other list items.

12 Save your file as c:\html\ch06-06.htm and view it with your browser.

► You have created your own custom-built list.

13 Close your browser and the current HoTMetaL document.

Using Horizontal Rules

Web pages that present a lot of textual information are sometimes hard to browse. It's the old needle in the haystack problem: when you are looking for a very specific piece of information, it can be hard to find if it is surrounded by a lot of other related material. *Horizontal rules* can alleviate this problem.

Horizontal rules—lines across the browser window—may not seem to be much of an innovation, but when applied well they divide Web pages into logical sections and organize browser displays. This enables Web users to spend less time reading and more time browsing, helping them quickly find information of interest on your Web pages.

A horizontal rule is indicated by the **<HR>** tag. When used without any attributes, it will result in a thin, shaded, engraved, horizontal line. There are a number of horizontal rule attributes that can add to its effects, as shown in the following table. As with most new attributes, they originate with Netscape and HTML 3.0.

ATTRIBUTE	ORIGIN	EFFECT
SIZE	Netscape	Sets the vertical thickness of the line in pixels
WIDTH	Netscape	Sets the horizontal width of the line in pixels
ALIGN	Netscape	Aligns the horizontal rule with the left edge, right edge, or center of the browser display
NOSHADE	Netscape	Prevents the horizontal rule from being shaded
SRC	HTML 3.0	Allows an image to be used as a horizontal rule

The **SIZE** and **WIDTH** attributes control the vertical and horizontal dimensions of the horizontal rule. The **ALIGN** attribute takes on the values of **LEFT**, **CENTER**, or **RIGHT** (the default value is **CENTER**). The **NOSHADE** attribute must be specified to turn off shading, since shading is performed by default. The **SRC** attribute is provided to allow images to be used as horizontal rules; however, it is not widely supported. Many Web page designers simply insert colorful images, using the **IMG** tag, in place of horizontal rules.

The following example illustrates a few ways to use horizontal rules.

1. Open a HoTMetaL document, create a level 1 heading, and type **Horizontal Rules** for the title and heading.

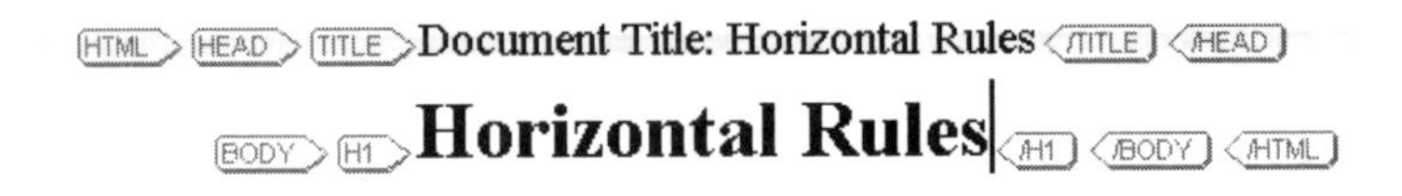

2. Move the cursor between the **/H1** and **/BODY** tags and type **normal**.

3. Click on the **Horizontal rule** toolbar button.

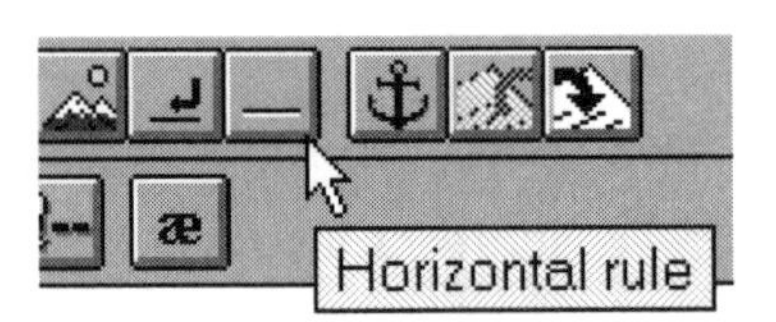

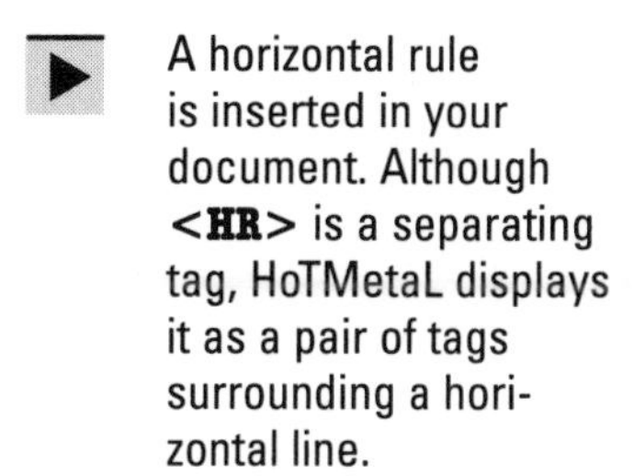

A horizontal rule is inserted in your document. Although **<HR>** is a separating tag, HoTMetaL displays it as a pair of tags surrounding a horizontal line.

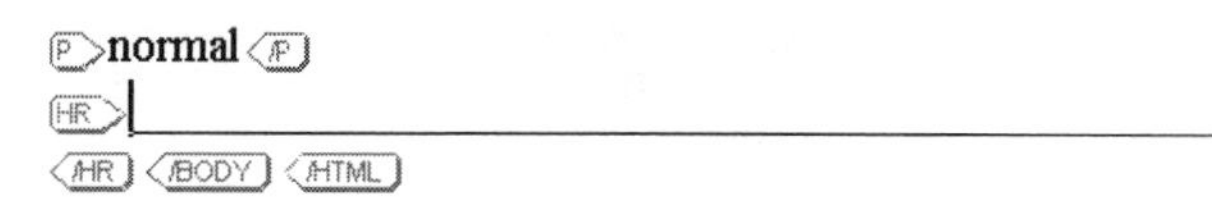

4. Type **width = 100, align = right, size = 25** and click on the **Horizontal rule** toolbar button.

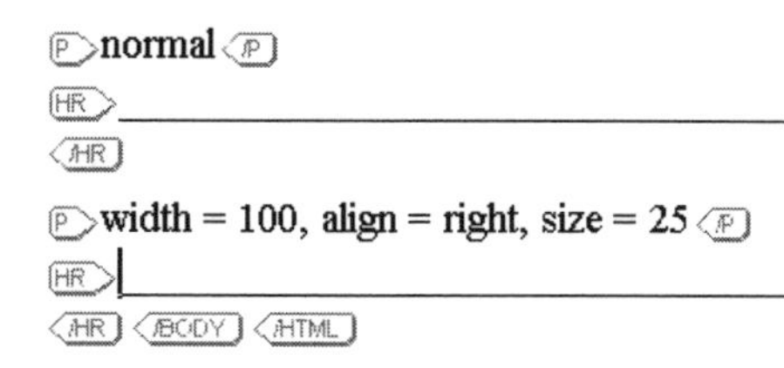

Another horizontal rule is inserted in your document.

5. Press **F6** to bring up the Edit Attributes dialog box.

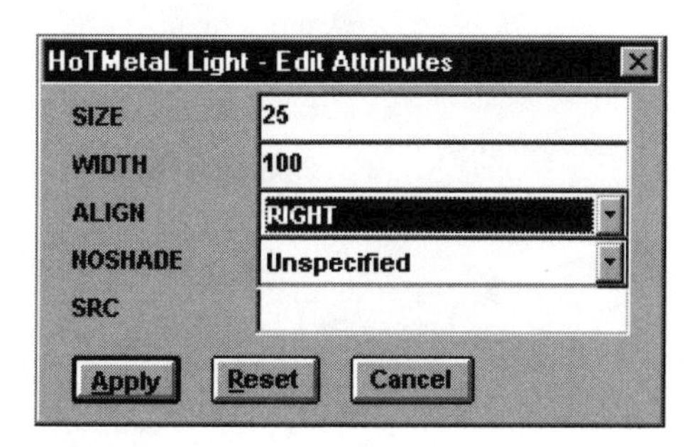

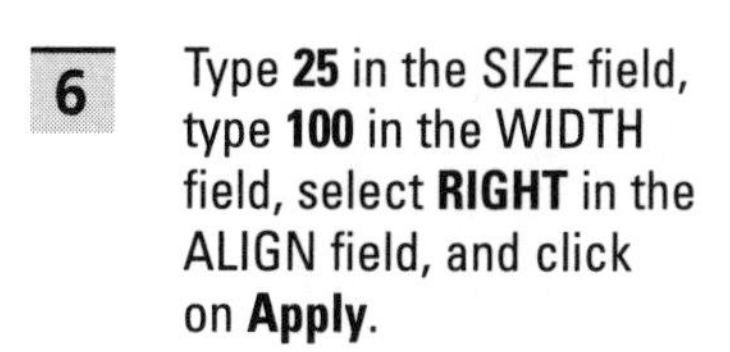

6. Type **25** in the SIZE field, type **100** in the WIDTH field, select **RIGHT** in the ALIGN field, and click on **Apply**.

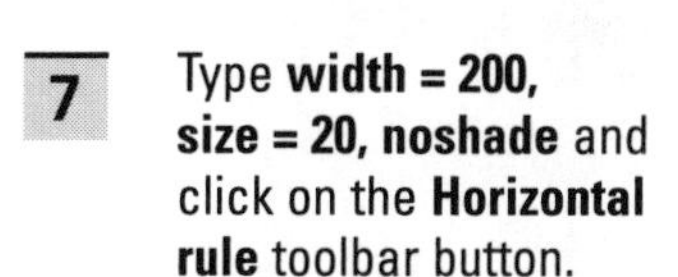

7. Type **width = 200, size = 20, noshade** and click on the **Horizontal rule** toolbar button.

width = 100, align = right, size = 25

width = 200, size = 20, noshade

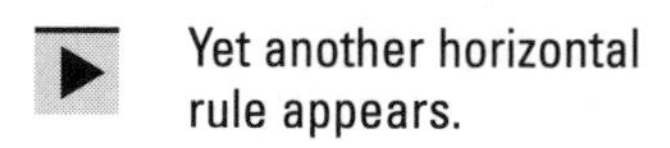

Yet another horizontal rule appears.

8 Press **F6** to bring up the Edit Attributes dialog box.

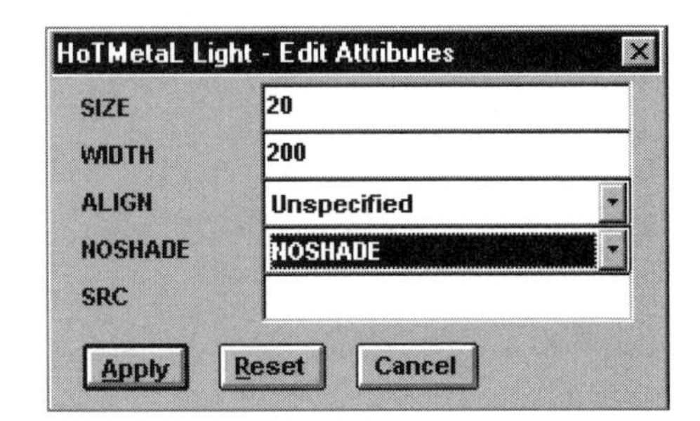

9 Type **20** in the SIZE field, type **200** in the WIDTH field, select **NOSHADE** in the NOSHADE field, and click on **Apply**.

10 Type **custom image**.

11 Move the cursor between the **/P** and **/BODY** tags and click on the **Image** toolbar button.

► The Edit Image dialog box appears.

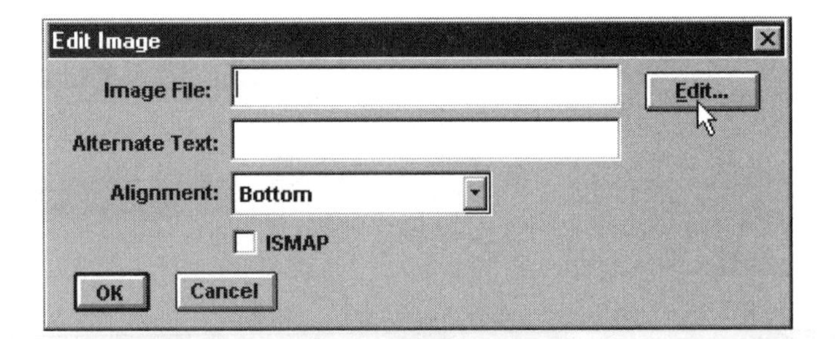

12 Click on the **Edit** button.

► The Edit IMG Source dialog box appears.

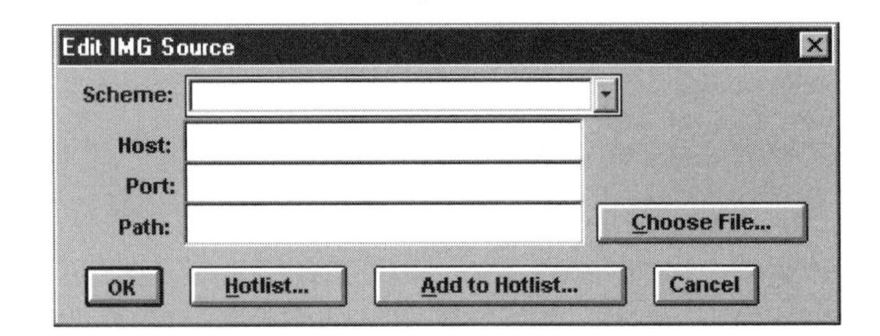

13 Click on the **Choose File** button to bring up the Choose Image File Image dialog box.

14 Type **c:\html\images\rainbow.gif** in the File name field and click on **Open**.

15 Click on **OK** twice more to close the Edit IMG Source and Edit Image dialog boxes.

▶ A rainbow-colored image is inserted.

16 Save your file as c:\html\ch06-07.htm and view it using your browser.

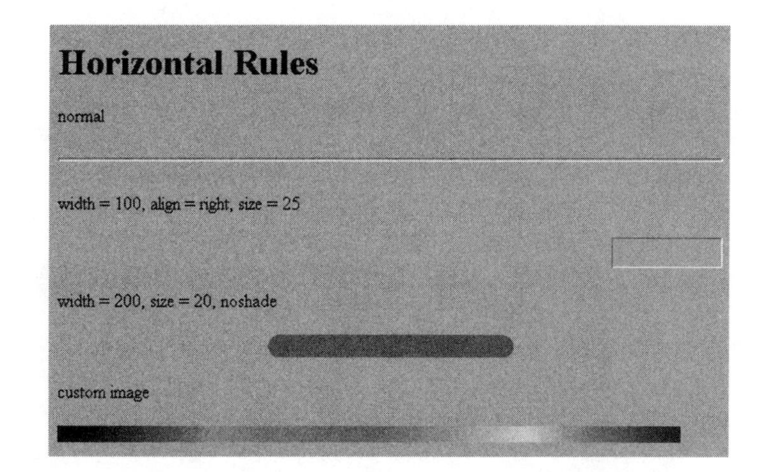

▶ Notice the variety of horizontal rules you've created.

17 Close your browser and HoTMetaL.

In this lesson, you learned how to organize your Web pages using lists and horizontal rules. You now know how to develop attractive and well-structured Web pages using a combination of text and graphics.

In the next lesson, you will learn how to link your Web pages to other Web pages and Internet services—one of the most exciting features of the Web. After completing the next lesson, you will be well on your way to understanding Web page design.

CREATING LINKS

Up to now, you have been working with Web pages that have been isolated from the rest of the Web. These pages have been information dead ends in the sense that they did not provide any connections to other documents. In this lesson, you will learn how to link your pages with each other and with pages and other services on the Web. You will also learn to use images in your links.

The lesson begins with some background information on link terminology and then shows you how to use HoTMetaL to start creating links. When you finish this lesson, you will be able to develop Web pages with links to your favorite Web destinations.

Understanding Links

Links, also called *hyperlinks*, are the essence of the Web. Without them, the Web would be nothing more than a disjointed collection of interesting facts. With them, you can quickly follow an interesting trail of information from page to page. Links make browsing possible.

Links connect *source pages* to *destination pages.* The particular part of the source page that contains the link is referred to as the *tail* of the link. The tail is usually colored, underlined, or set off in some other manner so that its nature is obvious. The specific location within the destination page that is the object of the link is referred to as the *head* of the link. Most of the time the head of a link is an entire Web page, but in some cases it may be a named offset within a Web page. (See the section entitled "Linking within a Web Page" later in this lesson for more about named offsets.) The tail and head of a link are referred to as the *anchors* of the link. The tail is the *source anchor* and the head is the *destination anchor.*

The important point to remember in learning this terminology is that two anchors—a source anchor and a destination anchor—are needed to construct a link.

Constructing Local Links

Links are constructed from the source anchor and the destination anchor. You insert a link into a Web page using the anchor tag. The anchor tag is a surrounding tag that surrounds the portion of a Web page that is to be the source or destination of the link. Its syntax is as follows:

<A>all text and images between the tags become the anchor</A>

Anchors have attributes that name the destination of a link. If an anchor is the source of a link, it uses the **HREF** attribute to identify the destination of the link. If an anchor is the destination of a link, it is named using the **NAME** attribute. This makes it available as a named offset within a Web document.

An anchor can be the source of one link and the destination of another.

Linking to Another Web Page

The easiest and most common way to construct a link is to surround the source of the link with anchor tags and set its **HREF** attribute to the destination Web page. You'll do just that in the following example. In this example, you'll create two Web pages: the first will contain the source anchor of the link and the second will serve as the destination of the link.

1 
Launch HoTMetaL, open a new document, create a level 1 heading, and type **Source Web Page** as the title and heading.

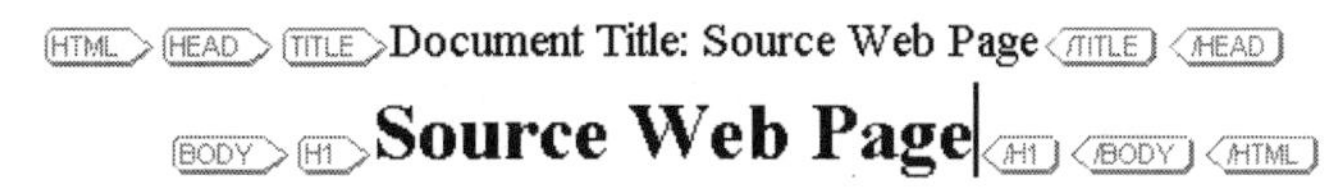

2 Move the cursor between the **/H1** and **/BODY** tags and type **This link connects this source Web page to the destination Web page.**

HTML HEAD TITLE Document Title: Source Web Page /TITLE /HEAD

BODY H1 **Source Web Page** /H1

P This link connects this source Web page to the destination Web page.
/P /BODY /HTML

3 Select the word **link** by double-clicking on it.

P This link connects this source Web page to the destination Web page.
/P /BODY /HTML

4 Click on the **Anchor** toolbar button.

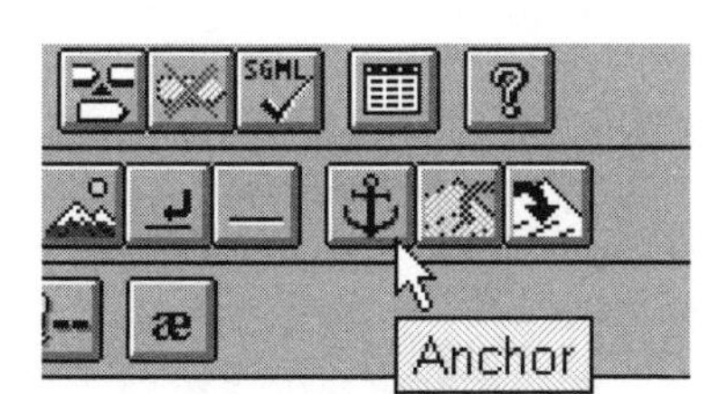

▶ The Edit URL dialog box appears.

5 Click on the **Choose File** button.

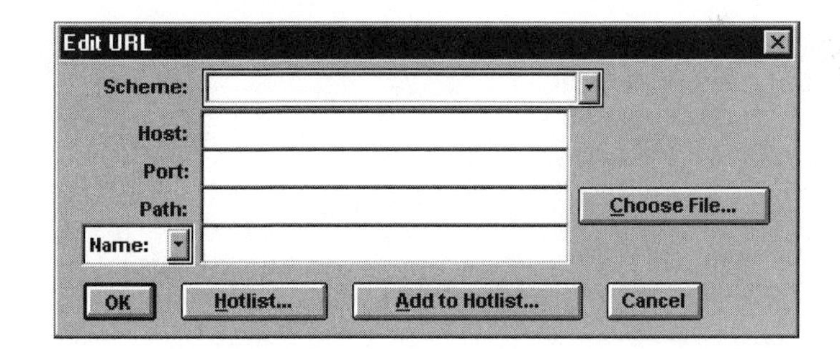

▶ The Choose File for URL dialog box appears.

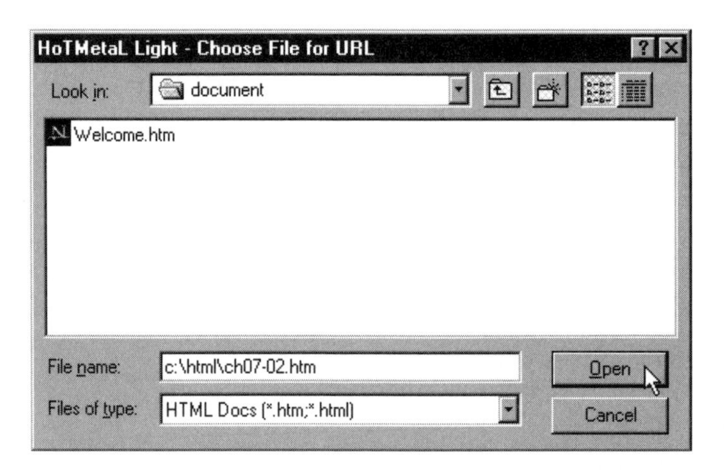

▶ Since the destination file doesn't exist yet, you have to type in the file's name.

6 Type **c:\html\ch07-02.htm** in the File name field and click on the **Open** button.

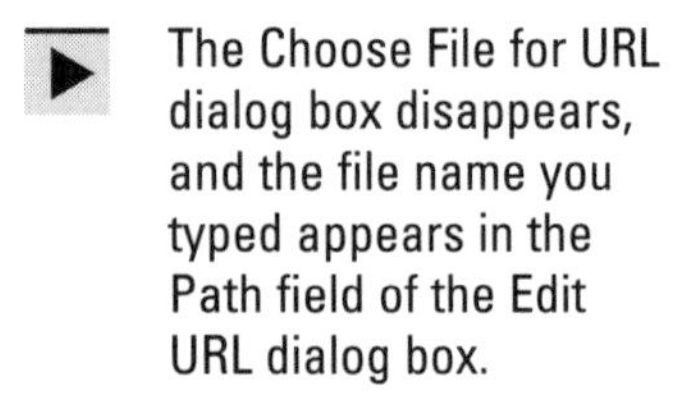

▶ The Choose File for URL dialog box disappears, and the file name you typed appears in the Path field of the Edit URL dialog box.

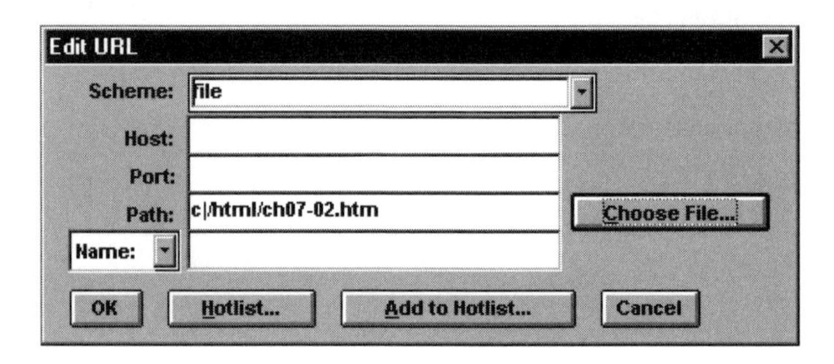

7 Click on **OK** to close the dialog box.

▶ HoTMetaL inserts a source anchor into your file. The **HREF** attribute points to ch07-02.htm as the destination of the link. You can verify this by pressing F6 to edit the anchor's attributes.

P This A [file:///c|/html/ch07-02.htm] link /A connects this source Web page to the destination Web page. /P /BODY /HTML

8 Save this document as c:\html\ch07-01.htm, but do not close it.

9 Open a new HoTMetaL document, create a level 1 heading and type **Destination Web Page** as the title and heading.

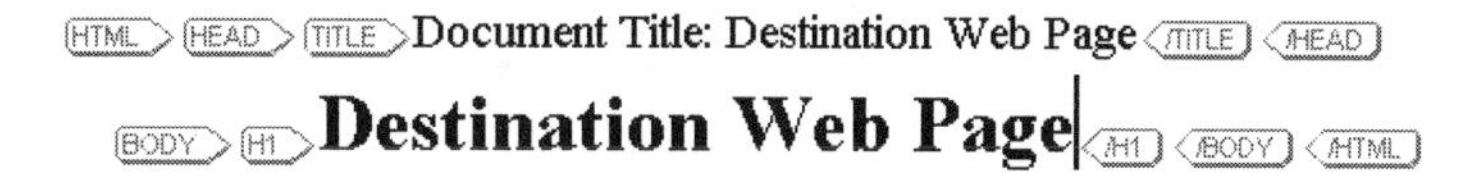

10 Move the cursor between the **/H1** and **/BODY** tags and type **The link worked!**

P The link worked! /P /BODY /HTML

11 Save your file as c:\html\ch07-02.htm.

12 Select **Window ➢ ch07-01.htm**.

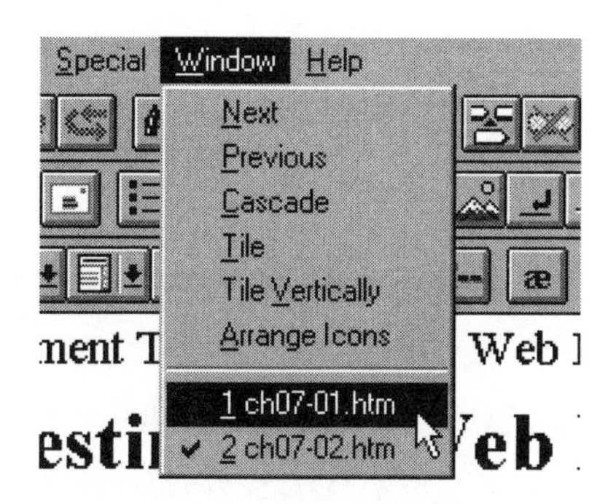

13 View this document with your Web browser.

Source Web Page

This link connects this source Web page to the destination Web page.

14 Click on the word **link**.

▶ Your browser switches to the destination Web page.

Destination Web Page

The link worked!

15 Close your browser and the current HoTMetaL document.

Linking within a Web Page

The previous example showed you how to link one Web page to another. You can also construct links that connect different parts of the same Web page by inserting source and destination anchors within the same document.

To do this in HTML, you set the **NAME** attribute of the destination anchor to a value that names its location within the document. You then set the **HREF** attribute of the source anchor to the name of the destination anchor. HoTMetaL greatly simplifies this process with the Name target and Connect link toolbar buttons.

Named anchors within Web pages are sometimes referred to as *named offsets*.

The following example shows how to use HoTMetaL to create links within a Web page.

1. Open a new HoTMetaL document, create a level 1 heading, and type **Links within Documents** as the title and heading.

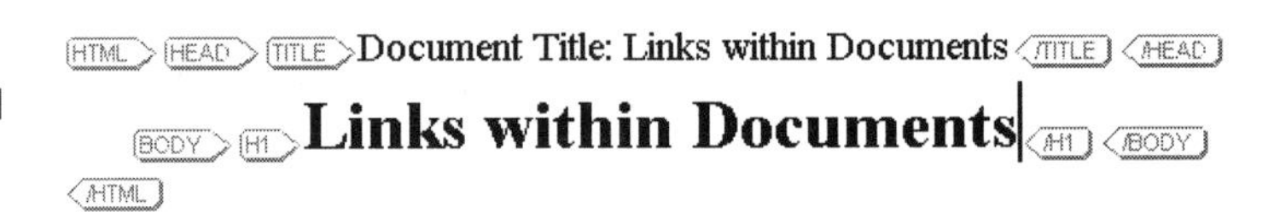
HTML HEAD TITLE Document Title: Links within Documents /TITLE /HEAD
BODY H1 Links within Documents /H1 /BODY
/HTML

2. Move the cursor between the **/H1** and **/BODY** tags and type **Go to Z**.

P Go to Z /P /BODY /HTML

3. Move the cursor between the **/P** and **/BODY** tags and click on the **H2** toolbar button.

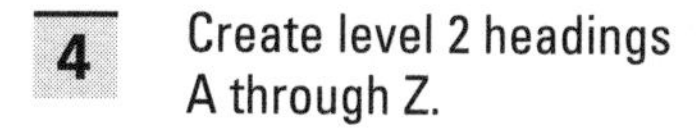

4 Create level 2 headings A through Z.

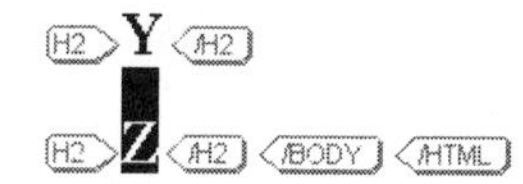

5 Select the last heading (Z).

6 Click on the **Name target** toolbar button.

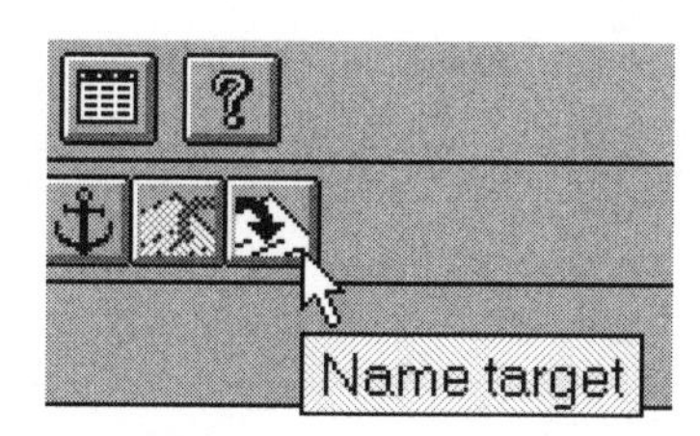

▶ The Insert Named Location dialog box appears.

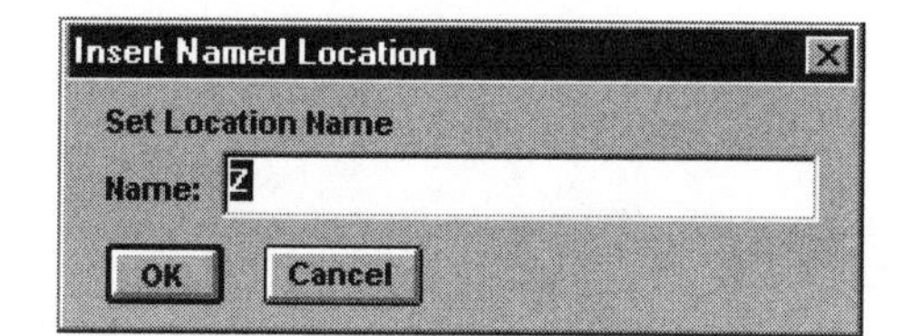

7 Type **Z** in the Name field and click on **OK**.

▶ Anchor (**A**) tags are inserted around the *Z*.

8 Go back to the top of your document and select **Go to Z**.

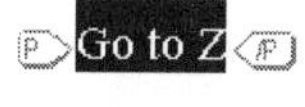

9 Click on the **Connect link** toolbar button.

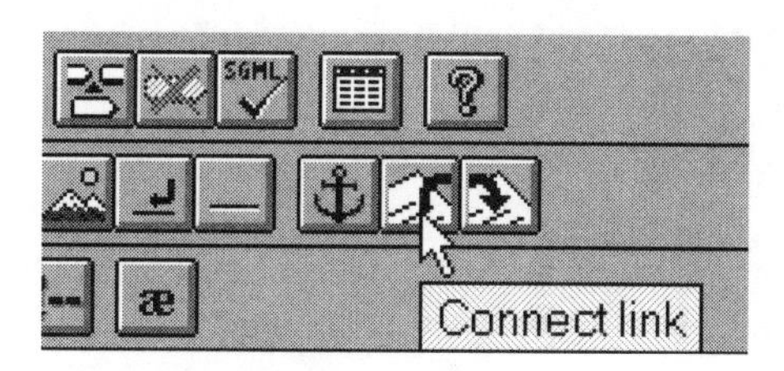

▶ Anchor tags and the link's named destination are placed around the selected text.

10 Save your document as c:\html\ch07-03.htm and view it with your Web browser.

Links within Documents

Go to Z

A

B

C

D

E

11 Click on the link **Go to Z**.

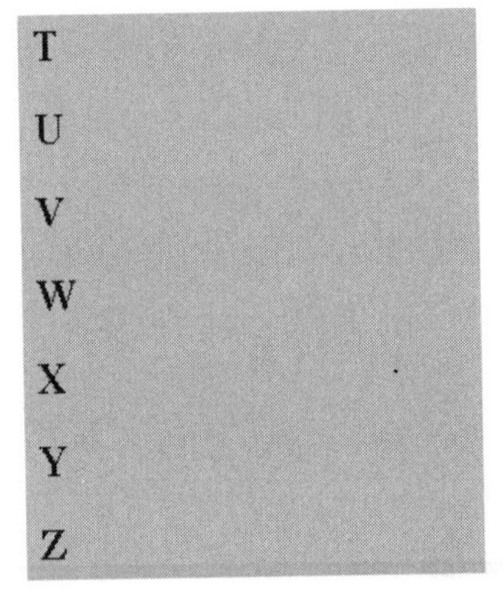

▶ You zoom to the *Z* at the end of your document.

12 Close your browser and the current HoTMetaL document.

Constructing Remote Links

The preceding examples showed you how to link Web pages that are local to your computer. You'll soon learn how to link your Web pages to pages on other computers around the Web. Before you do that, you'll have to learn a little bit about how remote Web pages are identified.

Working with Uniform Resource Locators

A *universal resource locator,* or *URL,* is a standard address for files, services, and other resources that are available over the Internet. Internet resources are identified by URLs in the same way that you can be identified by a social security number or an e-mail address.

URLs enable links between Web pages on different computers as well as links between Web pages and other Internet services. They provide an important foundation for the Web.

A URL may consist of some or all of the following address components: a protocol, a host name, a port name, a path name, a file name, and file parameters.

The *protocol* is the first component of a URL. It tells you how to communicate with the resource being located. For example, you use the Hypertext Transfer Protocol, or HTTP, with Web pages; the File Transfer Protocol, or FTP, with other types of Internet files; and your local file system protocol with files that are on your computer or local area network. These three protocols are identified as **http**, **ftp**, and **file** within URLs. There are several other Internet protocols besides those mentioned here that may used in URLs. These will be covered in the section "Links to Other Internet Services" later in this lesson.

The *host name* is usually the second component of a URL. It is the Internet domain name of the computer that is making the resource available. Examples of host names are **www.w3.org**, **hoohoo.ncsa.uiuc.edu**, and **ftp.cdrom.com**.

The *port name* tells you how to connect to the host using the specified protocol. The port name is implied by the protocol being used and is usually not specified. For example, most Web servers use port 80 with HTTP. The port address need only be specified when the port handling a particular protocol differs from the default, or *well-known port number.*

The *path name* identifies a particular directory on the host system, the *file name* identifies a specific file within that directory, and the *file parameters* may be used to identify a named location within the file.

► ► ► Not all address components are used with every type of URL.

Now that you have become familiar with the basic structure of URLs, let's use this information to construct some remote Web links.

Linking to a Remote Web Page

In order to construct a link from a Web page on your computer to a page that is on a remote computer, you identify the URL of the remote Web page using the **HREF** attribute of the source anchor. This gives the source Web page the information it needs to tell browsers how to fetch the destination Web page. The following example shows how this is done.

The remaining examples in this lesson require you to be connected to the Internet in order to carry out the final steps of each example.

1. Open a new HoTMetaL document, create a level 1 heading, and type **Links to Remote Documents** as the title and heading.

Document Title: Links to Remote Documents
Links to Remote Documents

2. Move the cursor between the **/H1** and **/BODY** tags and type the paragraph shown here.

Links to Remote Documents

This link connects to the home page of the World Wide Web Consortium, a great place to learn what's new on the Web.

3. Select the phrase **World Wide Web Consortium**.

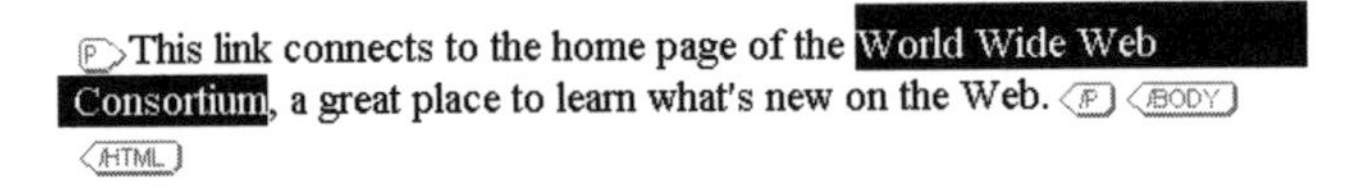
This link connects to the home page of the World Wide Web Consortium, a great place to learn what's new on the Web.

4. Click on the **Anchor** toolbar button.

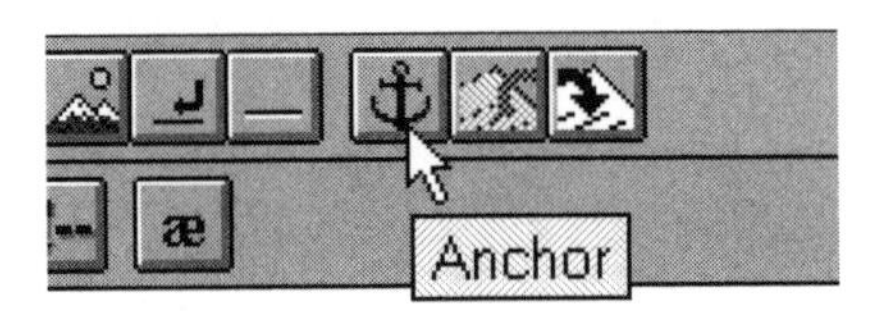
Anchor

▶ The Edit URL dialog box appears.

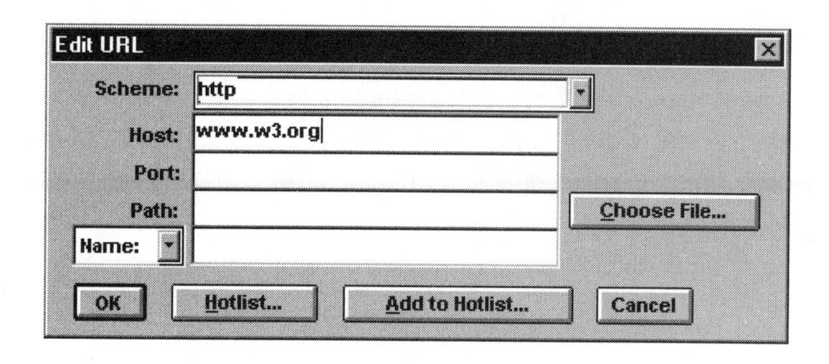

5 Select **http** in the Scheme field.

6 Type **www.w3.org** in the Host field.

7 Click on **OK** to close the dialog box.

▶ HoTMetaL inserts anchor tags around the selected text. The **HREF** attribute is set to the selected URL. You can verify this by pressing F6.

BODY H1 **Links to Remote Documents** /H1

P This link connects to the home page of the A [http://www.w3.org/] World Wide Web Consortium /A, a great place to learn what's new on the Web. /P /BODY /HTML

8 Save your document as c:\html\ch07-04.htm.

9 View it with your Web browser.

Links to Remote Documents

This link connects to the home page of the World Wide Web Consortium, a great place to learn what's new on the Web.

10 Click on **World Wide Web Consortium**.

▶ Your browser links to the home page of the W3C.

The World Wide Web Consortium

The World Wide Web is the universe of network-accessible information. The World Wide Web Consortium exists to realize the full potential of the Web.

W3C works with the global community to produce specifications and reference software. W3C is funded by industrial members but its products are freely available to all. The Consortium is run by MIT LCS and by INRIA, in collaboration with CERN where the web originated. Please see the list of members to learn about individual members and visit their World Wide Web sites.

11 Close your browser but leave this document open in HoTMetaL; we'll use it in the next section.

Linking to a Named Offset in a Remote Web Page

If a destination Web page contains a destination anchor, it is possible to link directly to the named offset within the destination file. This allows you to construct links from your Web pages right into the middle of pages on other computers. This capability is handy if the page that you want to link to is quite large and you are only interested in a specific section of that page. The following example shows you how to construct a link to a named offset in a remote Web page.

1. Select the document title from ch07-04.htm and type **Links to Named Offsets** over it; do the same with the heading.

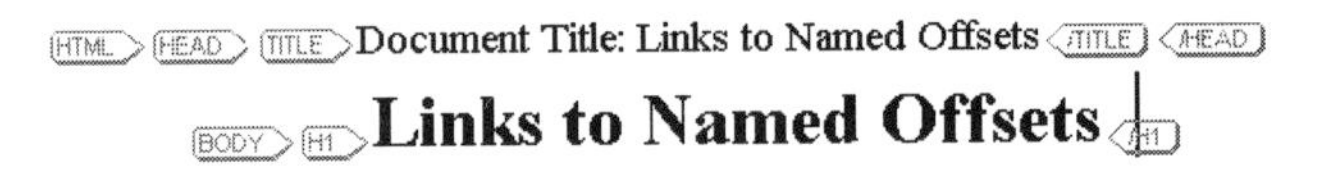

2. Click anywhere between the anchor tags and press **F6** to bring up the Edit Attributes dialog box.

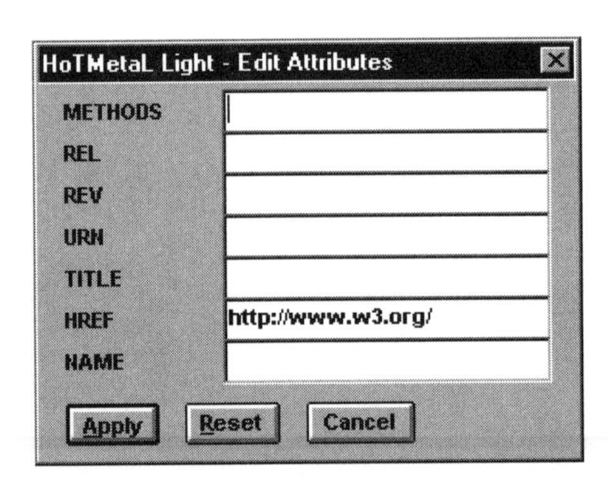

3. In the HREF field, place your cursor after the final slash and type **pub/WWW/#News**.

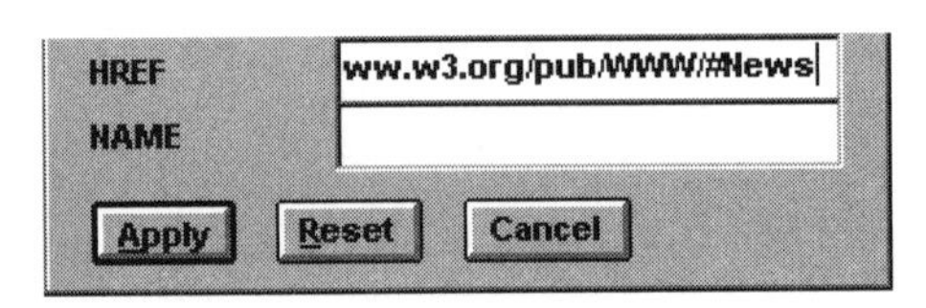

4. Click on **Apply**.

▶ HoTMetaL changes the **HREF** attribute shown in the anchor tags.

<P>This link connects to the home page of the <A>[http://www.w3.org/pub/WWW/#News] World Wide Web Consortium </A>, a great place to learn what's new on the Web. </P> </BODY> </HTML>

5 Save your document as c:\html\ch07-05.htm.

6 View it with your browser.

7 Click on **World Wide Web Consortium**.

Links to Named Offsets

This link connects to the home page of the World Wide Web Consortium, a great place to learn what's new on the Web.

▶ Your browser connects to the News and Updates section of the W3C home page.

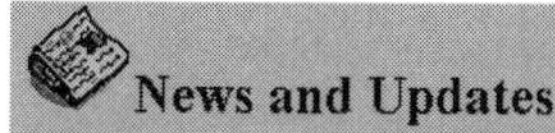

News and Updates

- **Joint Electronic Payment Initiative Launch Report**:
  Approximately forty-five participants attended the December 18th launch of the CommerceNet/ W3C Joint Electronic Payments Initiative. Details are available on the W3C Electronic Payments overview and the Joint Electronic Payment Initiative project page.
- **W3C Working Draft: Inserting multimedia objects into HTML3** (21 Dec 95)
  A work in progress, not to be considered as the final specification.
- **CSCW and the Web**, Sankt Augustin, Germany, February 7-9, 1996:
  The ERCIM World-Wide Web Working Group (W4G) and GMD invite you to participate in an open international workshop on support for collaboration on the Web.

8 Close your browser and the current HoTMetaL document.

Linking to Other Internet Services

Even though most links you encounter are to other pages on the Web, links are by no means limited to Web pages. You can construct links to many other types of Internet services by using the protocol, host name, and other parameters for that service in your URLs. The following table identifies the protocols that are supported by HoTMetaL. These protocols may be used in the scheme field of the Edit URL dialog box to specify that other Internet services be used as the destination of a link.

PROTOCOL	DESCRIPTION
file	Access local files on your computer or local area network
http	Access HTML documents
ftp	Access files located at FTP sites
gopher	Access information provided by gopher servers
telnet	Log in to other computers
wais	Access wide area information search capabilities
prospero	Access the Prospero virtual file system
nntp	Access a netnews server
rlogin	Remotely log in to another computer using the rlogin command
tn3270	Remotely log in to a computer with an IBM 3270 terminal emulator
news	Link to a specific newsgroup
mailto	Send e-mail to a particular address

The following example shows you how to use HoTMetaL to set up links from your Web pages to other Internet services. The example constructs a link to the world-famous Walnut Creek FTP site. Walnut Creek is one of the most popular places for obtaining software over the Internet.

1. Open a new HoTMetaL document, create a level 1 heading, and type **Links to Other Internet Services** as the title and heading.

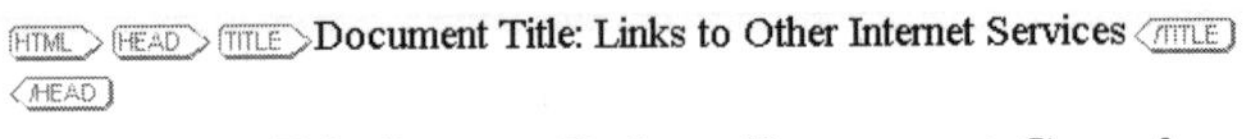
HTML HEAD TITLE Document Title: Links to Other Internet Services /TITLE
/HEAD

BODY H1 **Links to Other Internet Services**
/H1 /BODY /HTML

2. Move the cursor between the **/H1** and **/BODY** tags and type the paragraph shown here.

P This link connects to the Walnut Creek FTP site. It's a great place to find software on the Internet. /P /BODY /HTML

3. Select the text **Walnut Creek FTP site.**

P This link connects to the Walnut Creek FTP site. It's a great place to find software on the Internet. /P /BODY /HTML

4 Click on the **Anchor** toolbar button to open the Edit URL dialog box.

Edit URL
Scheme: ftp
Host: ftp.cdrom.com
Port:
Path: /pub
Name:
Choose File...
OK Hotlist... Add to Hotlist... Cancel

5 Select **ftp** in the Scheme field, type **ftp.cdrom.com** in the host field, type **/pub** in the path field, and click on **OK**.

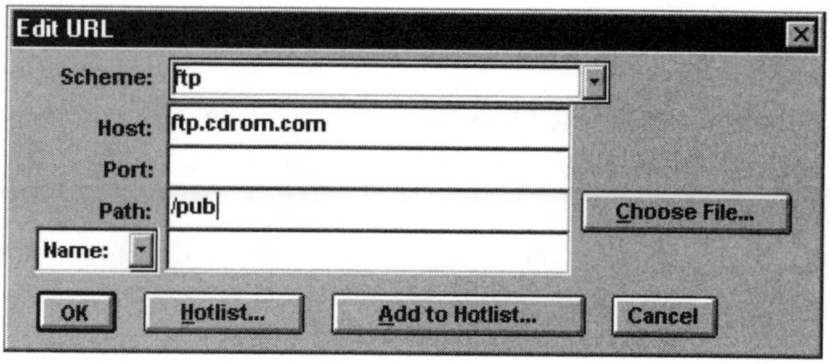

▶ Anchor tags and the URL are inserted into your document.

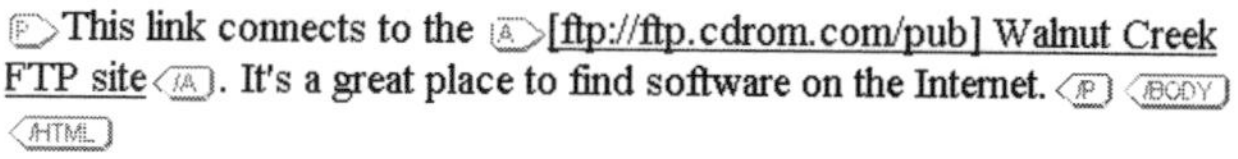

P This link connects to the A [ftp://ftp.cdrom.com/pub] Walnut Creek FTP site /A. It's a great place to find software on the Internet. /P /BODY /HTML

6 Save your document as c:\html\ch07-06.htm.

7 View it with your browser.

Links to Other Internet Services

This link connects to the Walnut Creek FTP site. It's a great place to find software on the Internet.

8 Click on **Walnut Creek FTP site**.

▶ You may or may not be able to connect to the Walnut Creek FTP site, shown here, depending on how busy it is at the moment.

Current directory is /pub

Welcome to wcarchive - home ftp site for Walnut Creek CDROM.
There are currently 300 users out of 300 possible.

Most of the files in this area are also available on CDROM. You can send email to (or finger) info@cdrom.com for more information or to order. For tech support about our products, please email support@cdrom.com. You may also call our toll-free number: 1-800-786-9907 or +1-510-674-0783. Orders are taken 24 hours.

9 Close your browser and the current HoTMetaL document.

Changing Link Colors

In Lesson 4, you learned how to change the color of the document background and text using the **BGCOLOR** and **TEXT** attributes of the **BODY** tag. HoTMetaL also supports the **LINK**, **VLINK**, and **ALINK** attributes, which allow you to change the colors of your links. You can access these attributes by placing the cursor immediately after the **BODY** tag and pressing F6.

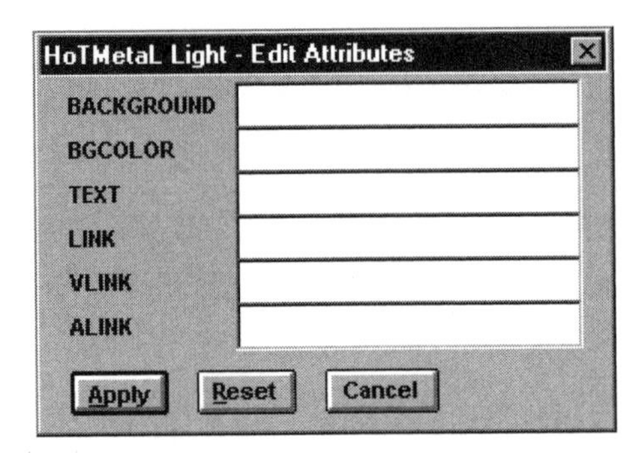

The **LINK** attribute lets you change the default color of a link before it is clicked on. The **ALINK** attribute allows you to change the color of an *active* link—one that is being clicked on. The **VLINK** attribute allows you to change the color of a *visited* link—one that has already been selected. To specify the link colors, you enter the appropriate red, green, and blue color intensity values.

We won't go through an example here because this grayscale book can't show the varying colors of links. For a refresher on how to apply color, see "Document Color Attributes" in Lesson 4.

Using Images as Anchors for Links

Now that you've learned how to construct links to other Web pages and Internet resources, you're probably wondering about all those websites that use fancy graphics with their links.

There are two major ways of using graphics with links: *image maps* and *image anchors.* Image maps make use of special programs, called *CGI programs,* to process links. They are covered in Lesson 9. Image anchors are simply images that are embedded in the source anchor of a link. The following example shows you how to use image anchors in your Web pages.

1 Open a new HoTMetaL document, create a level 1 heading, and type **Using Images as Anchors for Links** for the title and heading.

<HTML> <HEAD> <TITLE>Document Title: Using Images as Anchors for Links </TITLE> </HEAD>

<BODY> <H1> **Using Images as Anchors for Links** </H1> </BODY> </HTML>

2 Move the cursor between the **/H1** and **/BODY** tags and type **This image is a link to an interesting website.**

<P>This image is a link to an interesting website. </P> </BODY> </HTML>

3 Move the cursor between **image** and **is** and click on the **Image** toolbar button.

<P>This image is a link to an interesting website. </P> </BODY> </HTML>

▶ The Edit Image dialog box appears.

4 Click on the **Edit** button.

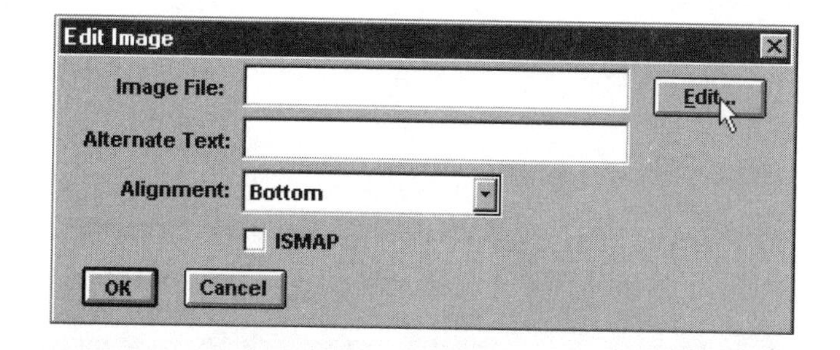

▶ The Edit IMG Source dialog box appears.

5 Click on the **Choose File** button to bring up the Choose Image File Image dialog box.

Edit IMG Source
Scheme:
Host:
Port:
Path:
Choose File...
OK
Hotlist...
Add to Hotlist...
Cancel

6 Select the file **c:\html\images\web-ti.gif** and click on the **Open** button.

▶ The selected file appears in the Path field of the Edit IMG Source dialog box.

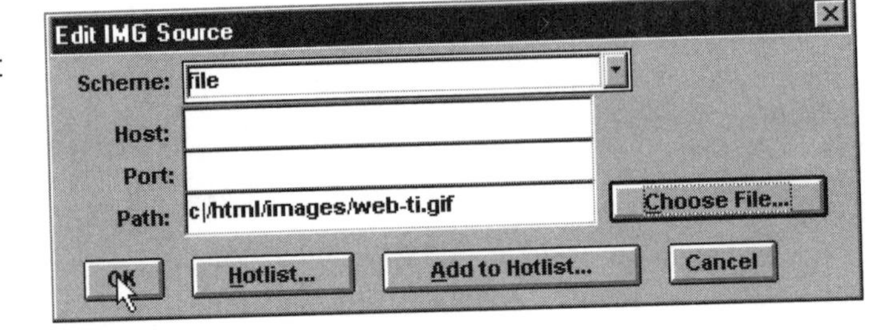

7 Click on **OK** to close the dialog box.

8 Click on **OK** to close the Edit Image dialog box.

▶ A partial image of a web is inserted into your document. This is a bug in HoTMetaL. Sometimes HoTMetaL does not correctly reformat the document window to display the full image.

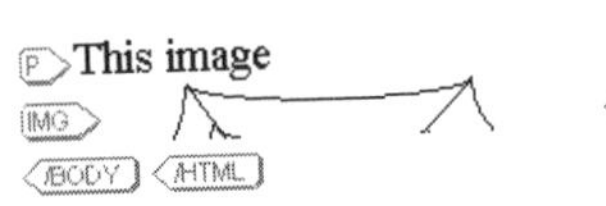

9 Select the image, including its tags.

10 Click on the **Anchor** toolbar button to bring up the Edit URL dialog box.

11 Select **http** in the Scheme field, type **miso.wwa.com** in the Host field, type **~boba/spider.html** in the Path field, and click on **OK**.

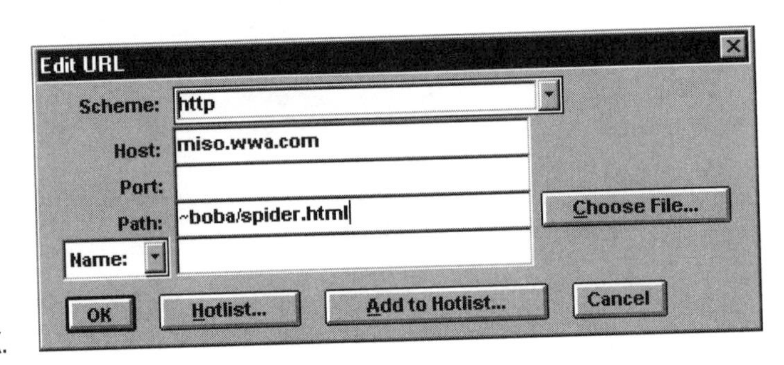

▶ The image is shown at full size, enclosed by anchor tags and the destination URL.

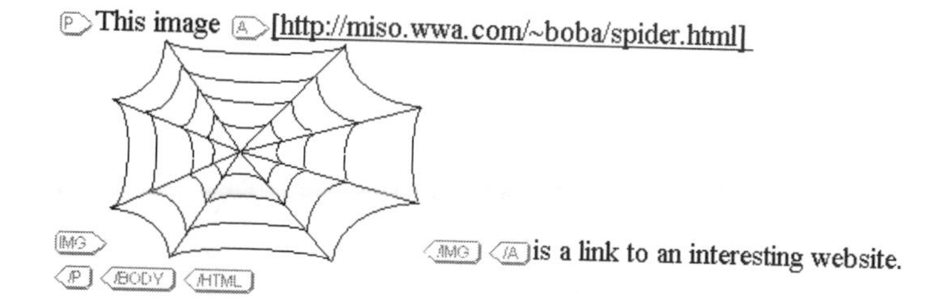

12 Save your file as c:\html\ch07-07.htm and view it with your browser.

13 Click on the spider web.

▶ Your browser links to a fun page on the Web.

14 When you're done, close your browser and HoTMetaL.

In this lesson, you took a giant step toward becoming a master Web publisher. Links are the essence of the Web, and you now know how to use them in your Web pages.

The following lesson will add more skills to your Web publishing repertoire. You'll learn all about using forms to collect information from Web users.

8

USING FORMS

The HTML tags that you've learned so far are great for providing information *to* Web users. However, these tags don't allow you to get any information *back* from them. Forms give you this capability. They make it possible to gather information using your Web pages. In this lesson, you'll learn how to use HoTMetaL to design forms that employ a full range of graphical user interface controls in collecting user data. When you finish this lesson, you will be able to develop forms for use in your Web pages.

Understanding Forms

If there's one thing that the pen-and-paper world has enough of, it's forms. From tax forms to fax forms, forms are everywhere. You fill them out when you go to a doctor, use a credit card, or apply for a job. The Web has forms, too, but Web forms are different from paper forms. They have special controls that help you fill them out, and they give you nearly instantaneous feedback. Unlike paper forms, which are usually "filled and filed," Web forms are usually a gateway to other Web services, such as information searches, software downloads, and online purchases.

Forms are implemented through a partnership among Web pages, browsers, servers, and other programs called *Common Gateway Interface,* or *CGI*, programs. Web browsers display pages containing forms to their users. The browsers implement the GUI controls of the form elements, allowing users to quickly and easily enter form data. When a form is completed and submitted by a user, the browser sends a request to process the data to the Web server identified by the form. The browser also tells the Web server what CGI program to use to process the data. The CGI program performs its processing and usually sends some status information back to the browser in the form of a Web page.

There are two major tasks to implementing a form: creating a Web page that collects form data from Web users and interacting with a CGI program to process the data collected via the form. HoTMetaL is used to simplify the first task. The following section shows you how to use HoTMetaL to create forms within your Web pages. The second task, interacting with a CGI program, is covered in Lesson 9. If you'd like to write your own CGI programs, read Lesson 9, then read the file \extra\morecgi.htm on the CD that came with this book.

Creating a Basic Form

Forms are created using the **FORM** tag, a surrounding tag that encloses all elements of the form. These elements may consist of form-specific tags or other HTML tags, such as formatted text, images, or links.

Form-specific tags are used to insert data fields and graphical user interface (GUI) controls into a form. They may only be used within a form and consist of the **INPUT**, **SELECT**, and **TEXTAREA** tags. These tags are covered in the following sections.

The general syntax for the **FORM** tag is as follows:

<FORM>contents of form</FORM>

Everything between the opening and closing tags is part of the form.

Setting Up the Form

The first form we'll create will be a simple one that asks the user for ID and password. We'll start by inserting the **FORM** tag and setting up the basic layout of the form.

1. Launch HoTMetaL, open a new document, create a level 1 heading, and type **First Form** for the title and heading.

2 Move the cursor between the **/H1** and **/BODY** tags and click on the **Form elements** toolbar button.

▶ A pop-up menu appears.

3 Select the **FORM** option.

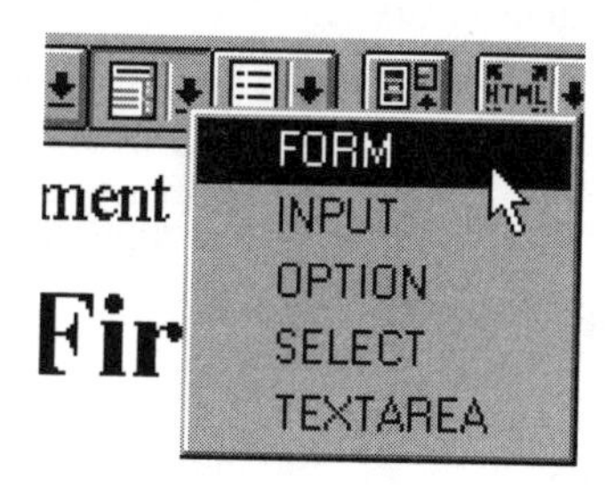

▶ **FORM** tags are inserted into your document.

4 Type **ID:** followed by a space, and press ↵.

5 Type **Password:** followed by a space.

FORM

P ID: /P

P Password: /P /FORM /BODY /HTML

Now we've told the reader what to type, but we need to give them fields to type in. Enter the **INPUT** tag.

Adding Input Elements

Most form elements are defined by the **INPUT** tag, a separating tag that is used to insert a variety of fields, check boxes, and buttons into your forms.

The **INPUT** tag has several attributes, the most important of which is the **TYPE** attribute. This attribute is used to identify the type of input element being defined. Valid values are **text**, **password**, **submit**, **reset**, **checkbox**, **radio**, **image**, and **hidden**. We'll work with the first four types in our first form, then learn about check boxes and radio buttons later in this lesson. The **image** and **hidden** types are covered in the next lesson. The other attributes of the **INPUT** tag are **NAME**, **VALUE**, **CHECKED**, **SIZE**, **MAXLENGTH**, **SRC**, and **ALIGN**. The **TYPE** attribute determines how these other attributes are used with an **INPUT** tag.

Adding Text and Password Fields

Text fields are used to collect a single line of text input from the user. They are defined by setting the **TYPE** attribute of an **INPUT** tag to **text**. Text fields use the **NAME**, **VALUE**, **SIZE**, and **MAXLENGTH** attributes of the **INPUT** tag.

The **NAME** attribute assigns an identifier to the text field. This identifier is passed to the CGI program that processes the form, along with the text entered by the user, so the CGI program can associate a name with data that is received from a form field.

The **VALUE** attribute specifies the default contents of an input field. When used with a text field, it identifies text that will initially appear in the text field.

The **SIZE** attribute sets the physical size of a text field, in characters. It only affects the number of characters that can be displayed, not the maximum number of characters that can be entered into the field. The **MAXLENGTH** attribute sets this property.

Password fields are defined by setting the **TYPE** attribute of an **INPUT** tag to **password**. They are the same as text fields in every respect, except that when the user types text into the field, it is displayed as a row of asterisks in order to prevent anyone from reading the password over the shoulder of the person typing.

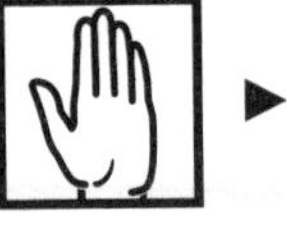

► ► ► Password fields provide no security other than hiding the text typed by users. Password data is sent out, in unencrypted form, from the Web browser to the CGI program.

Let's add text and password fields to our form now.

1. Move the cursor immediately before the first /**P** tag, click on the **Form elements** toolbar button, and select **INPUT**.

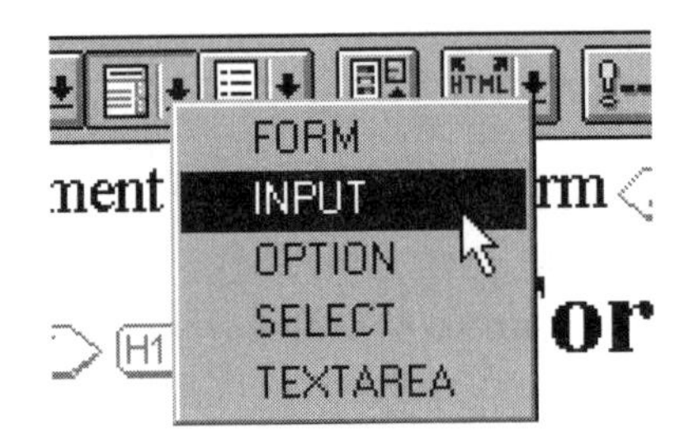

▶ **INPUT** tags are inserted in your document.

```
<FORM>
<P>ID: <INPUT>[NAME =  & TYPE = TEXT]</INPUT></P>
<P>Password: </P></FORM></BODY></HTML>
```

2 Press **F6** to access the Edit Attributes dialog box.

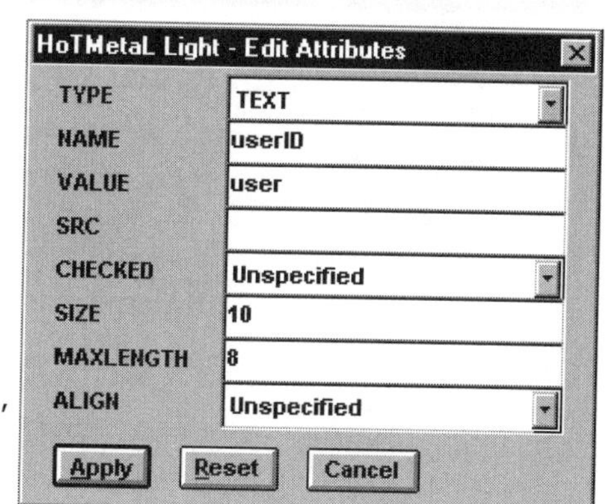

▶ The TYPE field is set to TEXT already, so we don't need to change it.

3 Type **userID** in the NAME field, **user** in the VALUE field, **10** in the SIZE field, and **8** in the MAXLENGTH field.

4 Click on the **Apply** button.

▶ The attributes of the **INPUT** tag are updated.

```
<FORM>
<P>ID: <INPUT>[NAME = userID & TYPE = TEXT]</INPUT></P>
<P>Password: </P></FORM></BODY></HTML>
```

5 Move the cursor immediately before the last **/P** tag, click on the **Form elements** toolbar button, and select **INPUT** to insert another set of **INPUT** tags.

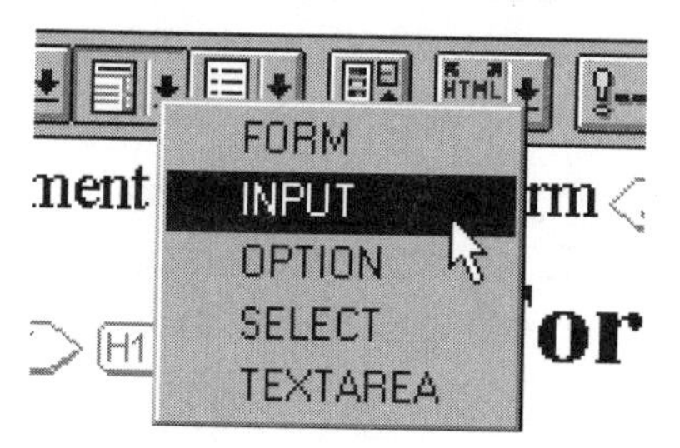

6 Press **F6** to bring up the Edit Attributes dialog box.

7 Select **PASSWORD** in the TYPE field, type **password** in the NAME field, and click on the **Apply** button.

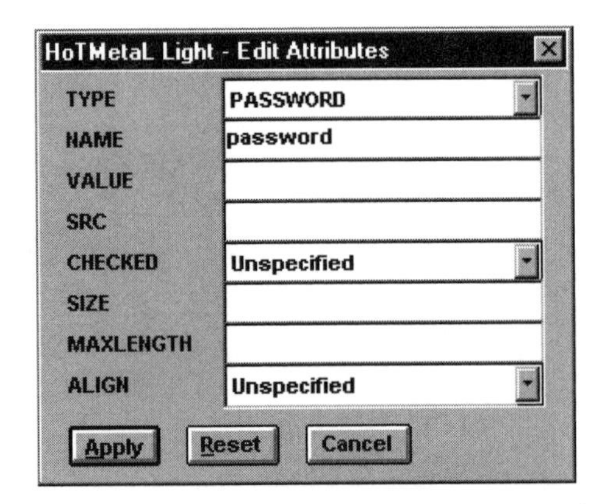

▶ The attributes of the **INPUT** tag are updated.

P ID: INPUT [NAME = userID & TYPE = TEXT] /INPUT /P

P Password: INPUT [NAME = password & TYPE = PASSWORD] /INPUT /P

Adding Submit and Reset Buttons

The beauty of Web forms is that when you fill them out, you usually get an immediate (or nearly so) response. In order to do that, there has to be a way to let the browser know that you're finished entering data. This is why all forms should include a *Submit button* that the user can click on. When the browser receives this signal, it sends the form to the CGI program for processing. To insert a Submit button in a form, set the **TYPE** attribute of an **INPUT** tag to **submit**.

What if your users goof up or change their minds in the middle of filling out your form? You can help them out by inserting a *Reset button,* which resets the values of the form fields to their default values. It removes any changes entered by the user and restores the form to its original state. To insert a Reset button, set the **TYPE** attribute of an **INPUT** tag to **reset**.

▶ ▶ ▶ In some browsers, different names may appear on the Submit and Reset buttons by default. You can control what the buttons say by using the **VALUE** attribute. For instance, if you wanted the Submit button to say "Send," your tag would say **<INPUT TYPE=reset VALUE=Send>**.

OK, let's add the Submit and Reset buttons.

1 Move the cursor immediately before the **/FORM** tag, click on the **Form elements** toolbar button, and select **INPUT** to insert another set of **INPUT** tags.

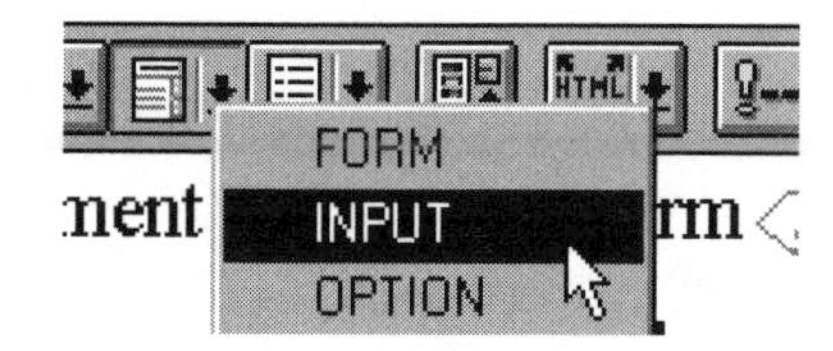

2 Press **F6** to bring up the Edit Attributes dialog box.

3 Select **SUBMIT** in the TYPE field and click on the **Apply** button.

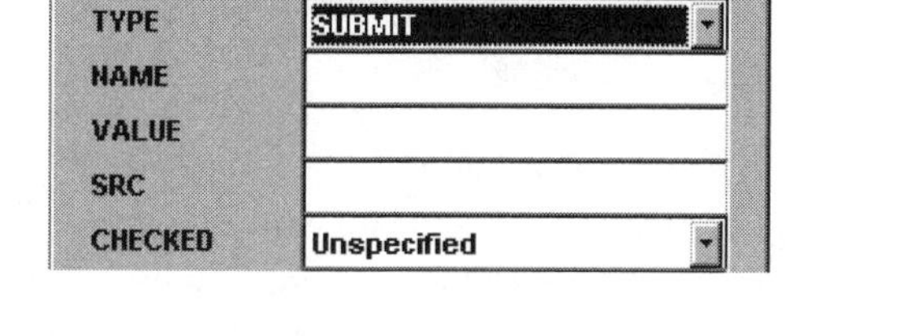

▶ The attributes of the **INPUT** tag are updated.

4 Move the cursor between the **/INPUT** and **/FORM** tags, click on the **Form elements** toolbar button, and select **INPUT** to insert **INPUT** tags in your document.

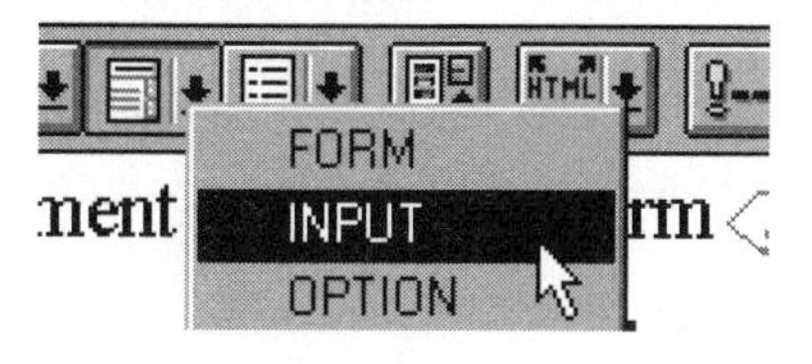

5 Press **F6** to bring up the Edit Attributes dialog box.

6 Select **RESET** in the TYPE field and click on the **Apply** button.

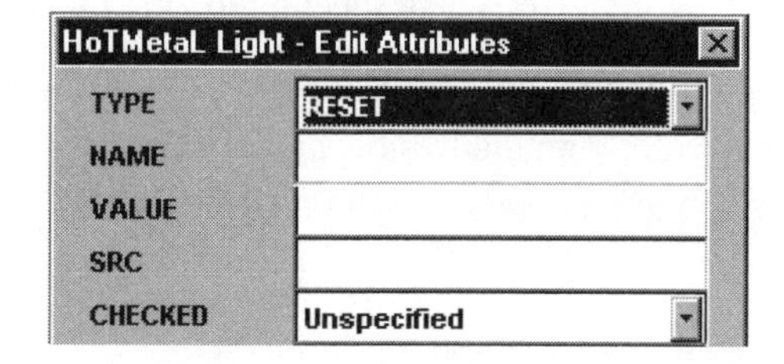

The attributes of the **INPUT** tag are updated.

<INPUT>[TYPE = SUBMIT]</INPUT> <INPUT>[TYPE = RESET]</INPUT> </FORM> </BODY> </HTML>

Now our basic form is ready; we just have to tell the browser what to do with it.

Preparing the Form for Processing

The **FORM** tag has three attributes that are used to control the processing of form data: **ACTION**, **METHOD**, and **ENCTYPE**.

The **ACTION** attribute tells the browser where to send the form; thus it takes a URL as its value. This URL identifies the Web server and gateway (CGI) program to be used to process the form data. The gateway program is usually located in a special directory on the Web server reserved for gateway programs.

The Web server used in this lesson's examples is a publicly available server that contains a CGI program called post-query that helps you test your forms. The program reads the form data sent to it by your browser and returns the values of the form fields submitted. The program's URL is **http://hoohoo.ncsa.uiuc.edu/htbin-post/post-query**. The **ACTION** attribute for all the forms in this lesson will use this URL.

You must be connected to the Internet in order to use the post-query program in the examples of this lesson.

The **METHOD** attribute specifies how data is to be passed to the CGI program; it takes either the **GET** or **POST** value. The **POST** method can handle larger forms, is more reliable, and thus is the preferred method. You'll use this method with all the forms in this lesson.

The last **FORM** attribute, **ENCTYPE**, tells the Web server how the form data is encoded. **ENCTYPE** only has one currently defined value: **application/x-www-form-urlencoded**. (You'll learn more about encoding and decoding in the next lesson. For now, we'll just use the default coding value.)

Now let's specify where and how to send the form.

1 Move the cursor immediately after the **FORM** tag.

2 Press **F6** to bring up the Edit Attributes dialog box.

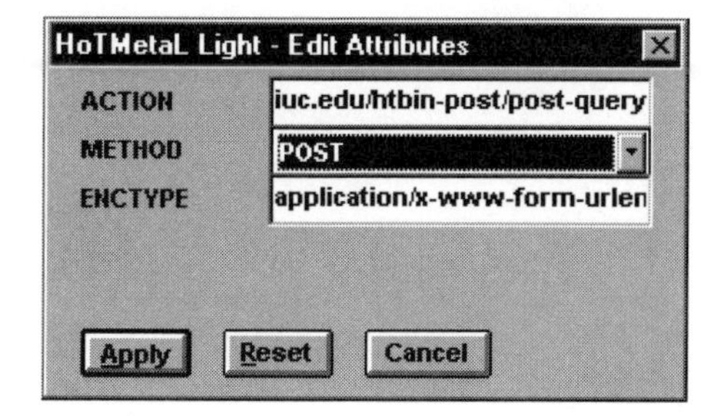

3 Type **http://hoohoo.ncsa.uiuc.edu/htbin-post/post-query** in the ACTION field, select **POST** in the METHOD field, and click on the **Apply** button.

► The **FORM** attributes are updated.

FORM [http://hoohoo.ncsa.uiuc.edu/htbin-post/post-query]

4 Save your file as c:\html\ch08-01.htm.

5 View it with your Web browser.

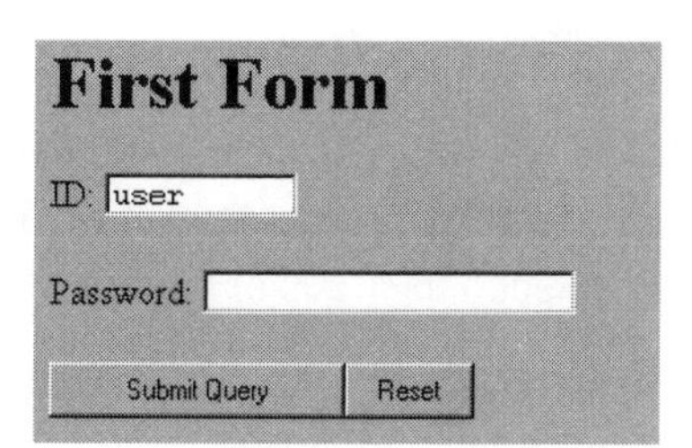

► Notice that the Submit button says "Submit Query." This is an example of the browser inserting its own default label, as discussed earlier.

Looks good. Let's take it for a spin.

6 Type a name in the ID field and a fake password in the Password field.

7 Click on the **Submit Query** button to submit your form to the post-query program.

First Form

ID: jamie

Password: ****

Submit Query Reset

The post-query program returns the field names and their corresponding values.

Query Results

You submitted the following name/value pairs:

- userID = jamie
- password = test

Close your browser and the current HoTMetaL document.

Getting Fancy

The form we just created was very basic and, as such, served its purpose well. But what if you want to get more information out of your users, give them a list of options to choose from, or elicit comments and questions from them? HoTMetaL allows you to do all these things by such methods as check boxes, radio buttons, selection lists, and text area fields.

First, we'll explore check boxes and radio buttons.

Adding Check Boxes and Radio Buttons

Check boxes are little boxes, placed next to a list of options, that the user can check or uncheck. Users can select as many check boxes as they like, so check boxes are useful for presenting nonexclusive options, such as areas of interest.

A check box is defined by setting the **TYPE** attribute of an **INPUT** tag to **checkbox**. It uses the **NAME**, **VALUE**, and **CHECKED** attributes of the **INPUT** tag.

The **NAME** attribute associates the check box with an identifier, which is used to tell the CGI program the state of the check box.

The **VALUE** attribute is used to specify the value of the check box when it is checked. The default value is **on**. You can change it to other values, such as **true**, **checked**, and so on. This value is not displayed to the user, but is passed on to the CGI program.

The **CHECKED** attribute determines the default value of the check box. It does not take a value. If it is present in the **INPUT** tag, the check box is initially checked. If it is absent, the check box is initially unchecked.

Radio buttons are similar to check boxes: they are little circles that present a series of choices to the user filling in a form. Unlike check boxes, however, radio buttons' choices are mutually exclusive (that is, only one button can be selected at a time, as in a car radio). Thus, radio buttons are useful for lists in which the user can have only one response, such as type of payment or marital status.

A radio button is defined by setting the **TYPE** attribute of an **INPUT** tag to **radio**. It uses the **NAME**, **VALUE**, and **CHECKED** attributes of the **INPUT** tag.

The radio buttons in one set of options are organized into a named group. The **NAME** attribute names the group to which the buttons belong, so all buttons in a form with the same name are assumed to belong to the same group. The group name is used in conjunction with the **VALUE** attribute to tell the CGI program which button in the group is selected.

The **VALUE** attribute specifies the value of the radio button when it is selected. The default value is **on**. Because all the radio buttons in a group have the same name, however, the CGI program can't distinguish which one has a value of **on**; it will simply know that the group is selected. Therefore, you must change the **VALUE** attribute for all the buttons so that each one is unique.

The **CHECKED** attribute determines the default value of a radio button. It does not take a value. If it is present in the **INPUT** tag, then the radio button is initially selected. If it is absent, then the radio button is selected. Only one button in a group may be initially selected.

The following example shows how to use check boxes and radio buttons in forms.

1. Open a new HoTMetaL document, create a level 1 heading, and type **Check Boxes and Radio Buttons** for the title and heading.

2. Move the cursor between the **/H1** and **/BODY** tags.

3 Click on the **Form elements** button and select **FORM** to insert **FORM** tags into your document.

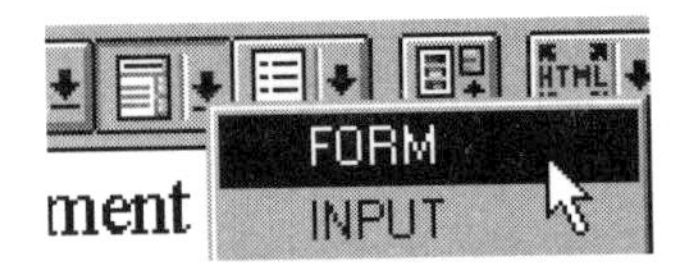

4 Press **F6** to bring up the Edit Attributes dialog box.

5 Type **http://hoohoo.ncsa.uiuc.edu/htbin-post/post-query** in the ACTION field, select **POST** in the METHOD field, and click on the **Apply** button.

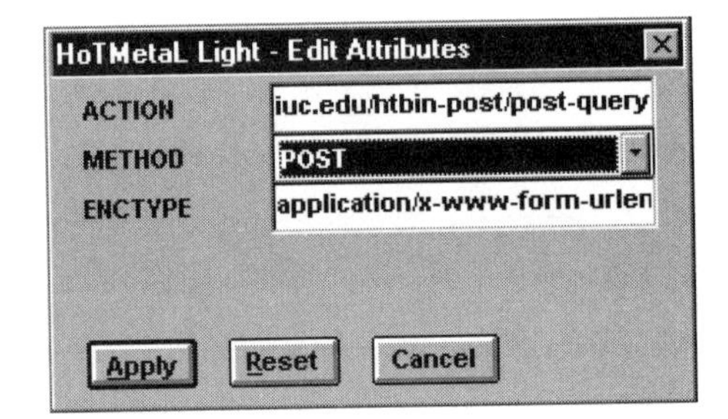

▶ The **FORM** attributes are updated.

FORM [http://hoohoo.ncsa.uiuc.edu/htbin-post/post-query] /FORM /BODY /HTML

6 Type the following, inserting a line break after each entry except the last: **Interests:**, **reading, watching TV**, **skydiving, Sex:**, **male**, **female, Age:**, **under 30**, and **30 and over**.

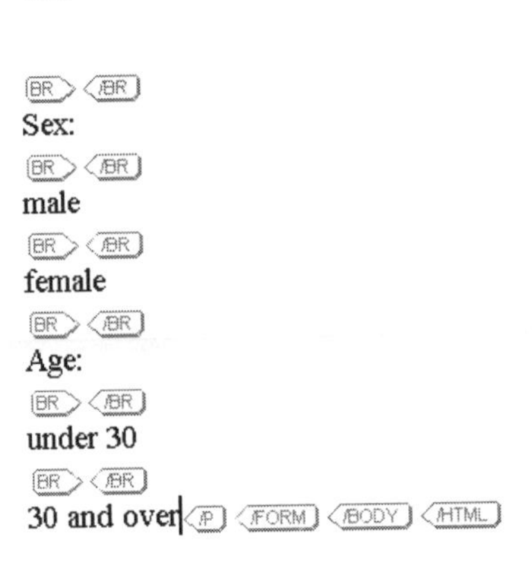

7 Move the cursor immediately before **reading**.

P Interests:
BR /BR
reading

8 Insert a set of **INPUT** tags by clicking on the **Form elements** button and selecting **INPUT**.

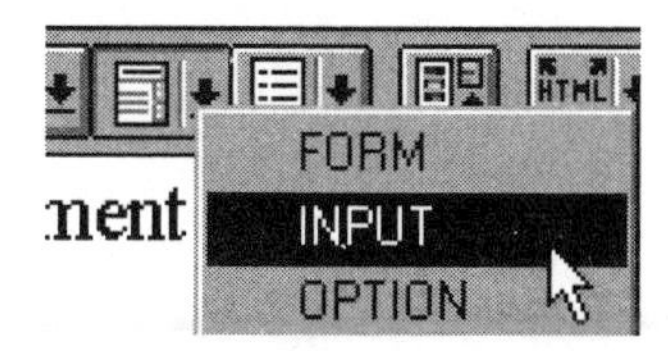

9 Press **F6** to bring up the Edit Attributes dialog box.

10 Select **CHECKBOX** in the TYPE field, type **reading** in the NAME field, select **CHECKED** in the CHECKED field, and click on the **Apply** button.

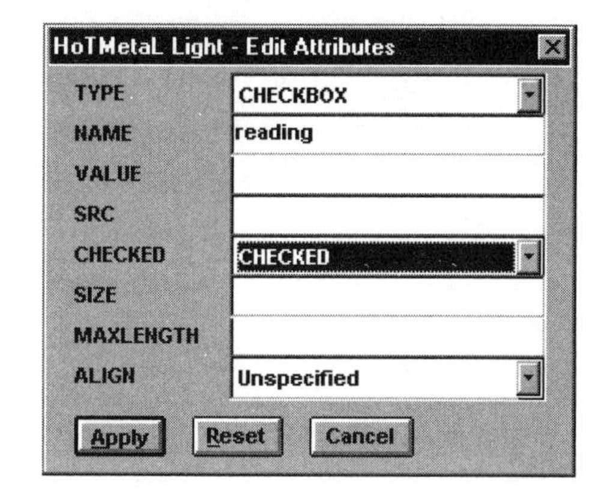

▶ The attributes of the **INPUT** tag are updated.

P Interests:
BR /BR
INPUT [NAME = reading & TYPE = CHECKBOX & VALUE =
] /INPUT reading
BR /BR
watching TV

11 Move the cursor immediately before **watching TV** and insert an **INPUT** tag into your document.

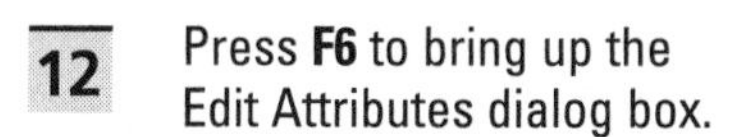

12 Press **F6** to bring up the Edit Attributes dialog box.

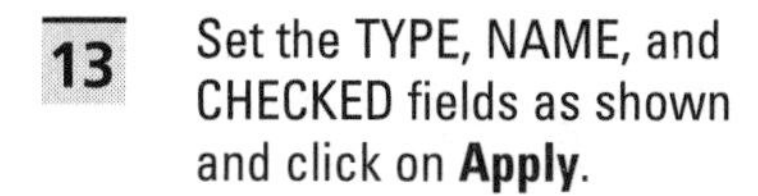

13 Set the TYPE, NAME, and CHECKED fields as shown and click on **Apply**.

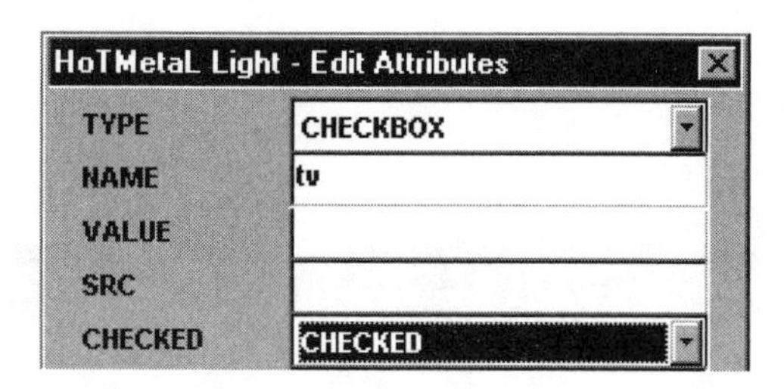

14 Move the cursor immediately before **skydiving** and insert an **INPUT** tag into your document.

15 Press **F6** to bring up the Edit Attributes dialog box.

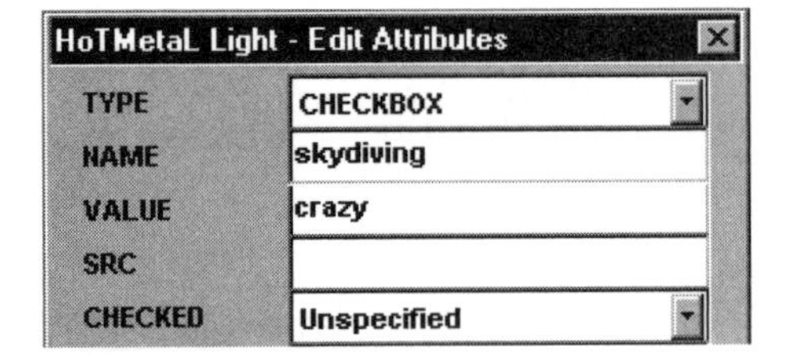

16 Set the TYPE, NAME, and VALUE fields as shown and click on **Apply**.

▶ All three check box tags are in place in your document.

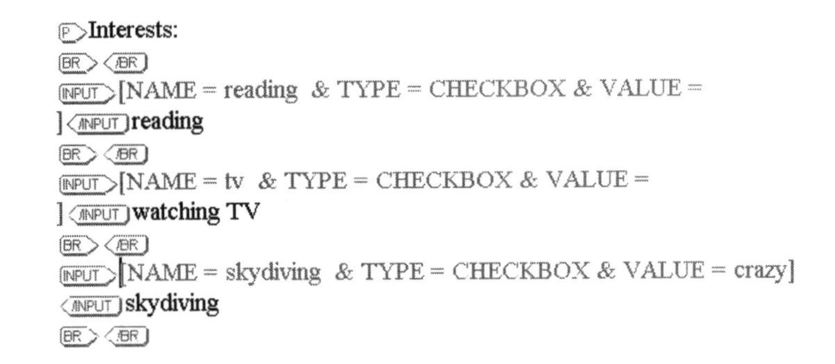

Interests:
[NAME = reading & TYPE = CHECKBOX & VALUE =
]reading
[NAME = tv & TYPE = CHECKBOX & VALUE =
]watching TV
[NAME = skydiving & TYPE = CHECKBOX & VALUE = crazy]
skydiving

Let's move on to the radio buttons.

1 Move the cursor immediately before **male** and insert an **INPUT** tag into your document.

2 Press **F6** to bring up the Edit Attributes dialog box.

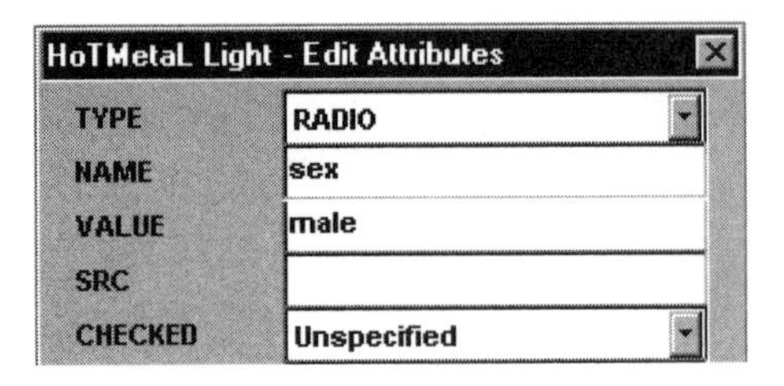

3 Select **RADIO** in the TYPE field, type **sex** in the NAME field, type **male** in the VALUE field, and click on **Apply**.

4 Move the cursor immediately before **female** and insert an **INPUT** tag into your document.

5 Repeat steps 2 and 3, except type **female** in the VALUE field.

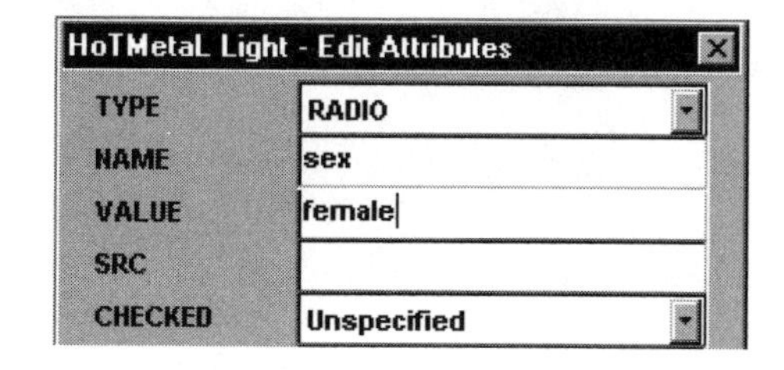

▶ Two radio button tags are in place in your document.

Sex:

</BR>
<INPUT>[NAME = sex & TYPE = RADIO & VALUE = male]</INPUT>**male**

</BR>
<INPUT>[NAME = sex & TYPE = RADIO & VALUE = female]</INPUT>**female**

</BR>

6 Using steps 1–3 above as a guide, insert radio buttons before the **under 30** and **30 and over** options, giving them the group name **age**. Give the first option a value of **under** and the second option a value of **notUnder**.

Age:

</BR>
<INPUT>[NAME = age & TYPE = RADIO & VALUE = under]</INPUT>**under 30**

</BR>
<INPUT>[NAME = age & TYPE = RADIO & VALUE = notUnder]</INPUT>**30 and over**</P></FORM></BODY></HTML>

7 Move the cursor immediately before the **/FORM** tag and insert a Submit button.

<INPUT>[TYPE = SUBMIT]</INPUT></FORM></BODY></HTML>

8 Save your file as c:\html\ch08-02.htm.

9 View it with your browser.

10 Click on the check boxes and radio buttons to fill in the form.

11 Click on the **Submit Query** button to submit your form to the post-query program.

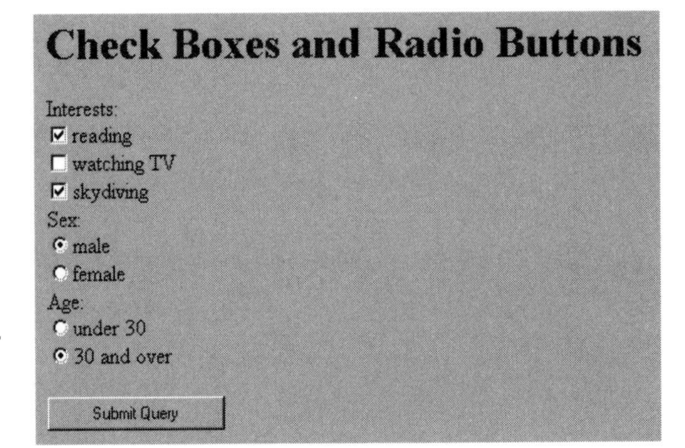

▶ The post-query program returns the field names and their corresponding values.

12 Close your browser and the current HoTMetaL document.

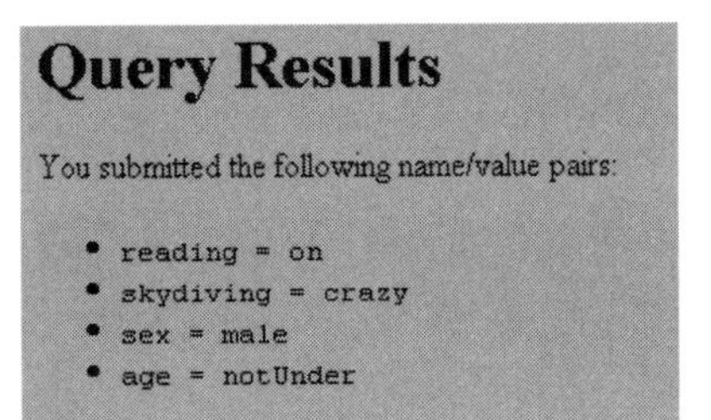

Adding Menus and Selection Lists

The **SELECT** tag supports three types of form elements: option menus, single selection lists, and multiple selection lists. *Option menus,* the most compact of the **SELECT** tags, are pull-down menus that allow the user to select a single option. *Single selection lists* also allow the user to select a single option, but they occupy more space than option menus and provide a scrollable window for the values that may be selected. *Multiple selection lists* are like single selection lists, except that the user can select more than one option from the list. To select multiple options, the user holds down the Ctrl key while clicking on items in the list.

The **SELECT** tag is a surrounding tag. It surrounds a group of option tags, as follows:

```
<SELECT>
  <OPTION>option</OPTION>
  <OPTION>option</OPTION>
  <OPTION>option</OPTION>
</SELECT>
```

The **OPTION** tags are used to list the items in the option menu or selection list.

The **SELECT** tag has three attributes: **NAME**, **SIZE**, and **MULTIPLE**. The **NAME** attribute is used in a similar manner as in the **INPUT** tag—it tells the CGI program what form element to associate with a particular value. The **SIZE** attribute is used to specify the physical size of the option menu or selection list. If the **SIZE** attribute is not specified or is set to **1**, then the **SELECT** tag is an option menu; otherwise it is a selection list. The **MULTIPLE** attribute forces a **SELECT** tag to be rendered as a multiple selection list even if the **SIZE** attribute is **1**. It does not take a value.

The **OPTION** tag also has two attributes: **SELECTED** and **VALUE**. The **SELECTED** attribute specifies that an option is selected by default. It does not take a value. Unless specified, the value of an option is the same as its text. To change this, you must give the option a different value using the **VALUE** attribute.

The following example shows how to use HoTMetaL to insert option menus and selection lists into your forms.

1. Open a new HoTMetaL document, create a level 1 heading, and type **Menus and Selection Lists** as the title and heading.

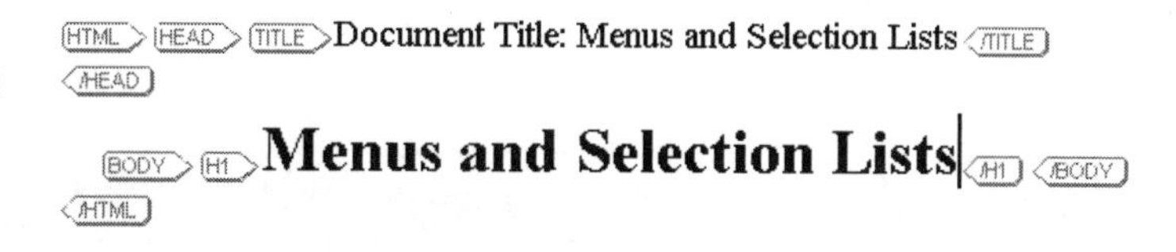

2. Move the cursor between the **/H1** and **/BODY** tags and insert a set of **FORM** tags.

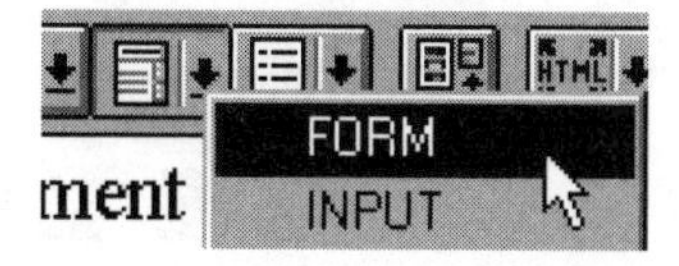

3 Press **F6** to bring up the Edit Attributes dialog box.

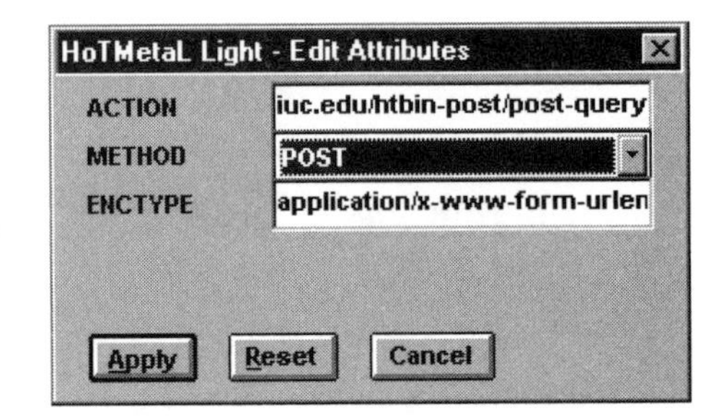

4 Type **http://hoohoo.ncsa.uiuc.edu/htbin-post/post-query** in the ACTION field, select **POST** in the METHOD field, and click on the **Apply** button.

▶ The **FORM** attributes are updated.

<FORM>[http://hoohoo.ncsa.uiuc.edu/htbin-post/post-query] </FORM> </BODY> </HTML>

5 Type **Hardware:** followed by a space and press ↵.

6 Type **Operating System:** followed by a space and press ↵.

<FORM>[http://hoohoo.ncsa.uiuc.edu/htbin-post/post-query]
<P>Hardware: </P>
<P>Operating System: </P>
<P>Multimedia: </P>
<P></P> </FORM> </BODY> </HTML>

7 Type **Multimedia:** followed by a space and press ↵.

8 Move the cursor immediately before the first **/P** tag.

9 Click on the **Form elements** button and select **SELECT**.

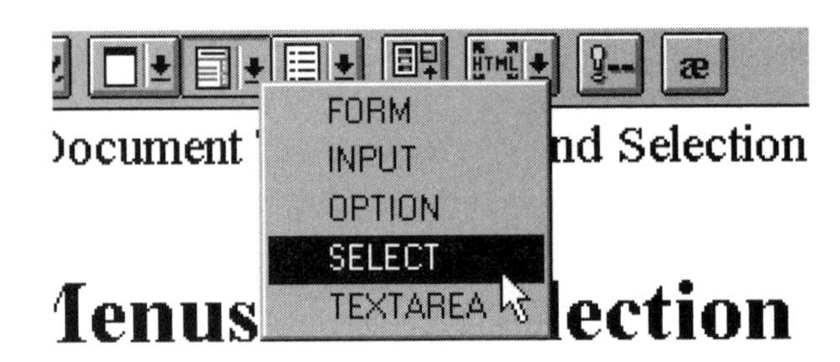

▶ **SELECT** tags are inserted into your document, along with an initial set of **OPTION** tags.

10 Type **386** and press ↵.

```
<FORM>[http://hoohoo.ncsa.uiuc.edu/htbin-post/post-query]
<P>Hardware: <SELECT>[NAME =  & SIZE = ]
   <OPTION>[VALUE = ]386</OPTION>
   <OPTION>[VALUE = ]486</OPTION>
   <OPTION>[VALUE = ]Pentium</OPTION>
   <OPTION>[VALUE = ]Other</OPTION></SELECT></P>
```

▶ As you press ↵, a new set of **OPTION** tags is inserted in your text.

11 Type **486** and press ↵.

12 Type **Pentium** and press ↵.

13 Type **Other**.

14 Click the cursor anywhere between the **SELECT** tag and the first **OPTION** tag, and press **F6** to bring up the Edit Attributes dialog box.

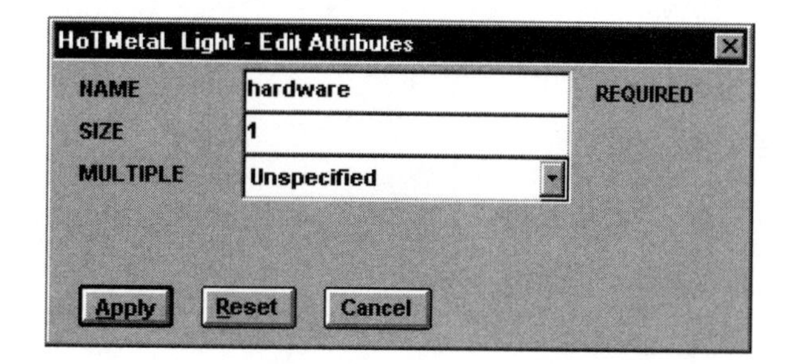

15 Type **hardware** in the NAME field and **1** in the SIZE field.

16 Click on the **Apply** button.

▶ The attributes of the **SELECT** tag are updated.

```
<P>Hardware: <SELECT>[NAME = hardware & SIZE = 1]
```

You've created an option menu; now let's add a single selection list.

1 Move the cursor immediately before the second **/P** tag and insert a set of **SELECT** tags.

2 Type the following, pressing ↵ after each entry except the last: **Windows 3.1**, **Windows 95**, **Windows NT**, and **Other**.

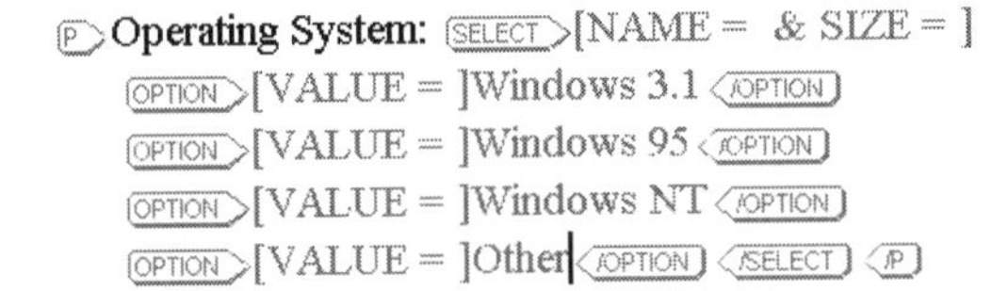

3 Click the cursor after the **SELECT** tag and before the first **OPTION** tag, and press **F6** to bring up the Edit Attributes dialog box.

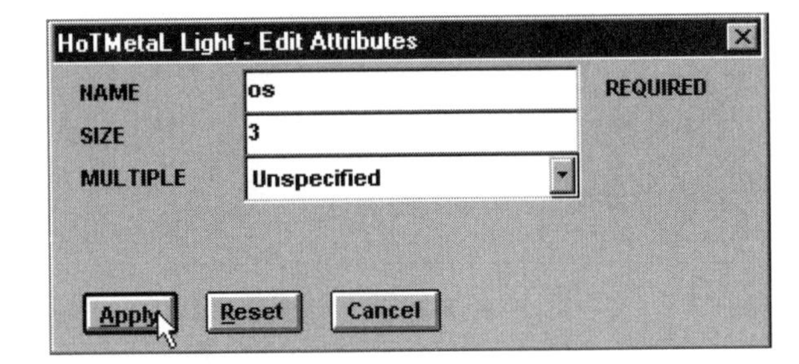

4 Type **os** in the NAME field and **3** in the SIZE field.

5 Click on the **Apply** button.

▶ The attributes of the **SELECT** tag are updated.

P Operating System: SELECT [NAME = os & SIZE = 3]

There's your single selection list. Now for the multiple selection list.

1 Move the cursor immediately before the last **/P** tag and insert a set of **SELECT** tags.

2 Type **Sound Card** and press ↵.

P Multimedia: SELECT [NAME = & SIZE =]
OPTION [VALUE =]Sound Card /OPTION
OPTION [VALUE =]CD-ROM /OPTION /SELECT /P

3 Type **CD-ROM**.

4 Click the cursor after the **SELECT** tag and before any **OPTION** tags, and press **F6** to bring up the Edit Attributes dialog box.

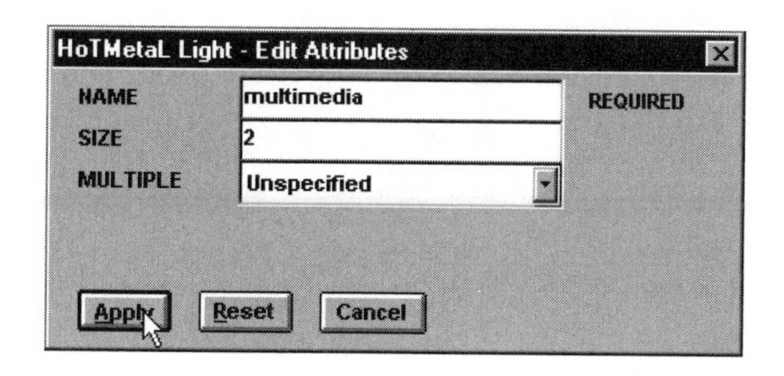

5 Type **multimedia** in the NAME field and **2** in the SIZE field.

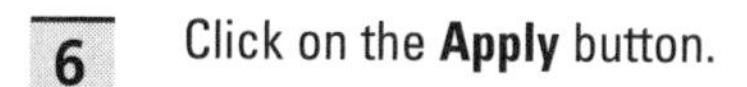

6 Click on the **Apply** button.

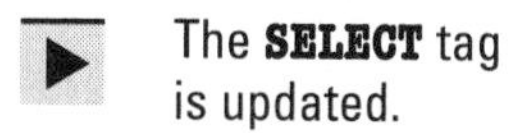

► The **SELECT** tag is updated.

P Multimedia: SELECT [NAME = multimedia & SIZE = 2]

7 Move the cursor immediately before the **/FORM** tag and insert a Submit button.

P Multimedia: SELECT [NAME = multimedia & SIZE = 2]
OPTION [VALUE =]Sound Card /OPTION
OPTION [VALUE =]CD-ROM /OPTION /SELECT /P
P INPUT [TYPE = SUBMIT] /INPUT /P /FORM /BODY /HTML

8 Save your file as c:\html\ch08-03.htm.

9 View it with your browser.

10 Make your selections in the form and click on the **Submit Query** button to submit your form to the post-query program.

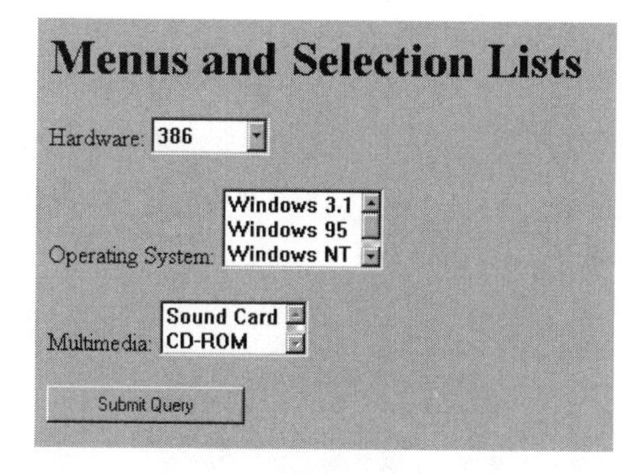

▶ The post-query program returns the field names and their corresponding values.

Query Results

You submitted the following name/value pairs:

- hardware = 486
- os = Windows 95
- multimedia = Sound Card
- multimedia = CD-ROM

11 Close your browser and the current HoTMetaL document.

Adding Text Area Fields

Sometimes you'll want to let users of your Web pages enter more than one line of text in a form field. For example, suppose you want to solicit comments and suggestions about your Web pages. It would be limiting to offer only a one-line text field. The **TEXTAREA** tag lets you insert multiline text fields in your Web pages. It is a surrounding tag and is used as follows:

<TEXTAREA>default text to be inserted in the field</TEXTAREA>

All text between the opening and closing tags is displayed as default data in the text field.

The **TEXTAREA** tag has three attributes: **NAME**, **ROWS**, and **COLS**. The **NAME** attribute identifies the field to the CGI program. The **ROWS** and **COLS** attributes specify the physical dimensions of the text field. Scroll bars are provided to move past the physical boundaries of the field.

1 Open a new HoTMetaL document, create a level 1 heading, and type **Text Area Fields** as the title and heading.

HTML HEAD TITLE Document Title: Text Area Fields /TITLE /HEAD

BODY H1 **Text Area Fields** /H1 /BODY /HTML

2 Move the cursor between the **/H1** and **/BODY** tags and insert **FORM** tags.

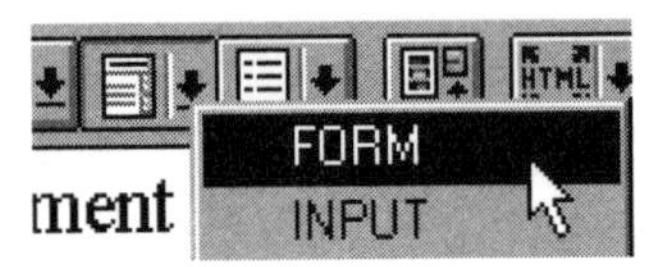

3 Press **F6** to bring up the Edit Attributes dialog box.

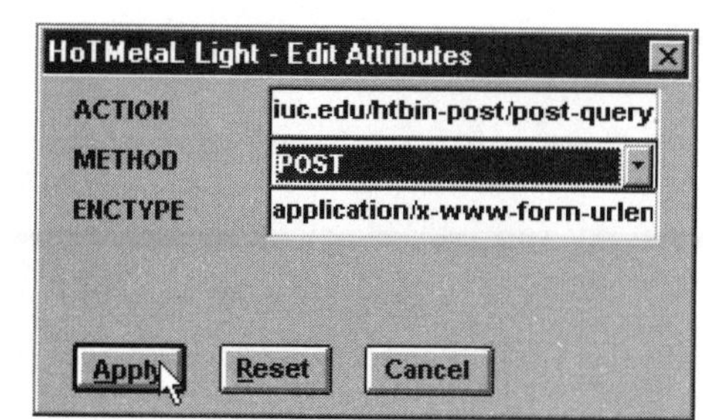

4 Type **http://hoohoo.ncsa.uiuc.edu/htbin-post/post-query** in the ACTION field, select **POST** in the METHOD field, and click on **Apply**.

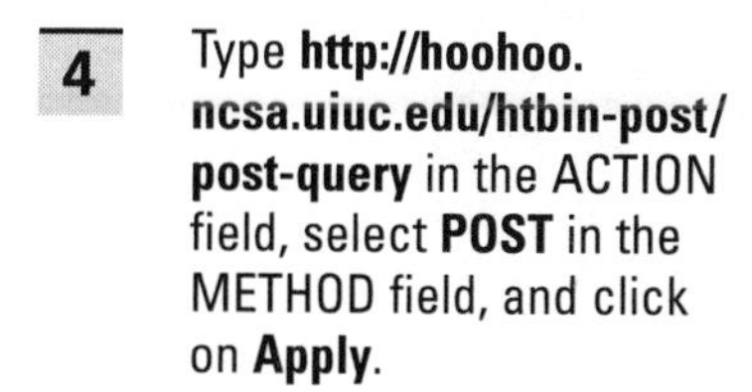

▶ The **FORM** attributes are updated.

<FORM>[http://hoohoo.ncsa.uiuc.edu/htbin-post/post-query] </FORM> </BODY> </HTML>

5 Type **Tell me a story:** and press ↵.

<FORM>[http://hoohoo.ncsa.uiuc.edu/htbin-post/post-query]

<P>Tell me a story: </P>

<P></P> </FORM> </BODY> </HTML>

6 Click on the **Form elements** button and select **TEXTAREA**.

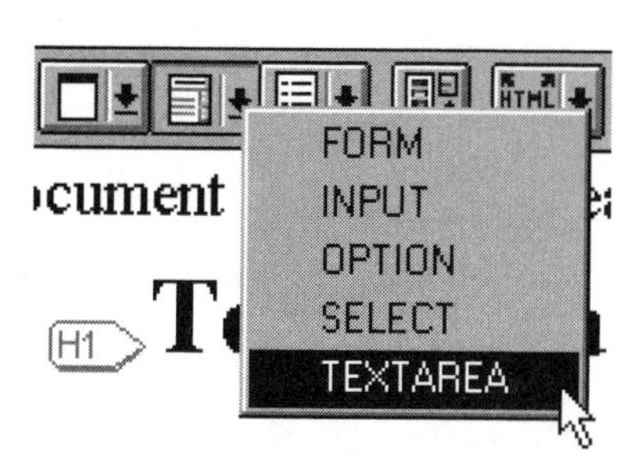

▶ **TEXTAREA** tags are inserted into your document.

<FORM>[http://hoohoo.ncsa.uiuc.edu/htbin-post/post-query]

<P>Tell me a story: </P>

<P> <TEXTAREA>[NAME = & ROWS = & COLS =]</TEXTAREA> </P> </FORM> </BODY> </HTML>

7 Press **F6** to bring up the Edit Attributes dialog box.

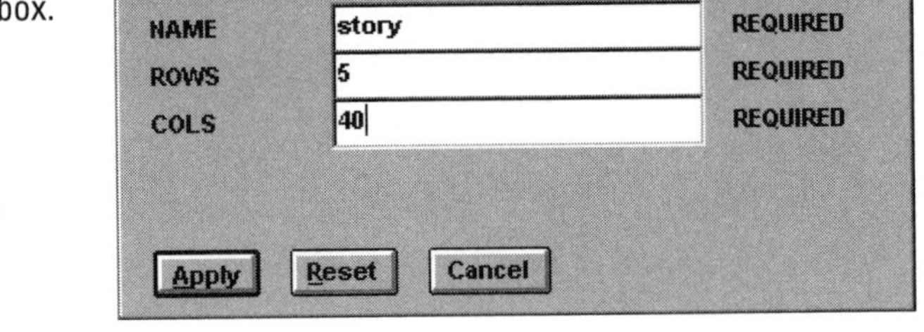

8 Type **story** in the NAME field, **5** in the ROWS field, and **40** in the COLS field.

9 Click on the **Apply** button.

▶ The attributes of the **TEXTAREA** tag are updated.

10 Type **Once upon a time,**.

<P> <TEXTAREA>[NAME = story & ROWS = 5 & COLS = 40]Once upon a time, </TEXTAREA> </P> </FORM> </BODY> </HTML>

11 Move the cursor immediately before the **/FORM** tag and insert a Submit button.

<P> <TEXTAREA>[NAME = story & ROWS = 5 & COLS = 40]Once upon a time, </TEXTAREA> </P>
<INPUT>[TYPE = SUBMIT] </INPUT> </FORM> </BODY> </HTML>

12 Save your file as c:\html\ch08-04.htm.

13 View it using your browser.

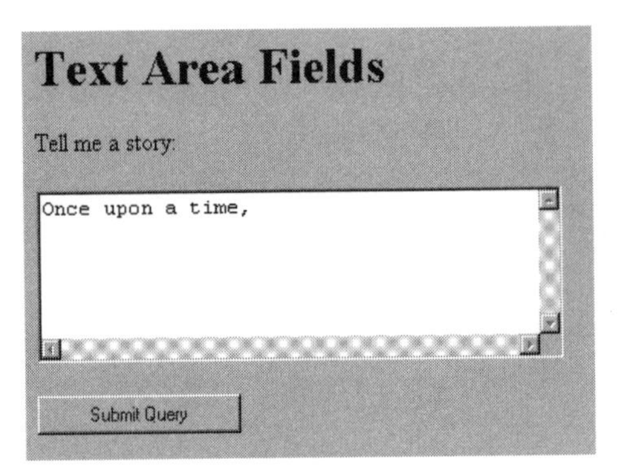

14 Fill in the text area field and click on the **Submit Query** button to submit your form to the post-query program.

▶ The post-query program returns the data that you typed in.

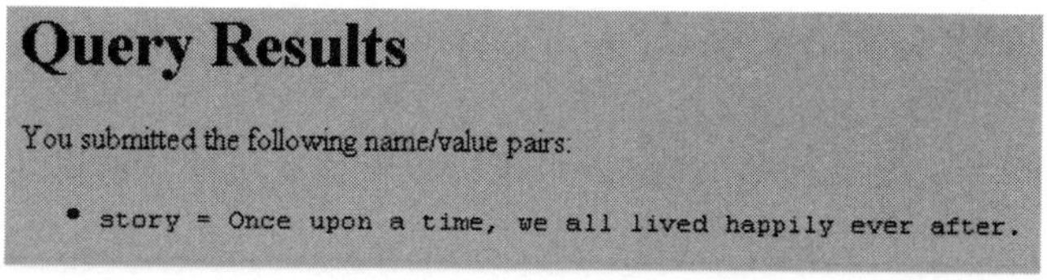

Query Results

You submitted the following name/value pairs:

- story = Once upon a time, we all lived happily ever after.

15 Close your browser and HoTMetaL.

In this lesson, you learned how to use forms in your Web documents. Forms provide you with the ability to collect information from Web users. In the next lesson, you will learn how form data is processed by CGI programs. You'll also learn how to work with clickable images.

9

Working with CGI Programs

In the previous lesson, you learned how to create forms using HoTMetaL. You used a predefined CGI program to process your form data. In this lesson, you will learn more about CGI programs. You will be given a short introduction to the CGI and shown how to use CGI programs to process form data and implement custom links. You will also learn to use clickable image maps.

The examples in this lesson don't require you to do any programming. If you want to create your own CGI programs, see the file \extra\morecgi.htm on the CD that came with this book for more advanced CGI information and programming techniques.

Understanding the CGI

The Common Gateway Interface is a standard for interfacing external programs with Web servers. These external programs are used to implement custom links, process form data, and provide a way to access other services, such as database and financial applications.

CGI programs are executed in response to user actions, such as clicking on a link or submitting a form. The **HREF** attribute of the link the user clicks on or the **ACTION** attribute of the form the user submits specifies the URL address of the CGI program. Data, such as that entered on a form, is passed from the browser to the CGI program via the Web server at the address specified in the URL. The CGI program performs its processing and returns data to the browser by way of the Web server. The CGI specifies how data is to be passed from the server to the CGI program and back again. The illustration on the next page outlines this process.

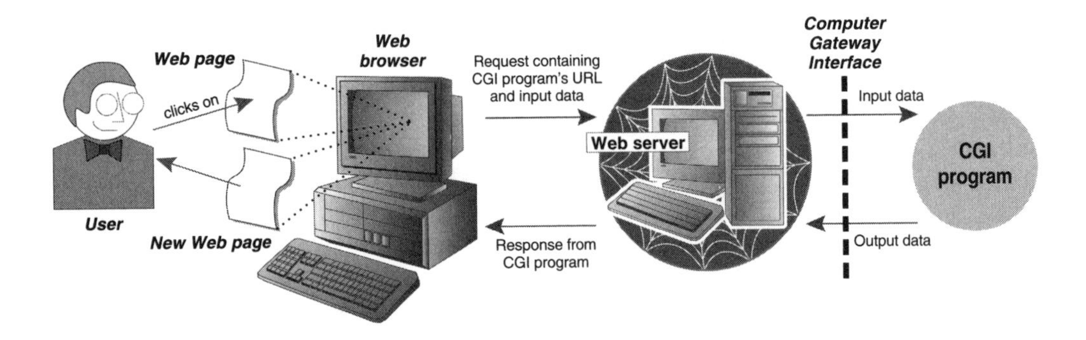

CGI programs are usually kept in a special directory on the Web server. This is done for two reasons: to ensure that the Web server will know when a URL points to a CGI program, as opposed to a Web page or other document, and to enforce security controls on what programs may be executed as CGI programs. Typical directory names are /cgi-bin or /htbin. When a browser requests a URL containing this directory in its path, the Web server executes the CGI program pointed to by the URL.

▶ ▶ ▶ CGI programs are also referred to as *scripts* when they are written in a scripting language, such as that provided by most operating system shells.

Linking to CGI Programs

The simplest way to integrate a CGI program with a Web page is to make it the destination of a link. You do this by putting a source anchor in your Web page and setting the **HREF** attribute to the URL of the CGI program. For example, the following anchor can be used to retrieve the date and time via the datetime CGI program:

```
<A HREF="http://www.jaworski.com/cgi-bin/datetime">current date
and time</A>
```

The datetime program does not read any input data—its sole function is to return the date and time. The following example illustrates the use of the datetime program.

1 Launch HoTMetaL, open a new document, create a level 1 heading, and type **Get Date and Time** for the title and heading.

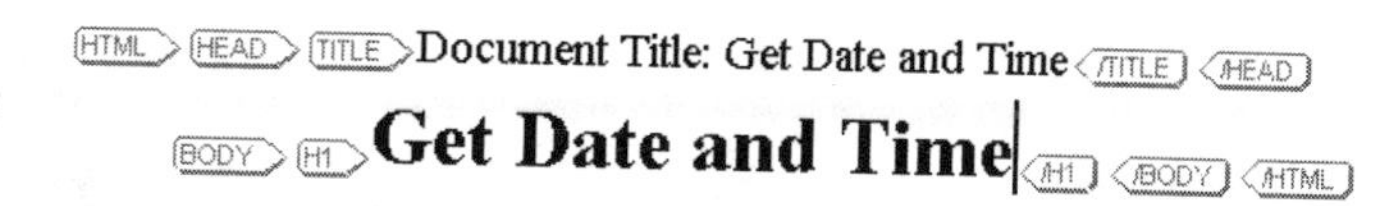

2 Move the cursor between the **/H1** and **/BODY** tags and click on the **Anchor** toolbar button.

▶ The Edit URL dialog box appears.

3 Select **http** in the Scheme field, type **www.jaworski.com** in the Host field, type **/cgi-bin/datetime** in the Path field, and click on **OK**.

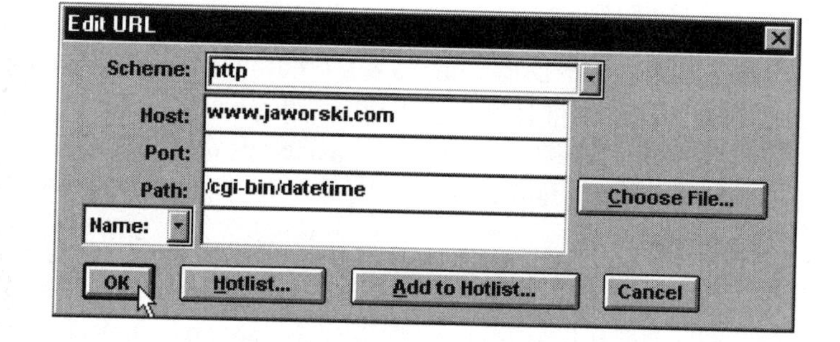

▶ Anchor tags are inserted into your document.

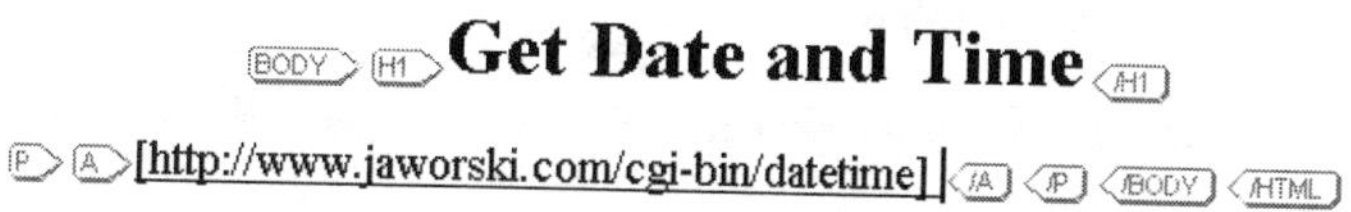

4 Type **Click here for the date and time in San Diego.**

5 Save your document as c:\html\ch09-01.htm.

6 View it with your browser.

Get Date and Time

Click here for the date and time in San Diego.

7 Click on the link to activate the CGI program.

▶ The datetime program returns San Diego's current date and time.

Current Date and Time in San Diego

Mon Jan 15 01:33:44 PST 1996

8 Close your browser and the current HoTMetaL document.

Adding Data to URLs

The datetime program shows how a CGI program generates output, but it doesn't process any user input. In order to send data to a CGI program using a source anchor, the data must be included in the URL. There are two ways that data may be included in a URL: a query string and extra path information.

A *query string* appends program data to the URL of the CGI program. It consists of a **?** followed by the data. The Web server removes the appended data and passes it to the CGI program using the **QUERY_STRING** environment variable. For example, the following URL results in the text *this+is+a+test* being passed to the echo-query program via the **QUERY_STRING** variable:

http://www.jaworski.com/cgi-bin/echo-query?this+is+a+test

Spaces are encoded with plus (+) signs when they appear in a query string. Other codings are used to pass special characters and binary data as discussed in the file \support\coding.htm on this book's CD.

Extra path information is data that is added to the URL as additional path information following the CGI program. Extra path information is passed to the CGI program using the **PATH_INFO** environment variable. For example, in the following URL, the path **/extra/path/info** following **echo-query** would be passed to the echo-query program via the **PATH_INFO** environment variable as **/extra/path/info**:

http://www.jaworski.com/cgi-bin/echo-query/extra/path/info

In the following example you'll develop a Web page that provides a link to the echo-query program using a URL that contains a query string and extra path information. The URL points to the echo-query program on my Web server. This program returns the values of any command line arguments, environment variables, and standard input that is passed to it. (See the file \extra\morecgi.htm on the CD for more information about these terms.) It is a very handy program for testing URLs.

1 Open a new HoTMetaL document, create a level 1 heading, and type **Query Test** for the title and heading.

2 Move the cursor between the **/H1** and **/BODY** tags and click on the **Anchor** button.

▶ The Edit URL dialog box appears.

3 Select **http** in the Scheme field, type **www.jaworski.com** in the Host field, and type **/cgi-bin/echo-query/extra/path** in the Path field.

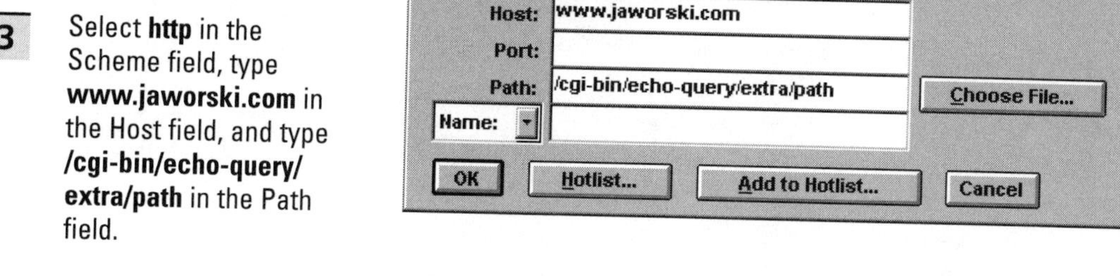

4 Select the **Query** field from the pull-down menu and type **p1=this&p2=that** as its value.

5 Click on **OK**.

▶ Anchor tags are inserted in your document.

P A [http://www.jaworski.com/cgi-bin/echo-query/extra/path?p1=this&p2=that] /A /P /BODY /HTML

6 Type **Click here to run echo-query.**

P A [http://www.jaworski.com/cgi-bin/echo-query/extra/path?p1=this&p2=that] Click here to run echo-query. /A /P /BODY /HTML

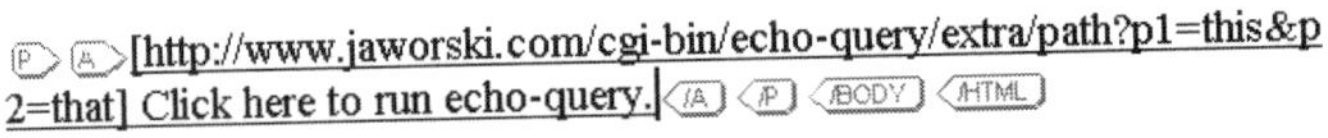

7 Save your document as c:\html\ch09-02.htm.

8 View it with your Web browser.

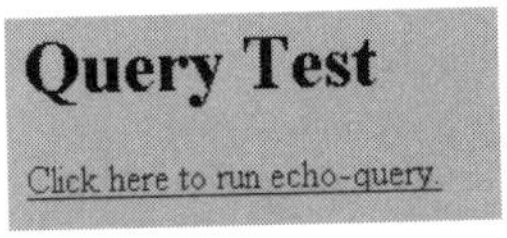

Query Test

Click here to run echo-query.

9 Click on the link to activate the CGI program.

▶ The echo-query program returns the data it received. Notice that the extra path information and query string are reported by the **PATH_INFO** and **QUERY_STRING** environment variables.

CGI Request

Command Line Arguments

Number of command line arguments: 0

Command line arguments:

Environment Variables

```
AUTH_TYPE =
CONTENT_LENGTH =
CONTENT_TYPE =
GATEWAY_INTERFACE = CGI/1.1
HTTP_ACCEPT = image/gif, image/x-xbitmap, image/jpeg, image/pjpeg, */*
HTTP_USER_AGENT = Mozilla/2.0b5 (Win95; I)
PATH_INFO = /extra/path
PATH_TRANSLATED = /usr/local/etc/httpd/htdocs/extra/path
QUERY_STRING = p1=this&p2=that
```

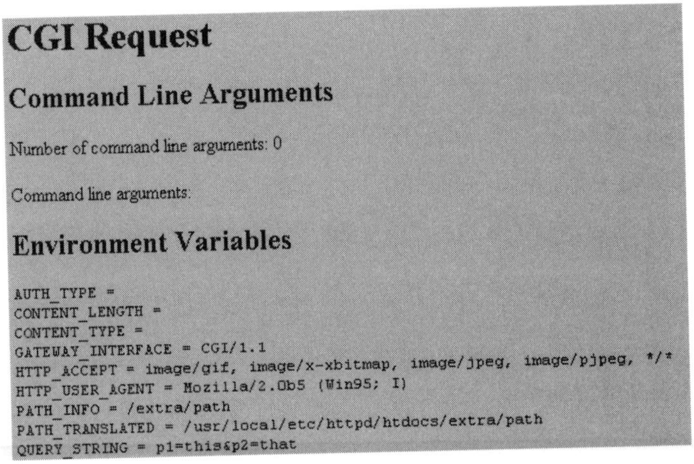

10 Close your browser and the current HoTMetaL document.

Using ISINDEX to Request Input from Users

So far, the CGI programs that you've looked at haven't provided a way for Web users to enter data. They just passed along whatever data was added to the CGI program's URL. The **ISINDEX** tag allows the CGI program to query Web users for additional data. It works like this:

You create a source anchor to a CGI program, as in the previous examples. The user clicks on the link, which executes the CGI program. The CGI program checks for any user input in its URL. Finding none, it returns a Web page containing the **ISINDEX** tag in the page's **HEAD**. The user's browser processes the **ISINDEX** tag by displaying a text entry field. The user enters data into the field and submits the field to the CGI program. The second time the CGI program is executed, it checks for data input, finds it, processes it, and returns status information to the user.

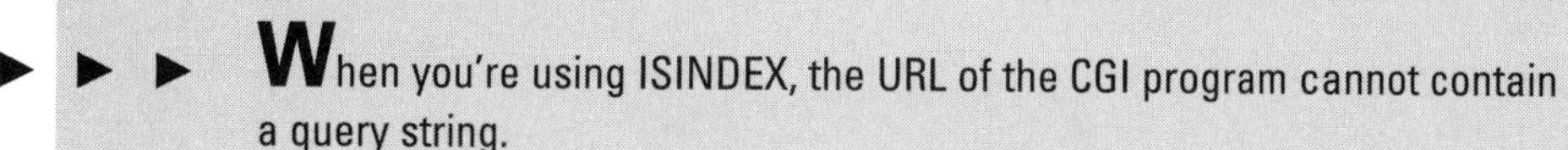

When you're using ISINDEX, the URL of the CGI program cannot contain a query string.

Let's test it out.

1 Open a new document, create a level 1 heading, and type **ISINDEX Test** for the title and heading.

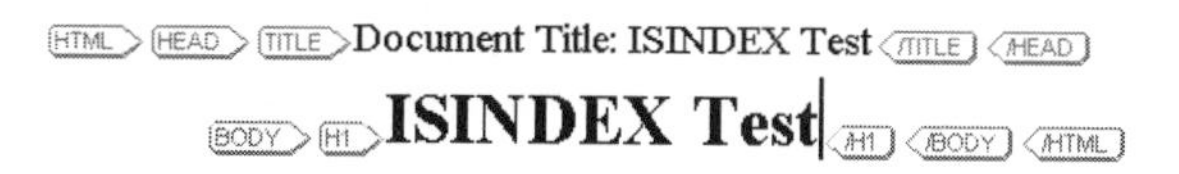

2 Move the cursor between the **/H1** and **/BODY** tags and click on the **Anchor** button.

► The Edit URL dialog box appears.

3 Select **http** in the Scheme field, type **www.jaworski.com** in the Host field, type **/cgi-bin/isindex-test** in the Path field, and click on **OK**.

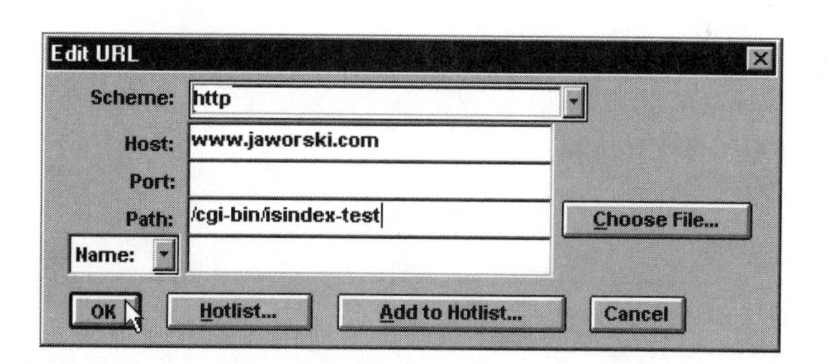

► Anchor tags appear in the document.

BODY H1 **ISINDEX Test** /H1

P A [http://www.jaworski.com/cgi-bin/isindex-test] /A /P /BODY
/HTML

4 Type **Click here to start the ISINDEX test.**

<P><A>[http://www.jaworski.com/cgi-bin/isindex-test] Click here to start the ISINDEX test.</A></P></BODY></HTML>

5 Save your document as c:\html\ch09-03.htm.

6 View it with your browser.

ISINDEX Test

Click here to start the ISINDEX test.

7 Click on the link to activate the CGI program.

► The ISINDEX form appears.

This is a searchable index. Enter search keywords:

Just enter some text.

8 Type some text and press ↵.

This is a searchable index. Enter search keywords: some text

► The CGI program displays the data you typed.

The text you entered is: *some text*

9 Close your browser and the current HoTMetaL document.

► ► ► The **ISINDEX** tag has one attribute, **PROMPT**, that you can set to change the default prompt displayed with the text entry field. This attribute is a Netscape extension.

Processing Forms

The **ISINDEX** tag provides a quick and easy way to implement user queries. However, its capabilities are far surpassed by forms. Forms provide much more attractive user interface controls and allow much more information to be passed to CGI programs.

Form data may be submitted to a browser using either the **GET** or **POST** method. As mentioned in Lesson 8, the **POST** method is preferred to the **GET** method. The primary reason for this lies in the way that data is passed to the CGI program. The **GET** method encodes the form data as a query string that is appended to the URL of the CGI program. The data is then passed to the program via the **QUERY_STRING** variable. The disadvantage of this is that the amount of data that can be stored in an environment variable is limited; any data over the limit is lost. The **POST** method does not have this shortcoming. Since it provides data to the CGI program via standard input, the amount of form data that can be processed does not have any practical limit.

The following example uses the echo-query program to illustrate how form data is provided to CGI programs using the **POST** method.

1. Open a new document, create a level 1 heading, and type **The POST Method** as the title and heading.

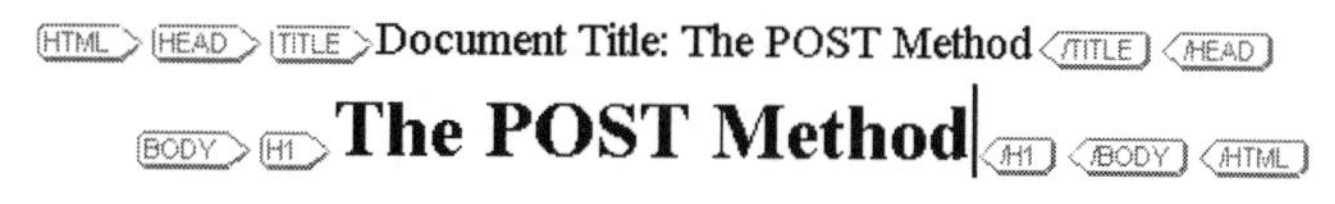

2. Move the cursor between the **/H1** and **/BODY** tags.

3. Click on the **Form elements** button and select **FORM** to insert **FORM** tags.

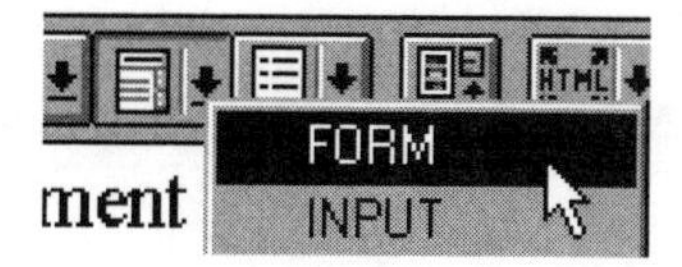

4 Press **F6** to bring up the Edit Attributes dialog box.

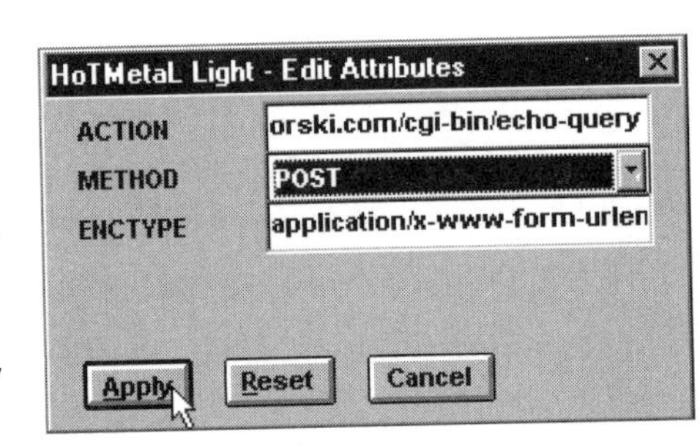

5 Type **http://www.jaworski.com/cgi-bin/echo-query** in the ACTION field, select **POST** in the METHOD field, and click on the **Apply** button.

▶ The attributes of the **FORM** tag are updated.

FORM [http://www.jaworski.com/cgi-bin/echo-query] /FORM /BODY /HTML

6 Click on the **Form elements** button and select **INPUT**.

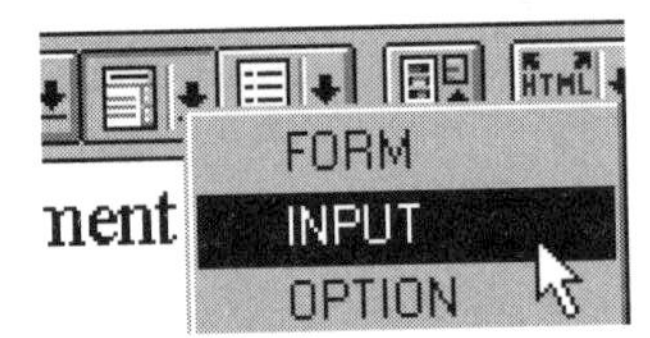

7 Press **F6** to bring up the Edit Attributes dialog box.

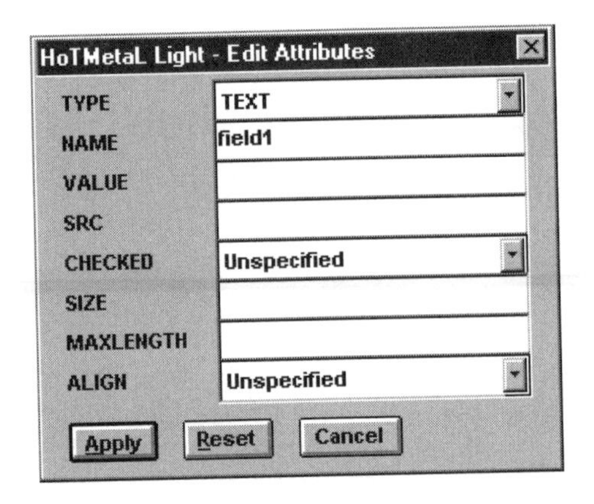

8 Type **field1** in the NAME field and click on **Apply**.

▶ The attributes of the **INPUT** tag are updated.

FORM [http://www.jaworski.com/cgi-bin/echo-query] INPUT [NAME = field1 & TYPE = TEXT] /INPUT /FORM /BODY /HTML

9 Move the cursor between the **/INPUT** and **/FORM** tags and click on the **Paragraph** button to insert a new paragraph.

10 Follow steps 6 through 8 to insert another input field. This time, type **field2** in the NAME field.

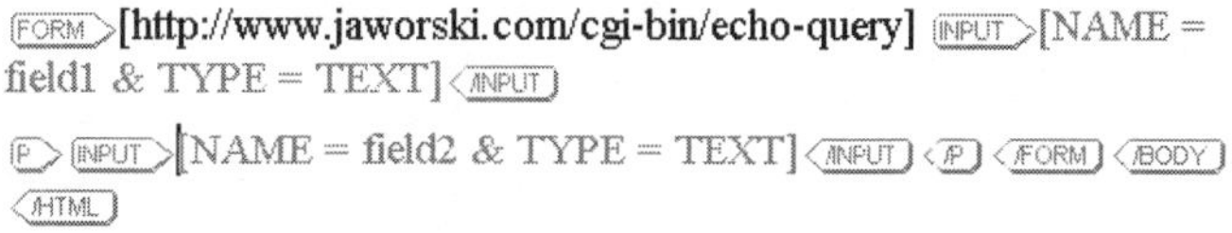

```
<FORM>[http://www.jaworski.com/cgi-bin/echo-query] <INPUT>[NAME = field1 & TYPE = TEXT]</INPUT>
<P><INPUT>[NAME = field2 & TYPE = TEXT]</INPUT></P></FORM></BODY></HTML>
```

11 Move the cursor between the **/P** and **/FORM** tags and insert a new paragraph.

12 Insert a Submit button. (See "Adding Submit and Reset Buttons" in Lesson 8 if you've forgotten how.)

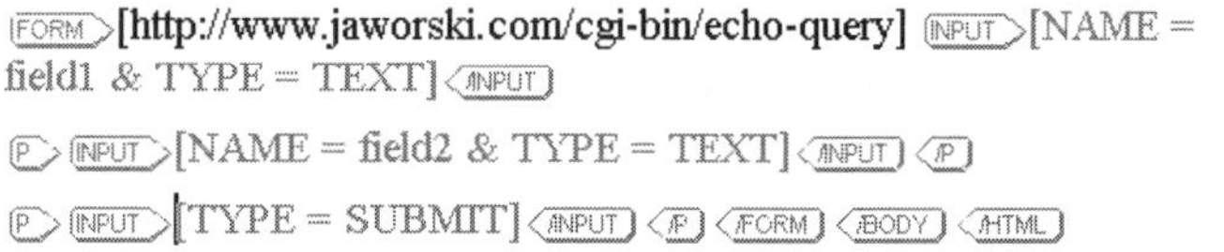

```
<FORM>[http://www.jaworski.com/cgi-bin/echo-query] <INPUT>[NAME = field1 & TYPE = TEXT]</INPUT>
<P><INPUT>[NAME = field2 & TYPE = TEXT]</INPUT></P>
<P><INPUT>[TYPE = SUBMIT]</INPUT></P></FORM></BODY></HTML>
```

13 Save your file as c\html\ch09-04.htm.

14 View it with your Web browser.

15 Enter data into the text fields as shown here and click on the **Submit Query** button.

```
The POST Method

[abcd]

[xyz]

[Submit Query]
```

▶ The echo-query program returns the data it received. Notice that the data was received through the standard input stream rather than as an environment variable. (You may have to scroll down to see the standard input data.)

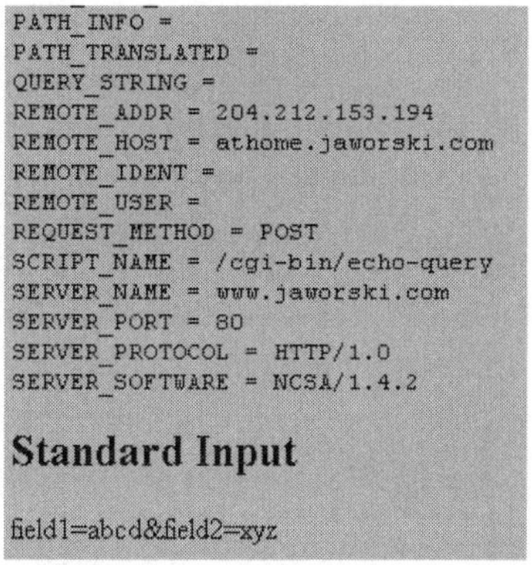

```
PATH_INFO =
PATH_TRANSLATED =
QUERY_STRING =
REMOTE_ADDR = 204.212.153.194
REMOTE_HOST = athome.jaworski.com
REMOTE_IDENT =
REMOTE_USER =
REQUEST_METHOD = POST
SCRIPT_NAME = /cgi-bin/echo-query
SERVER_NAME = www.jaworski.com
SERVER_PORT = 80
SERVER_PROTOCOL = HTTP/1.0
SERVER_SOFTWARE = NCSA/1.4.2

Standard Input

field1=abcd&field2=xyz
```

16 Close your browser and the current HoTMetaL document.

Form data is encoded before it is passed to the CGI program. The fields of the form are described using a series of *field=value* pairs joined by ampersands (&). This coding scheme is described in \support\coding.htm on the CD.

Using Hidden Fields in Forms

The forms that you've developed so far are said to be *stateless* because their processing does not depend in any way on data that was previously entered by the user. There are situations in which you will want the processing of one form to be dependent on the processing of forms that were previously submitted by a user. For example, you may wish to have a user complete a series of forms where the first form collects general information such as name, address, and phone number, and subsequent forms collect more specific information such as employment data.

Hidden fields make it possible to retain information between forms. Key data, previously submitted, may be encoded in subsequent forms provided to the user. This keeps the user from having to enter the same data more than once and allows CGI programs to associate the input from different forms with each other. When a CGI program receives subsequent forms from the same user, it uses the hidden user ID to update the user's database record.

To add a hidden field to a form, insert an **INPUT** tag and set its **TYPE** attribute to **hidden**.

Using Images in Forms

A form may also include an image as an input field. When a user clicks on the image, the location of the user's click within the image is sent to the CGI program processing the form. This allows the user to select parts of the image as inputs for further processing.

Image fields are identified by setting the **TYPE** attribute of an **INPUT** tag to **image**. The **SRC** attribute is then set to the location of the image in the same way that it is used in **IMG** tags. The **NAME** attribute of the image identifies the image field to the CGI program. For example, the following tag identifies the circle.gif image as an image field:

```
<INPUT TYPE=image NAME=circle SRC="images/circle.gif"></INPUT>
```

The *x* and *y* coordinates of the user's click are passed to the CGI program by constructing field names with **.x** and **.y** appended to the **NAME** attribute of the image field.

The **ALIGN** attribute may be used with image fields in the same way that it is used with **IMG** tags. (See "Aligning Images" in Lesson 5.)

When an image is clicked on by the user, the entire form is submitted. There is no need to include a Submit button on forms that contain an image field.

The following example illustrates the use of the image field. The echo-query program is used to show the data that is generated by this field.

1 Open a new document, create a level 1 heading, and type **Using Images in Forms** for the title and heading.

2 Move the cursor between the **/H1** and **/BODY** tags and insert **FORM** tags into the document.

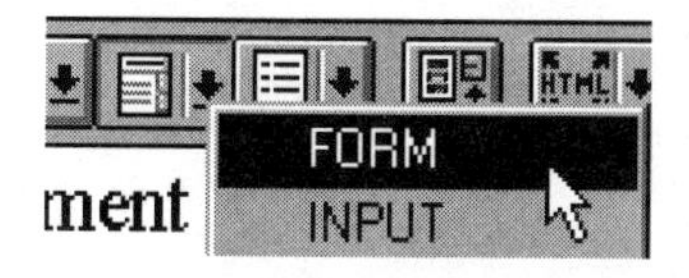

3 Press **F6** to edit the form's attributes.

4 Type **http://www.jaworski.com/cgi-bin/echo-query** in the ACTION field, select **POST** in the METHOD field, and click on the **Apply** button.

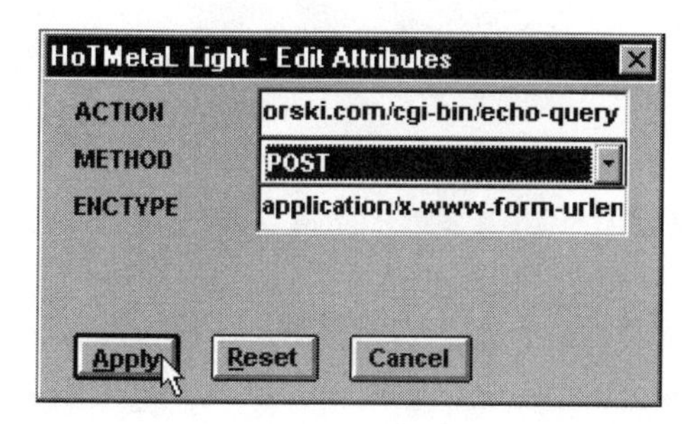

▶ The **FORM** attributes are updated.

FORM [http://www.jaworski.com/cgi-bin/echo-query] /FORM /BODY /HTML

5 Insert a set of **INPUT** tags.

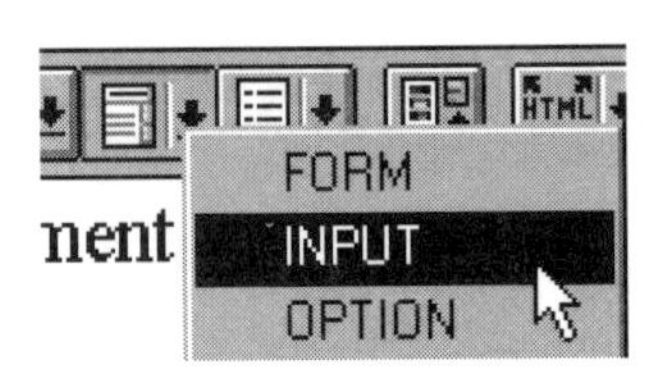

6 Press **F6** to edit the tag's attributes.

7 Select **IMAGE** in the TYPE field, type **circle** in the NAME field, type **images/circle.gif** in the SRC field, and click on the **Apply** button.

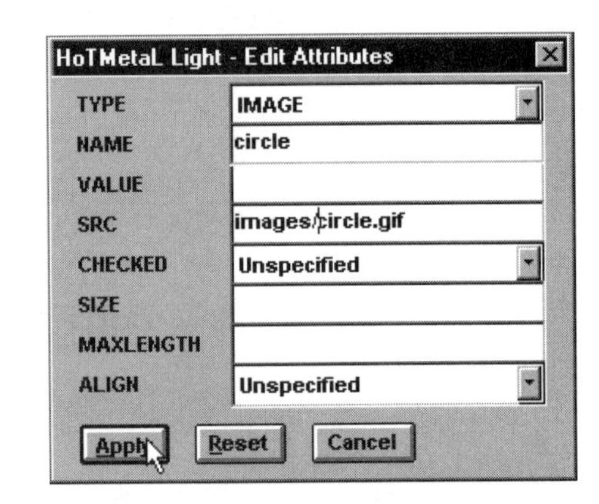

▶ The image field is inserted in your document.

FORM [http://www.jaworski.com/cgi-bin/echo-query]
INPUT [images/circle.gif] |[NAME = circle & TYPE = IMAGE] /INPUT
/FORM /BODY /HTML

8 Save your document as c\html\ch09-05.htm and view it with your browser.

9 Click anywhere on the image.

▶ The echo-query program displays the data received from your browser.

10 Close your browser and the current HoTMetaL document.

```
PATH_INFO =
PATH_TRANSLATED =
QUERY_STRING =
REMOTE_ADDR = 204.212.153.194
REMOTE_HOST = athome.jaworski.com
REMOTE_IDENT =
REMOTE_USER =
REQUEST_METHOD = POST
SCRIPT_NAME = /cgi-bin/echo-query
SERVER_NAME = www.jaworski.com
SERVER_PORT = 80
SERVER_PROTOCOL = HTTP/1.0
SERVER_SOFTWARE = NCSA/1.4.2
```

Standard Input

circle.x=79&circle.y=84

▶ ▶ ▶ The previous example used a very simple image in which the location of the user's click doesn't matter. More complex images can transmit different meanings to the CGI program depending on where the user clicks, as demonstrated in the following section.

Using Image Maps

Image maps are similar to image fields, but they are not used as part of a form. They allow users to click on an image and have the coordinates of the click select a link to the next Web page. They make use of a special CGI program, usually named imagemap, to process the coordinates of the user clicks. The processing performed by the image map is governed by image-specific *map files.*

Any image with well-defined features may be used as an image map. To designate an image as an image map, you make it the source anchor of a link and include the **ISMAP** attribute in its **IMG** tag. For example, the following anchor identifies the *shapes.gif* image as an image map:

```
<A HREF="http://www.jaworski.com/cgi-bin/imagemap/maps/shapes.map">
<IMG SRC="images/shapes.gif" ISMAP>
</A>
```

The **HREF** attribute of the link is set to the URL of the image map program; the extra path information identifies the location of the map file. In the above example, the imagemap program is located in the **/cgi-bin** path on the server host **www.jaworski.com**. The map file, *shapes.map,* is located in the **/maps** directory.

Once you've identified the image to be used as the image map, the next step is to create the map file. The map file identifies regions within the image and identifies the URL to be used as the destination of a link when the user clicks on that region. For now, I'll provide a map file to use. For an explanation of how to create map files, see "Working with Map Files" in the text file \extra\imagemap.htm on the CD.

In the following example, you will create a Web page that includes shapes.gif as an ISMAP image. It will reference the map file shapes.map, located on my Web server.

1 Open a new document, create a level 1 heading, and type **Using Image Maps** as the title and heading.

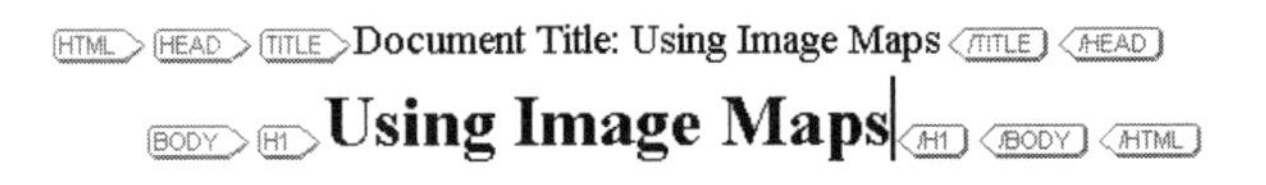

2 Move the cursor between the **/H1** and **/BODY** tags and click on the **Anchor** toolbar button.

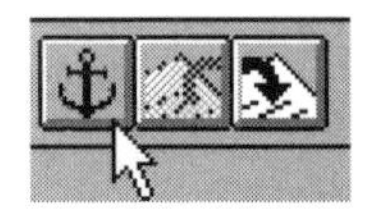

▶ The Edit URL dialog box appears.

3 Select **http** in the Scheme field, type **www.jaworski.com** in the Host field, type **/cgi-bin/imagemap/maps/shapes.map** in the Path field, and click on the **OK** button.

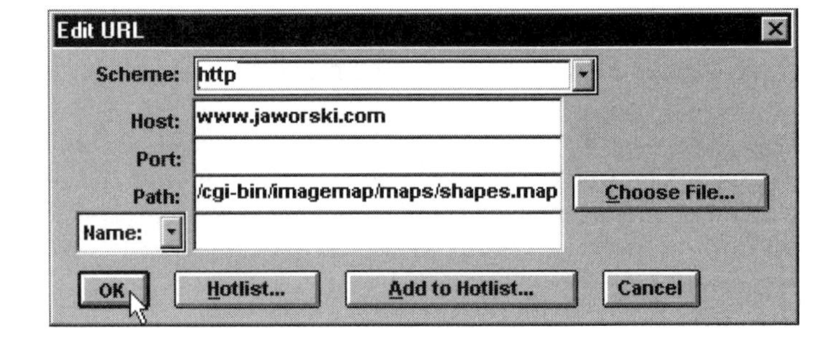

▶ Anchor tags are inserted into your document.

[http://www.jaworski.com/cgi-bin/imagemap/maps/shapes.map]
/A /P /BODY /HTML

4 Click on the **Image** toolbar button.

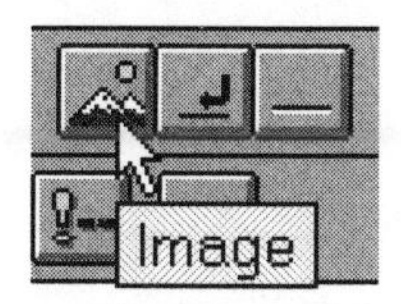

▶ The Edit Image dialog box appears.

5 Type **images/shapes.gif** in the Image File field, type **[image map]** in the Alternate Text field, check the **ISMAP** check box, and click on **OK**.

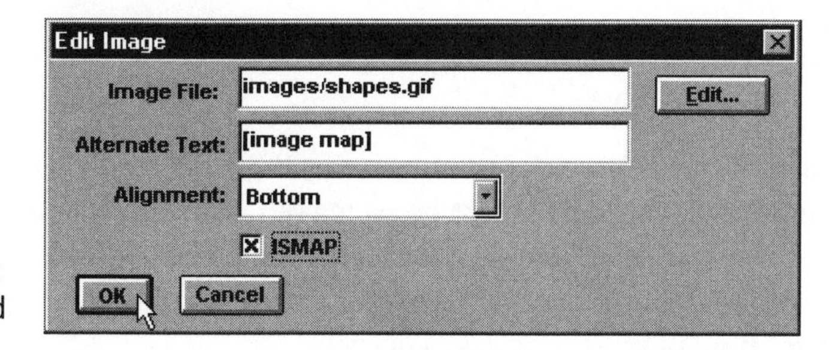

▶ The image shapes.gif appears in your document.

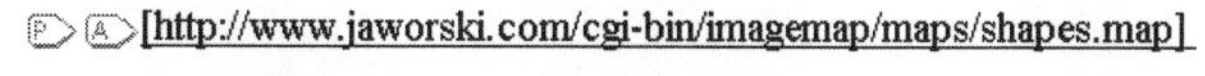

6 Save your document as c:\html\ch09-06.htm.

7 View it with your browser.

8 Click anywhere on the image.

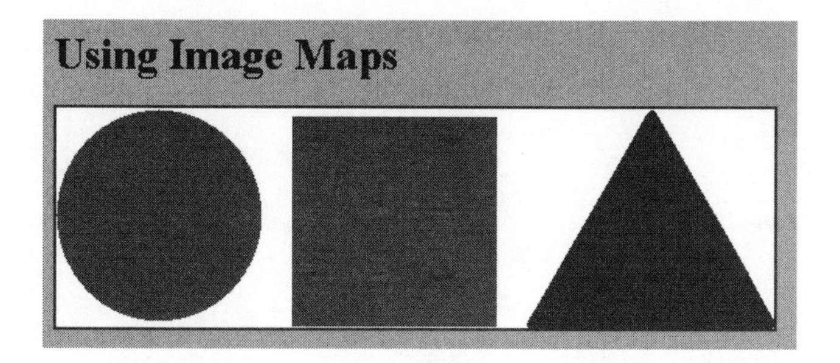

▶ The image map uses the map file to link to pages that identify the part of the image you clicked on.

You have selected the red circle.

Press the back icon to return to the image map.

9 Try clicking on different portions of the image map to see how it responds. When you're done, close your browser and HoTMetaL.

In this lesson, you learned a great deal about CGI programs. You learned how data is passed to and from these programs via the CGI. You learned how to access CGI programs through specialized URLs and how to process data generated by forms and the **ISINDEX** tag. You covered advanced form features, including hidden fields and clickable images, and you learned how to use image maps.

The next lesson will be somewhat of a break. You'll focus on creating tables, a new feature of HTML 3.0.

10

USING TABLES

In this lesson, you'll learn how to use tables, a new feature of HTML 3.0. Tables help you to organize information so that it can be easily accessed by the users of your Web pages. You'll learn how to use a number of table features, such as table captions, row and column headings, and borders. You'll also learn how to work with table cells that span multiple rows and columns. Most importantly, you'll learn how to use HoTMetaL to create and update your tables easily. When you finish this lesson, you'll be able to include a variety of eye-catching and informative tables in your Web pages.

Tables are a great way to present and summarize data. They help you organize information in a clearer and more accessible fashion. Their format makes it easy to find information of interest. Tables are organized as a set of intersecting *rows* and *columns*. Rows are displayed horizontally and columns are displayed vertically. Together they form a rectangular grid. The intersection of a row and a column is called the table *cell* located at the specified row and column.

You can use tables in Web pages in the same manner you use them in paper and other electronic documents. For example, you can use them to present financial transactions, analytical data, or scheduling information. Any type of data that can be cross-indexed is a good candidate for a table.

Creating Tables

HTML tables are identified by **TABLE** tags, surrounding tags that enclose the contents of the table, as shown here:

```
<TABLE>contents of table</TABLE>
```

The contents of HTML tables are defined by row. Rows are identified by the **TR** (table row) tags, which surround each row of the table, as follows:

```
<TABLE>
<TR>row</TR>
<TR>row</TR>
<TR>row</TR>
</TABLE>
```

Finally, each row of a table is organized into cells that are identified by the **TD** (table data) tags. The following tags identify a 3-row by 5-column table containing the first 15 letters of the alphabet.

```
<TABLE>
<TR><TD>A</TD><TD>B</TD><TD>C</TD><TD>D</TD><TD>E</TD></TR>
<TR><TD>F</TD><TD>G</TD><TD>H</TD><TD>I</TD><TD>J</TD></TR>
<TR><TD>K</TD><TD>L</TD><TD>M</TD><TD>N</TD><TD>O</TD></TR>
</TABLE>
```

Some table cells may be surrounded by **TH** (table header) tags instead of **TD** tags. The **TH** tags are used to identify the cells to be used as row and column headers. **TH** tags are identical to **TD** tags except that the data in the header cells is centered and displayed using a bold font.

At this point, you are probably thinking that tables are a syntactic nightmare—and you are right. It involves a lot of work to create a table using HTML directly. That's where HoTMetaL comes in handy. It automatically handles all of the intricacies of table-related tags and makes creating and modifying tables a cinch.

Creating a Simple Table

The following example shows how to use HoTMetaL to create a simple table.

1 Launch HoTMetaL, open a new document, create a level 1 heading, and type **A Simple Table** for the title and heading.

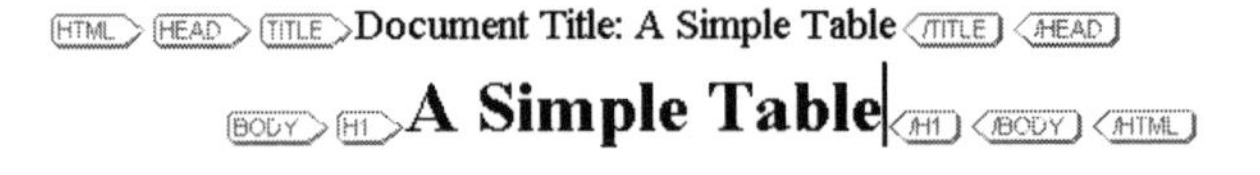
HTML HEAD TITLE Document Title: A Simple Table /TITLE /HEAD
BODY H1 A Simple Table /H1 /BODY /HTML

2 Move the cursor between the **/H1** and **/BODY** tags and click on the **Insert Table** toolbar button.

▶ The Insert Table dialog box appears.

3 Type **5** in the Rows field and **4** in the Columns field, and click on the **Insert** button.

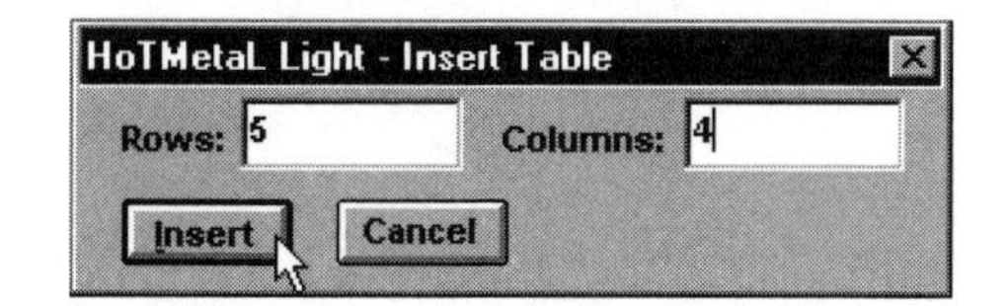

▶ A table 4 columns wide by 5 rows tall is inserted into your document.

TABLE

/TABLE /BODY /HTML

4 Type **Team** in the upper-left cell of the table and press the → key to move the cursor one cell to the right.

5 Type **Wins**, **Losses**, and **Ties**, pressing → to move to the right each time.

TABLE

Team	Wins	Losses	Ties

/TABLE /BODY /HTML

6 Fill in the rest of the table as shown here.

TABLE

Team	Wins	Losses	Ties
Rebels	6	0	0
Longhorns	3	2	1
Bolts	1	4	1
Hawks	1	5	0

/TABLE /BODY /HTML

7 Save your document as c:\html\ch10-01.htm and view it with your browser.

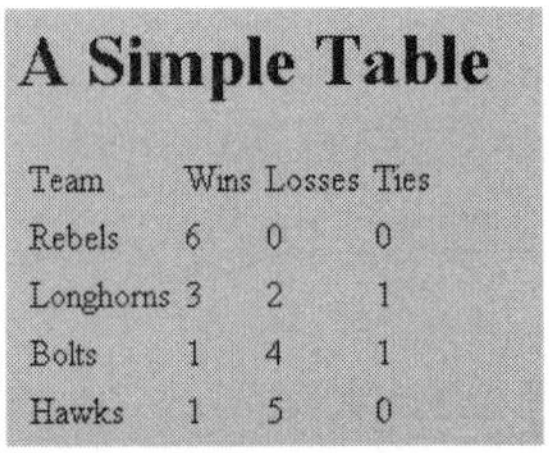

A Simple Table

Team	Wins	Losses	Ties
Rebels	6	0	0
Longhorns	3	2	1
Bolts	1	4	1
Hawks	1	5	0

8 Now view the document source file.

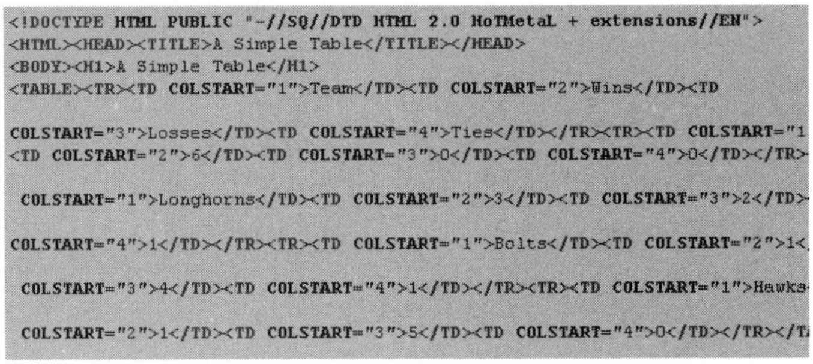

```
<!DOCTYPE HTML PUBLIC "-//SQ//DTD HTML 2.0 HoTMetaL + extensions//EN">
<HTML><HEAD><TITLE>A Simple Table</TITLE></HEAD>
<BODY><H1>A Simple Table</H1>
<TABLE><TR><TD COLSTART="1">Team</TD><TD COLSTART="2">Wins</TD><TD

COLSTART="3">Losses</TD><TD COLSTART="4">Ties</TD></TR><TR><TD COLSTART="1
<TD COLSTART="2">6</TD><TD COLSTART="3">0</TD><TD COLSTART="4">0</TD></TR>

 COLSTART="1">Longhorns</TD><TD COLSTART="2">3</TD><TD COLSTART="3">2</TD>

COLSTART="4">1</TD></TR><TR><TD COLSTART="1">Bolts</TD><TD COLSTART="2">1<

 COLSTART="3">4</TD><TD COLSTART="4">1</TD></TR><TR><TD COLSTART="1">Hawks

 COLSTART="2">1</TD><TD COLSTART="3">5</TD><TD COLSTART="4">0</TD></TR></T
```

► Notice all the tags needed just to generate this simple table. Aren't you glad you have HoTMetaL?

Adding a Border

Table borders are lines that surround each cell of a table. By default, tables do not have borders. You add a border to a table using the **BORDER** attribute of the **TABLE** tag. The **BORDER** attribute takes a numeric value from **0** to **10** that identifies the thickness of the border in pixels, as shown here:

<TABLE BORDER=2>contents of table</TABLE>

Giving the Table a Caption

A table may also contain a caption that identifies the table's purpose or contents. You designate a caption by inserting **CAPTION** tags immediately after the initial **TABLE** tag. **CAPTION** tags surround the caption text, as shown here:

<TABLE><CAPTION>this is the caption</CAPTION>contents of table</TABLE>

A caption may use the **ALIGN** attribute with values of **TOP**, **BOTTOM**, **LEFT**, and **RIGHT** to specify how it should be aligned with respect to the table. The default alignment is **TOP**.

Creating a Table Header

You may change **TD** cells to **TH** cells (and vice versa) by selecting Markup ➢ Change. This convenient feature makes it easy to toggle the cell type without having to mess with any HTML.

The following example shows how to add a border to the table we created in the previous example, give it a caption, and identify column headers.

1. Close your browser, but keep ch10-01.htm open in your HoTMetaL window.

2. Type **An Enhanced Table** over the old title and heading.

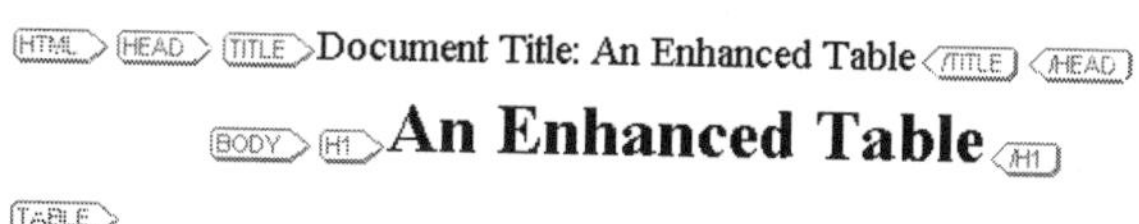

HTML HEAD TITLE Document Title: An Enhanced Table /TITLE /HEAD

BODY H1 An Enhanced Table /H1

TABLE

Team	Wins	Losses	Ties
Rebels	6	0	0
Longhorns	3	2	1
Bolts	1	4	1
Hawks	1	5	0

/TABLE /BODY /HTML

3. Save your document as c:\html\ch10-02.htm.

4. Move the cursor immediately after the opening **TABLE** tag and press **F6** to bring up the Edit Attributes dialog box.

5. Select **3** in the BORDER field and click on the **Apply** button.

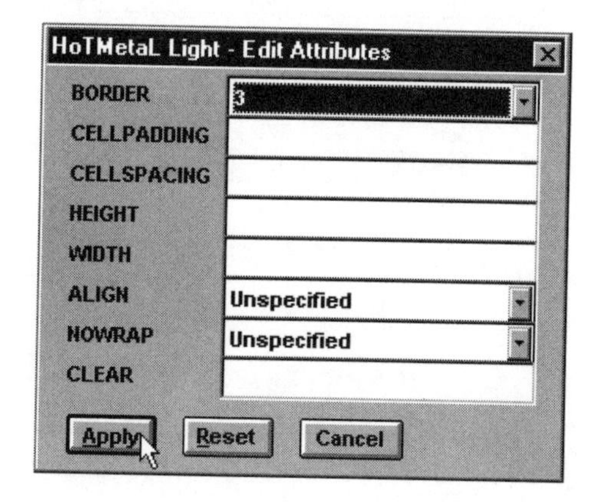

6 Click on the **Insert Element** toolbar button.

► The Insert Element dialog box appears with CAPTION highlighted.

7 Click on the **Insert Element** button.

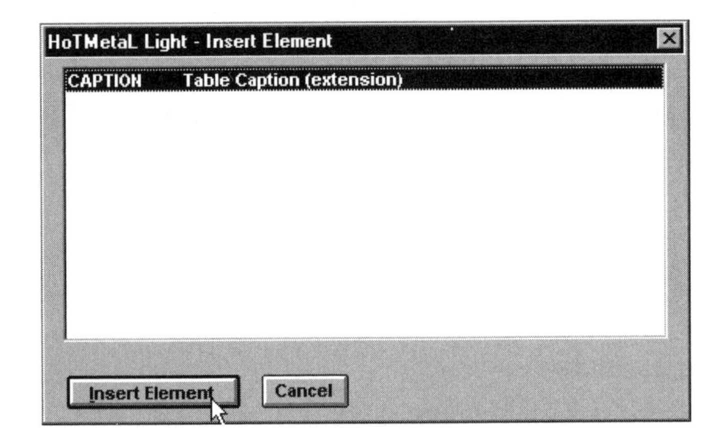

► **CAPTION** tags are inserted into your document.

<TABLE> <CAPTION> </CAPTION>

Team	Wins	Losses	Ties

8 Type **Rebels Win Them All!**

► The top border of the table may disappear and reappear in HoTMetaL. This is a HoTMetaL formatting problem and does not affect the way the table is displayed by browsers.

<TABLE> <CAPTION>Rebels Win Them All!</CAPTION>

Team	Wins	Losses	Ties
Rebels	6	0	0
Longhorns	3	2	1
Bolts	1	4	1
Hawks	1	5	0

</TABLE> </BODY> </HTML>

9 Click in the **Team** cell and select **Markup ➢ Change**.

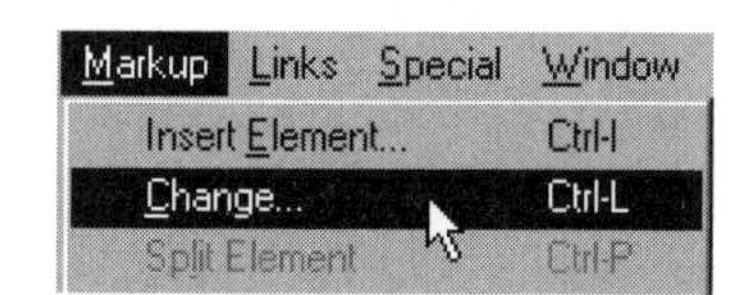

► The Change dialog box appears with TH highlighted.

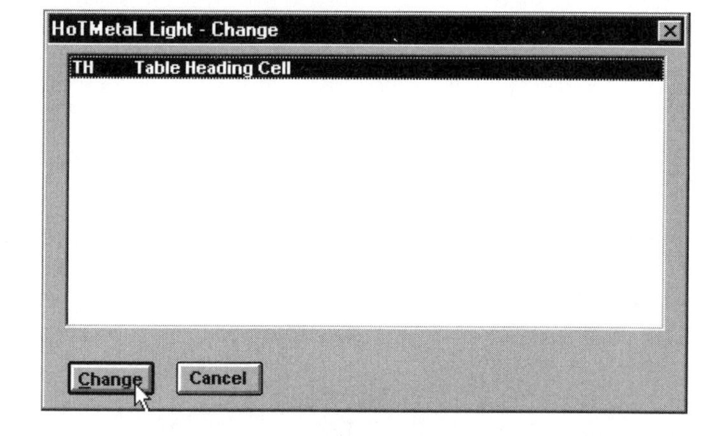

10 Click on the **Change** button.

11 Repeat steps 9 and 10 for the Wins, Losses, and Ties cells.

► The top row has become a row of table headers.

TABLE CAPTION Rebels Win Them All! /CAPTION

Team	Wins	Losses	Ties
Rebels	6	0	0
Longhorns	3	2	1
Bolts	1	4	1
Hawks	1	5	0

/TABLE /BODY /HTML

12 Save your document and view it with your Web browser.

13 When you're finished, close your browser and the current HoTMetaL document.

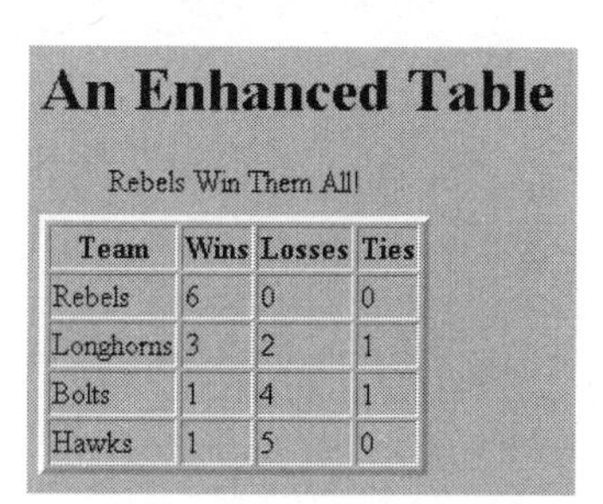

Spanning Cells

Sometimes you may want a particular table cell to span more than one row or column. These *spanning* cells can be used to define tables that break away from the traditional tabular grid. A common example of the use of spanning cells is in TV listings where the size of the cell containing a TV program is used to identify its time span.

The following example shows how HoTMetaL can be used to create special table effects using spanning cells.

1 Open a new HoTMetaL document, create a level 1 heading, and type **Spanning Cells** for the title and heading.

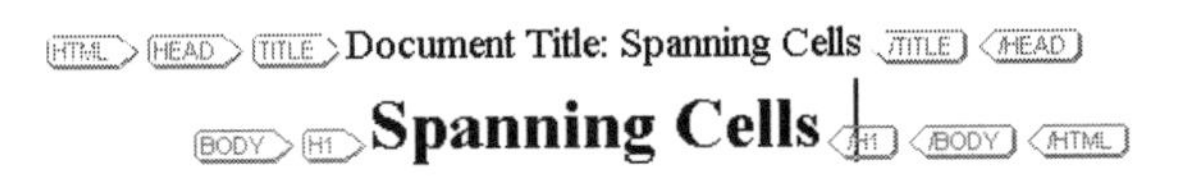

2 Move the cursor between the **/H1** and **/BODY** tags and click on the **Insert Table** toolbar button.

▶ The Insert Table dialog box appears.

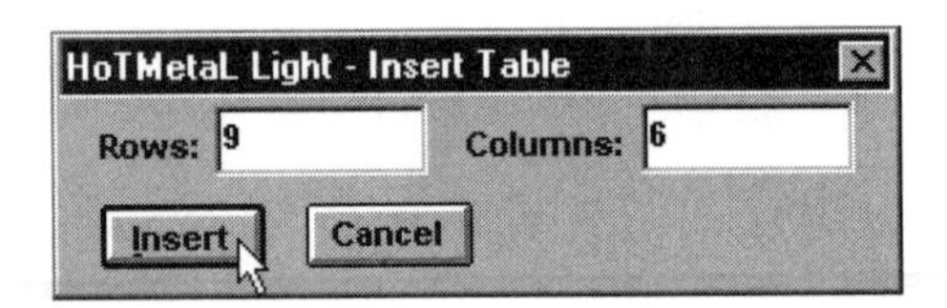

3 Type **9** in the Rows field and **6** in the Columns field, and click on the **Insert** button.

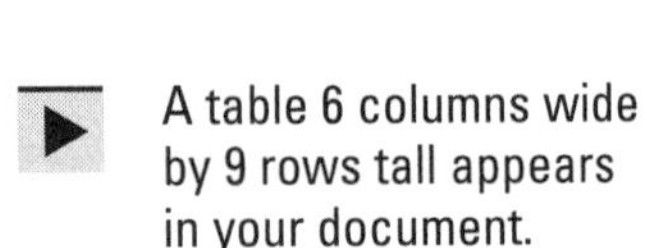

▶ A table 6 columns wide by 9 rows tall appears in your document.

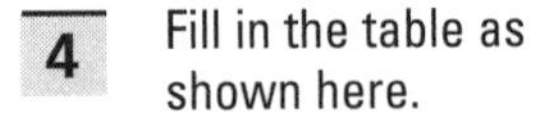

4 Fill in the table as shown here.

Time	Mon	Tue	Wed	Thu	Fri
9:00	Betty		Art		Manny
10:00		Frank		Tom	Moe
11:00				Jerry	Jack
12:00	Lunch				
1:00	Sue	Moe	Beach	Sally	Early Weekend
2:00		Curly		Jesse	
3:00	Larry			Raphael	
4:00					

5 Select **Markup ➢ Edit Table**.

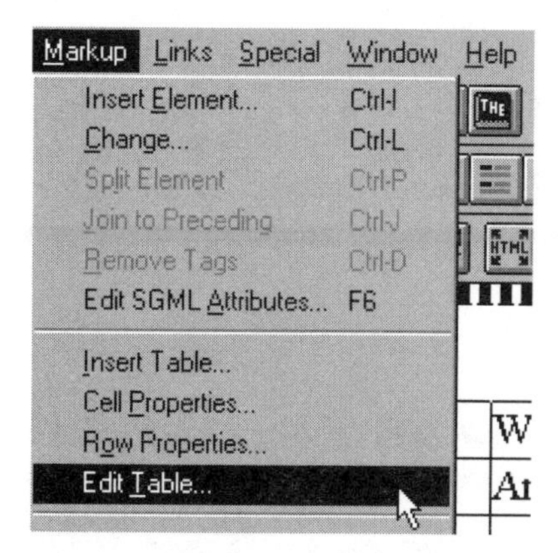

▶ The Edit Table palette appears. (If it's in your way, you can move the palette by dragging its title bar.)

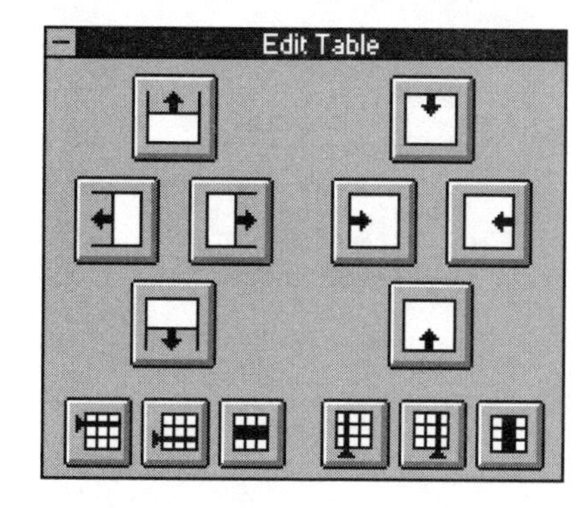

6 Click in the cell under Betty.

9:00	Betty
10:00	

7 Click on the **Extend Cell Down** button on the Edit Table palette.

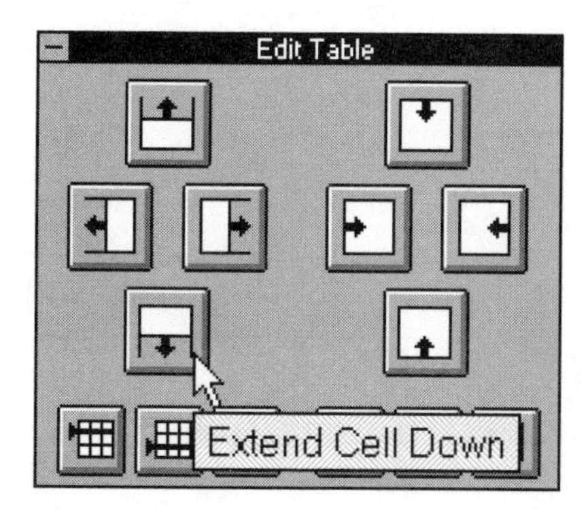

▶ The cell directly underneath Betty is combined with the one below it.

<TABLE>

Time	Mon	Tue
9:00	Betty	
10:00		Frank
11:00		

8 Click in the **Lunch** cell.

9 Click on the **Extend Cell Right** button.

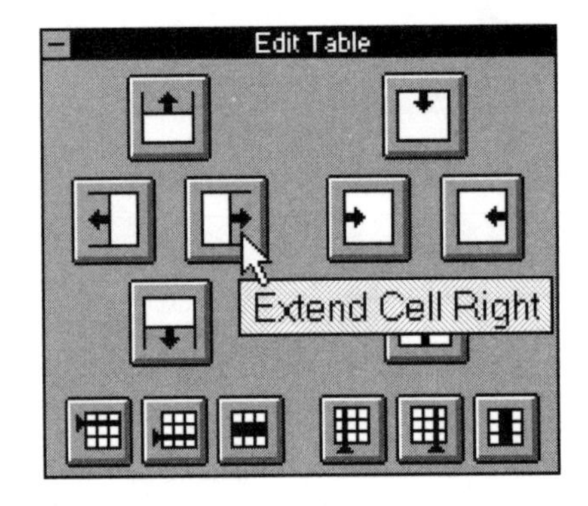

▶ The Lunch cell is combined with the one to its right.

10:00		Frank	
11:00			
12:00	Lunch		
1:00	Sue	Moe	Beach

10 Click on the **Extend Cell Right** button three more times to extend Lunch from the Mon column to the Fri column.

10:00		Frank		Tom	Moe
11:00				Jerry	Jack
12:00	Lunch				
1:00	Sue	Moe	Beach	Sally	Early Weekend

11 Click in the **Larry** cell.

12 Click on the **Extend Cell Down** button, then the **Extend Cell Right** button.

2:00		Curly	
3:00	Larry		
4:00			

</TABLE> </BODY> </HTML>

13 Use the Extend Cell Down button to extend the Art, Beach, and Early Weekend cells as shown here.

<TABLE>

Time	Mon	Tue	Wed	Thu	Fri
9:00	Betty		Art		Manny
10:00		Frank		Tom	Moe
11:00				Jerry	Jack
12:00	Lunch				
1:00	Sue	Moe	Beach	Sally	Early Weekend
2:00		Curly		Jesse	
3:00	Larry			Raphael	
4:00					

</TABLE> </BODY> </HTML>

14 Now click in the **Beach** cell.

15 Click on the **Contract Cell From Bottom** button.

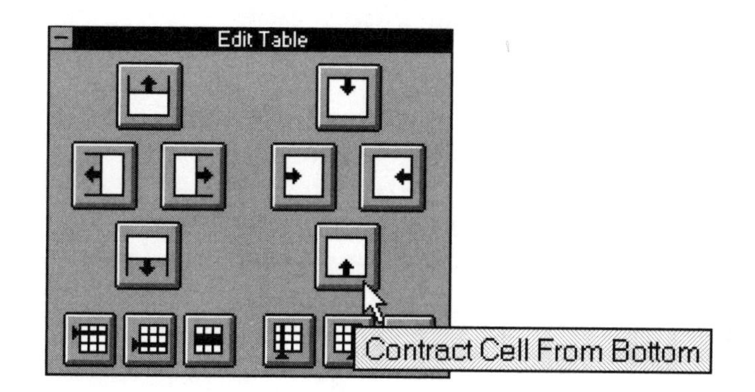

▶ The cell height decreases by one row.

Beach	Sally
	Jesse
	Raphael

16 Click on the **Contract Cell From Bottom** button two more times.

Beach	Sally
	Jesse
	Raphael

17 Close the **Edit Table** palette.

18 Click immediately after the **TABLE** tag and press **F6** to bring up the Edit Attributes dialog box.

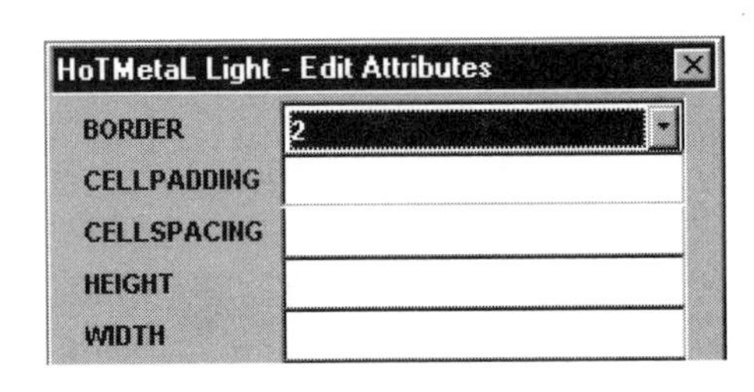

19 Type **2** in the BORDER field and click on **Apply**.

20 Click on the **Insert Element** toolbar button.

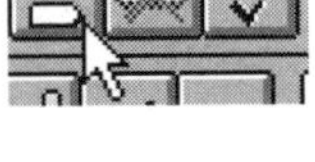

21 Click on the **Insert Element** button to insert **CAPTION** tags.

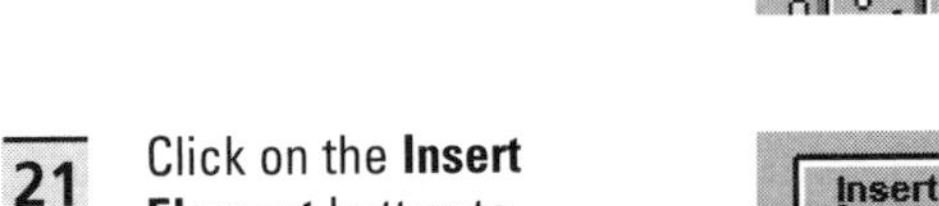

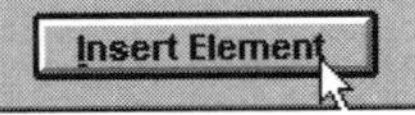

22 Type **Appointment Schedule** as the caption.

TABLE CAPTION Appointment Schedule /CAPTION

23 As we did earlier in the lesson, use the Markup ➢ Change command to make each cell in the top row a table heading.

TABLE CAPTION Appointment Schedule /CAPTION

Time	Mon	Tue	Wed	Thu	Fri
9:00	Betty		Art		Manny

24 Save your document as c:\html\ch10-03.htm and view it with your Web browser.

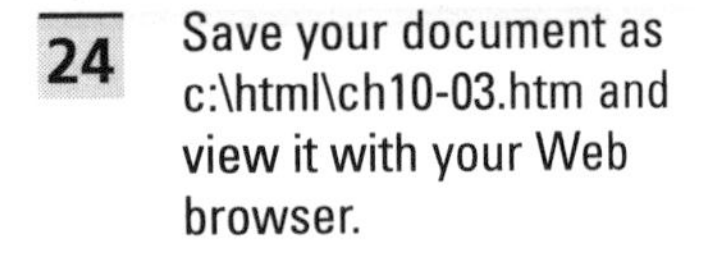

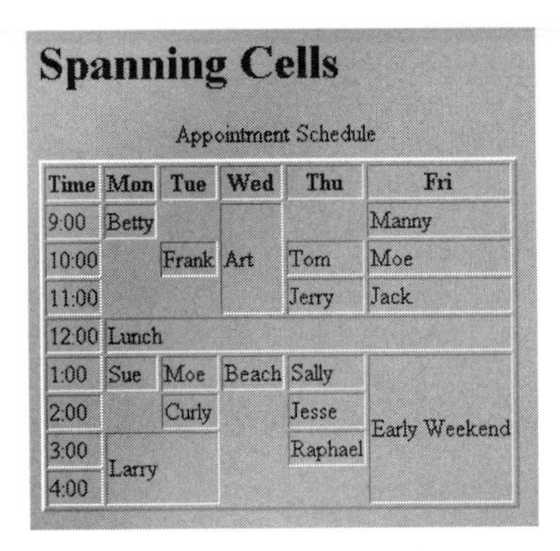

Appointment Schedule

<table>
<tr><th>Time</th><th>Mon</th><th>Tue</th><th>Wed</th><th>Thu</th><th>Fri</th></tr>
<tr><td>9:00</td><td>Betty</td><td></td><td rowspan="3">Art</td><td></td><td>Manny</td></tr>
<tr><td>10:00</td><td></td><td>Frank</td><td>Tom</td><td>Moe</td></tr>
<tr><td>11:00</td><td></td><td></td><td>Jerry</td><td>Jack</td></tr>
<tr><td>12:00</td><td colspan="5">Lunch</td></tr>
<tr><td>1:00</td><td>Sue</td><td>Moe</td><td>Beach</td><td>Sally</td><td rowspan="4">Early Weekend</td></tr>
<tr><td>2:00</td><td></td><td>Curly</td><td></td><td>Jesse</td></tr>
<tr><td>3:00</td><td colspan="2" rowspan="2">Larry</td><td></td><td>Raphael</td></tr>
<tr><td>4:00</td><td></td><td></td></tr>
</table>

Applying Table Attributes

So far you have encountered only one of the attributes used with the **TABLE** tag—the **BORDER** attribute. HoTMetaL supports a total of eight **TABLE** tag attributes via the Edit Attributes dialog box: **BORDER**, **CELLSPACING**, **CELLPADDING**, **HEIGHT**, **WIDTH**, **ALIGN**, **NOWRAP**, and **CLEAR**. Of these eight attributes, **BORDER**, **ALIGN**, **CELLPADDING**, and **CELLSPACING** are the most commonly used.

The **ALIGN** attribute determines the alignment of the whole table with respect to the Web page. It may take on the values **LEFT**, **CENTER**, **RIGHT**, **JUSTIFY**, **BLEEDRIGHT**, and **BLEEDLEFT**. The **LEFT** and **RIGHT** values align the table with the left and right text margins, while the **BLEEDLEFT** and **BLEEDRIGHT** values align the table with the left and right edges of the browser window. The other attribute values are used in the same way as with the **ALIGN** attribute of headings and paragraphs.

You can use the **CELLPADDING** and **CELLSPACING** attributes to make your table more spacious or compact, depending on your needs. **CELLPADDING** determines the amount of space in pixels between a cell's contents and its border. **CELLSPACING** determines the amount of space in pixels between individual cells in a table.

The **HEIGHT** and **WIDTH** attributes specify the dimensions of the table in pixels. You are almost always better off letting browsers figure out the best size for a table. The **NOWRAP** attribute prevents text that is too big to fit in a cell from wrapping. Using this attribute can cause cell text to be truncated and information to be left out of your table, so I recommend you don't use it. The **CLEAR** attribute specifies how surrounding text is to be displayed around a table. It is used in the same manner as the **CLEAR** attribute of the line break tag (see "Controlling Text Placement around Images" in Lesson 5).

The following example shows how to apply table attributes.

1. Close your browser, but leave ch10-03.htm open.

2. Type **Applying Table Attributes** over the old title and heading.

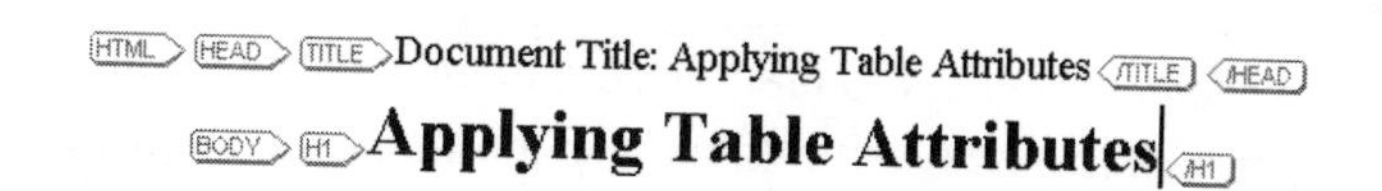
HTML
HEAD
TITLE
Document Title: Applying Table Attributes
/TITLE
/HEAD
BODY
H1
Applying Table Attributes
/H1

3. Save the document as c:\html\ch10-04.htm.

4. Move the cursor immediately after the opening **TABLE** tag and press **F6** to bring up the Edit Attributes dialog box.

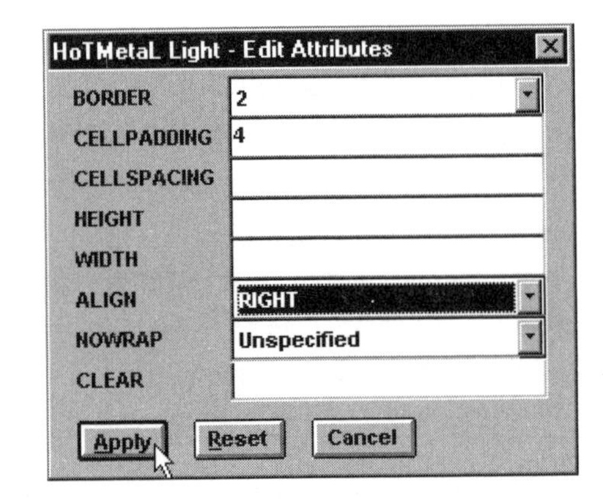

5. Type **4** in the CELLPADDING field, select **RIGHT** in the ALIGN field, and click on **Apply**.

6. Save your document and view it with your Web browser.

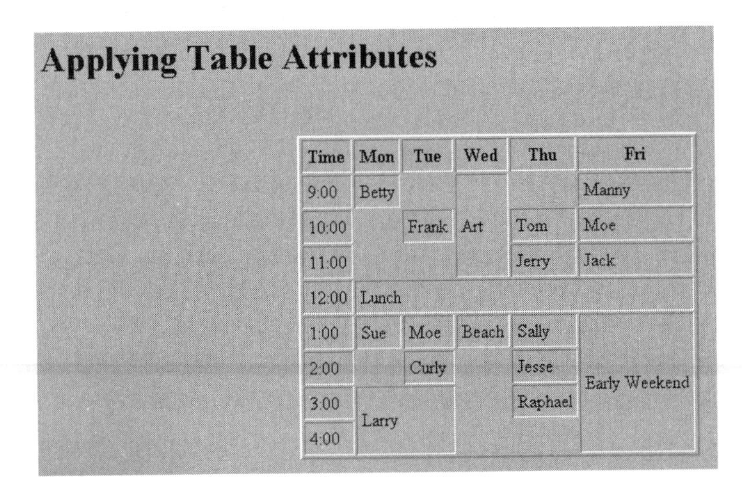

Applying Table Attributes
Time
Mon
Tue
Wed
Thu
Fri
9:00
Betty
Manny
10:00
Frank
Art
Tom
Moe
11:00
Jerry
Jack
12:00
Lunch
1:00
Sue
Moe
Beach
Sally
2:00
Curly
Jesse
Early Weekend
3:00
Raphael
Larry
4:00

▶ The table is now aligned with the right margin, and the cell padding has produced extra space around the contents of your cells.

7. Close your browser and the current HoTMetaL document.

Applying Cell Attributes

In the previous example, you learned how to change the attributes of a table as a whole. It is also possible to modify the attributes of individual cells. HoTMetaL supports the following eight cell attributes: **VALIGN**, **ALIGN**, **COLSTART**, **COLSPAN**, **ROWSTART**, **ROWSPAN**, **NOWRAP**, and **WIDTH**.

The **VALIGN** attribute controls the vertical alignment of data within a cell, while **ALIGN** controls its horizontal alignment. These attributes can be used together to align data in many different ways.

The **COLSTART**, **COLSPAN**, **ROWSTART**, and **ROWSPAN** attributes are used for spanning cells, but you should not set them directly. Instead, use the Edit Table tool palette to create and modify spanning cells.

The **NOWRAP** attribute is the same as with the **TABLE** tag, except that it only affects a single cell. The **WIDTH** attribute allows you to determine the width of a cell in pixels. It is much better to let browsers do this for you.

When you edit the attributes of a cell, you will notice the SQTABLE field at the top of the Edit Attributes dialog box. This field is for use by HoTMetaL and cannot be modified.

The following example shows how to modify the attributes of table cells.

1. Open ch10-03.htm and type **Applying Cell Attributes** over the old document title and heading.

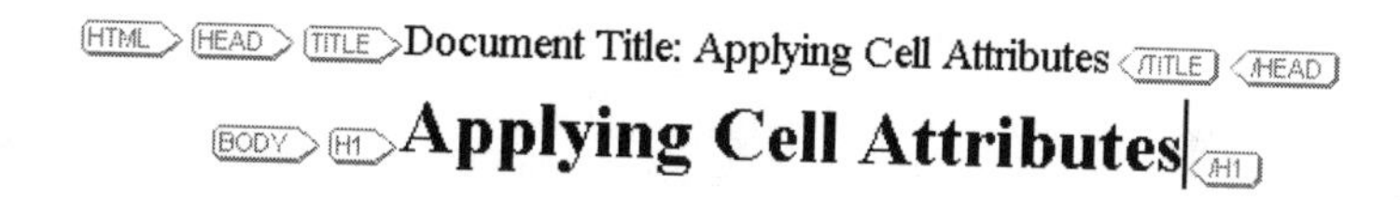
HTML HEAD TITLE Document Title: Applying Cell Attributes /TITLE /HEAD
BODY H1 Applying Cell Attributes /H1

2. Save it as c:\html\ch10-05.htm.

3 Click in the **Lunch** cell and press **F6** to bring up the Edit Attributes dialog box.

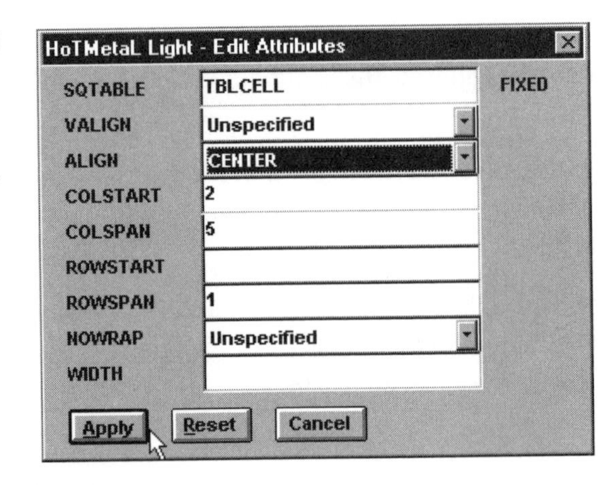

▶ Notice that the COLSTART and COLSPAN fields have values in them (because the Lunch cell spans five rows), but don't change them.

4 Select **CENTER** in the ALIGN field and click on **Apply**.

5 Click in the **Larry** cell and press **F6** to bring up the Edit Attributes dialog box.

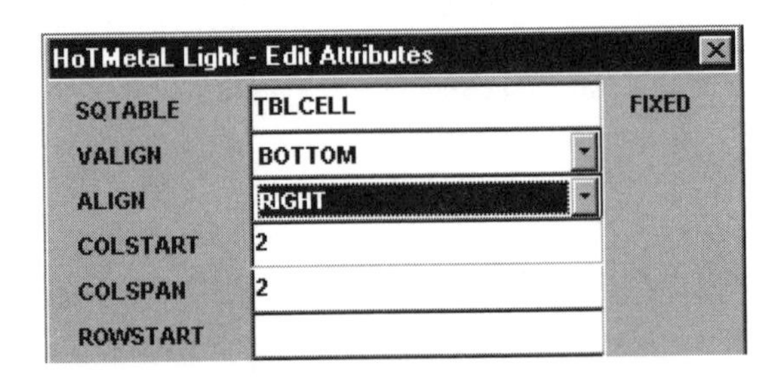

6 Select **BOTTOM** in the VALIGN field and **RIGHT** in the ALIGN field, then click on **Apply**.

7 Click in the **Art** cell and press **F6**.

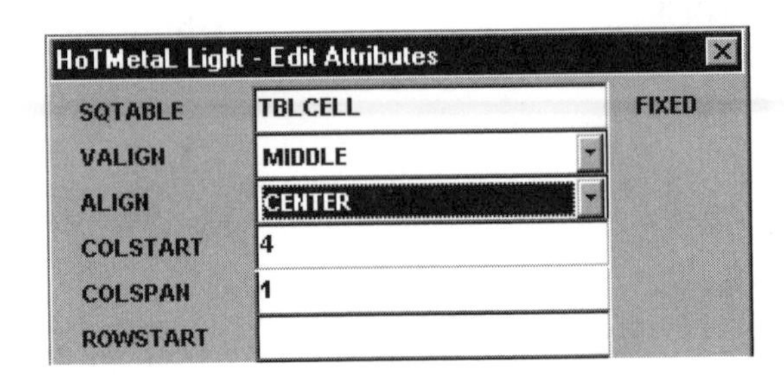

8 Select **MIDDLE** in the VALIGN field and **CENTER** in the ALIGN field, then click on **Apply**.

9 Save the document and view it with your Web browser.

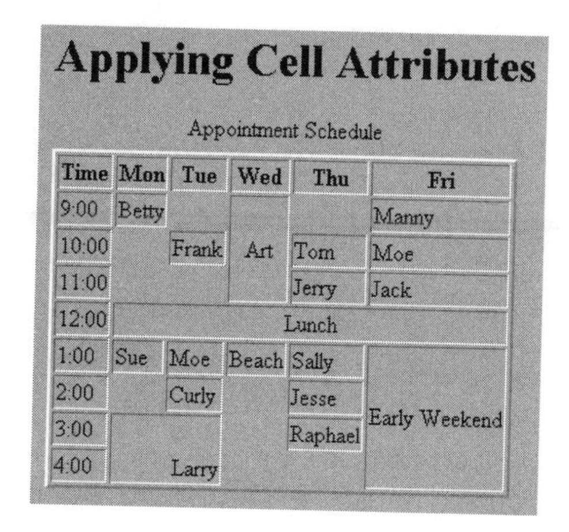

Modifying Tables

When working with tables, you will find many times that you need to add or delete a row or column. This would be overwhelmingly complicated if you were working directly with a table's HTML tags, but it's easy with HoTMetaL. HoTMetaL's Edit Table palette lets you add or delete a row or column with a single mouse click. The following example will show you how to use this feature.

1 Close your browser, but leave ch10-05.htm open.

2 Type **Adding and Deleting** over the old document title and heading, and save the document as c:\html\ch10-06.htm.

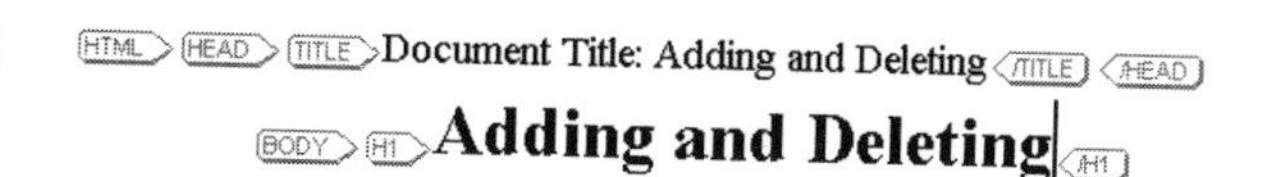

3 Click in the **12:00** cell and select **Markup ➢ Edit Table** to bring up the Edit Table palette.

4 Click on the **Delete Row** button.

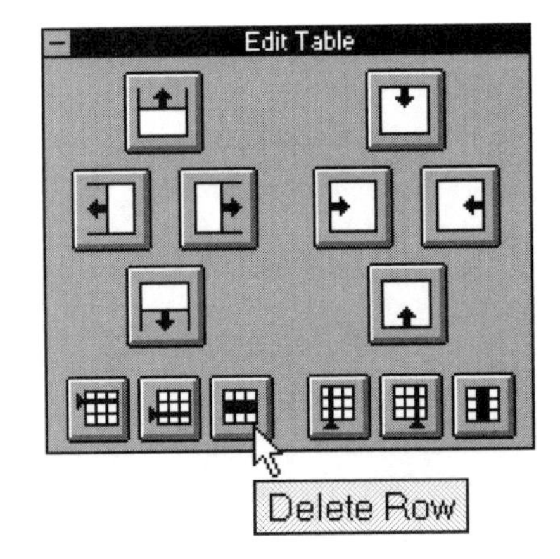

▶ The row is deleted.

11:00				Jerry	Jack
1:00	Sue	Moe	Beach	Sally	Early

5 Click in the **Wed** cell, then click on the **Delete Column** button.

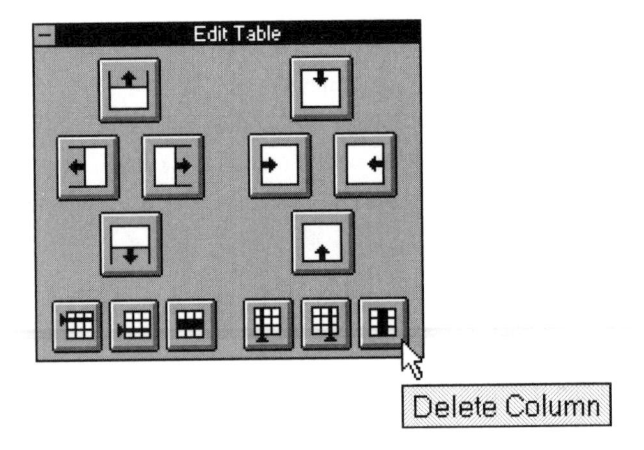

▶ The column is deleted.

hedule <CAPTION>

Tue	Thu
Frank	Tom
	Jerry
Moe	Sally
Curly	Jesse
	Raphael
Larry	

6 Click in the **Fri** cell, then click on **Insert Column Right**.

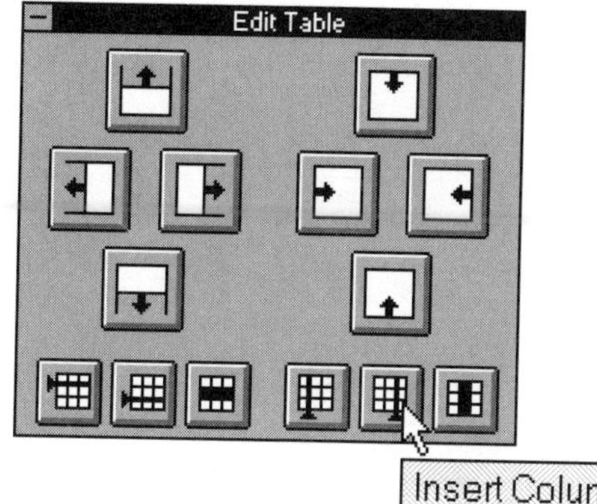

▶ A new column is added.

Thu	Fri	
	Manny	
Tom	Moe	
Jerry	Jack	
Sally	Early Weekend	
Jesse		
Raphael		

7 Click in the **11:00** cell, then click on the **Insert Row Below** button.

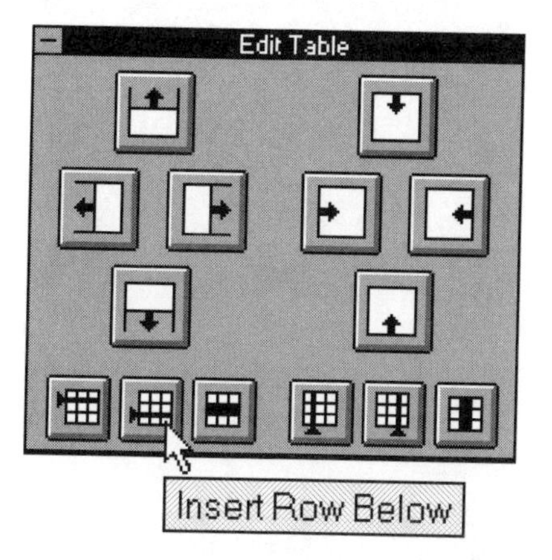

▶ A new row is inserted in the table.

11:00			Jerry	Jack	
1:00	Sue	Moe	Sally	Early	

8 Update the table as shown here.

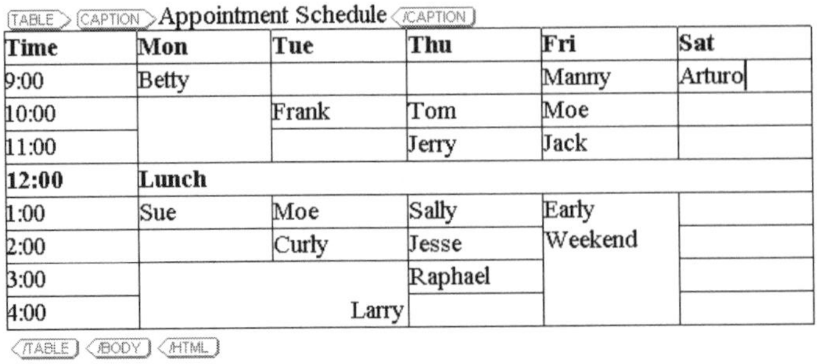

TABLE CAPTION Appointment Schedule /CAPTION

Time	Mon	Tue	Thu	Fri	Sat
9:00	Betty			Manny	Arturo
10:00		Frank	Tom	Moe	
11:00			Jerry	Jack	
12:00	Lunch				
1:00	Sue	Moe	Sally	Early Weekend	
2:00		Curly	Jesse		
3:00			Raphael		
4:00	Larry				

/TABLE /BODY /HTML

▶ HoTMetaL inserted the cells in the 12:00 row as header cells. It does this by default if another header cell has been defined in the table.

9 Since we don't want the 12:00 row to be header cells, select **Markup ➢ Change** and change them to table data cells.

TABLE CAPTION Appointment Schedule /CAPTION

Time	Mon	Tue	Thu	Fri	Sat
9:00	Betty			Manny	Arturo
10:00		Frank	Tom	Moe	
11:00			Jerry	Jack	
12:00	Lunch				
1:00	Sue	Moe	Sally	Early Weekend	
2:00		Curly	Jesse		
3:00			Raphael		
4:00	Larry				

/TABLE /BODY /HTML

10 Close the **Edit Table** palette.

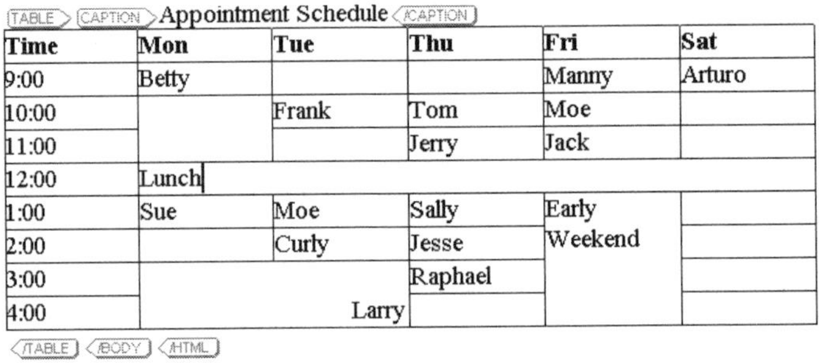

11 Save the document and view it with your browser.

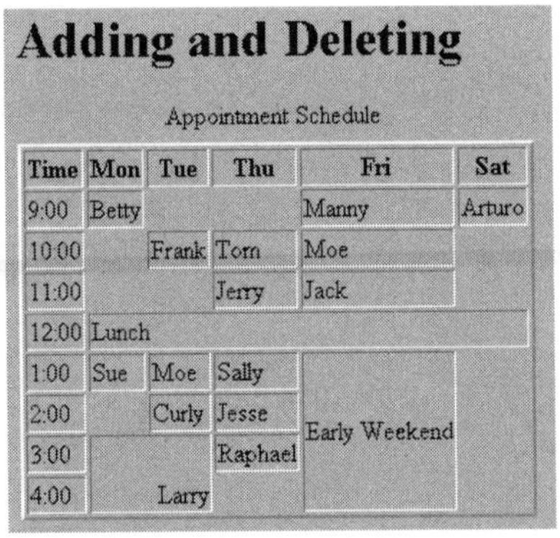

Adding and Deleting

Appointment Schedule

Time	Mon	Tue	Thu	Fri	Sat
9:00	Betty			Manny	Arturo
10:00		Frank	Tom	Moe	
11:00			Jerry	Jack	
12:00	Lunch				
1:00	Sue	Moe	Sally	Early Weekend	
2:00		Curly	Jesse		
3:00			Raphael		
4:00	Larry				

12 When you're done, close your browser and HoTMetaL.

In this lesson, you learned how to use HoTMetaL to create a variety of tables. You learned how to work with spanning cells and how to apply table and cell attributes. In the next lesson, you will learn how to include multimedia features, such as audio and video clips, in your Web pages.

11

Developing Multimedia Applications

In this lesson, you'll learn how to dress up your Web pages using multimedia files. You'll learn about external viewers and browser plug-ins and how they work with your browser to display multimedia and application-specific file formats. You'll learn how MIME types are used to associate different file formats with the appropriate viewers. You'll also receive some pointers on where to get audio and video viewers. When you finish this lesson, you'll be able to include multimedia and other types of documents in your Web pages.

External Viewers and Plug-Ins

First generation browsers supported the display of text and some images, such as GIF and XBM files. These browsers could also use external programs to view unsupported file formats, such as JPEG and PostScript. *External viewers* were developed to support a variety of image, audio, video, and other file formats.

Gradually, browsers such as Netscape and Mosaic began to provide internal support for some file formats, such as JPEG. Realizing the impracticality of trying to accommodate all potential file formats, the second generation Netscape and Microsoft browsers provided support for supplements, known as *plug-in* or *add-in modules.* These modules are executed with the browser and display multimedia, virtual reality markup, and application-specific files inline with the browser display. Inline display is more visually appealing because application-specific files are fully integrated within the browser window.

Whether a browser uses an external viewer or a plug-in to display a particular file type has no bearing on the way the file is presented within a Web page. You simply create a link to the URL of the file and let the browser figure out how to display it, using an external viewer or a plug-in module. This lesson shows you how to construct these links, provides you with background information on how they work, and introduces the most common types of external media found on the Web.

Netscape has recently introduced the **EMBED** tag to identify regions within a Web page that are set aside for use by a plug-in module. This tag is not currently supported by HoTMetaL.

Understanding MIME Types

Browsers and servers use the Multipurpose Internet Mail Extensions, or *MIME*, to specify the type of file referenced on a Web page. MIME types were originally developed to include images, sounds, videos, and application-specific objects within e-mail messages.

The primary MIME types used on the Web are text, image, audio, video, and application. Each type is associated with a number of subtypes that identify file formats within the major type category. For example, plain and html are two subtypes of the text type. Normal text documents are of the type text/plain, while Web pages are text/html. MIME types are also identified for application-specific file formats, such as Microsoft Word, PostScript, and ZIP files (types application/msword, application/postscript, and application/zip, respectively). An *x-* preceding a type indicates that it is an unregistered type. For example, the common WAV files used by Windows programs are of type audio/x-wav.

When a browser requests a file from a server, the server informs the browser of the file's MIME type. The browser maintains a list of MIME types that it is capable of displaying. The browser may display some types internally, for example, as an inline image, or via a plug-in module. Other types may be displayed using external viewers. The browser maps each MIME type that it knows about to the specific manner in which files of that type are to be displayed.

What happens when a browser comes across a file with a MIME type it can't display? It typically prompts the user to pick a program that can display the file or allows the user to save the file to disk. By allowing the user to pick a program, the browser is able to incrementally expand its external viewing capabilities. By allowing the user to save a file to disk, the user is given a chance to go out and obtain a viewer for the file, without having to download the file again. This can be a very helpful feature for large files, such as video files.

Configuring Your Browser

Where does one find external viewers and browser plug-ins? The best place to find information about Windows viewers and plug-ins is Forrest Stroud's Consummate Windsock Applications List, located at **http://cwsapps.texas.net/cwsa.html** or **http://cws.wilmington.net/cwsa.html**. Also, consult the Appendix for information on the external viewers included on this book's CD.

The following sections show how to include audio, video, and application-specific files with your Web pages. To work the examples for these sections, configure your browser with external viewers for WAV audio files, MPEG videos, and Microsoft Word documents. I use the following viewers with my Netscape browser: WHAM for audio/x-wav files, NET TOOB for video/mpeg, and Word Viewer for application/msword. These programs will work with almost any Windows-based browser. Consult the Appendix for more information about installing them. They are all located in the \programs directory on the CD. The WHAM viewer is donation-ware. If you like it, send a donation to Andrew Bulhak, its developer. NET TOOB is shareware. It will work for only two weeks after it is installed. To use it longer than this, you must register it. Check out **http://www.duplexx.com** for more information about NET TOOB. Word Viewer is freeware from Microsoft.

Copying the Multimedia Files

Several multimedia files are used in the examples in this lesson. Before continuing with this lesson, copy these files from the \multimed directory of this book's CD to the c:\html\multimed directory of your hard disk (you will need to create this directory). The files are fairly large; you may wish to delete them when you are finished with this lesson.

Using Audio Files

The easiest way to include multimedia features with your Web pages is to add audio files. Audio files are easy and inexpensive to develop. If you have a sound card and a microphone, you can record your own files. You can even use the audio software that comes with your sound board to alter your voice. The sound files used in the examples of this lesson were recorded by my daughter, Emily, and digitally filtered to soften her voice.

Sound files come in a variety of formats, with the Sun audio file (.au) and the Windows WAV formats being the most popular.

When including a link to an audio file, it is a good idea to identify the link as an audio link. I like to use a sound icon. You can use icons or text messages, depending on your preferences.

Audio files can be somewhat large, although they are typically much smaller than video files. When you publish a page containing a sound link, it is a good idea to identify the size of the file so users can decide whether they want to wait around to download the file. The sound and video files used in the following examples will be loaded from your hard disk, so there is no need to worry about waiting.

If you don't have a sound card, you can still work the following example; you just won't hear anything.

The following example shows how to include audio files with your Web pages.

1. Launch HoTMetaL, open a new HoTMetaL document, create a level 1 heading, and type **Using Audio** for the title and heading.

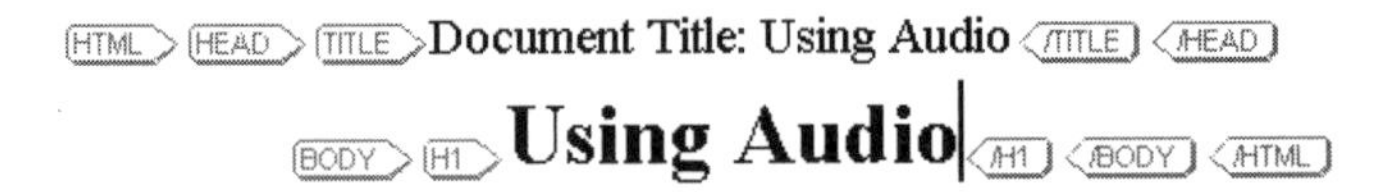

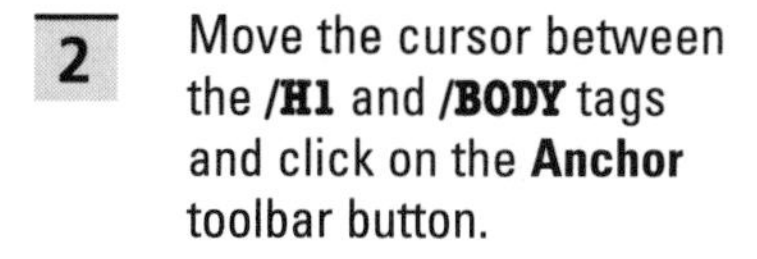

2 Move the cursor between the **/H1** and **/BODY** tags and click on the **Anchor** toolbar button.

▶ Anchor tags are inserted into your document and the Edit URL dialog box appears.

3 Type **multimed/hello.wav** in the Path field and click on **OK**.

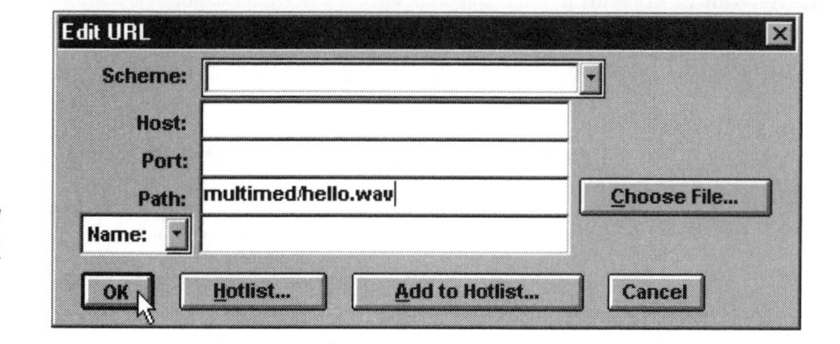

▶ The anchor tags are updated.

P A [multimed/hello.wav] /A /P /BODY /HTML

4 Click on the **Image** toolbar button.

▶ The Edit Image dialog box appears.

5 Click on the **Edit** button.

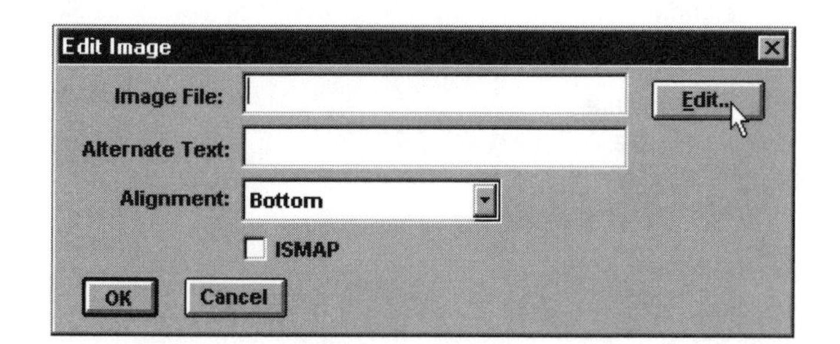

▶ The Edit IMG Source dialog box appears.

6 Type **images/sound.xbm** in the Path field and click on **OK** twice to close both dialog boxes.

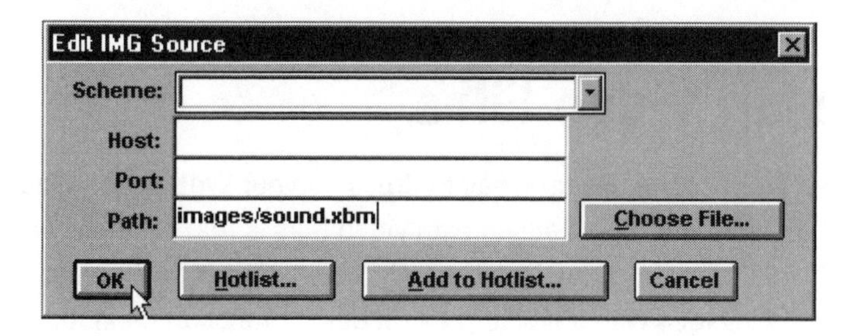

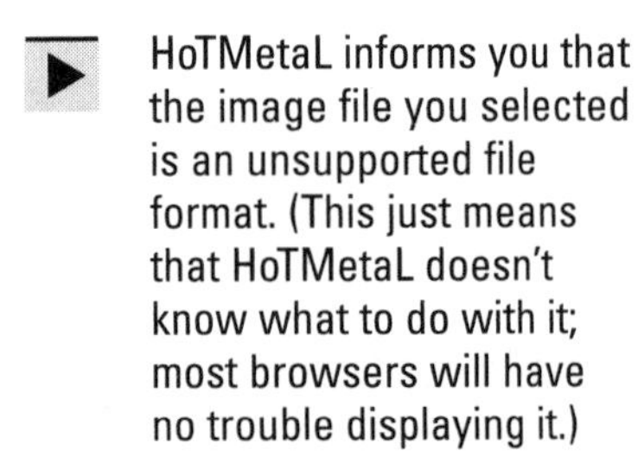

▶ HoTMetaL informs you that the image file you selected is an unsupported file format. (This just means that HoTMetaL doesn't know what to do with it; most browsers will have no trouble displaying it.)

7 Move the cursor between the **/P** and **/BODY** tags and insert a level 2 heading.

HTML HEAD TITLE Document Title: Using Audio /TITLE /HEAD

BODY H1 **Using Audio** /H1

P A [multimed/hello.wav] IMG Unsupported Format /IMG /A /P

H2 **Welcome to my home page!** /H2 /BODY /HTML

8 Type **Welcome to my home page!**

9 Save your file as c:\html\ch11-01.htm.

10 View it with your browser.

11 Click on the audio icon.

▶ A short audio message welcomes you to the home page.

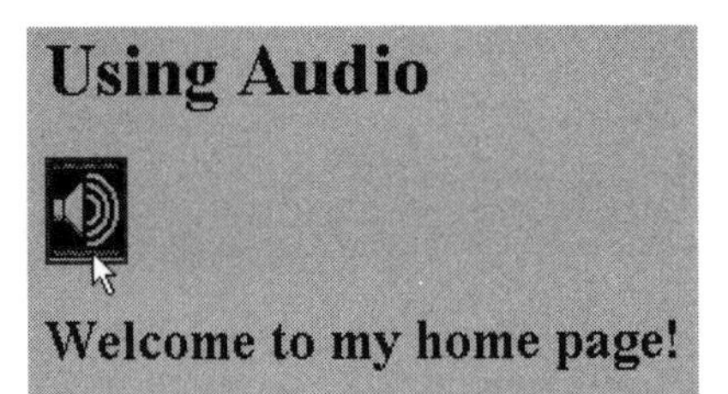

12 Close your browser and the current HoTMetaL document.

Using Video Files

Video files are the ultimate way to dress up your Web pages. They are usually informative and entertaining. The problem with video files is that they are very large and can be costly to develop. Typical video files range from .5 to 5 megabytes in size. If a user is browsing your Web pages with a typical 14.4K modem, they can be in for a long wait if you link to a large video file. The development of video files is more expensive than audio files. Typical video capturing hardware and software costs several hundred dollars. The time required to edit and process video files is also usually longer than it is for audio files.

The most common video file formats are MPEG and the Apple QuickTime video format (.mov). The file included with the following example is in the MPEG format. It is taken from the NASA Space Telescope Science Institute Office of Public Outreach archive located at **http://www.stsci.edu/public.html**.

When including a link to a video file, it is a good idea to identify the link as a video link. I like to use a movie icon; others include an image that describes the subject matter of the video. You should also identify the size of the video file.

The following example shows how to include video files with your Web pages.

1. Open a new document, create a level 1 heading, and type **Combining Audio and Video** for the title and heading.

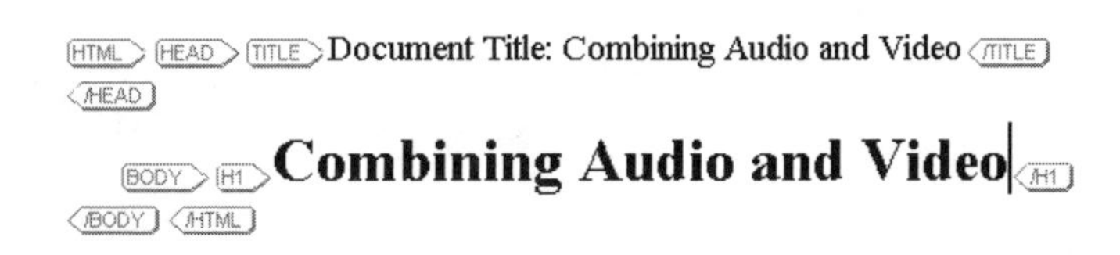

2. Move the cursor between the **/H1** and **/BODY** tags and click on the **Anchor** toolbar button to bring up the Edit URL dialog box.

3. Type **multimed/mars.wav** in the Path field and click on **OK**.

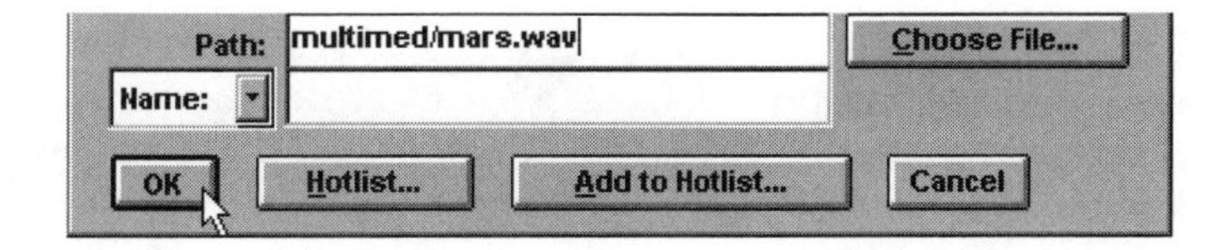

4. Click on the **Image** toolbar button to bring up the Edit Image dialog box.

5. Click on the **Edit** button to bring up the Edit IMG Source dialog box.

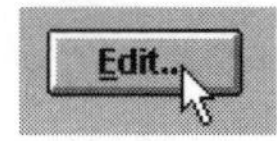

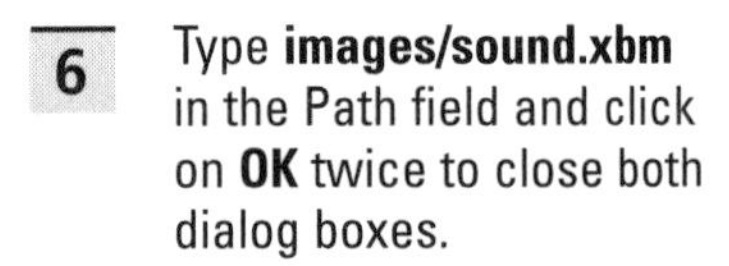

6 Type **images/sound.xbm** in the Path field and click on **OK** twice to close both dialog boxes.

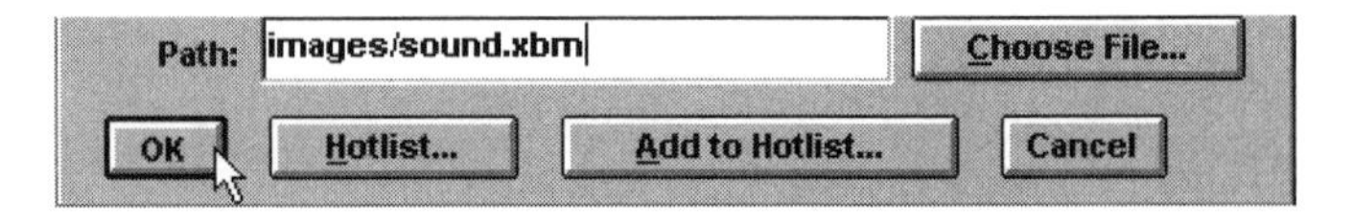

7 Move the cursor between the **/A** and **/P** tags.

P A [multimed/mars.wav] IMG Unsupported Format /IMG /A /P /BODY
/HTML

8 Press the space bar and then the **Anchor** toolbar button to bring up the Edit URL dialog box.

9 Type **multimed/mars.mpg** in the Path field and click on **OK**.

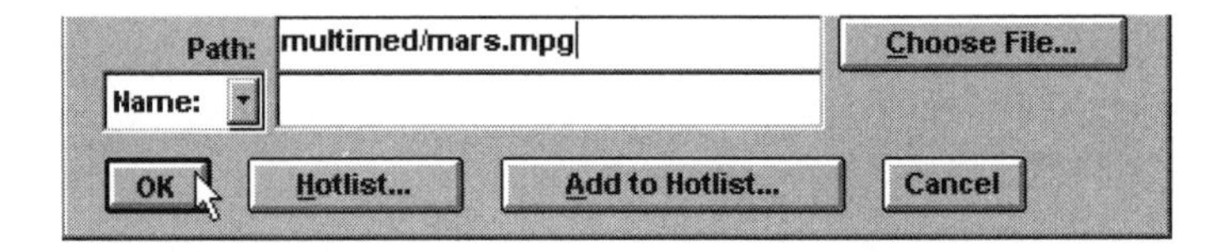

10 Click on the **Image** toolbar button to bring up the Edit Image dialog box.

11 Click on the **Edit** button to bring up the Edit IMG Source dialog box.

12 In the Path field, type **images/movie.xbm** and click on **OK** twice to close both dialog boxes.

13 Move the cursor between the **/A** and **/P** tags.

14 Type a space and then **My Home Planet!**

HTML HEAD TITLE Document Title: Combining Audio and Video /TITLE
/HEAD

BODY H1 **Combining Audio and Video** /H1

P A [multimed/mars.wav] IMG Unsupported Format /IMG /A
A [multimed/mars.mpg] IMG Unsupported Format /IMG /A My Home Planet!
/P /BODY /HTML

15 Save the document as c:\html\ch11-02.htm and view it with your Web browser.

16 Click on the audio icon.

▶ You hear a short introduction to the video.

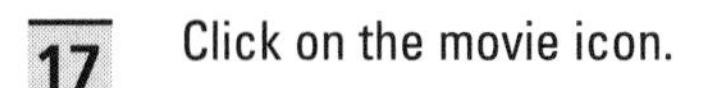

17 Click on the movie icon.

▶ The NET TOOB viewer appears and displays a video of the planet Mars.

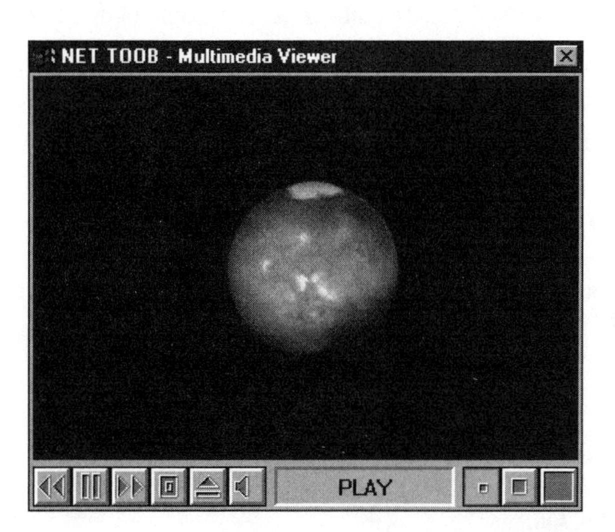

18 When you are finished with the video, close the external viewer, your browser, and the current HoTMetaL document.

Working with Application-Specific Viewers

You can include *application-specific files* with your Web pages in the same manner you include audio and video files. These application-specific files are files that are used with common application programs. For example, Microsoft Word files are a common file type for word processor documents, PostScript files are a common format for published documents, and ZIP files are a common file type for compressed files. If you want to make these types of files available through your Web pages, you can do so by constructing links to them in the same way you did for the audio and video files in the previous examples.

When you link to application-specific files in your Web pages, you should identify the application types of these files so users will know they need a compatible viewer to display the linked files. You should also identify the files' sizes.

The development of application-specific files is usually inexpensive. To develop PostScript files, all you need is access to software that supports text-to-PostScript conversion. To develop Word documents, you need Microsoft Word or a word processor that supports it. The problem with application-specific files is that your users need to have a viewer that is compatible with the file format. Microsoft gives away its Word Viewer for free via its website. PostScript viewing software is also available over the Internet. However, the viewing software itself can be quite large, and some people may be reluctant to install it.

The following example shows how to include application-specific files with your Web pages. You will create a link to a Word document that contains the text "Now I can add Word documents to my Web pages!"

1. Open a new HoTMetaL document, create a level 1 heading, and type **Application-Specific Viewers** for the title and heading.

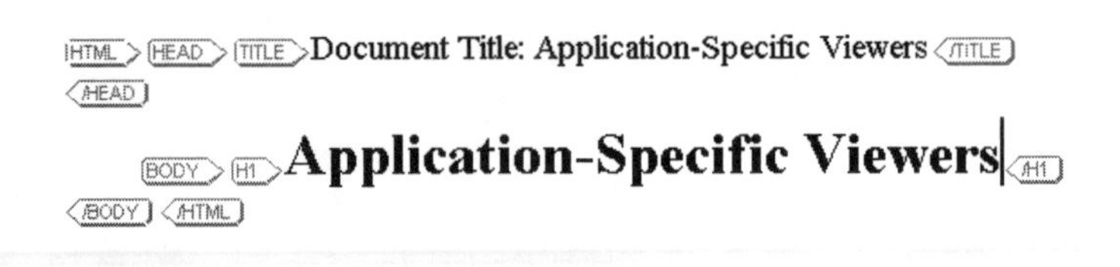

2. Move the cursor between the **/H1** and **/BODY** tags and press the **Anchor** toolbar button to bring up the Edit URL dialog box.

3 Type **multimed/word.doc** in the Path field and click on the **OK** button.

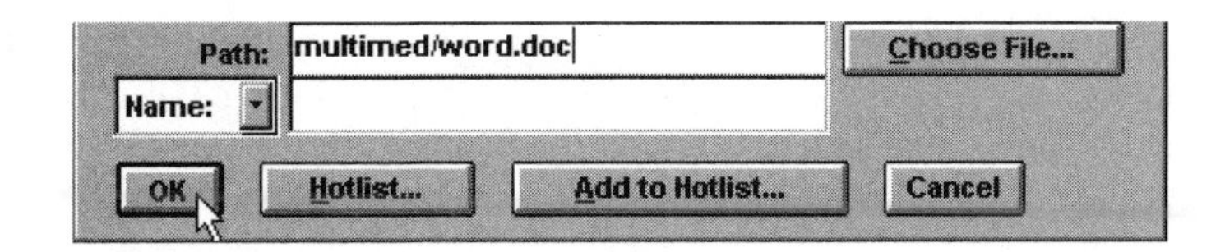

4 Click on the **Image** toolbar button to bring up the Edit Image dialog box.

5 Click on the **Edit** button to bring up the Edit IMG Source dialog box.

6 Type **images/paper.xbm** in the Path field and click on **OK** twice to close both dialog boxes.

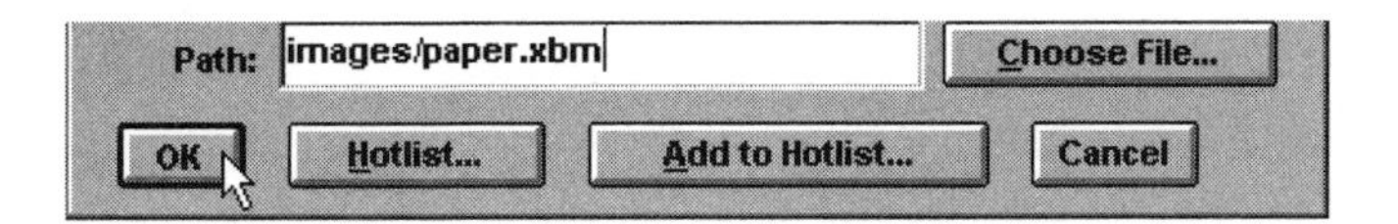

7 Move the cursor between the **/A** and **/P** tags.

8 Type a space and then the text **A Word document.**

9 Save your file as c:\html\ch11-03.htm and view it with your Web browser.

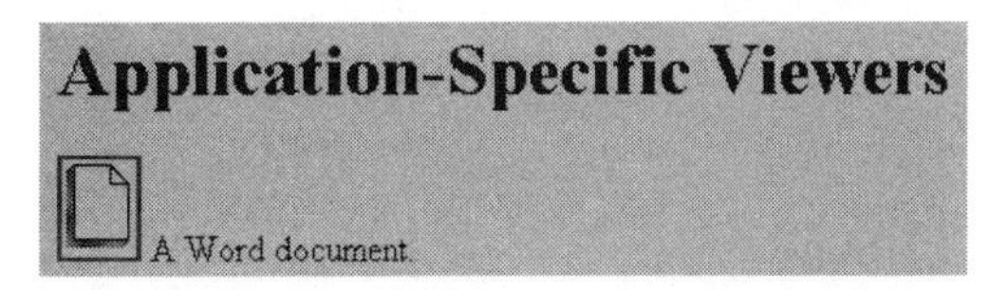

10 Click on the paper icon.

▶ Word Viewer launches and displays the document in the file multimed\word.doc. This document contains the text "Now I can add Word documents to my Web pages!"

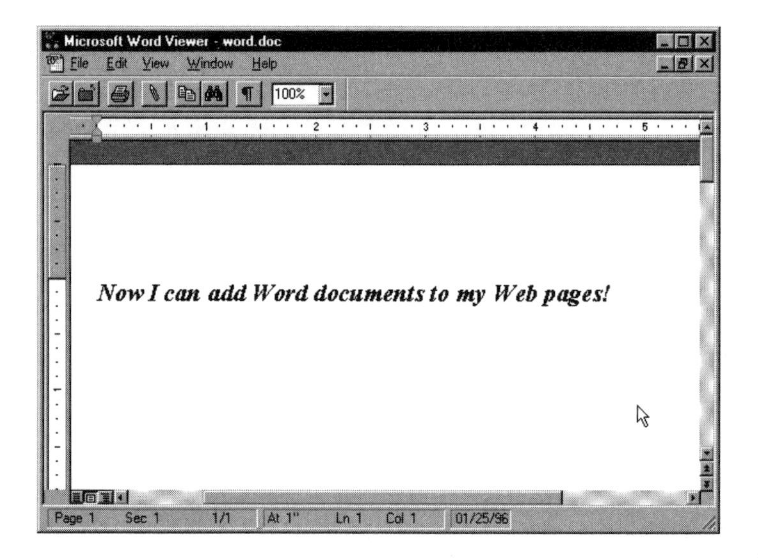

11 Close Word Viewer, your browser, and HoTMetaL.

In this lesson, you learned how to enhance your Web pages using audio, video, and application-specific files. You learned about external viewers and browser plug-ins and how they work with your browser to display multimedia and application-specific file formats. You were also introduced to MIME types and learned how they are used to associate different file formats with the appropriate viewers. In the next lesson, you'll learn some additional HoTMetaL features that will help automate the process of Web page development.

12

More HoTMetaL Features

In this lesson, you'll learn about more HoTMetaL features that are designed to simplify the process of Web publishing. You'll learn how to use document templates to construct prototype Web pages that can be easily tailored to support different Web applications. You'll be introduced to HoTMetaL's macro capabilities and learn how to create macros that can be quickly accessed via selected keystrokes. You'll also cover some additional HTML header tags that can be useful in special circumstances. Finally, you'll learn how to use HoTMetaL's internal style controls to facilitate the process of Web page development. When you finish this lesson, you will know how to use HoTMetaL more efficiently, and you will have covered all HTML tags that it supports.

Working with Templates

There are many times when you may use an old document as the basis for writing a new one. For example, you may be new to a project and have to write a monthly report. You can ask for a copy of the previous month's report, update it for the current month's activities, and send it along its way. It's generally easier to modify or update something that's already written than it is to start from scratch. That's because you don't have to reinvent the structure of the document; you only have to update its details.

Using HoTMetaL's Templates

HoTMetaL's templates follow the same line of reasoning. If you're going to develop several Web pages with the same structure, or if you're periodically going to revise and update the pages that you publish, templates are for you. Templates function as Web page prototypes that provide the structure for the creation of new Web pages.

When you open a HoTMetaL template, you open a document that is already structured and only needs to be filled in and tailored to a particular purpose. You can make any changes you need, and your modifications are saved as a new HTML document; the template itself remains unmodified.

HoTMetaL comes with several templates that can be used as a basis for Web page development. Some of the templates are focused toward business needs; others are provided for the development of personal home pages. You can experiment with these templates to select the ones that are best for you. In the next section, you'll learn how to develop your own templates. Right now, you'll learn how to use the templates that are provided with HoTMetaL.

1. Launch HoTMetaL and select **File ➢ Open Template**.

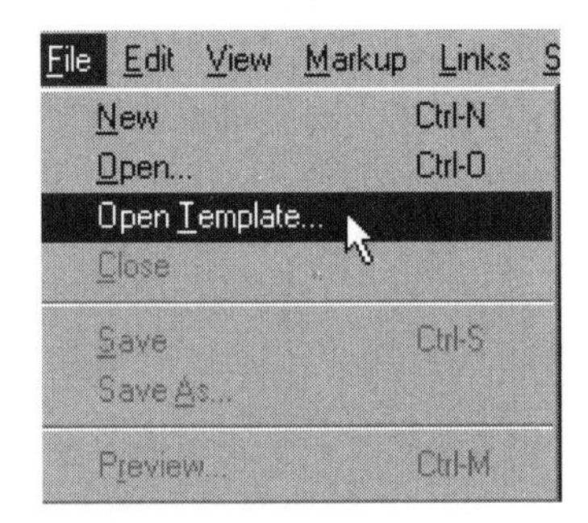

▶ The Open Template dialog box appears.

2. Select the template **c:\hmlight2\template\perscool.htm** and click on the **Open** button.

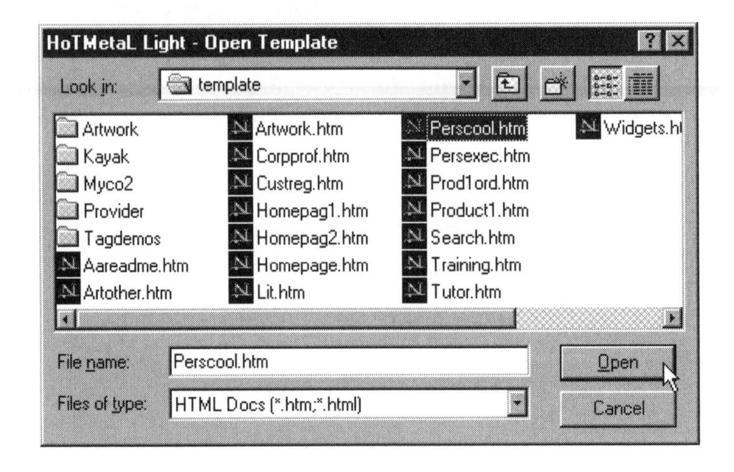

The template opens in your HoTMetaL window.

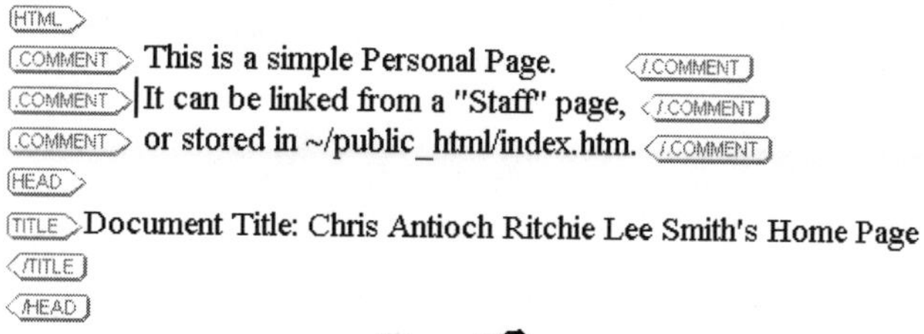
HTML
COMMENT This is a simple Personal Page. /COMMENT
COMMENT It can be linked from a "Staff" page, /COMMENT
COMMENT or stored in ~/public_html/index.htm. /COMMENT
HEAD
TITLE Document Title: Chris Antioch Ritchie Lee Smith's Home Page
/TITLE
/HEAD

BODY H1 IMG
/IMG Chris

3. In the title, select **Chris Antioch Ritchie Lee** and type **Joe**.

HEAD
TITLE Document Title: Joe Smith's Home Page /TITLE
/HEAD

4. In the H1 heading, delete the image, then select **Chris Antioch Ritchie Lee** and type **Joe**.

BODY H1 **Joe Smith** /H1

5. Delete the paragraph containing the text "Me on a bad hair day."

BODY H1 **Joe Smith** /H1

H1 **My Likes, Dislikes** /H1

6. In the My Likes, Dislikes list, delete the list items **Strawberry layer cake (dislike)** and **Crappy window systems (dislike)**.

H1 **My Likes, Dislikes** /H1

UL
LI Chocolate (like) /LI
LI Computer Graphics (like) /LI
LI Dogs (smart) /LI
LI Cats (dumb animals anyway) /LI
/UL

7. Select the word **smart** and type **like**.

8. Select the text **dumb animals anyway** and type **dislike**.

My Likes, Dislikes

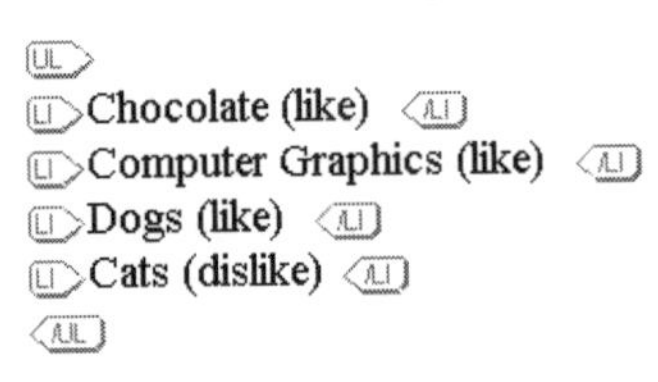

9. Click on the **Save** toolbar button.

► The Save As dialog box appears. This dialog box will appear any time you click on Save while using a template.

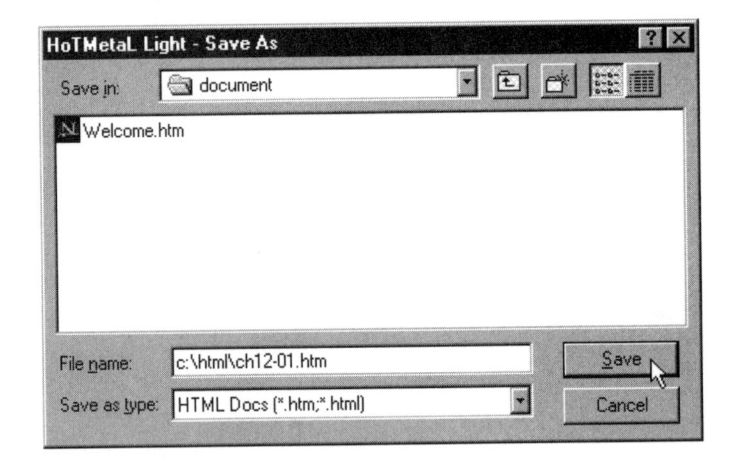

10. Save your file as c:\html\ch12-01.htm.

11. View it with your browser.

► Notice that the text within the comment tags at the top of the document is not displayed.

Joe Smith

My Likes, Dislikes

- Chocolate (like)
- Computer Graphics (like)
- Dogs (like)
- Cats (dislike)

Fave Web Sites

- Wired, for Weird Ideas
- SoftQuad Panorama!
- GNN, for Web guidance

12. Close your browser and the HoTMetaL document.

13 Reopen the template c:\hmlight2\template\perscool.htm.

▶ The template is unchanged.

14 Close the template.

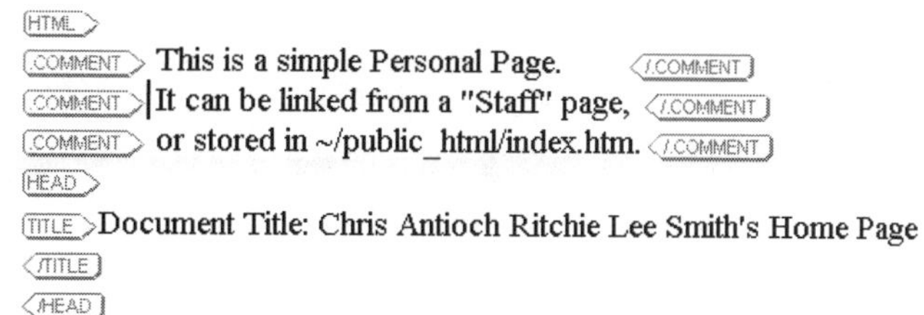
HTML
COMMENT This is a simple Personal Page. /COMMENT
COMMENT It can be linked from a "Staff" page, /COMMENT
COMMENT or stored in ~/public_html/index.htm. /COMMENT
HEAD
TITLE Document Title: Chris Antioch Ritchie Lee Smith's Home Page
/TITLE
/HEAD

BODY H1 IMG
/IMG Chris

Creating Your Own Templates

In the previous example, you learned how to use the templates that are provided with HoTMetaL. Now you're going to learn how to create your own templates. If you have to create or modify several Web pages that follow the same overall structure, you may want to create a template to minimize the amount of duplication involved with each new document. You may also want to use templates to standardize your Web pages.

1 Open a new HoTMetaL document and type **My Title** for the document title.

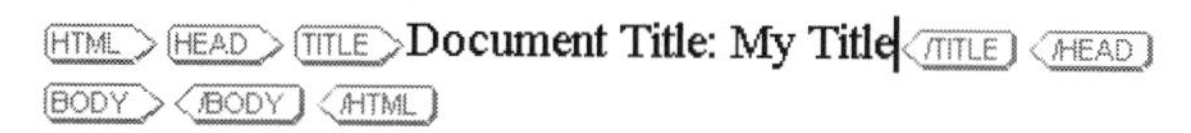
HTML HEAD TITLE Document Title: My Title /TITLE /HEAD
BODY /BODY /HTML

2 Insert an H1 heading and type **My Heading**.

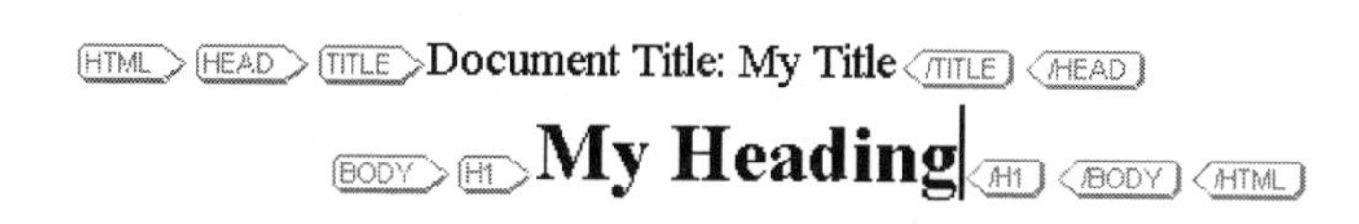
HTML HEAD TITLE Document Title: My Title /TITLE /HEAD
BODY H1 My Heading /H1 /BODY /HTML

3 Move the cursor between the **/H1** and **/BODY** tags and type **My text**.

BODY H1 My Heading /H1
P My text. /P /BODY /HTML

4 Save your file as c:\hmlight2\template\mytemp.htm.

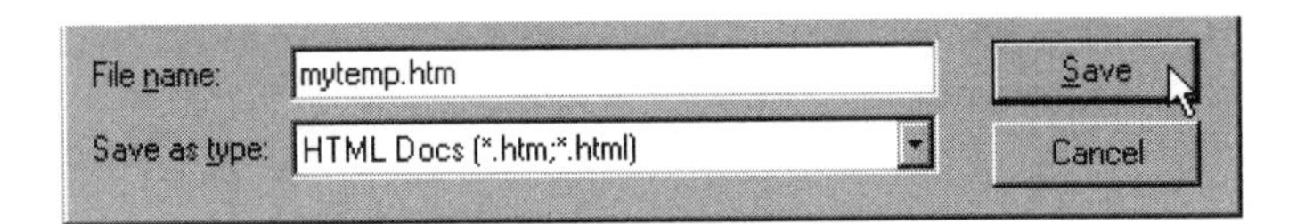

5 Close the document.

You created a HoTMetaL template by saving your document to the template directory. Now, you'll use that template as the basis for creating a new Web page.

1 Select **File ➢ Open Template**.

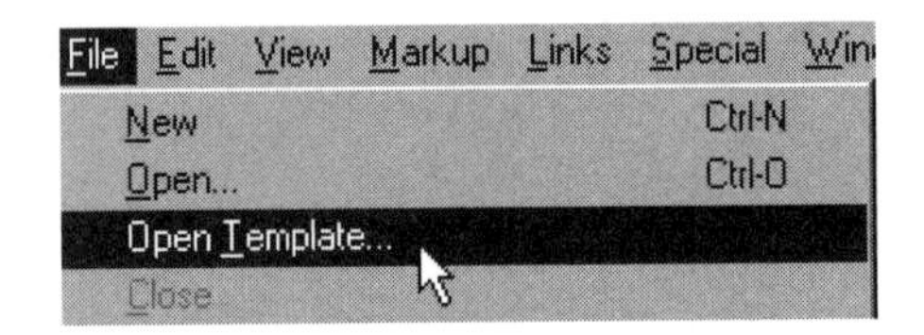

► The Open Template dialog box appears.

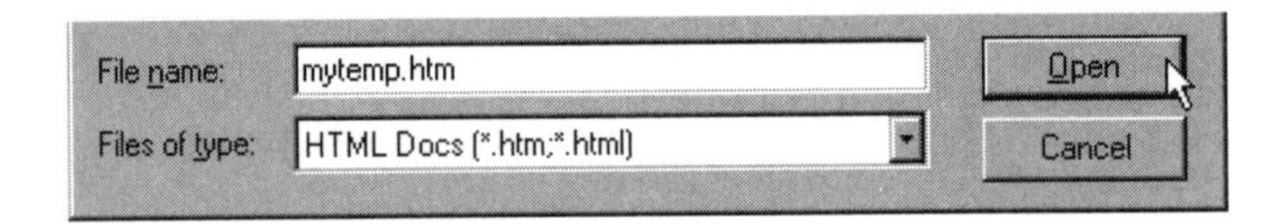

2 Select **mytemp.htm** and click on the **Open** button.

► The document template appears in the HoTMetaL window.

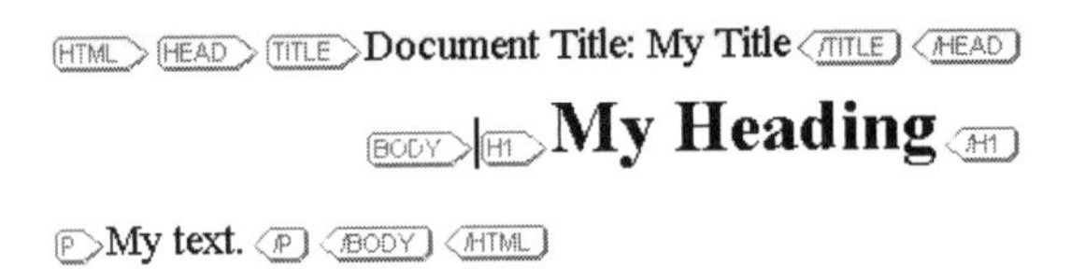

3 Type **Creating Templates** over the title and H1 heading.

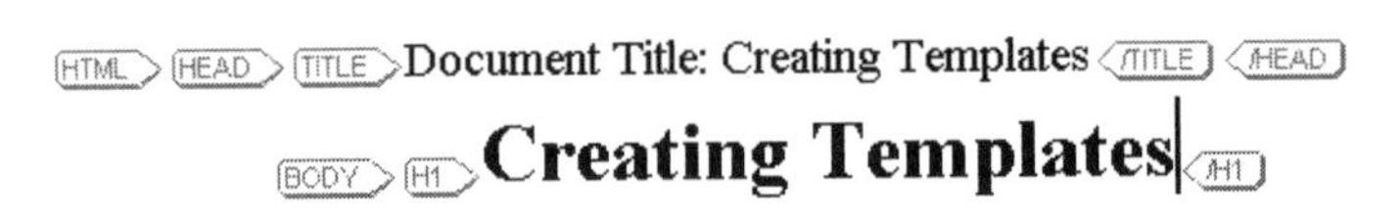

4. Save the document as c:\html\ch12-02.htm and view it with your Web browser.

Creating Templates

My text.

5. Close your browser and the current HoTMetaL document.

Working with Macros

HoTMetaL's macros are useful tools for minimizing the work involved in performing repetitive tasks. If you find yourself entering the same keystrokes and making the same button and menu selections over and over again when developing Web pages, you may want to assign those keystrokes and selections to a HoTMetaL macro. Macros are invoked using *hot keys* (also called *keyboard accelerators*), combinations of the Ctrl, Alt, and Shift keys and other characters you assign. When a macro's hot keys are pressed, the macro is invoked, and it enters all the commands and keyboard characters assigned to it—a real time-saver!

Creating Macros

To create a macro, you simply have HoTMetaL record the keystrokes, menu selections, and toolbar buttons associated with a particular task. When you're finished recording, you select the macro's hot keys. It's that simple.

There are some command sequences that cannot be used with a macro. These include any actions that require additional user inputs for the macro to be completed, such as filling out a dialog box. In general, any menu selections that end with an ellipsis (...) should not be used in a macro.

► ► ► When recording a macro, you can use your mouse to make menu and toolbar selections, but don't use it to move around the document itself. Instead, use the ↑, ↓, ←, and → arrow keys.

The following example shows you how to create a macro that can be used to sign your Web documents.

1 Open a new HoTMetaL document and select **Special ➢ Record Macro**.

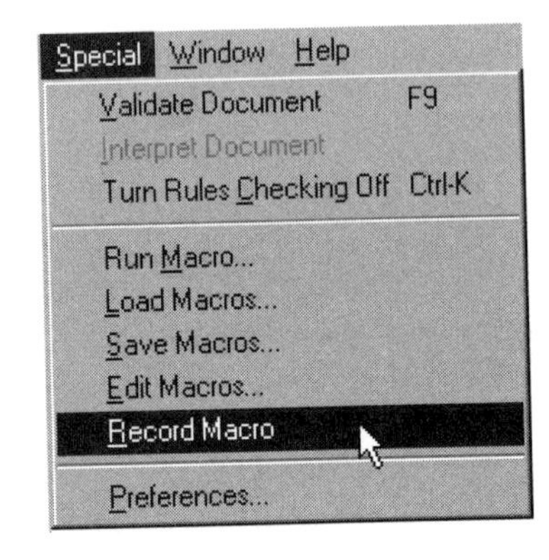

▶ The message area of the HoTMetaL window displays the words *Recording Macro*.

2 Click on the **Horizontal rule** button to insert a horizontal rule.

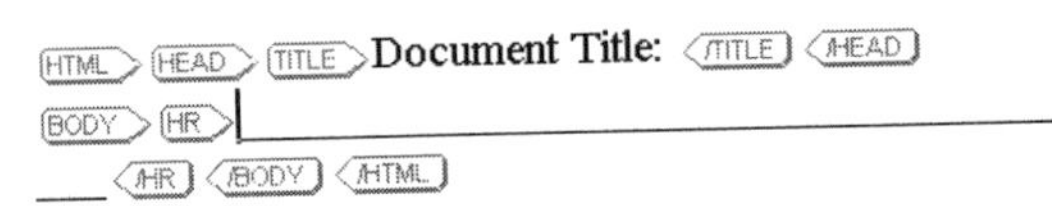

3 Move the cursor between the **/HR** and **/BODY** tags by pressing the → key once.

4 Click on the **Address** toolbar button to insert **ADDRESS** tags.

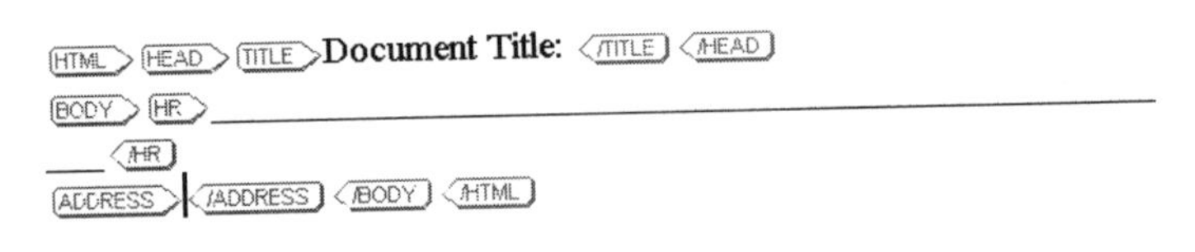

5 Type your e-mail address.

ADDRESS *jamie@jaworski.com* /ADDRESS /BODY /HTML

6 Select **Special ➢ Stop Recording**.

▶ The New Macro dialog box appears.

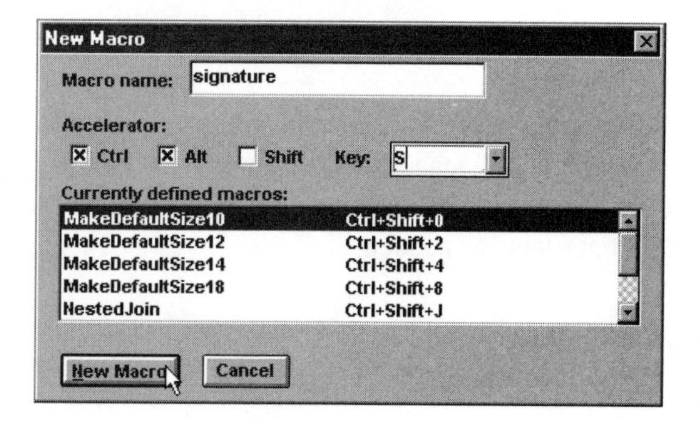

7 Select the contents of the Macro name field and type **signature**.

8 Check the **Ctrl** and **Alt** check boxes in the Accelerator field and type **S** in the Key field to assign the hot keys Ctrl+Alt+S to the macro.

9 Click on the **New Macro** button.

10 Select **Special ➢ Save Macros**.

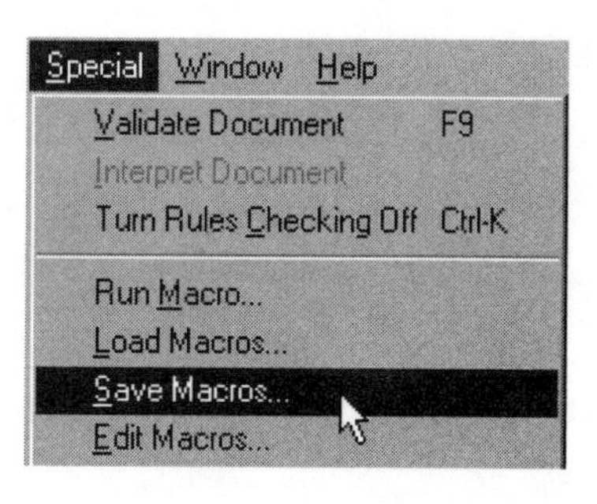

▶ The Save Macros dialog box appears.

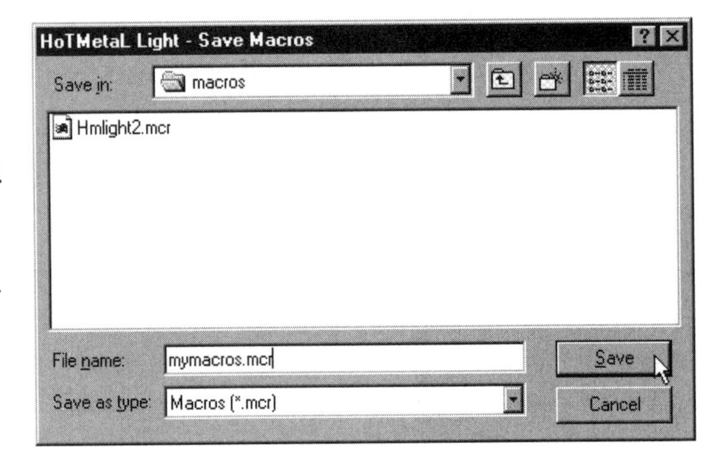

11. Save your macro as c:\hmlight2\mymacros.mcr.

12. Close the document and select **No** when HoTMetaL prompts you to save changes to the document. (You've already saved the macro; you don't need to save the document.)

After you've created a macro, you can go back and edit it using the Special ➢ Edit Macros command. You can also delete it using this command. The Special menu has options for saving and loading macros. You can use these commands to save your macros to a file and then load them later, as needed.

Running Macros

Macros are easy to use. All you do is type their hot keys, and the macros insert the keystrokes and commands that you've assigned to them. You must be sure that the cursor is positioned in the correct part of your document before you invoke a macro, or else you may not get the results you want.

The following example will show you how to use the macro that you just created.

1. Open a new HoTMetaL document, insert a level 1 heading, and type **Using Macros** for the title and heading.

2. Move the cursor between the **/H1** and **/BODY** tags and type the text shown here.

P This Web page used a macro to insert the horizontal rule and my e-mail address. /P /BODY /HTML

3 Move the cursor between the **/P** and **/BODY** tags and press **Ctrl+Alt+S** at the same time.

▶ The signature macro inserts the horizontal rule and your e-mail address.

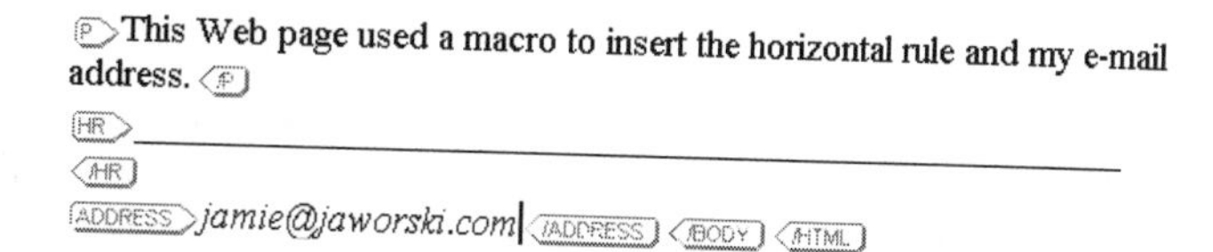
P This Web page used a macro to insert the horizontal rule and my e-mail address. /P
HR
/HR
ADDRESS jamie@jaworski.com /ADDRESS /BODY /HTML

4 Save your document as c:\html\ch12-03.htm and view it with your browser.

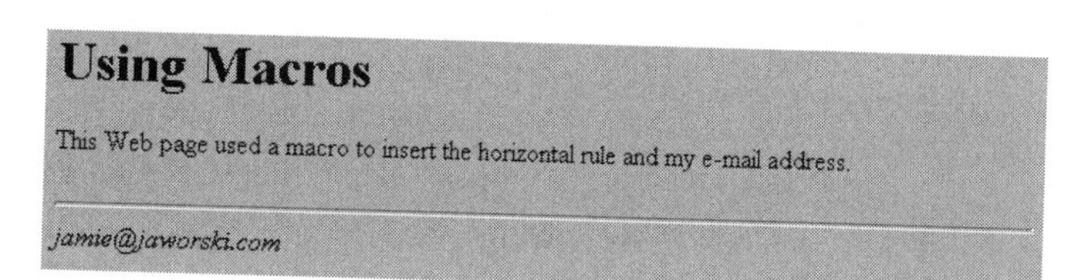
Using Macros
This Web page used a macro to insert the horizontal rule and my e-mail address.
jamie@jaworski.com

5 Close your browser and the current HoTMetaL document.

Using Special Header Tags

HoTMetaL provides all the tags necessary to ensure full compliance with HTML 2.0. Among these tags are a few header tags that may be useful in special circumstances, but are not found in the majority of Web pages.

1 Open a new HoTMetaL document.

2 Click on the **Head elements** toolbar button.

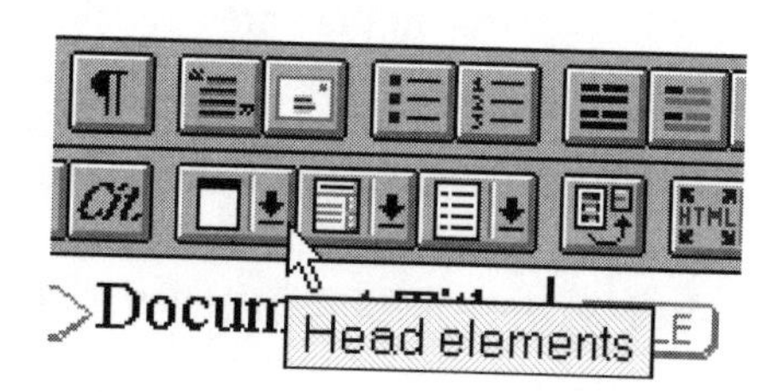
Head elements

A menu appears. The Head elements toolbar button provides access to the **BASE**, **ISINDEX**, **LINK**, **META**, and **TITLE** tags. You've already learned how to use the **TITLE** and **ISINDEX** tags. The **BASE**, **LINK**, and **META** tags are the subject of this section.

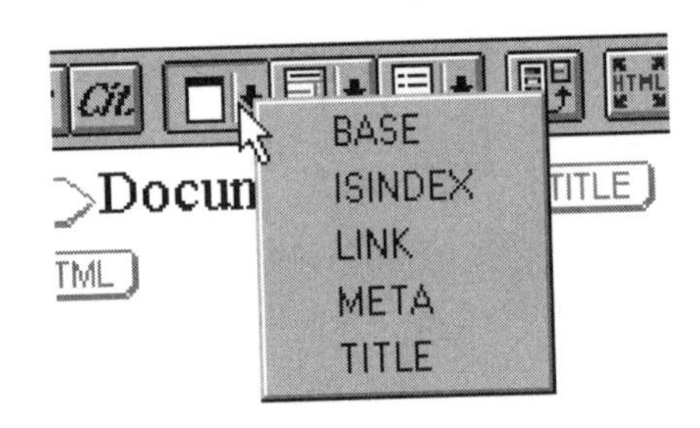

The **BASE** tag is used to identify the *base address* of a Web page, the address that browsers use when resolving relative URLs. Normally, the base address is taken from the page's URL, but you can reassign the base address by using the **BASE** tag and giving it an absolute URL as an attribute. Why would you ever want to do this? If someone saves one of your Web pages as a file on their computer, all URLs will be calculated relative to their machine. By using the **BASE** tag, you can force these URLs to be calculated relative to the original Web page's location. But you must take care when using the **BASE** tag: by changing the base address, you change the URL address calculation of all relative URLs found on the Web page, which can really mess up your links. I'd advise against using it at all.

The **LINK** tag is used to place the source of a link in the **HEAD** of a Web page. It takes the URL of the link's destination as its only attribute. It is usually much more useful to implement links using anchor tags within the body of a Web page.

The **META** tag is used to specify "meta-information" about a Web page, such as its expiration date, the national language in which it is written, or special keywords associated with the page. This information may be reported to Web browsers by a Web server. The **META** tag does not add to the information content of a Web page as displayed by browsers.

When you insert **BASE** and **LINK** tags into a HoTMetaL document, the Edit URL dialog box appears and prompts you to enter a URL. However, the **META** tag does not automatically solicit the information it requires because meta-information is not formally defined. You must manually edit the meta-information you choose to supply.

Using HoTMetaL Styles

HoTMetaL provides a feature that allows you to change the style of your documents as they appear in the HoTMetaL window. This style control feature only applies to the way your documents appear within HoTMetaL and does not affect the way they are rendered by browsers.

HoTMetaL's styles allow you to adjust its screen formatting capabilities to fit your needs and tastes. These styles may not help you produce better Web pages, but they will help you feel more comfortable in constructing the pages you produce.

HoTMetaL allows you to change a number of its screen formatting properties, including fonts, colors, spacing, indentation, and justification. Changing these properties is easy. All you have to do is select the Styles command and make your adjustments using the Styles dialog box.

The following example will show you how to use HoTMetaL's styles to change the colors used with headings and paragraphs.

1. Open a new HoTMetaL document, create a level 1 heading, and type **Using Styles** for the title and heading.

2. With the cursor still in the heading, select **View ➢ Styles**.

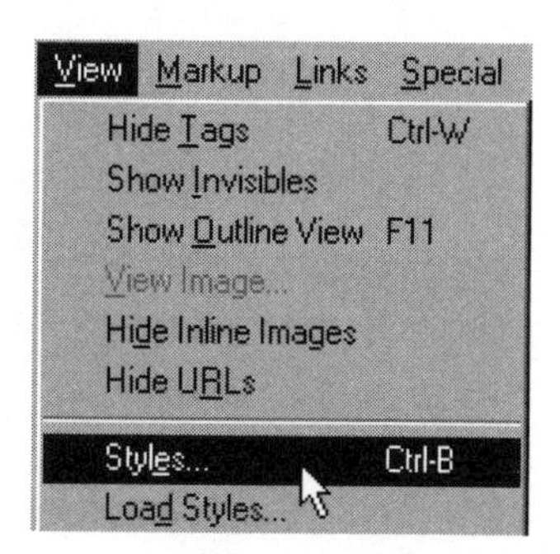

▶ The H1 Styles dialog box appears.

3 Click on the **Colors** button.

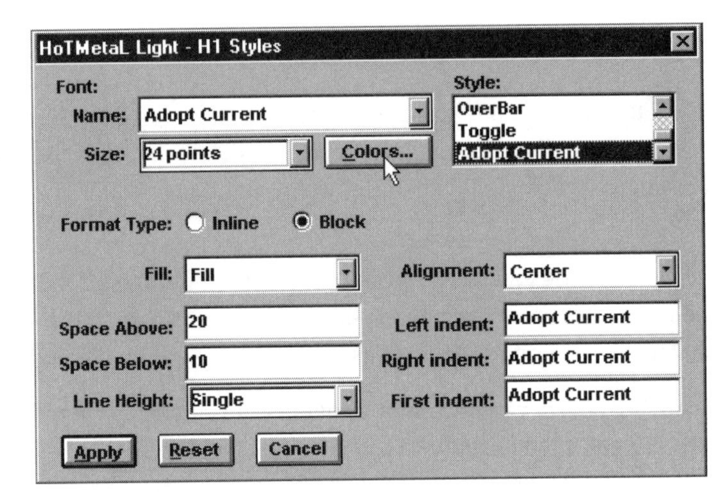

▶ The Colors for H1 dialog box appears.

4 Select **blue** from the Foreground list and click on the **Apply** button.

5 Click on the **Apply** button in the H1 Styles dialog box.

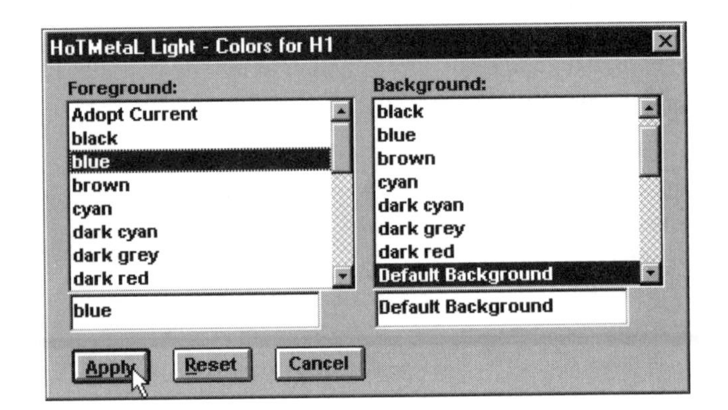

▶ The H1 heading is displayed with a blue foreground color.

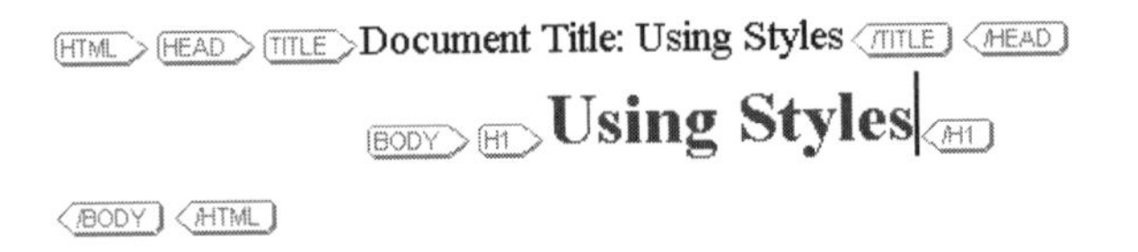

6 Move the cursor between the **/H1** and **/BODY** tags and type the text shown here.

P HoTMetaL styles are for editing purposes. They are not displayed by browsers. /P /BODY /HTML

7 Select **View ➢ Styles**.

▶ The P Styles dialog box appears.

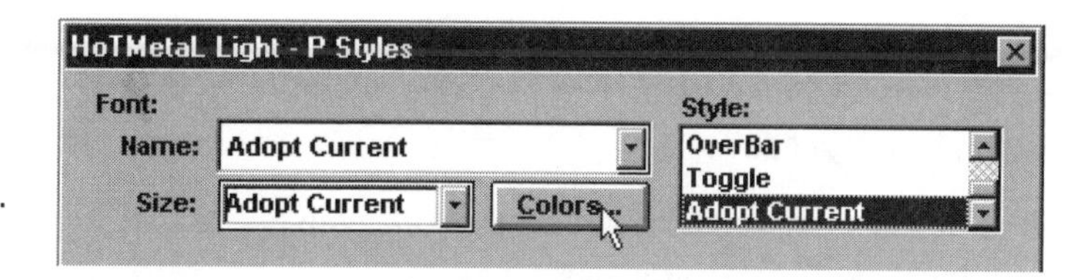

8 Click on the **Colors** button.

▶ The Colors for P dialog box appears.

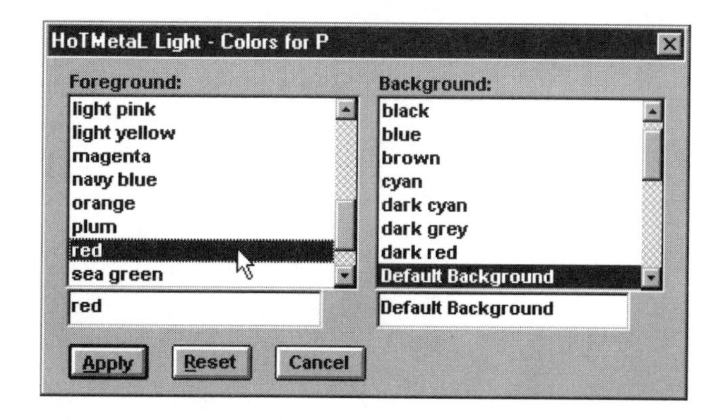

9 Scroll down the list and select the **red** foreground color.

10 Click on **Apply** twice to close both dialog boxes.

▶ A red foreground color is used to display the text between the **P** tags.

11 Save your file as c:\html\ch12-04.htm.

12 View it with your browser.

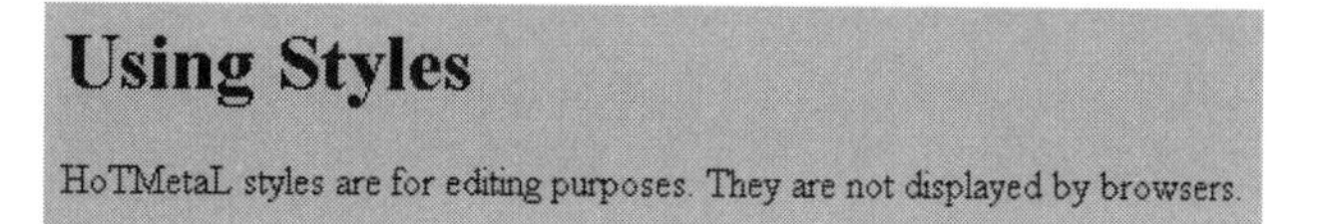

▶ The HoTMetaL styles do not affect the way the text is displayed by your browser.

13 Exit your browser and HoTMetaL.

In this lesson, you learned how to streamline the Web page development process by creating templates and macros and using them in developing your Web pages. You also learned about the additional HTML header tags supported by HoTMetaL. Finally, you learned how to use HoTMetaL's styles to control how your documents appear in the HoTMetaL window.

In the next lesson, you'll learn how to write Web pages with style, using some of the helpful tools HoTMetaL provides.

13

PUBLISHING WITH STYLE

In this lesson, you'll receive some tips on how to style your Web pages to make them visually appealing, easy to navigate, and responsive to user needs. You'll learn the minimum capabilities that Web users expect and how to provide those capabilities in your Web pages. You will also learn how to use HoTMetaL to validate your Web documents, check your spelling, and provide the perfect word when needed. Finally, you'll learn what to do when it's time to put your pages on the Web.

Meeting Web Users' Expectations

In retailing, location and presentation determine business success. On the Web, content and style are the key. To be successful, you have to provide the information people want, and you have to present it in a way that meets their needs. If your Web pages provide value in terms of information, understanding, entertainment, or some other measure, then people will find them. If your Web pages don't measure up, they will surely be sidestepped.

While I can't pretend to tell you what information is of value, I can give you some basic suggestions on how to present it. This advice is from the perspective of Web users and is based on the minimum capabilities that they expect.

Availability and Responsiveness

It is easy to get to any Web page—the user either clicks on a link to the page or types in its URL. What happens after that depends on the data communication capabilities of the website where the page is located, the current load on its server, and the speed at which the user is communicating with the Internet. One of the most frustrating experiences for a Web user is to point their browser at a website and wait a seemingly interminable amount of time for a Web page to load. In some cases, the availability of your Web pages may have nothing to do with their design; in other cases it does.

For example, your Web server could be connected to the net via a 14.4K modem, a fairly slow connection by today's standards. However, if your server is reasonably responsive and your Web pages are short and succinct, users may not notice any significant delays. On the other hand, you may be connected to the net via a high-speed T3 connection, but if your Web pages are long and contain an inordinate number of inline graphics, the users may have to wait twice as long to access your Web pages than if they were short, succinct, and served over the 14.4K connection.

The first principle of Web page design is *Never make Web users wait too long.* If you violate this principle, you will fail to get low data rate users interested in your Web pages. This means that your home page must load quickly and just as quickly catch the interest of its users. Some people put too many graphics on their home pages. This is a big mistake. By the time your Web page is fully loaded, your users may have lost interest. If you must put a whole lot of graphics on your home page, take advantage of interlaced graphics and some of the new Netscape attributes that allow low-resolution graphics to set the stage while high-resolution graphics are loading.

Web users generally won't mind waiting if they know before they click on the link that they will have to wait. If you create a link to a page with several images or to a large multimedia file, label the link with a warning such as "This page contains several images and may take a few minutes to load," or "[MPEG video, 2 Mbytes]." That way you give users a chance to decide whether your link is worth their wait. Remember, there are quite a few Web users who pay by the hour for Web access.

Page length is another consideration for responsiveness. If you are putting a large document such as a thesis or your latest novel on the Web, don't put it all in one file. There are two reasons to avoid this. First, if a user has to wait for a 100 Kbyte+ file to load, you are violating the principle of never making users wait too long. Second, the Web is a hypertext medium. If you put everything in one page, you aren't using the medium correctly. When information isn't carefully linked, it comes across like a black-and-white television show. People may put up with it, but it's not what they prefer.

Navigation and Searchability

When users browse your home page, they should have quick visibility into the structure of your website. The purpose of your home page isn't to impress users with a massive number of image map graphics; it's to provide them with information about you, your interests, your organization, and so on. Image maps and graphic icons are helpful tools, as long as they are used for the right purpose.

The second principle of Web page design is *Make sure that users can easily navigate your Web pages to find the information they want.* Many people suggest specific navigational structures for organizing your Web pages, such as tree-like page organizations or hub-oriented designs. The Web is a free-form medium; whatever structure you choose to organize your pages is fine, as long as users are able to easily move among your pages and find what they are looking for.

It is important that users understand how your pages are organized and that you provide the tools necessary for them to move among the pages to find what they are looking for. Your Web pages should not be an adventure game with hard to find passages between pages of interest and blind alleys leading to no further links. It is common to see navigational buttons attached to Web pages that help users move forward and backward, up and down within large collections of Web pages. These navigational aids are useful, but they solve only half the problem. Users need to know not only what direction they're going in, but also what kind of information is available in each direction. If you provide *content-oriented* pointers, they'll know which way to go. The objective of hypertext is to enable users to easily find and follow a path to the information they desire.

Large websites usually contain search capabilities that help users find pages of interest by searching for keywords. These search capabilities are important for large collections of Web pages because they are usually the most efficient way to find pages on a particular topic. However, searchability alone is not enough. Most people expect to be able to wander around a website to find something of interest, something that they didn't know about when they arrived at your home page. A website that is limited to keyword searches denies users this ability to wander and explore.

Look and Feel

It may be hard to admit, but much of what we do is based on look and feel. It is a factor in how we select the clothes we wear, the people we date, and the software we use. Why shouldn't it be a factor in how we value a Web page? We may not like it, but the visual aesthetics of a Web page determine how we respond to it. These aesthetics include, among other features, the page background color, the background image, the text color, the type and placement of images and links, the use of headers, the way pages are physically laid out, etc. Every decision you make about how a page *appears* determines its look, and every decision on how a page *behaves* affects its feel.

Appearance and behavior are important elements of style. The way we value these elements depends on our taste. What is pleasing to a teenager may not be attractive to a senior citizen. What is useful to a businessperson may be a burden to a student. In deciding what should appear in your Web page and how your page should be organized and used, you must consider its intended audience. If your Web page is about your life as a Grateful Dead fan, it should take on a different style than it would if it were providing information about your child-care facilities.

Because the appearance and use of your Web pages will vary with your target audience, there are no hard and fast rules that govern how you should design them. However, it is very important to keep your audience in mind and tailor the appearance and behavior of your pages to fit their needs. The third principle of Web page design is *Make sure your Web pages interest and appeal to your target audience.*

Compatibility

As long as innovative technologies continue to flow into the Web, browser compatibility will be a problem. In the old days of the Web, compatibility meant that you had to support text-limited browsers, such as Lynx, as well as graphics-oriented browsers, such as Mosaic. Nowadays, you have to provide Java applets and real-time audio to keep power users happy, while still maintaining text-mode compatibility for your graphically-challenged users.

Browser compatibility is a hard problem to solve. There is no law that says you have to support text-mode browsers; it's just a common courtesy. On the other hand, there isn't always a compelling need to provide the latest Web technology in your pages; it just contributes to their appeal. Finding the right balance between innovation and compatibility is difficult, but there is an approach to solving this dilemma (and it is, coincidentally, the fourth principle of Web page design): *Provide compatibility when necessary; support innovation when it adds value to your Web pages.*

Your home page, since it is the entry point to your website, should support text-mode browsers. This doesn't mean that you can't have graphics, but it does mean that your home page must be understandable without them. The pages that are linked to your home page can then include additional technologies, such as Java applets, multimedia, etc., as long as you notify users what to expect.

Some websites provide duplicate sets of Web pages, one set for graphical browsers and the other for text-mode browsers. This is one way to solve the compatibility problem, but it requires quite a bit of extra effort. However, if complete compatibility is your goal, this may be the best option.

Quality and Reliability

Your Web pages are a reflection of you and your organization. If they contain invalid HTML or links to nonexistent Web pages, or if they're filled with spelling, grammar, and punctuation errors, they will detract from your image. There really is no excuse for these types of errors—especially since you have HoTMetaL. You can use HoTMetaL to validate your Web page's HTML and check its spelling, as you'll learn later in this lesson. You'll have to perform your own checks for grammar, punctuation, and incorrect links.

The bottom line on Web page quality and reliability (and the fifth principle of Web page design) is *Always validate your HTML, review your Web page for any errors, and test it to make sure that it works correctly.* This is not difficult; it just requires a concern for quality, careful attention to detail, and a little extra effort.

Minimum Information Requirements

If you are using the Web to publish something you aren't ashamed of or afraid to be associated with, you should provide contact information so that Web users can get in touch with you to ask questions, make suggestions, and provide feedback. You don't have to give away your home address and telephone number, but you should at least provide an e-mail address.

Businesses should supply as much information as they can, including points of contact, e-mail addresses, and phone numbers. The webmaster shouldn't be the only point of contact unless that person runs the company. It doesn't make sense to send e-mail to **webmaster@company.com** to ask questions about a company's products and services.

Web pages should always display the date on which they were last updated and identify the areas that were added or changed, if possible. This makes it easy for return users to find out what's new. If you want to have return visitors, you have to give them something new. If you don't plan on periodically updating your Web pages, don't count on anyone returning to them.

Good websites should include links to other sites that provide related or supporting information. Business websites are almost always guilty of confining their links to company-related information. While I'm not suggesting that you link to your competition, you can and should provide value-added information by linking your Web pages to other topics related to your products and services. For example, suppose you work for the ACME Widget Company and you want to include a Web page about your new XYZ widget. It may not be a bad idea to link to the home pages of customers who use your product, pages on current university widget research, or pages on technology that is related to widgets.

In summary, the sixth principle of Web page design is *Provide contact information, identify the date when the page was last updated, and provide links to related information outside of your website.*

Validating Your Documents

While HoTMetaL can't ensure the overall quality of your Web pages, it does provide several features that will help you avoid common errors. Among these features is its capability to validate that the HTML specifications of your Web pages are correct and complete.

If your Web pages use incorrect or incomplete HTML, they may still appear fine when viewed by your browser. Depending on the nature and extent of your errors, however, they may be severely mangled by less-forgiving browsers, which will adversely affect the overall quality of your Web pages.

HoTMetaL can keep you from publishing Web pages that contain HTML errors and omissions. All you need to do is click on the Validate SGML toolbar button, and HoTMetaL checks your document for any violations of the HTML specifications. This one-click approach to document quality helps you to spend your time focusing on the content of your Web pages without having to be concerned with their correctness.

The following example shows how to use HoTMetaL's document validation feature.

1 Launch HoTMetaL, open a new document, create a level 1 heading, and type **Document Validation** for the title and heading.

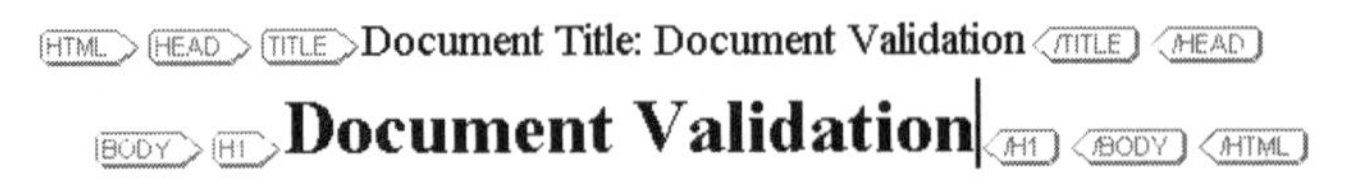
HTML HEAD TITLE Document Title: Document Validation /TITLE /HEAD
BODY H1 Document Validation /H1 /BODY /HTML

2 Move the cursor between the **/TITLE** and **/HEAD** tags, click on the **Head elements** toolbar button, and select **LINK**.

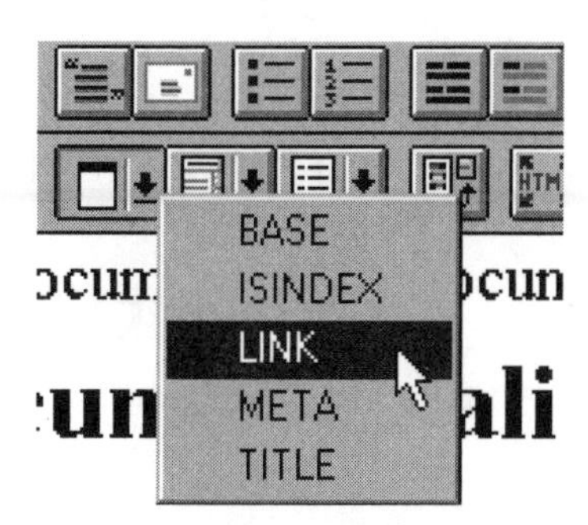

▶ The Edit URL dialog box appears.

3 Click on **OK** to dismiss the dialog box.

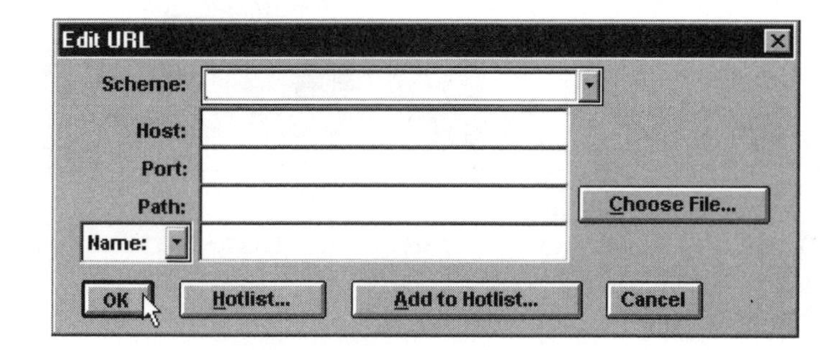

▶ **LINK** tags are inserted into your document.

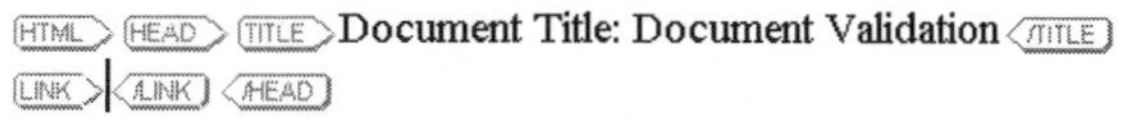

4 Move the cursor between the **BODY** and **H1** tags and click on the **Image** toolbar button.

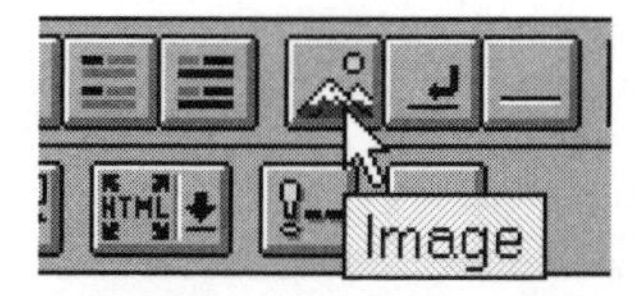

▶ The Edit Image dialog box appears.

5 Click on **OK** to close the box.

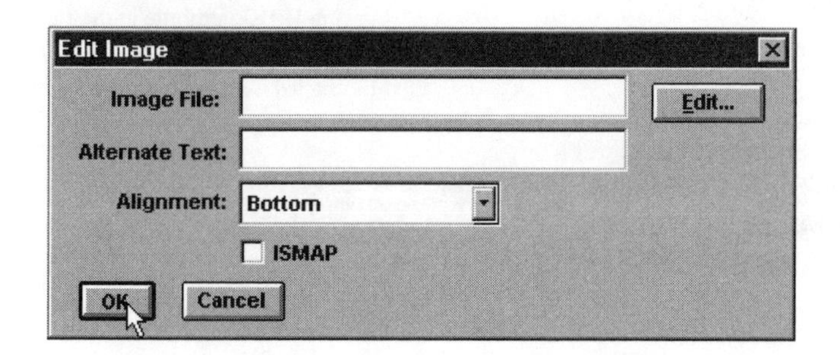

▶ **IMG** tags and the *Image not available* graphic are inserted in your document.

LINK /LINK /HEAD
BODY IMG Image not available /IMG
H1 **Document Validation** /H1 /BODY /HTML

6 Move the cursor between the **/H1** and **/BODY** tags and type **Here's a list of errors for HoTMetaL to find:**.

H1 **Document Validation** /H1
P Here's a list of errors for HoTMetaL to find: /P /BODY /HTML

7 Move the cursor between the **/P** and **/BODY** tags and click on the **Unordered list** toolbar button.

▶ **UL** tags are inserted into your document, with **LI** tags nested inside.

P Here's a list of errors for HoTMetaL to find: /P
UL LI /LI /UL /BODY /HTML

8 Select and delete the **LI** tags.

P Here's a list of errors for HoTMetaL to find: /P
UL /UL /BODY /HTML

9 Move the cursor between the **/UL** and **/BODY** tags and insert another unordered list.

P Here's a list of errors for HoTMetaL to find: /P
UL /UL
UL LI /LI /UL /BODY /HTML

10 Type the list items shown here.

P Here's a list of errors for HoTMetaL to find: /P
UL /UL
UL LI Missing HREF attribute in the LINK tags /LI /UL
UL LI Missing SRC attribute for the IMG tag /LI /UL
UL LI Missing list item in the first unordered list /LI /UL /BODY /HTML

11 Click on the **Validate SGML** toolbar button.

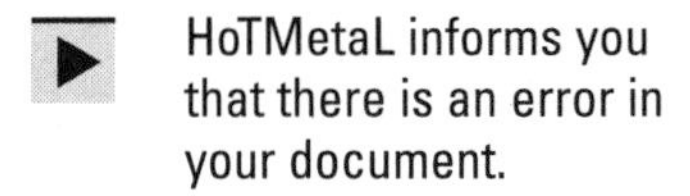

▶ HoTMetaL informs you that there is an error in your document.

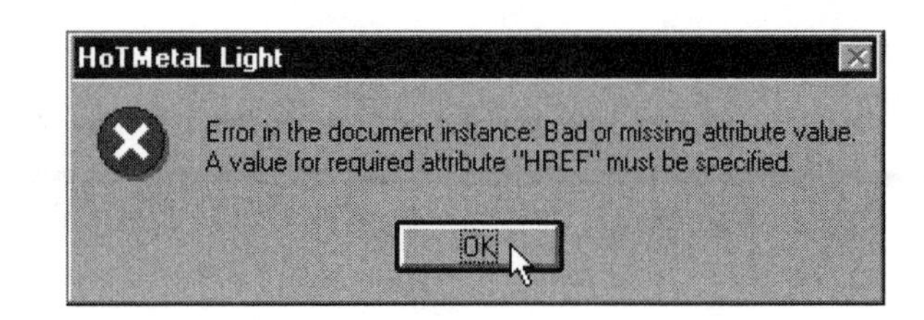

12 Click on **OK** to dismiss the error notification.

▶ HoTMetaL moves the cursor between **LINK** tags, the location of the first error in your document.

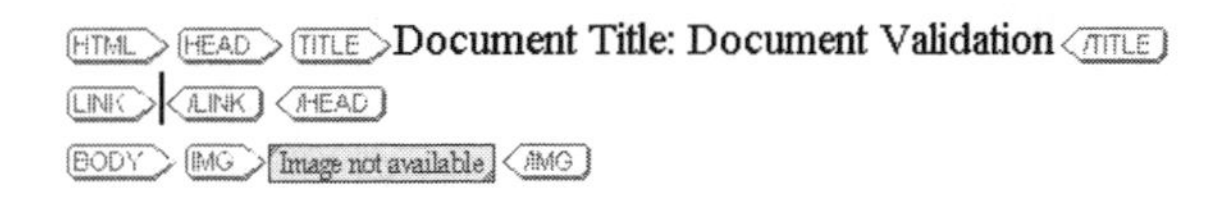

13 Select and delete the **LINK** tags.

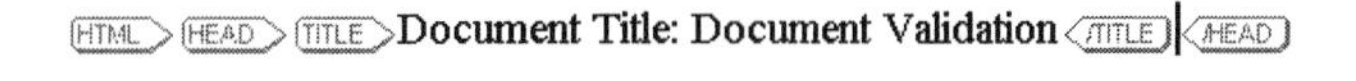

14 Click on the **Validate SGML** toolbar button.

▶ HoTMetaL finds another error in your document.

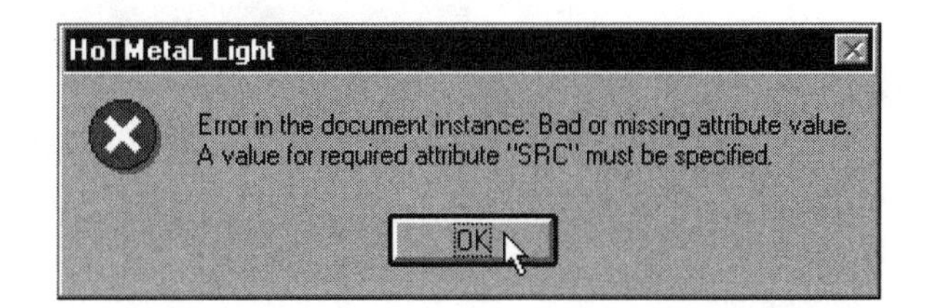

15 Click on **OK**.

▶ HoTMetaL places the cursor between the **IMG** tags.

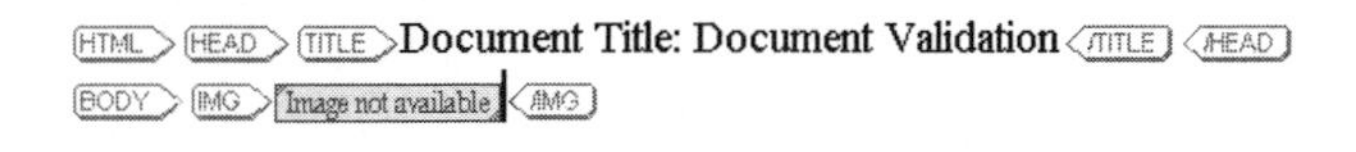

16 Select and delete the **IMG** tags.

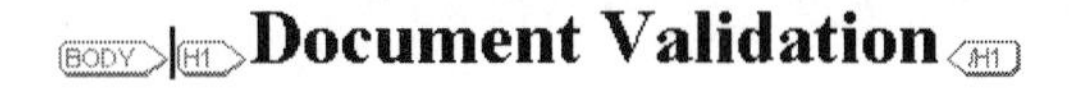

17 Click on the **Validate SGML** toolbar button.

▶ HoTMetaL identifies yet another error.

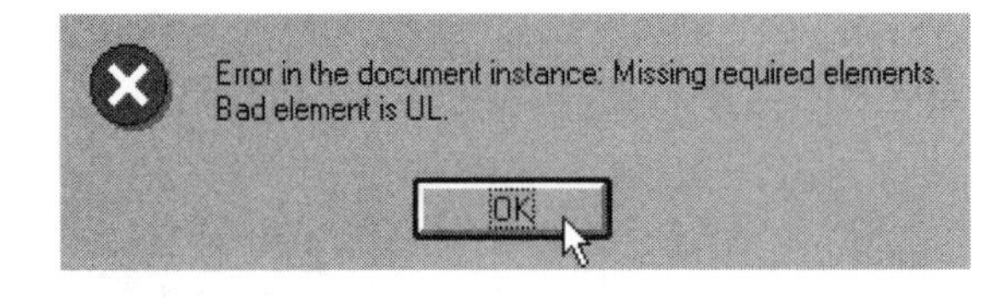

18 Click on **OK**.

▶ HoTMetaL places the cursor between the first set of **UL** tags.

P Here's a list of errors for HoTMetaL to find: /P
UL /UL
UL LI Missing HREF attribute in the LINK tags /LI /UL

19 Select and delete these **UL** tags.

P Here's a list of errors for HoTMetaL to find: /P
UL LI Missing HREF attribute in the LINK tags /LI /UL

20 Click on the **Validate SGML** toolbar button.

▶ HoTMetaL reports that your document was successfully validated.

21 Click on **OK**.

22 Save your document as c:\html\ch13-01.htm.

23 Close the document.

Checking Your Spelling

I've always considered myself to be a great speller, yet I still make several typos in any long document I create. It may be that my fingers are getting older and fatter, or maybe I'm just experiencing the statistical odds of making a mistake. In any case, using a spell checker helps me eliminate most spelling errors from the documents I produce.

The spell checking feature is a tremendous addition to the capabilities that HoTMetaL has to offer. It's very discouraging to go through the time and trouble of developing a Web page, only to find out that you spelled *the* or *Internet* incorrectly. HoTMetaL's spell checker is easy to use and is of great help in improving the quality of your Web pages. The following example shows how to use it to check the spelling of a Web document.

1 Open a new HoTMetaL document, create a level 1 heading, and type **Spell Checking** for the title and heading.

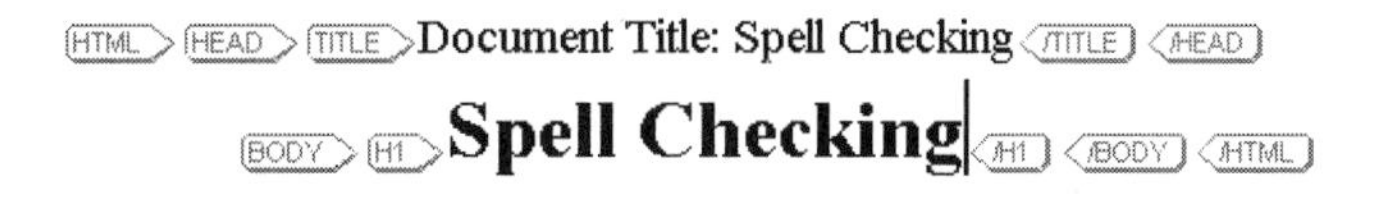

2 Move the cursor between the **/H1** and **/BODY** tags and type the text shown here.

<P>THis iz a tets to see how weel the spell cheker werks. Let's see how well it handles acronyms like HTML, UCSD, and VRML. Finally, let's create "framazam" and add it to our dictionary.</P> </BODY> </HTML>

3 Move the cursor to the beginning of the document and click on the **Check Spelling** toolbar button.

▶ The Check Spelling dialog box appears for the word *THis.*

4 Click on the word **This** and then on the **Replace** button.

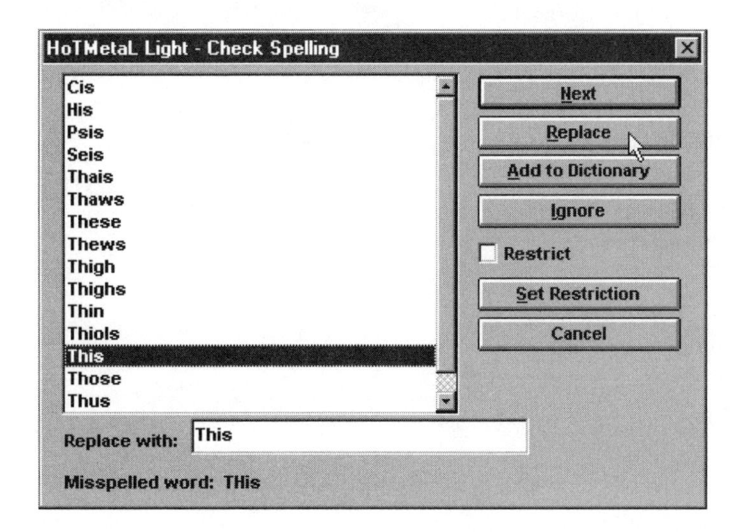

▶ The Check Spelling dialog box appears for the next misspelled word, *iz.*

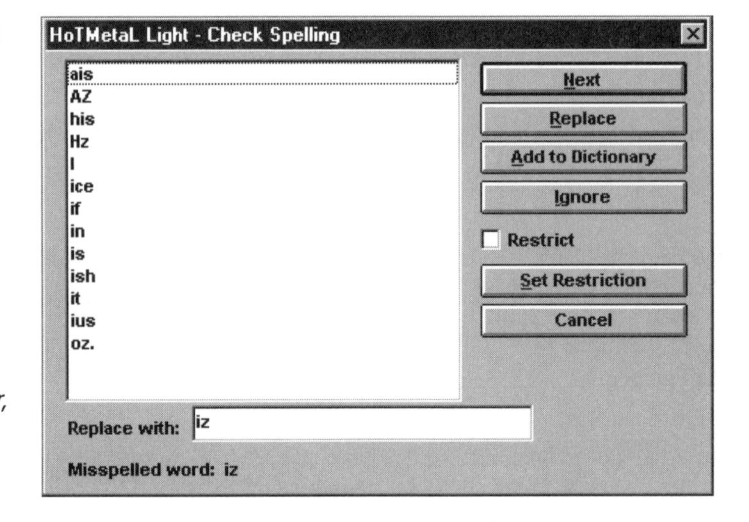

5 Replace *iz* with *is.*

6 Fix the rest of the misspelled words in the first sentence in the same manner: replace *tets* with *test, weel* with *well, cheker* with *checker,* and *werks* with *works.*

▶ Next, the Check Spelling dialog box appears for the acronym *UCSD.* (It skipped over the acronym *HTML.* You probably expected HoTMetaL to know that *HTML* is a valid word.) The list of words shown as alternatives to *UCSD* are the words in HoTMetaL's dictionary that are closest to *UCSD* based upon HoTMetaL's word-matching algorithm.

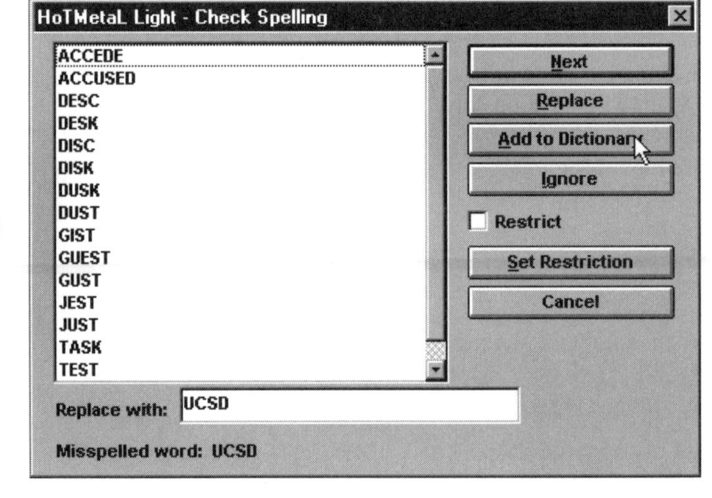

7 Click on the **Add to Dictionary** button.

8 Do the same to add *VRML* and *framazam* to the dictionary.

▶ HoTMetaL informs you that it has found no more misspelled words.

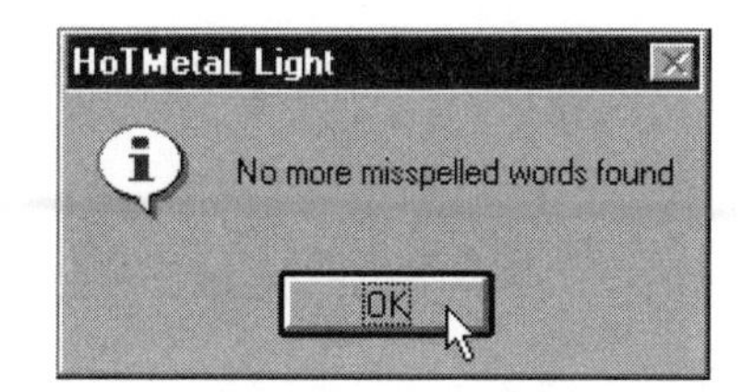
HoTMetaL Light
No more misspelled words found
OK

9 Click on **OK** to dismiss the notification.

10 Click on **Cancel** in the Check Spelling dialog box to close it.

▶ Your document is now spelled correctly.

HTML HEAD TITLE Document Title: Spell Checking /TITLE /HEAD
BODY H1 Spell Checking /H1
P This is a test to see how well the spell checker works. Let's see how well it handles acronyms like HTML, UCSD, and VRML. Finally, let's create "framazam" and add it to our dictionary. /P /BODY /HTML

11 Save the document as c:\html\ch13-02.htm and close it.

Using the Thesaurus

A thesaurus is an invaluable tool for anyone faced with the task of putting pen to paper—or fingers to keyboard—and coming up with text that is accurate and interesting to read. Sometimes I'll be writing away on a subject and come to a dead stop when I can't think of the right word to use in a given context. The way I solve this problem is to think of a word that is close to what I want, then use a thesaurus to home in on the perfect word for the occasion. HoTMetaL's thesaurus provides the same capabilities for Web page development. It allows you to quickly and easily find the words you need to make your Web pages say exactly what you want them to say.

The following example shows how to use HoTMetaL's thesaurus.

1 Open a new document, create a level 1 heading, and type **Using the Thesaurus** for the title and heading.

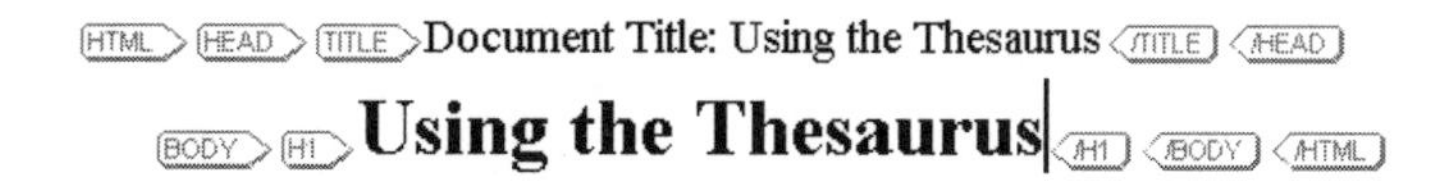
HTML HEAD TITLE Document Title: Using the Thesaurus /TITLE /HEAD
BODY H1 Using the Thesaurus /H1 /BODY /HTML

2 Move the cursor between the **/H1** and **/BODY** tags and type the text shown here.

HoTMetaL's thesaurus picks the good word for every happening.

3 Double-click on the word **good** to select it.

is picks the good word for every

4 Click on the **Thesaurus** toolbar button.

▶ The Thesaurus dialog box appears, showing a list of synonyms for the first meaning of *good.* None of the synonyms shown here is exactly what we want.

5 Click on the **Next Meaning** button.

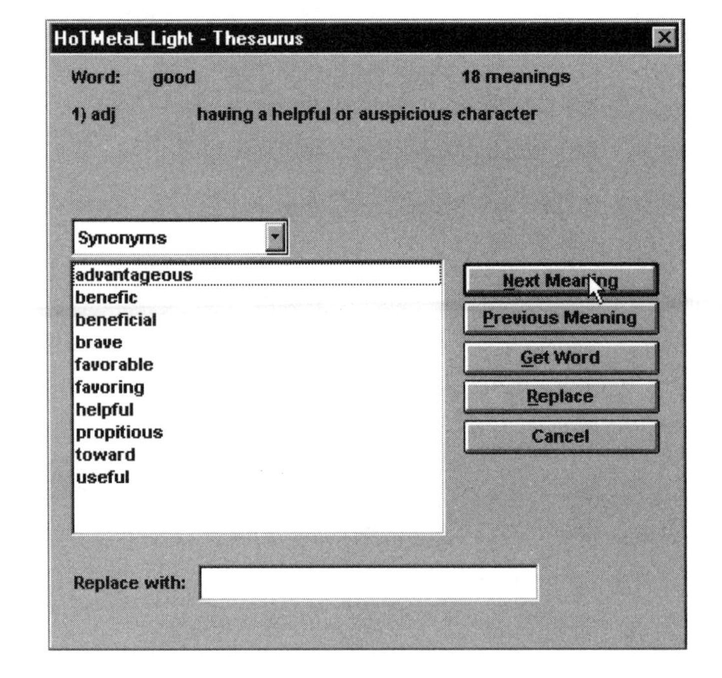

▶ HoTMetaL displays a second meaning of the word *good.*

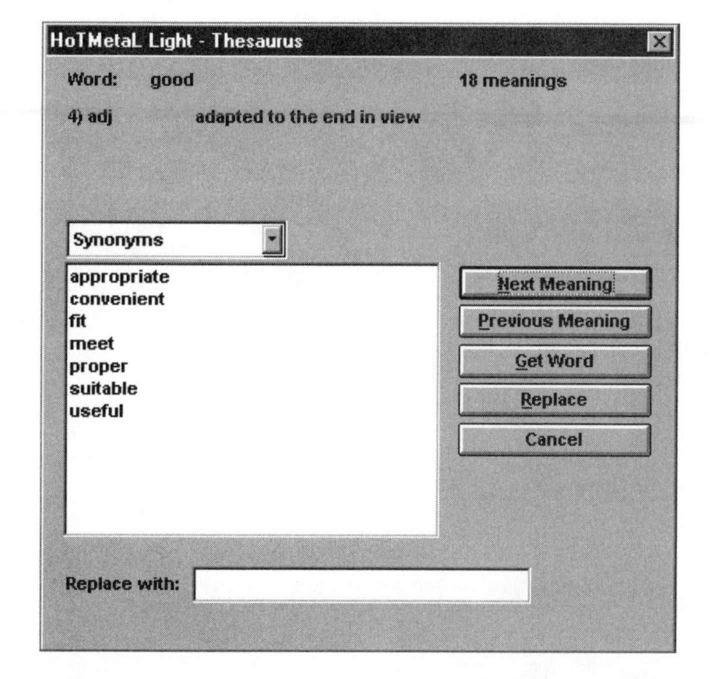

6 Click on the **Next Meaning** button two more times until the fourth meaning is shown.

7 Click on the word **proper** and then on the **Replace** button.

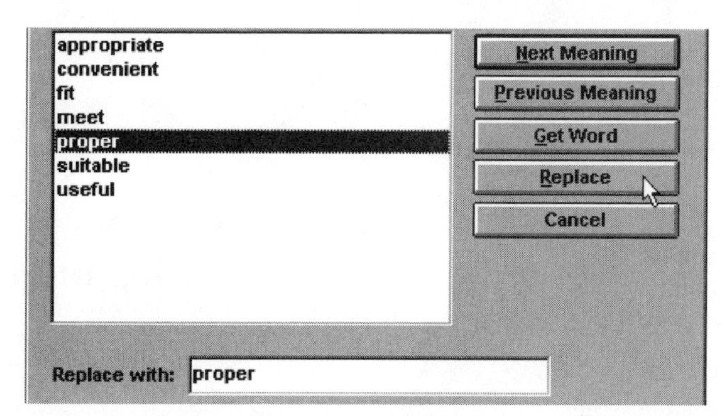

8 Click on the **Cancel** button to close the dialog box.

▶ The word *proper* replaces the word *good.*

<P>HoTMetaL's thesaurus picks the proper word for every happening. </P>
</BODY> </HTML>

9 Select the word **happening** and click on the **Thesaurus** toolbar button.

▶ The Thesaurus dialog box appears once again.

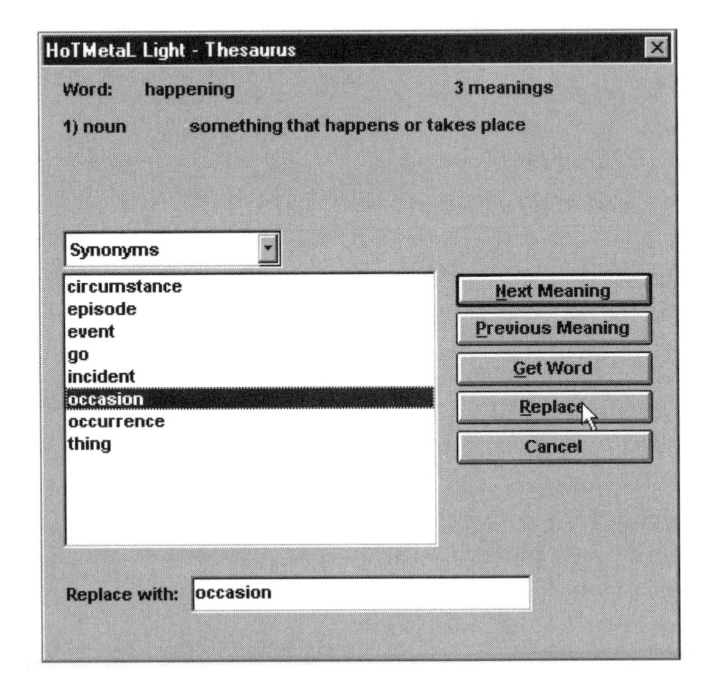

10 Click on the word **occasion** and then on the **Replace** button.

11 Click on the **Cancel** button to close the dialog box.

▶ The word *occasion* replaces the word *happening.*

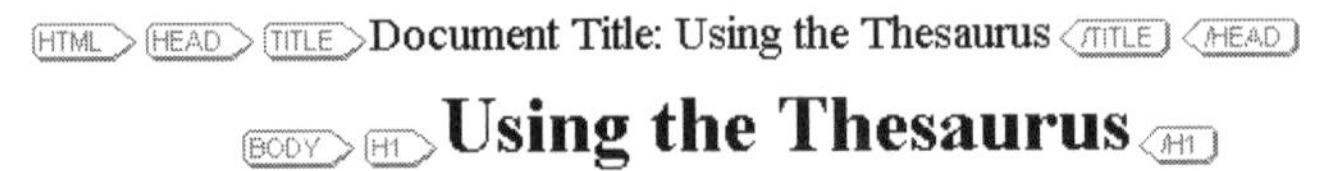

12 Click anywhere to deselect *occasion.*

13 Save your document as c:\html\ch13-03.htm and close it.

14 Close HoTMetaL.

Putting Your Pages on the Web

You've designed your pages with care, always keeping in mind the six principles of Web page design. You've validated your documents, checked your spelling, used the thesaurus, and tested all your links (you *have* tested all your links, haven't you?) to make sure everything is perfect. Now is the moment you've been waiting for: actually putting your pages out there for all the world to see.

Putting your pages on the Web turns out to be the easiest step in the Web publishing process. To put your pages on the Web, you must first identify a Web server where you'll publish your Web pages. Then all you have to do is move the HTML files containing your pages from your computer to the appropriate location on the server.

Finding a Server

Where do you find a Web server to publish your pages? This is easier than it seems. If you're a student, check with your school's website to see if you can put your Web pages on the school's server. Most schools with a Web server have some sort of system set up for publishing students' Web pages. If your company has a Web server, check with your company's webmaster. Some companies allow personal Web pages to be published on company servers, as long as they meet certain guidelines. If you can't publish through school or work, check around to see if you know someone who has their own Web server. I've set up a few friends with Web publishing accounts on the server that I keep at home.

If you can't find anyone who'll publish your pages for free, you have two choices: set up your own Web server or use a Web publishing service. If you are technically inclined, you may want to look into setting up your own server. The book's website (located at **http://www.jaworski.com/htmlbook/**) provides links to a variety of Web servers that can be downloaded from the Internet. If you elect to use a Web publishing service, the easiest way to find one is to check with your local Internet service provider.

Moving Your Files

Once you have found a Web server, the webmaster will either set you up with a directory where you can locate your HTML files, or set up some sort of system where you pass her your files and she moves them to the appropriate locations on the server. She will also tell you how to identify the URLs of your Web pages.

If you are responsible for moving your HTML files from your computer to a directory on the Web server, the webmaster will tell you what directory to put them in. All you have to do is get them there.

The easiest way to move files from your computer to another computer on the Internet is to use an FTP client program. Windows 95 comes with a basic FTP program, named ftp.exe. You can run it from an MS-DOS command window by entering the command **ftp**. The best source of information on how to use this program is the U.S. Army. If you point your browser at **http://www.army.mil/ftptutor.htm**, you will find a quick tutorial that explains the use of FTP.

Publicizing Your Pages

Once you have moved the HTML files containing your Web pages to your Web server, your Web pages will be published on the Web. Anyone with a Web browser and Internet connection will be able to view them. But how do they know your Web pages exist?

The best way to let the world know about your Web pages is by registering them with Web page catalogs. When you register your pages with a catalog, a description of your pages goes into the catalog's database. Anyone searching the catalog for pages that match your description will be provided with links to your pages.

There are a number of ways to register Web pages. The easiest way that I've found is to use the free registration service provided by wURLd Presence™. This service automatically registers your pages in the most popular Web catalogs. All you have to do is fill out a simple HTML form that describes them. The URL for wURLd Presence is **http://www.ogi.com/wurld/**.

That's all there is to it.

In this lesson, you've learned how to design your Web pages with a style that is responsive to user expectations. You've also learned how to use HoTMetaL to validate your Web documents, check your spelling, and select the right word for the right occasion. Finally, you've learned how to put your pages on the Web.

The next lesson is the final lesson in this book. It will take you through an extended example that integrates the HoTMetaL features you've learned in the previous lessons.

14

A Web Publishing Example

In this lesson, you'll learn how to design, develop, publish, and test an example Web application. You'll start with a concept for a personal home page, lay out its design and supporting pages, develop a working template, and use the template to create each of the pages you've designed. After that, you'll add graphics to the Web pages and test them on your computer. You'll then learn how to publish the Web pages on a typical Web server. Finally, you'll perform actual online testing of the published example.

The Example Application

The example for this lesson is the development of a personal home page for a hypothetical individual named Willie Web. Willie has access to a friend's Web server and wants to put together a simple home page that introduces himself and his family. He wants to provide links to his employer, his hobbies, his family members, and his favorite Web pages. He doesn't want to bog his pages down with a lot of graphics or multimedia links, because his friend has a low-bandwidth dial-up connection. He just wants to publish a simple home page and periodically update it to include additional features. Now that you're an expert at using HoTMetaL, he's come to you for help.

Planning the Design

The first thing that you and Willie do is figure out how many Web pages you need and how those pages are to be organized. You decide on a total of five pages. One page will be the home page, and the four other pages will address Willie's work, hobbies, family, and favorite Web pages. The home page will provide links to the other four pages. Since the number of pages is small, you decide to link each page with the four others. In addition, the pages on Willie's work, hobbies, and favorite Web pages will contain links to other pages on the Web outside of Willie's website.

Developing a Working Template

You decide to develop a template to standardize and simplify the creation of the Web pages. The template will contain partial information for the document title and heading, set the page background color, provide links to all five pages, and place a horizontal rule and e-mail link at the bottom of each page.

You create the template as follows:

1. Launch HoTMetaL, open a new document, and type **Willie Web - My** followed by a space as the document title.

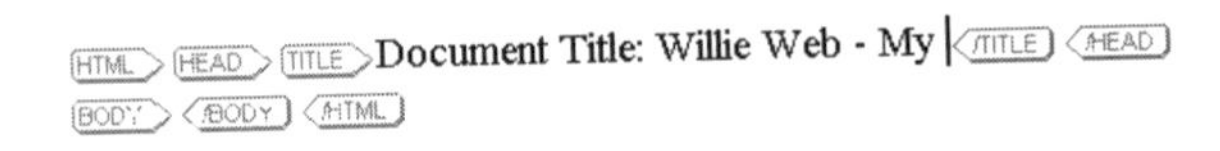

2. Create an H1 heading and type **My** followed by a space.

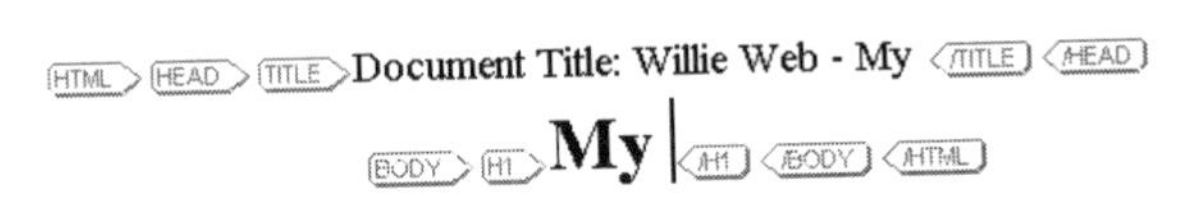

3. Move the cursor between the **/H1** and **/BODY** tags and type **My Home Page**.

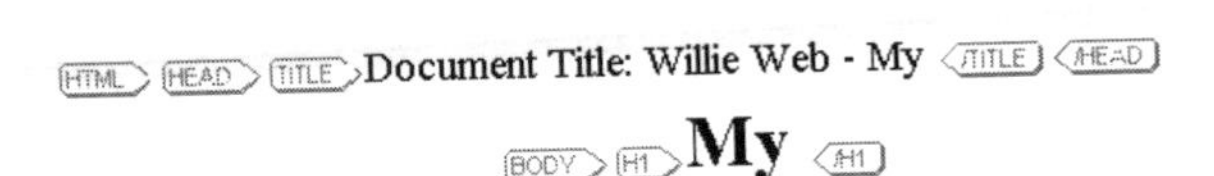

P My Home Page
BR /BR /P /BODY /HTML

4. Click on the **Break** toolbar button to insert a line break.

5. Type the following, inserting a line break after each: **My Work**, **My Hobbies**, and **My Family**.

P My Home Page
BR /BR
My Work
BR /BR
My Hobbies
BR /BR
My Family
BR /BR
My Favorite Links /P /BODY /HTML

6. Type **My Favorite Links**.

7 Press **F6** to bring up the Edit Attributes dialog box.

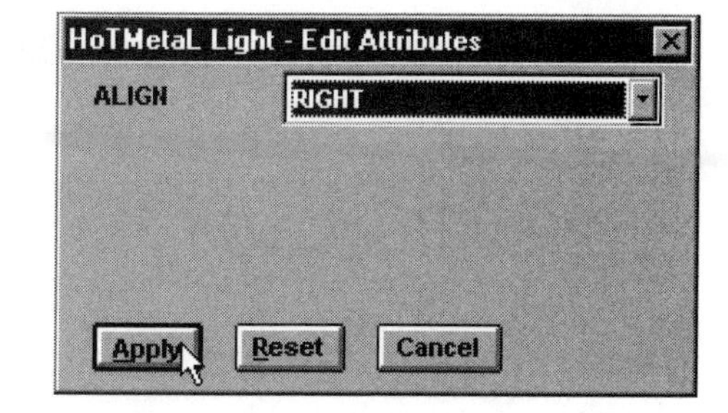

8 Select **RIGHT** in the ALIGN field and click on **Apply**.

► The paragraph is right-aligned within the HoTMetaL window.

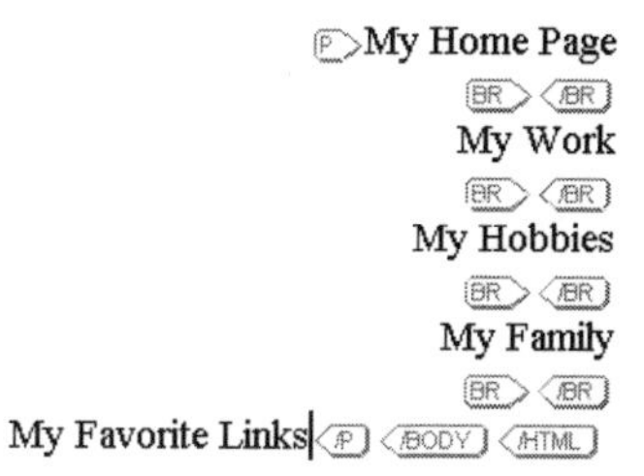

9 Click on the **Horizontal rule** toolbar button.

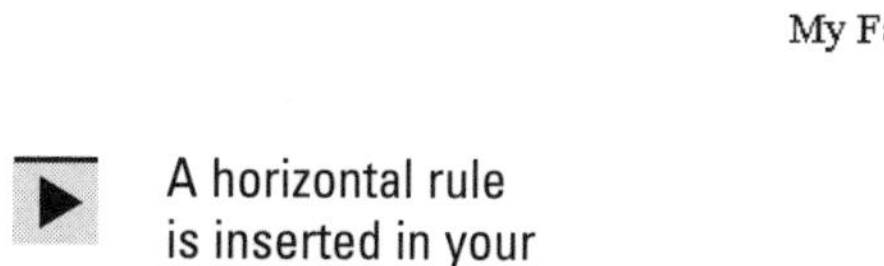

► A horizontal rule is inserted in your document.

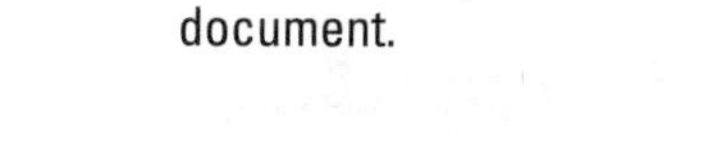

10 Type **willie@jaworski.com**.

11 Move the cursor between the **/P** and **/BODY** tags and press **F6** to bring up the Edit Attributes dialog box.

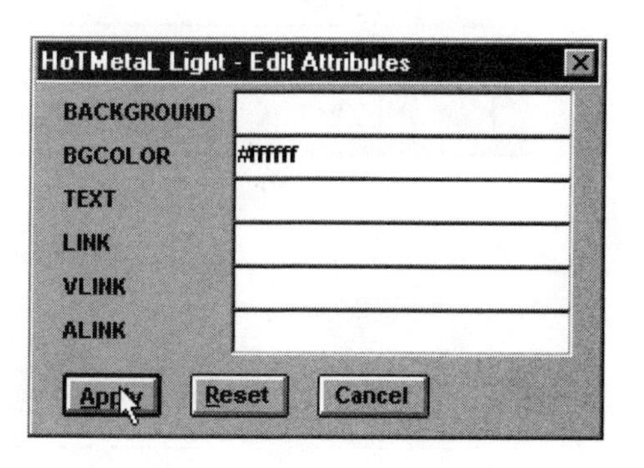

12 Type **#ffffff** in the BGCOLOR field and click on **Apply**.

13 Select the text **My Home Page** and click on the **Anchor** toolbar button to bring up the Edit URL dialog box.

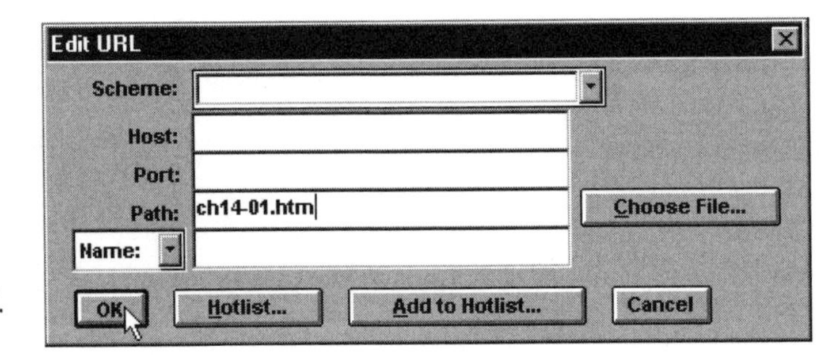

14 Type **ch14-01.htm** in the Path field and click on **OK**.

15 Repeat steps 13 and 14 for the other items in the paragraph, giving them the URLs shown here.

<P> <A>[ch14-01.htm] My Home Page </A>

 </BR>
<A>[ch14-02.htm] My Work </A>

 </BR>
<A>[ch14-03.htm] My Hobbies </A>

 </BR>
<A>[ch14-04.htm] My Family </A>

 </BR>
<A>[ch14-05.htm] My Favorite Links </A> </P>
<HR>
</HR>

16 Select **willie@jaworski.com** and click on the **Anchor** button to bring up the Edit URL dialog box.

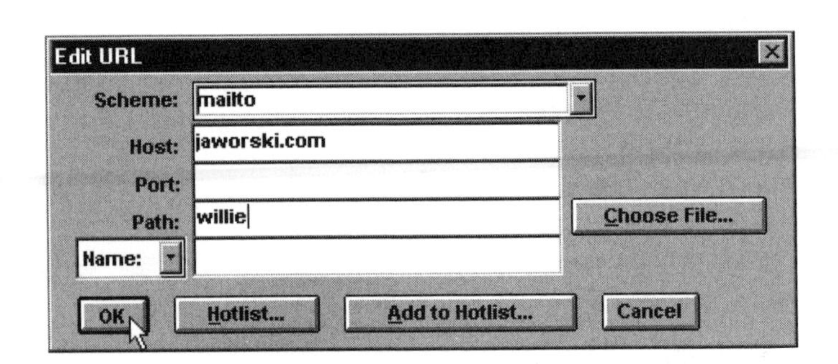

17 Select **mailto** in the Scheme field, type **jaworski.com** in the Host field, type **willie** in the Path field, and click on **OK**.

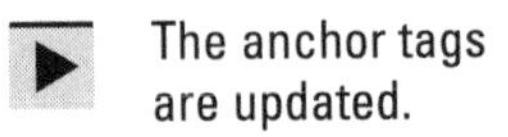

The anchor tags are updated.

 </BR>
<A>[ch14-05.htm] My Favorite Links </A> </P>
<HR>
</HR>
<P> <A>[mailto:willie@jaworski.com] willie@jaworski.com </A> </P> </BODY>
</HTML>

18 Save your file as c:\hmlight2\template\willie.htm and close it.

Creating and Linking the Web Pages

Now that you've developed the template, let's use it to create each of the five Web pages. We'll create Willie's home page first, followed by each of the four subordinate Web pages.

1 Select **File > Open Template** and open willie.htm.

2 Type **Willie Web's Home Page** over the old document title and H1 heading.

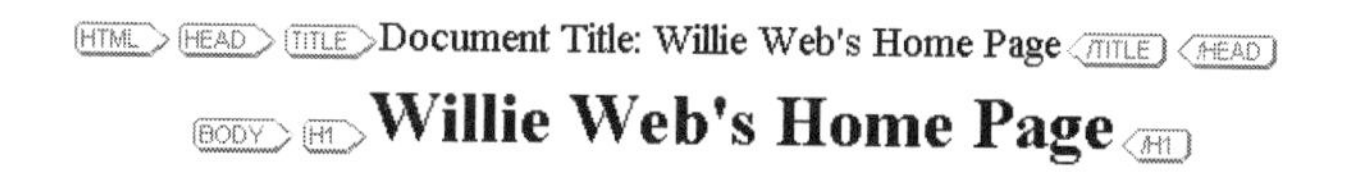

3 Select everything between and including the first set of anchor tags and click on the **H2** button.

► The paragraph tags are replaced by **H2** heading tags.

[ch14-01.htm] My Home Page

4 Click between the **H2** and **A** tags and press **F6** to bring up the Edit Attributes dialog box.

5 Select **LEFT** in the ALIGN field and click on **Apply**.

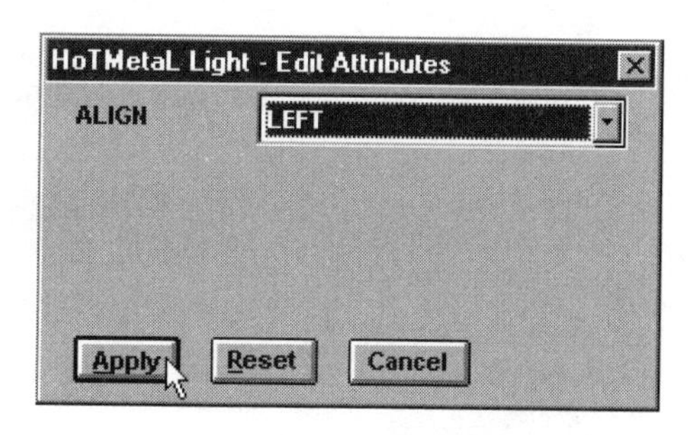

6 Delete the My Home Page anchor and its subsequent break tags.

Willie Web's Home Page

[ch14-02.htm] My Work

7 Move the cursor immediately after the horizontal rule and type **Last updated:** followed by today's date.

HR /HR
P Last updated: January 30, 1996 /P
P A [mailto:willie@jaworski.com] willie@jaworski.com /A /P /BODY
/HTML

8 Save your document as c:\html\ch14-01.htm and close it.

OK, we've set up the basic home page. Now let's do the work page.

1 Open the willie.htm template as in step 1 above.

2 Type **Work** at the end of the title and H1 heading.

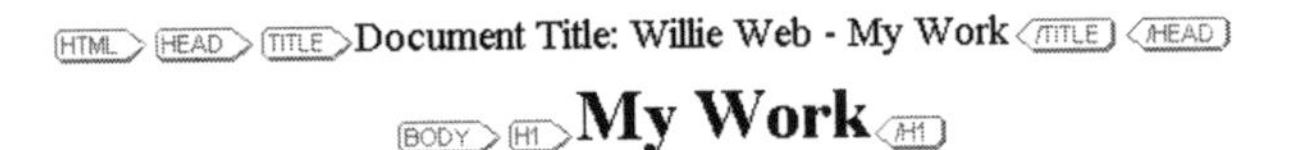

3 Delete the My Work anchor and its subsequent break tags.

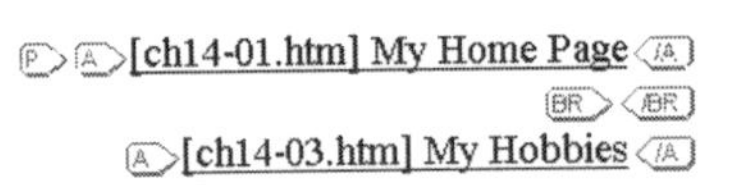

4 Move the cursor between the **/H1** and **P** tags and type the text shown here.

BODY H1 **My Work** /H1

P I am a biologist with the U.S. Department of Agriculture's Forest Service. I study the effects of global climate changes on insects. /P

5 Select **Forest Service** and click on the **Anchor** toolbar button to bring up the Edit URL dialog box.

6 Select **http** in the Scheme field, type **www.fs.fed.us** in the Host field, and click on **OK**.

Edit URL
Scheme: http
Host: www.fs.fed.us
Port:
Path:
Name:
Choose File...
OK | Hotlist... | Add to Hotlist... | Cancel

▶ The anchor tags are updated with the Forest Service's URL.

<P>I am a biologist with the U.S. Department of Agriculture's <A>[http://www.fs.fed.us/] Forest Service</A>. I study the effects of global climate changes on insects.</P>

7 Save your document as c:\html\ch14-02.htm and close it.

Now for the hobbies page.

1 Open a new willie.htm template.

2 Type **Hobbies** at the end of the title and H1 heading.

<HTML><HEAD><TITLE>Document Title: Willie Web - My Hobbies</TITLE></HEAD>

<BODY><H1>**My Hobbies**</H1>

3 Delete the My Hobbies anchor and its subsequent break tags.

<A>[ch14-02.htm] My Work</A>

</BR>
<A>[ch14-04.htm] My Family</A>

4 Click between the **/H1** and **P** tags and add the level 2 headings and paragraphs shown here.

<BODY><H1>**My Hobbies**</H1>

<H2>**Fishing**</H2>

<P>I am an avid freshwater fisherman. I like to fish for largemouth bass and any kind of trout.</P>

<H2>**Hiking**</H2>

<P>I like to get out at least once a week, when the weather is nice.</P>

<H2>**Reading**</H2>

<P>I've read everything by Tom Clancy and Michael Crichton.</P>

5 Select **Fishing** and, using the Anchor toolbar button and the Edit URL dialog box, create a link to **http://www.gorp.com/gorp/activity/fishing.htm**.

<H2><A>**[http://www.gorp.com/gorp/activity/fishing.htm] Fishing**</A></H2>

<P>I am an avid freshwater fisherman. I like to fish for largemouth bass and any kind of trout.</P>

6 Select **Hiking** and create a link to **http://www.teleport.com/~walking/hiking.html**.

<H2> <A>[http://www.teleport.com/~walking/hiking.html] Hiking </A> </H2>

7 Select **Tom Clancy** and create a link to **http://www.auburn.edu/~sandlkr/tom_clancy.html**.

<H2>Reading </H2>
<P>I've read everything by
<A>[http://www.auburn.edu/~sandlkr/tom_clancy.html] Tom Clancy </A>
and <A>[http://www.cei.net/~cthomaso/mc.htm] Michael Crichton </A>. </P>

8 Select **Michael Crichton** and create a link to **http://www.cei.net/~cthomaso/mc.htm**.

9 Save your file as c:\html\ch14-03.htm and close it.

Next is the family page.

1 Open a new willie.htm template.

2 Type **Family** at the end of the title and H1 heading.

<HTML> <HEAD> <TITLE> Document Title: Willie Web - My Family </TITLE> </HEAD>
<BODY> <H1> **My Family** </H1>

3 Delete the My Family anchor and its subsequent break tags.

<A>[ch14-03.htm] My Hobbies </A>

 </BR>
<A>[ch14-05.htm] My Favorite Links </A> </P>

4 Click between the **/H1** and **P** tags and add the level 2 headings and paragraphs shown here.

<H2>**Wilma**</H2>

<P>My wife, Wilma, is a fashion designer for Blanc Fashions. She likes hiking and shopping.</P>

<H2>**Wanda**</H2>

<P>My daughter, Wanda, is a seventh grade student at George Washington Junior High School. She likes to listen to music with her friends.</P>

<H2>**Will Jr.**</H2>

<P>My son, Will Jr., is a fourth grade student at Benjamin Franklin Elementary School. He likes inline skating and playing video games.</P>

<P><A>[ch14-01.htm] My Home Page</A>

</BR>

5 Save the document as c:\html\ch14-04.htm and close it.

Finally, the favorite links page.

1 Open a new willie.htm template.

2 Type **Favorite Links** at the end of the title and H1 heading.

<BODY><H1>**My Favorite Links**</H1>

<P><A>[ch14-01.htm] My Home Page</A>

</BR>
<A>[ch14-02.htm] My Work</A>

</BR>
<A>[ch14-03.htm] My Hobbies</A>

</BR>
<A>[ch14-04.htm] My Family</A></P>

3 Delete the My Favorite Links anchor and the break tags immediately preceding it.

4 Click between the **/H1** and **P** tags and add the ordered list shown here.

<BODY><H1>**My Favorite Links**</H1>

<OL><LI>Cartoons</LI>
<LI>News</LI>
<LI>Outdoors</LI></OL>

5 Create links from **Cartoons** to **http://www.excite.com/Toon/Toon.html**, from **News** to **http://www.cnn.com**, and from **Outdoors** to **http://www.ono.com**.

<BODY><H1>**My Favorite Links**</H1>

<OL><LI><A>[http://www.excite.com/Toon/Toon.html] Cartoons</A></LI>
<LI><A>[http://www.cnn.com] News</A></LI>
<LI><A>[http://www.ono.com] Outdoors</A></LI></OL>

6 Save the document as c:\html\ch14-05.htm and close it.

Adding Images

While you were busy creating the Web pages, Willie went over to another friend's house, scanned in a few pictures of his family, and produced four GIF files. You told him that he would have been better off using JPEG, but he doesn't care. Let's add the images of Willie and his family to his Web pages.

1 Open c:\html\ch14-01.htm.

HTML HEAD TITLE Document Title: Willie Web's Home Page /TITLE /HEAD
BODY H1 **Willie Web's Home Page** /H1
H2 A [ch14-02.htm] My Work /A
BR /BR
A [ch14-03.htm] My Hobbies /A

2 Move the cursor immediately after the **H1** tag.

3 Click on the **Image** toolbar button to bring up the Edit Image dialog box.

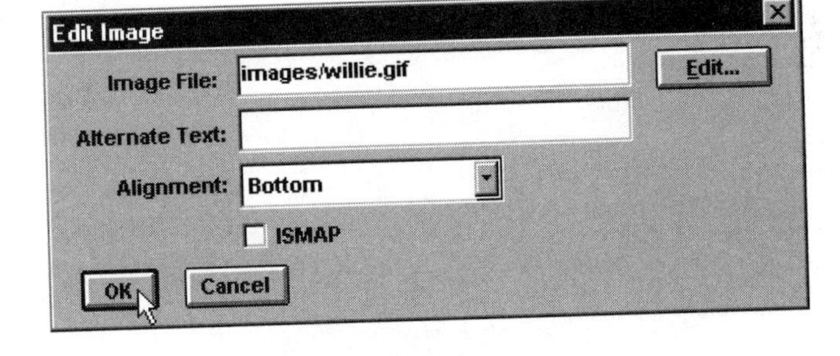

4 Type **images/willie.gif** in the Image File field and click on **OK**.

▶ An image of Willie Web appears in your document.

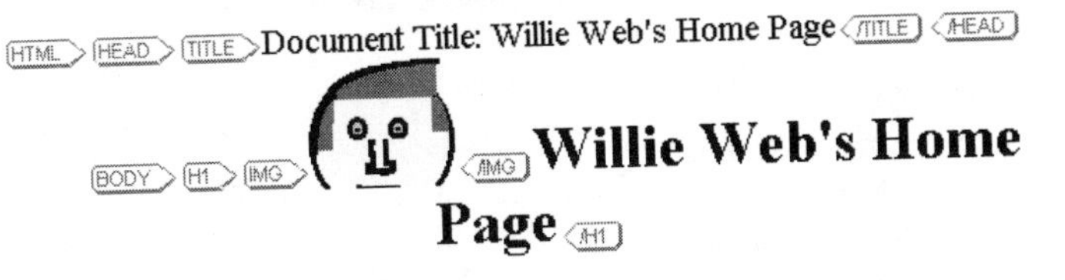

5 Save your file and then close it.

6 Open c:\html\ch14-04.htm.

7 Move the cursor between the **H2** tag and **Wilma**.

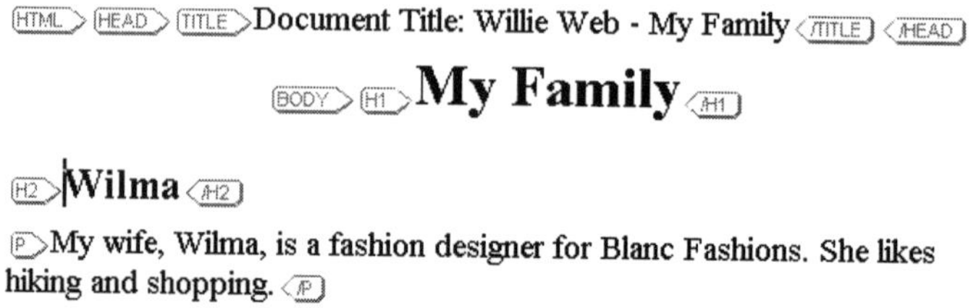
HTML HEAD TITLE Document Title: Willie Web - My Family /TITLE /HEAD
BODY H1 My Family /H1
H2 Wilma /H2
P My wife, Wilma, is a fashion designer for Blanc Fashions. She likes hiking and shopping. /P

8 Insert the image images/wilma.gif.

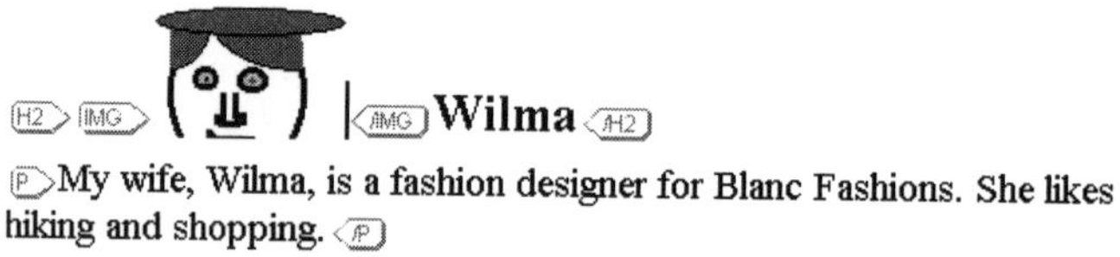
H2 IMG /IMG Wilma /H2
P My wife, Wilma, is a fashion designer for Blanc Fashions. She likes hiking and shopping. /P

9 Move the cursor between the **H2** tag and **Wanda**, and insert the image images/wanda.gif.

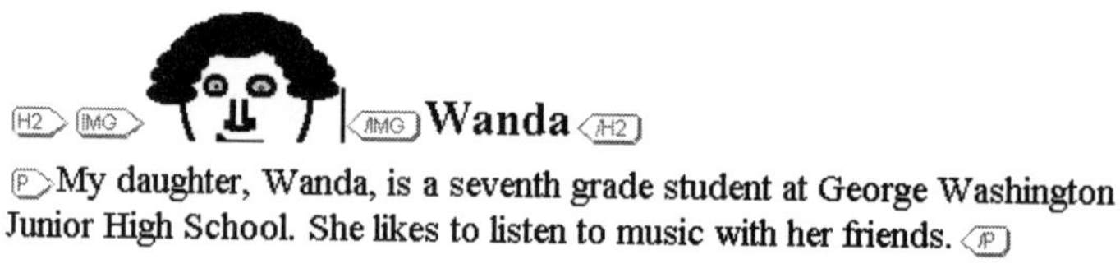
H2 IMG /IMG Wanda /H2
P My daughter, Wanda, is a seventh grade student at George Washington Junior High School. She likes to listen to music with her friends. /P

10 Move the cursor between the **H2** tag and **Will**, and insert the image images/willjr.gif.

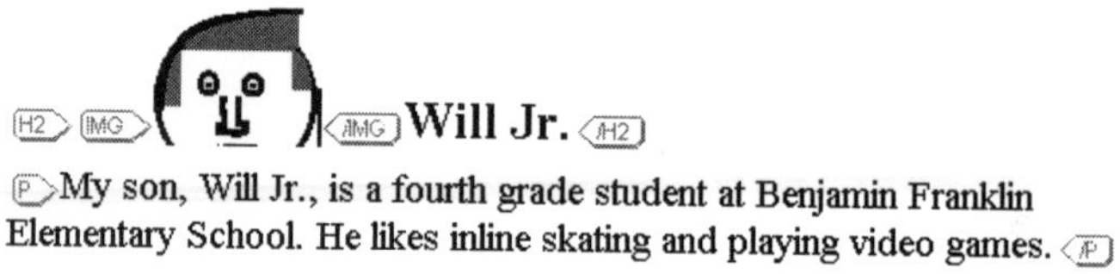
H2 IMG /IMG Will Jr. /H2
P My son, Will Jr., is a fourth grade student at Benjamin Franklin Elementary School. He likes inline skating and playing video games. /P

11 Save your file and close it.

Offline Testing

Now that you've put together Willie's Web pages, you decide to use HoTMetaL to validate them and check their spelling. You've also decided to test them to make sure that you have entered the correct URL for each link.

1 Open c:\html\ch14-01.htm and view it with your browser.

My Work
My Hobbies
My Family
My Favorite Links

Last updated: January 30, 1996

willie@jaworski.com

2 Click on the **My Work** link.

▶ The Willie Web - My Work page is displayed.

My Work

I am a biologist with the U.S. Department of Agriculture's Forest Service. I study the effects of global climate changes on insects.

My Home Page
My Hobbies
My Family
My Favorite Links

---

willie@jaworski.com

3 Click on the **My Home Page** link to return to Willie's home page.

4 Click on **My Hobbies**.

▶ The Willie Web - My Hobbies page is displayed.

My Hobbies

Fishing

I am an avid freshwater fisherman. I like to fish for largemouth bass and any kind of trout.

Hiking

I like to get out at least once a week, when the weather is nice.

Reading

I've read everything by Tom Clancy and Michael Crichton.

My Home Page

5 Click on the **My Home Page** link to return to Willie's home page.

6 Click on **My Family**.

▶ The Willie Web - My Family page is displayed.

My Family

Wilma

My wife, Wilma, is a fashion designer for Blanc Fashions. She likes hiking and shopping.

Wanda

My daughter, Wanda, is a seventh grade student at George Washington Junior High School. She

7 Scroll down and click on the **My Home Page** link to return to Willie's home page.

8 Click on **My Favorite Links**.

▶ The Willie Web - My Favorite Links page is displayed.

My Favorite Links

1. Cartoons
2. News
3. Outdoors

My Home Page
My Work
My Hobbies
My Family

---

willie@jaworski.com

9 Click on the **My Home Page** link to return to Willie's home page.

10 Test all the other links in all the pages to make sure that they are operable. When you're done, close your browser.

11 Return to Willie's home page.

12 Move the cursor to the beginning of the file and click on the **Validate SGML** toolbar button.

▶ HoTMetaL tells you that your document has passed the validation test.

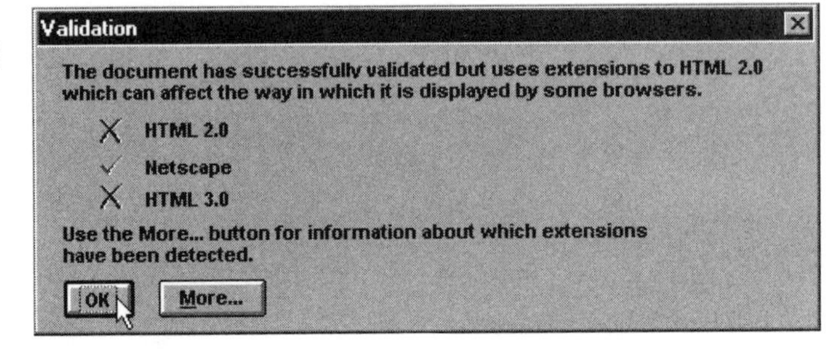

13 Click on **OK** to dismiss the dialog box.

14 Click on the **Check Spelling** button.

▶ Willie's e-mail address should be the only problem for the spell checker.

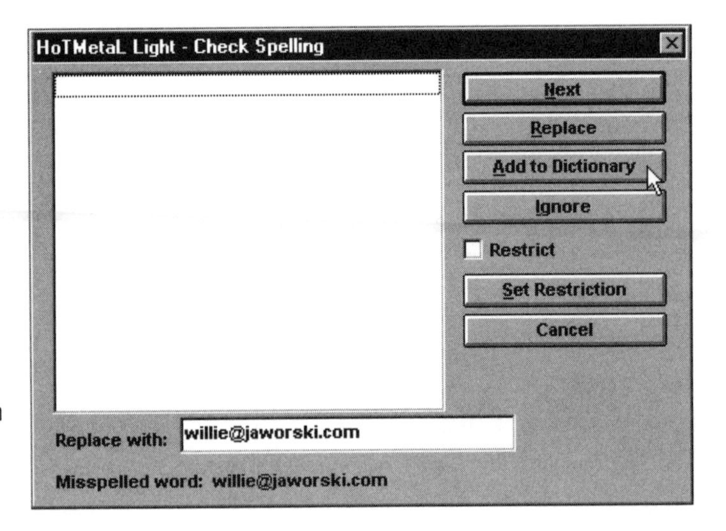

15 Click on **Add to Dictionary**, then click on **Cancel** to close the spell checker.

16 Close the current file, then validate and spell check ch14-02.htm through ch14-05.htm. When you're done, close HoTMetaL.

Publishing

Willie is ecstatic about the way his Web pages have turned out and can't wait to put them on the Web. You copy the five HTML files—ch14-01.htm through ch14-05.htm—from the c:\html directory to a diskette. You also copy the four GIF files—willie.gif, wilma.gif, wanda.gif, and willjr.gif—to the diskette. You take the disks over to Willie's friend's house, and he puts them on his Web server. Willie's friend is using the popular NCSA Web server, running under Linux. He copies the HTML files from Willie's disk to the /home/willie/public_html directory. He also copies the image files to the /home/willie/public_html/images directory. He then tells Willie that the URL for his home page is **http://www.jaworski.com /~willie/ch14-01.htm**. Willie asks what the tilde (~) is used for, and his friend tells him that it is used to identify Willie's "home" directory, /home/willie.

Online Testing

After loading his Web pages onto his friend's server, Willie rushes home to check them out, using his browser. He wants to make sure that everything works correctly, so he decides to check that each link in his pages makes the proper connection. You can do the same, by pointing your browser at **http://www.jaworski.com/~willie/ch14-01.htm**. Be sure to notify Willie if you find any errors.

In this lesson, you learned how to design, develop, publish, and test an example Web application. You helped Willie develop a concept for his home page and worked with him to lay out its design. You then developed a working template and used it to create all of Willie's Web pages. After that, you added some graphics, validated your HTML, checked your spelling, and tested the Web pages on Willie's computer. Finally, you performed actual online testing of the published pages.

Congratulations! You've successfully finished this book and are ready to begin using HoTMetaL to develop and publish your own pages on the Web.

APPENDIX

USING THE CD

The CD that accompanies this book contains several programs, multimedia and graphics files, and HTML files that will help you quickly get started producing high-quality Web pages. It is organized as follows:

- The *hotmetal* directory contains the HoTMetaL installation software. See Lesson 1 for information on how to install HoTMetaL.
- The *html* directory contains a copy of the HTML files that are developed in Lessons 2 through 14. It also contains the *images* and *multimed* subdirectories, which contain all of the images and multimedia files used in the book's examples.
- The *support* directory contains two HTML files, chars.htm and coding.htm, that provide reference information on coding mechanisms used with HTML, forms data, and URLs. The chars.htm file contains a list of named and numbered character codes used to insert special characters in HTML documents. The coding.htm file contains information on the way form and other data is encoded and passed to CGI programs. You can read these files by opening them with your Web browser.
- The *extra* directory contains additional information on developing CGI programs and image maps in the files morecgi.htm and imagemap.htm. These files are also accessible via your Web browser.
- The *programs* directory contains several freeware and shareware programs, including a Web browser, several external viewers, and a program to support forms processing. Installation of these programs is covered later in this Appendix.

The CD's root directory contains two files, readme.txt and readme.htm. The readme.txt file lists the CD's contents and provides pointers on how to install HoTMetaL and the other programs contained on the CD. The readme.htm file provides a clickable index to the CD.

In addition to the files included on the CD, the website located at **http://www.jaworski.com/htmlbook/** provides updated links to sources of information related to this book.

Program Files

The *\programs* directory has seven subdirectories, each of which contains a unique freeware or shareware program:

- The *\programs\udiw3* directory contains the UdiWWW browser for Windows 95. It is a freeware Web browser authored by Bernd Richter and developed at the University of Ulm, Professoriate Organisation and Management of Information Systems, Professor Dr. H. P. Grossmann, D-89069 Ulm. To install UdiWWW, run the setup program in the \programs\udiw3 directory of the CD. A 16-bit version of the browser is also available. Browse the UdiWWW home page for more information. It is located at **http://www.uni-ulm.de/~richter/udiwww/index.htm**.
- The *\programs\webforms* directory contains the WebForms shareware program developed by Q&D Software Development. It is a useful tool for designing Web forms and for processing form data without having to develop CGI programs. To install the program, run the setup program in the \programs\webforms directory of the CD. More information on WebForms may be found at the Q&D Software Development website located at **http://www.q-d.com/wf.htm**. (Copyright ©1995 Q&D Software Development.)
- The *\programs\wham* directory contains the WHAM donation-ware program developed by Andrew Bulhak. WHAM provides excellent external audio support for Web browsers because it works with a large variety of audio formats. It can also be used to record and manipulate audio files. To install WHAM, simply copy the WHAM directory to your hard disk (e.g., c:\wham). You can then run the wham.exe program. I recommend that you also configure your browser to use it as an external audio player.
- The *\programs\nettoob* directory contains the NET TOOB shareware program developed by Duplexx Software, Inc. NET TOOB is the top program for viewing digital videos over the Web and supports many video formats. It is easy to install. Simply run the nettoob.exe self-extracting installation program and follow the setup instructions. You may also want to configure your browser to use NET TOOB as an external viewer. The shareware program will only run for two weeks after it is installed. Check out the Duplexx website at **http://www.duplexx.com** for more information about NET TOOB. (Copyright ©1996 Duplexx Software. All rights reserved worldwide. NET TOOB and Duplexx are trademarks of Duplexx Software, Inc. E-mail: **info@duplexx.com**.)

- The *\programs\word* directory contains the Microsoft Word Viewer for Windows 95. It is a freeware program that allows you to read Microsoft Word documents. It is used as an external viewer with Web browsers. To install Word Viewer, simply run the wd95vw71.exe self-extracting installation program. (Copyright ©1983–1995 Microsoft Corporation. All rights reserved.)
- The *\programs\excel* directory contains the Microsoft Excel Viewer. It is a freeware program that allows you to read Excel spreadsheets. To install Excel Viewer, run the xlvwrus.exe self-extracting installation program. (Copyright ©1983–1995 Microsoft Corporation. All rights reserved.)
- The *\programs\powerpnt* directory contains the Microsoft PowerPoint Viewer. It is a freeware program that allows you to read PowerPoint presentations. To install PowerPoint Viewer, run the pptvw32.exe self-extracting installation program. (Copyright ©1983–1995 Microsoft Corporation. All rights reserved.)

Page numbers in *italics* refer to figures; page numbers in **bold** refer to primary discussions of the topic.

Symbols & Numbers

A

B

C

D

E

H

J

K

L

M

N

O

P

Q

R

S

T

U

V

W

X

Y

Z

About This CD

In addition to the HoTMetaL Light 2.0 installation files, the CD contains freeware and shareware programs, graphics and multimedia files, and HTML files that will help you develop attractive Web pages.

The directories of the CD are organized as follows:

DIRECTORY	CONTAINS
\hotmetal	HoTMetaL Light 2.0 installation files
\win95	Windows 95 installation files for HoTMetaL Light 2.0
\Windows3.1	Windows 3.1 installation files for HoTMetaL Light 2.0
\html	HTML files developed in Lessons 2 through 14
\images	Images used with these lessons
\multimed	Multimedia files used with Lesson 11
\support	Information on HTML, forms, and URL coding
\extra	Information on developing CGI programs and image maps
\programs	Shareware and freeware applications
\udiw3	UdiWWW Web browser
\webforms	WebForms form development and processing program
\wham	WHAM audio file player/recorder
\nettoob	NET TOOB digital video viewer
\word	Microsoft Word Viewer
\excel	Microsoft Excel Viewer
\powerpnt	Microsoft PowerPoint Viewer

See the Appendix for a more complete description of the files on the CD. Also, be sure to read the README files that accompany various programs and libraries on the CD. Where specified in files on the CD, the owners retain copyright to their respective contents.

For HoTMetaL technical support, contact SoftQuad Inc.:

Phone: (416) 239-6851
Fax: (416) 234-9188
E-mail: hotmetal-support@sq.com

About the Web Resource

If you're looking for still more Web publishing know-how, the Do-It-Yourself Web Publishing with HoTMetaL Home Page, located at **http://www.jaworski.com/htmlbook/**, provides links to sources of information related to this book. Check this site periodically for new tips on how to use HoTMetaL.